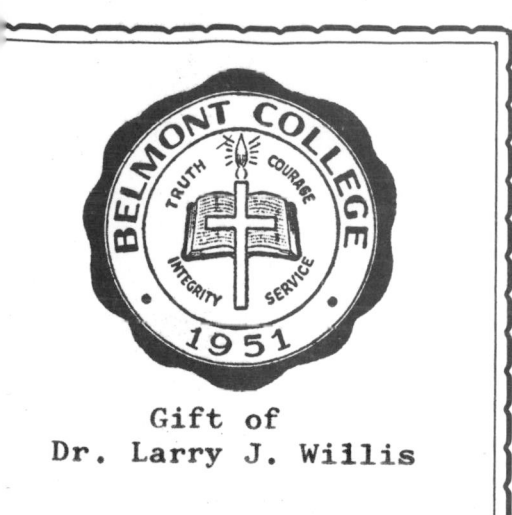

THE WORLD AND THE

AMERICAN TEACHER

The Preparation of Teachers in the Field of World Affairs

HAROLD TAYLOR

THE AMERICAN ASSOCIATION OF COLLEGES FOR TEACHER EDUCATION

Published by

THE AMERICAN ASSOCIATION OF COLLEGES FOR TEACHER EDUCATION
1201 Sixteenth Street, N.W., Washington, D.C. 20036

The research reported herein was performed pursuant to a contract with the U.S. Department of Health, Education, and Welfare, Office of Education, under the provisions of the Cooperative Research Program.

Library of Congress Catalog Card Number: 68-19800
Printed in the U.S.A.

64314

Additional copies of this publication are available at $6.50 each.

Order from:

DR. EDWARD C. POMEROY, *Executive Secretary*
THE AMERICAN ASSOCIATION OF COLLEGES FOR TEACHER EDUCATION
1201 Sixteenth Street, N.W., Washington, D.C. 20036

Foreword

The World and the American Teacher reflects in a significant way the growing contribution of the American Association of Colleges for Teacher Education to the development of a curriculum for prospective teachers which effectively represents the international relationships so much a part of today's world. Fortunately for the Association and for the remaking of American teacher education, the interest and scholarly efforts of Harold Taylor were secured to conduct the study which is so well reported in this volume.

Dr. Harold Taylor has long been an advocate of change and improvement in American education. Formerly president of Sarah Lawrence College, he has written and spoken effectively regarding the problems facing higher education, including teacher education. The Conference on World Education, held at Airlie House, Virginia, December 9-11, 1966, and reported by Dr. Taylor in an earlier publication of AACTE, was an integral part of a two-year effort represented by the present volume.

The study was instituted in 1965 as a result of the efforts of the AACTE Committee on International Relations and has been supported by a grant from the U.S. Office of Education. The Association's committee has provided general direction of the study from its inception and appointed the National Advisory Committee which worked closely with Dr. Taylor. The committee members include the following:

H. KENNETH BARKER, Dean of the College of Education and Dean of International Programs, University of Akron.

HENRY STEELE COMMAGER, Professor of American History, Amherst College.

PETER GILLINGHAM, Executive Associate of Education and World Affairs, Counsel to the House of Representatives Task Force on the International Education Act.

FRANCIS HAMBLIN, Chairman, International Relations Committee of the American Association of Colleges for Teacher Education; presently Vice-President for Academic Affairs, Northern Arizona University, Flagstaff, Arizona.

FRANK KLASSEN, Associate Secretary of the American Association of Colleges for Teacher Education.

BRIAN URQUHART, Office of the Secretary General of the United Nations.

HARRIS WOFFORD, President, State University of New York in Old Westbury.

AACTE commends its Committee on International Relations, the members of the National Advisory Committee, Dr. Taylor and his associates, and members of the AACTE staff who have brought the study to completion. The results will be added to other Association efforts to assist member institutions in improving their programs of instruction, the federal government in assessing and revising its international programs, and the Association itself in determining future activities in international education.

The views expressed in this report are those of Dr. Taylor and do not necessarily represent the position of AACTE. Dr. Taylor was encouraged from the beginning to conduct the study without restrictions other than those imposed by his own integrity as a scholar. Readers will undoubtedly find some viewpoints which are controversial as well as those with which they strongly agree. It is the expectation of AACTE that this study will be provocative and that it will push forward the improvement of teacher education by means of more effective consideration of world affairs as an integral part of every teacher's preparation.

EDWARD C. POMEROY
Executive Secretary

March 1968

iv

Contents

Introduction

The present study had its inception in conversations initiated in May 1962 by Dr. Kenneth Barker, then Associate Executive Secretary of the American Association of Colleges for Teacher Education (AACTE); Dr. George Angell, President of the State University College in Plattsburgh, New York, and Chairman of the International Relations Committee of AACTE for 1962; and the late Dr. Walter Anderson, then Dean of the School of Education of New York University and a member of the International Relations Committee. That Committee, with a membership of seven representatives of the member institutions of AACTE, had developed during previous years a program for extending the education of teachers into an international dimension. In 1963, the Committee had reached the conclusion that a study of the problems and possibilities of this kind of extension was a necessary prelude to further advance in the field and that such a study might best be undertaken by a person whose scholarly interests lay in the area of education and world affairs but who was not himself involved directly with existing organizations and institutions of teacher education.

The purpose of the study was to examine the way in which teachers in America are educated in the field of world affairs and the extent to which their preparation as teachers enables them to understand and to teach about the nature of world society and its problems, and to suggest ways in which the quality of education in a world dimension might be improved, where such improvement was indicated.

The project began formally on February 1, 1966, with a staff consisting of the Director, Harold Taylor; a research associate, Crane Haussamen; and an administrative and research assistant, Miss Miriam Willey. Michael Rossman served as research assistant for a two-month period in January and February 1967, Miss Clara Grossman from February until July 1967. An Advisory Committee was invited to serve throughout the project and consisted of—

H. Kenneth Barker, Dean of the College of Education and Dean of International Programs, University of Akron

1

Henry Steele Commager, Professor of American History, Amherst College

Peter Gillingham, Executive Associate of Education and World Affairs, Counsel to the House of Representatives Task Force on the International Education Act

Francis Hamblin, former Dean of the School of Education, George Washington University, and, in 1966, Chairman, International Relations Committee of the American Association of Colleges for Teacher Education; presently Vice-President for Academic Affairs, State University of Arizona, Flagstaff, Arizona

Frank Klassen, Associate Secretary of the American Association of Colleges for Teacher Education

Brian Urquhart, Office of the Secretary General of the United Nations

Harris Wofford, formerly Associate Director of the Peace Corps in charge of the Office of Planning, Evaluation, and Research; presently President, State University of New York in Old Westbury

The Committee met six times during 1965-66 for discussion of issues, ideas, and procedures; and although the Committee members are not responsible for the views expressed in this report, their thinking is an integral part of the ideas it contains. The Director also had the benefit of five meetings with the International Relations Committee of the AACTE for discussion of the study findings and of topics for further enquiry.

The method of research was to visit a cross section of 50 colleges and universities where teachers are prepared, chosen to include a variety of categories—small, large, rural, urban, private, public—in each region of the country; to review existing literature in the field; and to confer with educators, government officials, students, United Nations personnel, and others with direct experience in and knowledge of the field of world affairs, including officials and members of private organizations and public bodies. In addition to the campus visits by Harold Taylor and Crane Haussamen, two conferences were held: one on the role of students in educational reform, with a representative national group of 40 students engaged in educational reform and teacher education, on October 22-23, 1966, in New York City; the other on world education, with representatives from government (including some who were instrumental in developing the legislation for the International Education Act of 1966), educators, students, and university scholars and administrators, at Airlie House in Warrenton, Virginia, December 9-11, 1966, financed by the Kettering Foundation. An edited version of the proceedings of the World Education Conference has been published by and is available from AACTE.

The colleges and universities visited during the study were—
Antioch College, Yellow Springs, Ohio
Ball State University, Muncie, Indiana
Berea College, Berea, Kentucky

Bloomsburg State College, Bloomsburg, Pennsylvania
Brooklyn College, New York
University of California, Berkeley
University of Southern California, Los Angeles
University of North Carolina, Greensboro
Illinois Teachers College: Chicago—North
University of Colorado, Boulder
Columbia University, Teachers College, New York
University of South Florida, Tampa
Fisk University, Nashville, Tennessee
Flint Community College, Flint, Michigan
George Peabody College for Teachers, Nashville, Tennessee
Georgia Southern College, Statesboro
College of Great Falls, Great Falls, Montana
Hamline University, St. Paul, Minnesota
Harvard University, Cambridge, Massachusetts
California State College at Hayward
Hunter College, New York, New York
Southern Illinois University, Carbondale
University of Illinois, Urbana
Indiana University, Bloomington
State College of Iowa, Cedar Falls
Kent State University, Kent, Ohio
University of Kentucky, Lexington
West Liberty State College, West Liberty, West Virginia
Lady of the Lake College, San Antonio, Texas
Lincoln University, Lincoln, Pennsylvania
Los Angeles City College, Los Angeles, California
Michigan State University, East Lansing
Western Michigan University, Kalamazoo
New York University, New York, New York
Northwestern University, Evanston, Illinois
Ohio University, Athens
New York State University, International Studies and World Affairs,
    Planting Fields
State University of New York, College at Plattsburgh
Queens College, New York
San Francisco State College, San Francisco
Stanford University, Stanford, California
Temple University, Philadelphia, Pennsylvania
Texas Christian University, Fort Worth
North Texas State College, Denton
Southwest Texas State College, San Marco
Utah State University, Logan
West Virginia State College, Institute, West Virginia
Eastern Washington State College, Cheney
Wayne State University, Detroit, Michigan
Wilmington College, Wilmington, Ohio

At most of the institutions a general pattern was followed of a two-day visit consisting of (a) conferences with faculty members of the College of Education or the Department of Education and the administrative officers connected with the education of teachers; (b) conferences with members of the arts and science faculty involved in international programs or courses dealing with world affairs or non-Western cultures; (c) visits to education classes and others where possible; (d) conferences with students in teacher education programs and other students interested in education and world affairs; (e) conferences with appropriate administrative officers of the institution, including deans of arts and science, provosts, presidents, and directors of international programs and centers, depending on availability and areas of responsibility for educational policy.

Not all institutions were studied with the same amount of direct coverage, although in most cases the visits included the elements described above, along with the study of available materials, including mimeographed statements describing programs, curriculums, etc.; published documents; pamphlets; articles by faculty members; and the college or university catalogs. In a few other instances, regional conferences with faculty members and administrators took the place of single visits. More emphasis was placed on institutions primarily concerned with the education of teachers than on those in which this was a relatively minor interest. The generalizations drawn about the national system of teacher education and its possibilities in the future are based on examination of the cross section of colleges and universities listed above; specific references in the report to programs and practices are based on direct examination of the institutions where they are in effect.

On occasion, addresses were made to convocations of students and faculty members, at faculty meetings, or before groups of students; on other occasions, classes were taught in education and philosophy to evoke discussion of educational issues and to gain a sense of student concerns and interests. Nine conferences attended in connection with the study ranged from the U.S. National Student Association Congress in Urbana, Illinois, in August 1966 to a Conference on International Education and Teacher Education at the University of Kentucky and an NDEA Institute on teaching about peace and war at Wayne State University.

Other information was solicited from appropriate organizations and individuals through correspondence and conferences; file materials and memoranda were prepared on the basis of this information for the use of the staff, the Director, and the Advisory Committee.

After the completion of the schedule of visits to campuses, on December 20, 1966, a preliminary statement of the findings was presented at the Annual Meeting of the American Association of Colleges for Teacher Education on February 16, 1967, in Chicago; following the presentation, representatives of the member institutions discussed a series of 12 suggested projects for increasing the scope of education in its international dimension. The presentation of preliminary findings; comments by three members of the project Advisory Committee, Henry Steele Commager, Harris Wofford, and Brian Urquhart; and a summary of the discussion which followed are published in the 1967 *Yearbook* of the American Association of Colleges for Teacher Education, along with the talks of participants in an open meeting of the AACTE Committee on International Relations. These materials should be considered an integral part of the present Report.

Teacher Education and Internationalism

The history of American research in the education of teachers in world affairs is comparatively short; in fact the international education of teachers, or, more accurately, the education of American teachers in internationalism and cultural pluralism, has not yet become a matter for concentrated attention or full-scale effort on the part of the major educational organizations, government agencies, foundations, and universities. The efforts of the private foundations and government agencies through the development of area studies programs and centers, the Fulbright legislation, the Bureau of Educational and Cultural Affairs of the State Department, the Agency for International Development, the National Defense Education Act, the Peace Corps, the International Education Act of 1966, the universities, and many other government and nongovernmental bodies have all contributed to a growing amount of attention paid to the problems and solutions of internationalism in higher education. However, except for preliminary initiatives taken by the American Association of Colleges for Teacher Education and educational organizations with an interest in curriculum planning, little has been done as yet on a national or international scale to develop new concepts, programs, and organizations to deal with the international component in the education of teachers. The education of teachers—whether for the public schools, the colleges and universities, or the professional schools—has remained on the periphery of the main body of effort to develop scholars, research experts, and practitioners in the field of world affairs, foreign cultures, and foreign languages. It may, therefore, be useful at the outset to summarize the work of the Association to date in the field as a part of the setting for the present study.

Over the past 10 years, the International Relations Committee of AACTE—which has 795 member institutions, in which 90 percent of the country's teachers are prepared—has been the central planning body of the Association for international programs and activities to increase the involvement of educators of teachers in the field of world affairs. Through the Committee, international education has been an integral part of the agenda of the Association's annual meetings, to which some 50 foreign educators are invited. Regional conferences have been held each year at universities throughout the country at which proposals, projects, and suggestions for international education have been discussed, with consequent practical results on the home campuses.

Descriptions of some of the projects follow.

1. Overseas study tours for American educational administrators, comprising 30-day visits to examine educational systems and conditions in foreign countries, have been arranged through a contract with the Bureau of Educational and Cultural Affairs in the Department of State. Approximately 100 administrators have visited six European and Asian countries.

2. Interinstitutional affiliation projects have been carried out through

5

arrangements made by the Association with 30 American colleges and universities for direct links to foreign teacher education institutions for exchange of faculty, texts, curriculum material, college publications, and faculty and students, depending on the resources of the American institution.

3. Through arrangements made with AID, educational administrators from abroad have been brought to this country for administrative internships in American colleges and universities; the foreign visitor spends six to nine months at an American institution for study and practical experience in educational administration. Nineteen administrators from Asia, Africa, and Latin America have participated.

4. Four annual seminars for teachers in social studies to be attended by Central American teachers have been arranged under a contract with the Bureau of Educational and Cultural Affairs, with staff provided by American teacher education institutions. Two hundred teachers have participated.

5. In collaboration with the Office of Overseas Schools of the Department of State, the Association has provided educational aid to seven overseas schools in Europe, Asia, Africa, and Latin America for improvement of the quality of teaching, staffing, and curriculum.

6. A series of pilot projects in education for international understanding has been organized in 11 American colleges and universities, in collaboration with the National Council for the Social Studies, and have ranged, according to the interests and financial ability of the institutions involved, from introduction of international curriculums into the present programs and participation in travel-study programs abroad to the development of exchange programs with foreign students and faculty members.

7. Liaison has been established with the major foundations, private organizations, and government agencies with an interest in international education, including the U.S. Commission for UNESCO, the U.S. Committee for UNICEF, the Peace Corps, Education and World Affairs, the Ford Foundation, the Carnegie Corporation, and the Asia Society, which has developed valuable guidelines and materials for the use of Asian studies in the education of teachers.

Among the future research activities planned by the Association are—

1. A major review and assessment of American technical assistance overseas in the field of teacher education, beginning with a report on the character and content of the involvement of the Agency for International Development in education, to be carried out under a contract with AID.

2. A review of the administrative internship program (Number 3 above) with a view to considering the extension of the program in the future.

3. An analysis of the present state of staff resources, curricular practices, innovations, financial commitments, and possible involvement of col-

leges and universities in the education of teachers in world affairs, to be conducted under a grant from the U.S. Office of Education.

There are, of course, other projects in international education for teachers which have been set in motion by other organizations and institutions, but the extent of AACTE efforts, with stringent financial limitations both in the local institutions and in the Association itself, is an indication of the present scale of effort in national initiatives within the teacher education movement.

The International Education Act of 1966

In the meantime, the passage of the International Education Act in October of 1966 has provided a clear policy statement by the U.S. government on the relation between the American educational system and the involvement of the United States in world affairs, offering cooperation with educators of all other countries, "friend or foe alike," and linking the need for internationalism in the spirit and practices of American education with the position of the United States as a world power. Preliminary planning for carrying out the provisions of the International Education Act has already been under way during the past year in the Department of Health, Education, and Welfare, under the overall direction of the assistant secretary for education, Paul Miller, and his staff. The objectives of the Department and the new administrative organization now being designed, including the new Center for Educational Cooperation, are fourfold: (a) the enlargement of the international experience of American students and faculty members, (b) enlargement of the manpower resources in the United States in the field of international affairs, (c) the advance of public understanding of international affairs and world education, and (d) the development of a spirit of educational cooperation between Americans and educators in every part of the world.

In pursuit of these aims, a series of meetings has been held by the Department with members of the major academic organizations and with an advisory group of national educational leaders to work out appropriate strategies for the future. A series of 33 papers on international education have been commissioned for use by the Department on a series of topics ranging from economic development and education to comparative politics and government, in addition to papers on particular regions where new work in area studies is needed. A series of regional meetings sponsored by the Department in cooperation with universities and/or college associations have been held across the country for the presentation and discussion of issues in planning and execution of new programs in the international field.

The next step awaits the appropriation of funds to bring into existence the National Advisory Council, stipulated by the Act as the liaison group between the Center for Educational Cooperation and the universities and public bodies. The establishment of the Center itself will be possible only when these appropriations are granted, although, in the meantime, preliminary plans have been made for staffing and organizing the work of the Center. There are also direct connections between this work in the Department of Health, Education, and Welfare and the U.S. Office of Education bureaus, the Bureau of Educational and Cultural Affairs of the State Department, the Peace Corps, the Agency for International Development, and other government and educational bodies. It is worth noting that in this phase of the preliminary planning, the problems involved in developing specific programs for the education of teachers have again been included among the general problems of higher education rather than singled out for particular attention within the total structure of the educational system. Further information and comment on the implications of the International Education Act and the Center for Educational Cooperation are included in the proceedings of the World Education Conference cited above and throughout this Report.

Education and World Affairs

Aside from these activities in planning and project development, the most important recent work in the relation of internationalism to higher education is that of Education and World Affairs (EWA), established in 1962 with grants from the Ford Foundation and the Carnegie Corporation of New York. Previous foundation-supported studies, in particular that of the Committee on The University and World Affairs in 1959-60,[1] indicated the need for an organization to "study, analyze and assist in strengthening the international teaching, research and service dimensions of U.S. colleges and universities." Through its officers and staff and the members of its Board of Trustees, Education and World Affairs is continually in touch with colleges and universities, government agencies, and private organizations interested in international affairs and education. A great deal of what is known in the educational community about college and university activities in international education and world affairs has come from EWA, through staff research, the work of committees, and the direct relation among officers of the government, the EWA staff, and the EWA Board of Trustees. This organization has been the main source of stimulus and exhortation for the development of international studies and world affairs programs in the universities and colleges and has provided in the field the most substantial body of the literature of explanation and fact which is currently available.[2]

---

[1] Report of the Committee on The University and World Affairs, J. L. Morrill, chairman, December 1960, 84 pp., distributed by Education and World Affairs, 522 Fifth Avenue, New York, N. Y.

[2] Studies and reports issued by Education and World Affairs:
AID and the Universities, by John W. Gardner. Published by Education and World Affairs, 1964.
The U.S. Office of Education; A New International Dimension, 1964.
The Foreign Student: Whom Shall We Welcome? 1964. (Out of print)
The University Looks Abroad: Approaches to World Affairs at Six American Universities. Published by Walker & Co., 1966.

The International Programs of American Universities

The most important single document for detailed information about university work in international education is the second edition of *The International Programs of American Universities; an Inventory and Analysis,* prepared by the Institute of Advanced Projects at the East-West Center in Honolulu in cooperation with Education and World Affairs and Michigan State University. This 466-page report describes and analyzes briefly the 1,314 international educational programs going on in 396 institutions in the United States and gives the kind of information about their operations which can furnish a basis not only for further research but for planning by institutions wishing to enter the field.

As of September 1965, 199 colleges and universities, mostly in the Middle Atlantic and North East Central states, sent faculty members abroad; 88 institutions had overseas branches of some kind, 95 were training Americans for work abroad, 100 had specific programs for exchanging materials with educators in foreign countries, and 55 were engaged in some form of educational collaboration with foreign institutions. Since 1965, the number of institutions and programs has continued to increase.

Before reviewing the materials in the East-West Center report, I had

---

The Overseas Selection of Foreign Students, 1966.

Publications and information services provided by EWA:

Education and World Affairs: Report on Program 1963-1964, 1965.

Intercultural Education, 1965. (Out of print)

International Education Program, 1966. (Out of print)

Education and World Affairs: An Overview, 1966.

As Nations Become Neighbors. Reprinted from *Saturday Review,* August 20, 1966, issue.

The International Education Act of 1966, 1966.

Coordinating International Programs and Activities at U.S. Colleges and Universities: A Directory, 1966.

Occasional reports:

Guidelines for the Planning of External Aid Projects in Education, by Arthur J. Lewis, 1967.

Policy statements:

The University Community and Overseas Research: Guidelines for the Future, Board of Trustees of EWA, 1967.

In addition to these reports, the following publications are distributed by EWA:

The University and World Affairs. Report of the Committee on The University and World Affairs, J. L. Morrill, chairman. Published by the Ford Foundation, 1960.

The College and World Affairs. Report of the Committee on The College and World Affairs, John W. Nason, chairman. Published by the Hazen Foundation, 1964.

Some Facts About Serving in Educational Posts Abroad. Published by Overseas Educational Service, 1964.

Overseas Educational Service, Its Purpose and Program. Published by Overseas Educational Service, 1965.

The Professional School and World Affairs. Series of reports by Task Forces on—
1. Agriculture and Engineering
2. Law
3. Business Administration and Public Administration
4. Medicine and Public Health
5. Education.

assumed that it would be necessary to collect a good deal of this kind of information as part of the research project, in order to be able to provide a set of findings about the present range of work in international programs having to do with the education of teachers. I had also assumed before reviewing thoroughly the work of Education and World Affairs that it would be necessary to investigate in a variety of ways the relation of international affairs to the undergraduate and graduate programs of American colleges and universities, because of their direct connection with teacher education. However, the combination of the East-West Center document and the publications, activities, and studies of EWA have removed those necessities, and I now make the assumption that persons interested in gaining more information about the actual range of present international programs, in higher education in general as well as in the education of teachers, will turn to the work already done so capably and imaginatively by the staff of the above organizations.

The reader will find, for example, in the East-West Center report that, beginning in 1962, the University of Akron has annually held a month's Summer Session Abroad for teachers in elementary and secondary schools —60 of them in 1964—to "prepare them to translate more adequately the culture of the world to their students," financed by the participants' fees and held in India, Spain, and the United Kingdom. At St. Olaf College in Northfield, Minnesota, the senior class raises funds annually to send a member of the graduating class to the Martin Luther School in Rimbach, Germany, to teach English. To review the entire report is to find any number of ways in which ideas already in action through existing college and university programs could be transferred to additional institutions or could be used as a stimulus to further planning and extensions to projects already under way.

The Conference on World Education

Another part of the present study has had to do with the implications of the International Education Act and the present and future possibilities for collaborative effort in international programs of teacher education among private organizations, colleges and universities, schools, colleges of education, and the U.S. government. The Conference on World Education, mentioned above, brought together many of those in this country most directly concerned with the International Education Act, including some who were instrumental in developing both the legislation and the ideas on which the legislation was based. The Conference resulted in a document which not only contains the substance of the papers and the discussion, but serves as a report of this phase of the study findings. Rather than repeating either the generalizations or the specific details of the results of that Conference, I am assuming that the proceedings of the Conference will be read as an integral part of the present Report.

Additional Documents

I also refer the reader to two other sets of documents. The first set is the U.S. government publication of the hearings before the Task Force on International Education of the House Committee on Education and Labor of the Eighty-Ninth Congress in March and April of 1966,[3] and the accompanying government publication of selected readings to supplement the International Education Act, prepared by the Task Force on International Education, chaired by Congressman John Brademas of Indiana.[4] In the former document, the reader will find a set of statements about the problems and possibilities in international education presented by a cross section of the country's best informed representatives of higher education, private organization, and government. In the latter is to be found one of the finest compilations of research findings and writing on the subject of international education that is available anywhere, with individual sections on a full range of topics—from the problems of internationalizing the curriculum to those of strengthening the faculty and teaching resources in higher education and the schools.

The second set of materials is the series of pamphlets recently published by Education and World Affairs on international education and the professional schools, in agriculture, engineering, law, business administration, public administration, medicine, public health, and education.[5] The research was conducted with the overall supervision of a study committee of 20 educators, headed by T. Keith Glennan, president of Associated Universities, Inc., and involved the work of four task forces in the areas under consideration. The introductory section of these documents presents the problems of adapting the work of the professional schools to accommodate new international responsibilities and provides a basic rationale for the proposition that all institutions of higher education, in whatever field, have both opportunities and duties in connection with international education. The reports on the professional schools themselves provide valuable analysis of the present state of professional education in its international aspect and equally valuable suggestions and recommendations for further activity.

Other reference books, handbooks, and publications relevant to the education of teachers in world affairs are included among the standard publications of UNESCO, the United Nations, and other international organizations, as listed in the Foreign Policy Association regular bulletin, Intercom.[6] The September-October 1967 issue of Intercom contains a

---

[3] Hearings before the Task Force on International Education of the Committee on Education and Labor, House of Representatives, Eighty-Ninth Congress, Second Session on H.R. 12451 and H.R. 12452, Washington, D. C., March 30, 31; April 1, 4, 5, 6, and 7, 1966. Washington, D. C.: Government Printing Office, 1966. 453 pp.

[4] International Education; Past, Present, Problems and Prospects. Selected Readings to supplement H.R. 14643 prepared by the Task Force on International Education, John Brademas, chairman, Committee on Education and Labor, House of Representatives. Washington, D. C.: Government Printing Office. 564 pp.

[5] Op. cit. (3)

[6] Intercom, issued six times annually by the Foreign Policy Association, 345 East 46th Street, New York, N.Y. September-October 1967, 88 pp.

valuable survey by James M. Becker on the present state of teaching and curriculum in world affairs in American schools and an account of research and projects designed to improve the situation in the schools and colleges. Becker's article, the bibliographical and other references, along with the description of an 18-month research study of education in international affairs being conducted by the Foreign Policy Association, make this document a concise and basic reference work for those concerned with the education of teachers in internationalism.

The Point of View

In view of the availability of these documents, and others designated, I have not found it either necessary or desirable to go over ground already covered so well by those who have been at work in the field. What I have tried to do is to use the previous research and findings wherever they are relevant and to remain free to deal more explicitly than others have as yet done with the problems of educating teachers to acquire an international point of view and the knowledge to go with it, not merely for the public schools but for the whole system of education, from elementary schools to postgraduate training, from the arts and humanities to the social and natural sciences. I have therefore concentrated less on the analysis and reporting of existing programs and institutions and more on the development of ideas for using the entire culture as an instrument of education.

I have resisted the temptation to denounce weaknesses in the system of teacher education, since that kind of denunciation is already in unusual supply and, in any case, is about at the same level of significance as shooting fish in a barrel. I have tried to report what I have found, and where I have found weaknesses I have looked for their cause, with a view to laying a foundation for overcoming the weaknesses. I have also tried to think of education as a social and cultural system, not as a set of formal institutions with certain theories and practices, and have taken the view that in the reform of education, to keep it relevant to the society in which it exists it is necessary to see the way all the other parts of the social system are interlocked with education. Conversely, to make reform possible, it is necessary to use every possible part of the system as a whole—from the Peace Corps and the Office of Education to the United Nations Association and the Students for a Democratic Society.

I think it is fair to say that the problem of educating teachers in world affairs has not been sufficiently considered from this point of view, that is to say, as a problem interlocked with the going systems of politics, economics, and culture in world society. I have therefore begun at the beginning, with an analysis of the dimensions of the problem of educating teachers in the American educational system and its cultural and social setting, taking account of the fact that an understanding of the world at large depends for its accomplishment on a prior understanding of oneself in relation to one's own society.

12

I would like to express my thanks to the members of the project staff, Crane Haussamen, Miriam Willey, Clara Grossman, Michael Rossman, Martha Darling, and Muriel Taylor, for their contribution to the study; to Kenneth Barker, former associate executive secretary of the American Association of Colleges for Teacher Education, whose persistence in urging that the study be done and whose efforts in making the necessary arrangements are in large part responsible for its beginning; to Frank Klassen, who succeeded Kenneth Barker in his post; to Frank Hamblin, chairman, and to the members of the International Relations Committee of the AACTE who conceived the project in the first place; to the members of the Advisory Committee for the study; to Edward C. Pomeroy, executive secretary of AACTE; to Charles Foster of the U.S. Office of Education, who, as the government officer responsible for the study contract, gave all the help the Director needed; to his successor David Hattrick; to the many officers of government, foundations, and organizations who gave their time and thought to the questions they were asked; and to the students, faculty members, and administrators of the colleges and universities whose campuses we visited.

Chapter 1. The Dimensions of the Problem

> The unity of knowledge, the nature of human communities, the order of
> society, the order of ideas, the very notions of society have changed, and will not
> return to what they have been in the past. What is new is not new because it
> has never been before, but because it has changed in quality . . . so that the
> world alters as we walk in it, so that the years of a man's life measure not some
> small growth or rearrangement or moderation of what he learned in childhood,
> but a great upheaval. . . . The global quality of the world is new; our knowledge
> of and sympathy with remote and diverse people, our involvement with them in
> practical terms and our commitment to them in terms of brotherhood . . .
>
> Robert Oppenheimer,
> speaking at Columbia University,
> December 27, 1954

The child enters the world without knowledge of it and without
having adopted an attitude toward it. In the long run, what he can know
and believe about the world depends on the attitude he learns to adopt
toward it and toward himself. His early years are spent in exploring what
the world contains, how he feels about what he discovers, how to cope with
the small private sector which he occupies. Although this exploration is
not usually called education, that is what it is, except that it is not formal.
It is a set of personal experiences in which the child's senses and emotions
are so completely fused with his intellect that he does not separate the
knowledge he possesses from the way he feels about it; and, in a sense, he
can learn only what he wants to learn.

His capacity to go on learning about the world depends on his openness to it and the opportunities for extending his range. The child who
has never been more than three blocks from home or a mile from his
father's rice paddy, who can't read, and who knows no one who is not like
himself is condemned to a narrow orbit of self-awareness, a meager knowledge of the world at large, and a very slim chance that he will ever know
more than he does.

In one way or another, in more or less degree, everyone suffers from
a similar limitation, and that is the problem in teaching about world affairs,

or, to put it more accurately, in teaching and learning about the world. The narrow orbit in which each learns to move depends for its broadening on the arousal of interest in knowing what exists in the broader dimension of an environment which extends beyond one's own. It is not enough to be told about Africa, Asia, Europe, or Kansas in the classrooms of the world. Everything that is told or presented is told to persons in various states of capacity to respond. It is not so much what is said as what is heard. There is such a thing as total capacity to respond, which in the most fortunate of cases means that the children are interested in everything that is interesting, including the Africans, Asians, Europeans, Kansans, or mathematics. But that is a situation seldom to be found throughout the American public school system, or the American universities, or anywhere else in the schools and colleges of the world.

Through the normal course of growing up in his own culture, each child is taught what he is intended to know, and his sense of identity and his attitudes depend on the cultural milieu in which they are developed and on what he has been taught to believe about himself. In order to know anything, it is necessary to be able to relate it to something already known, to look at the world from one's own point of view. But to do that means narrowing what the world looks like to a single perspective, thus distorting the reality of what can only be seen clearly and truthfully from a larger view and many perspectives.

As Erik Erikson says—

> For men, not being a natural species any more, and not a mankind as yet—need to feel that they are of some special kind (tribe or nation, class or caste, family, occupation, or type), whose insignia they will wear with vanity and conviction, and defend (along with the economic claims they have staked out for their kind) against the foreign, the inimical, the not-so-human kinds. Thus it comes about that they can use all their proud skills and methods most systematically against other men, even in the most advanced states of rationality and civilization, with the conviction that they could not morally afford not to do so.[1]

We can read the history of world education as the way in which, in successive generations since civilization began, the size of the group to which one was attached gradually increased in the spread of its loyalties, from the family to the tribe, from the tribe to a village, from one village to other villages, until the shared loyalty and sense of identity could extend to a city-state. The sense of personal and group identity was sharpened and defined by conflict and war, reinforced by cultural and religious unity, and the rallying points for the assertion of that identity were around ideas of physical courage, faithfulness to one's own, and pride of conquest.

In the most optimistic reading of contemporary history, we could now say that we have reached a stage at which it has become necessary for the educated man to extend the dimension of his loyalty to the entire human race, and that the conception of education itself must be one which locates

---

[1] Erikson, Erik. "Youth: Fidelity and Diversity." *Conflict Resolution and World Education.* (Edited by Stuart Mudd.) The Hague: Dr. W. Junk Publishers, 1966. p. 40.

man intellectually in a universe described by scientists, artists, and writers, and in a cultural setting as big as the globe. To enjoy any longer the luxury of defining one's nation, one's society, or oneself in terms of pride of ancestry, social superiority, or power of destruction is not only supremely dangerous to the survival of the race, but intellectually and socially obsolete.

To be truly educated, man must have a full sense of the nature of modern man and of the world he lives in, and I do not see how that sense can be achieved by the kind of education now being provided by most of the schools, colleges, universities, and educational systems of the world. They have fallen behind the reality of world society and are presenting conceptions of man and his world comparable to the pre-Copernican system of ideas in the post-Copernican period.

To create a new beginning, it is necessary to understand modern man as a single member of the human race with infinite individual variations, and not as the representative of a single culture, nation, society, or continent. There is no East and West, North and South. There are just different people, living in different places, under different conditions; and, through the happy circumstance of the spread of modern knowledge, we now have access to the full variety of their lives and natures, with more to be learned the longer we live.

It is now the task of education, on a world scale, to put together the scattered fragments of the world's knowledge of itself in a form which can become the basis for a new kind of education in human affairs. I urge the effort to achieve this kind of education if for no other reason than that it lifts the conception of human nature to the level at which it belongs. There is new and global knowledge of man to be gained by those who care to seek it out—from poetry, theatre, sociology, philosophy, anthropology, religion, the arts, on every continent—and the fascination of the art of education in the modern world lies in the number of different ways one can learn to understand how human beings have created themselves out of the accidents of their own environment and their own history.

The principal characteristic of the modern world is not its massive unrest, although that is its most visible one, but its growing and necessary unity—the interpenetration of all lives by every other, the coming together of peoples, cultures, and societies to accomplish common purposes. The teacher is at the center of his own culture and of this process of interpenetration. By what he teaches and by what he learns, it is within his power to join with other teachers and their students in every part of the world to create the elements of unity in a world culture. That is what he must now do.

For a world transformation is under way, partly through the blind and unavoidable impulses in contemporary history which are driving societies into revolutionary situations, where the need for political and social reform has not kept pace with the legitimate expectations and demands of the dispossessed and the unprivileged; partly through conscious changes in the thinking and policies of countries who hold the major sources of political, military, and economic power. The social and political systems of the world are now affecting each other in fundamental ways, creating a fluid state of rapid change in international alignments and interrelationships.

In another dimension, ideological, secular, and religious beliefs are finding new accommodations with each other, of a kind few would have predicted at the middle of this century. Most of the great religions—Hinduism, Buddhism, Christianity, Islam—are in the process of discovering, through a worldwide ecumenical movement, a set of shared values which have to do, not with theological dogma, but with what Pope John in *Pacem in Terris* has called "the common good of the entire human family."

At the moment, the balance of forces that puts war, violence, hatred, and ignorance on one side and peace, security, human well-being, social progress, and education on the other seems tipped toward violence as the norm in world affairs, and it is clear that the present stage of world history demands more than ever before the intense commitment of those who have intellectual, educational, and social power at their disposal to do everything in their power to tip the balance in the opposite direction.

The necessity to do so becomes even more urgent when we face the fact that a new generation, larger than ever before in a worldwide population expansion of an alarming size, is growing up in an unstable environment in which the older forms of authority have lost their grip. Everywhere in the world, the new expectations of the young are challenging the authority of the older generation and its patterns of control. In this country, where by 1970 more than half of the population will be under the age of 25, a new generation of students has created a national community, a subculture within the larger society, with its own interests, attitudes, ideas, and ambitions. The educated young have become involved in the issues of international affairs, in which the problems of human rights, war and peace, the politics of change, and the reform of education have become of central concern. They see the problems of world society in the same light as those of their own.

The solutions they propose and act upon, the unifying beliefs, are based on the conviction that the older generation and the established order in any society cannot assume the right of control over the younger generation, either before or after it reaches its majority. The young, they are saying, have equal rights as citizens, regardless of their age group, and, as certified citizens, black or white, have their own ideas about how to run the society and its educational system. Since they are the ones education is "done" to, they claim special qualifications for knowing what it is, how it is working, and how it should work. Maximum participation by the poor, says the poverty legislation. Yes, say the students, and maximum participation by the young, poor or otherwise.

Elsewhere around the world there is a comparable constituency, alive to the fact that they can exercise political and social power, conscious of discrepancies between the privileges of the rich and the deprivations of the poor. The young Indonesians who united against Sukarno, the Korean youth who opposed the dictatorship of Rhee, the Spanish students who reject the educational control of Franco, the Soviet young who question, through poetry and the arts, the social policy and politics of their elders have their counterparts in other societies around the world, in Africa, Asia, Latin America, and Europe. They are forming their own leadership from their own ranks, and where there is no accommodation between them and their elders, they can and will form the basis for revolutionary action, responsible or irresponsible, as the circumstances provide.

It is in this sense that the education and accommodation of the new generation becomes a primary matter of concern for the societies of the world as they enter the second half of what has been announced as the "Development Decade," a time when the resources of the United Nations and allied organizations and governments are pledged to narrow the gap between the have and the have-not countries. The unhappy fact is that during the first half of the 10 years, the have-not countries have been finding that even with foreign help and their own development programs, food, supplies, production of goods, housing, and jobs have either barely kept up with their rising populations or have fallen behind. The gap has widened, not narrowed, and the basic problem grindingly returns to the lack of educated manpower to give leadership in planning and trained capacity in action.

The Context of Education

It is in the context of these considerations that I wish to deal with the education of teachers in the field of world affairs and to define the terms in which the idea of world education acquires its meaning. By *education,* I mean the process by which each person becomes aware of himself and his place in the world at large and learns how best to conduct himself in it and to contribute to it. To achieve such awareness, he needs the opportunity to explore the world's geography, its people, including those of his own society, to learn through science the physical characteristics and foundations of nature, and to learn through language, the arts, and philosophy the ideas and experience of mankind. These are the world's affairs, and although they include such matters as the history of governments, international relationships, wars, victories, defeats, and the rise and fall of empires and civilizations, the culminating point in education comes when one has learned to understand the nature and character of the world itself in its contemporary manifestation and to do something useful within it.

This is not to say that all education must deal with the contemporary, but that all education *is* ultimately contemporary and that it has links with the whole world. The mind of primitive man is, in history or in the present, linked directly to our own. The primitive, the preindustrial, and the postindustrial cultures and educational systems of the world are linked together by their common efforts to solve the problems of human existence,

18

no matter how different they may be in the ways they set about doing it. Says Margaret Mead—

> While anthropologists seek for ways of describing man that will apply to all cultures at all times in history, anthropology remains closely bound to the living detail of the way special men have lived at given times and places. . . . The precious concrete reference is never lost. Real Indians hunt real buffalo, or stare at the sun until they fall unconscious, or fast in the lonely wilderness seeking a guardian spirit for life. . . .[2]

The educator, like the anthropologist, the philosopher, the poet, or the psychologist, must take for his province the infinite variety of human nature and human cultures, blending the general characteristics one can find among the details with the concrete reality of specific men, women, and children who have lived under specific circumstances at certain times. The generalization without the detail is banal and essentially meaningless; the detail without the pattern in history and culture becomes meaningless by fragmentation.

Or, to put it in different terms, in the words of Joseph Campbell—

> In his life-form the individual is necessarily only a fraction and distortion of the total image of man. He is limited either as male or as female; at any given period of his life he is again limited as child, youth, mature adult, or ancient; furthermore, in his life-role he is necessarily specialized as craftsman, tradesman, servant or thief, priest, leader, wife, nun or harlot; he cannot be all. Hence, the totality—the fullness of man—is not in the separate member, but in the body of the society as a whole; the individual can be only an organ. From his group he has derived his techniques of life, the language in which he thinks, the ideas on which he thrives; through the past of that society descended the genes that built his body. If he presumes to cut himself off, either in deed or in thought and feeling, he only breaks connection with the sources of his existence.[3]

To make the connection with the sources of one's existence is the ultimate purpose of education, and it is with the process of making these connections that the education of the teacher must be concerned.

A shift in educational perspective to a world point of view is now made necessary by the shift in the circumstances of world society, and the education of teachers is the focal point at which the shift must be made. Without teachers whose own knowledge and attitudes are in tune with the demands of world society for the application of new knowledge, there is little chance that new perspectives can be introduced into the structure and content of modern education, in the United States or anywhere else.

Immediately then, the question is raised, Who will teach the teachers, how will they be taught, and how can they teach themselves?

That is the central question to which the present study is addressed. Although the study deals with the education of American teachers and is based on research having to do with American institutions, the effort has been made to find conclusions and proposals which relate themselves to the education of teachers in the world community.

---

[2] Mead, Margaret, and Bunzel, Ruth L., editors. *The Golden Age of American Anthropology.* New York: George Braziller, p. 1.

[3] Campbell, Joseph. *The Hero with a Thousand Faces.* New York: Pantheon Books, 1949. pp. 382-83.

At this point, we in the United States *are* the world's most powerful economic, social, military, and political force, and we possess a vast and latent power for taking initiatives in cultural and educational change on a world scale. Whether we like it or not, or whether anyone else likes it, with our mass media, our science, our technology, our cultural and educational institutions, our mass transport and urban problems, we are the forerunners of what mass societies will some day be. Despite our location here on a local continent, we live in the middle of the world and serve as a point of linkage among the thousands of elements which make up the cultural and social fabric of world society. Having been handed the leadership of the world as a gift from history, a gift seldom given and quickly taken away, we now have a chance to show what we can do with it. We have the opportunity to use our cultural and educational resources to make the entire country into a general friendly meeting ground and laboratory in social change, to which students and teachers from everywhere in the world may come to try to find solutions to the world's educational problems while working with us on ours and their own.

We have within our 50 states a fascinating assortment of underdeveloped areas, preindustrial societies, postindustrial urban centers, bad housing, ghettos, rural slums, wealthy suburbs, beautiful farms, bad schools, good schools, mediocre universities, great ones, anti-intellectuals, poets, Philistines, dancers, surf-riders, television programs, research centers, think tanks, anti-think tanks, rebels, conformists, mass culture, and high art—all of which has to be seen to be believed and is, in a curious way, the wonder of the world. There is no reason why we cannot make of this assortment a campus for the world, just as the world can, under the right circumstances, become a campus for everyone, including the Americans.

In saying this I am not proposing a new kind of cultural imperialism, or a program of making friends and allies through education, or a new display of the arrogance of power, but something quite simple and appropriate—the use of our money, our institutions, and our cultural resources to improve the quality of education throughout the world, considering America to be a part of the world where this can be done most effectively. We have already come part way to this point of view, with the 100,000 students and 10,000 scholars here from abroad each year, with the new International Education Act of 1966, with the international work of our foundations, universities, and voluntary organizations. The initiatives for the next steps will have to come from the joint efforts of educators here and abroad, from the American campuses where teachers are now being educated, and from the schools where American teachers are already teaching.

The Argument for Internationalism

There are, of course, other reasons for supporting the cause of American involvement and initiative in world education. Among them is the necessity of achieving a common understanding among cultures, nation-states, and societies through cooperative educational programs, simply to ensure the continuity of what civilization we now have, before we blow it up—a straightforward, practical reason, good enough by itself. Another and compelling reason is the moral obligation of the West to share what we know with those in other countries who wish to make use of the kind of knowledge we have accumulated in our own climb toward social and economic security. By knowing more about other cultures and their situation we can help to adapt and reshape our knowledge to their needs, so that others may adapt what they need to their own social and personal use. The injection of new knowledge and ideas from one culture into another gives greater vitality to both. It makes each culture more interesting and varied by the influence one has on the other; it gives each culture something to assimilate, something with which to compare and to judge itself.

Until recently, the major argument for American international involvement in cultural and educational affairs has had to do with our national and international security. It has been argued that our educational system should make provision for teaching world affairs and non-Western cultures in order that American citizens can understand the nature of world society and the problems of American foreign policy. It is obvious that without a broad educational base in foreign languages and foreign cultures, the educational system as a whole will be unable to develop enough citizens, scholars, and experts in foreign cultures and international affairs to supply the manpower needed to cope with the formation and application of our foreign policy, both inside and outside of government. Nor could it deal with the need for a broader professional education for lawyers, businessmen, public administrators, and engineers who conduct American affairs overseas. This is the rationale behind the National Defense Education Act. Education in this instance becomes an instrument of national security. Foundation and government grants for area studies, international affairs centers, and research institutes have been based on similar reasoning.

The difficulty is that although these areas of research and scholarship are an essential ingredient in the store of American knowledge, to whatever use it may be put, the knowledge itself has not permeated the educational system as a whole, largely because there is no direct connection between the developments within the knowledge industry and the education of teachers within the schools and colleges. It is time now to put these elements together, and the place to do it is in the universities and schools where teachers are prepared and in the schools where the young are now being educated.

The Community and Its Culture

It will be clear at the outset that the achievement of a broad and enlightened outlook toward the world is the result not merely of what is done by teachers in the classrooms or scholars in the universities, no matter how well they have been prepared for their mission. The American child in early and in later life is immersed in a total context, and the context shifts from big cities in the North to rural areas in the South, from poverty to affluence, from Negroes to whites, from Spanish-Americans to Puerto Ricans, from ghettos to suburbs. The teaching problem shifts from one subculture to another, and the pervasive social and cultural values carried through the mass media are absorbed by the young in their life in the American community.

The vehicles for these values range from Little League baseball and the Kiwanis Club to Sunday School and the Beatles. The pervasiveness and the emotional power of community institutions and the mass media are greater in affecting the attitudes of the young American than are those which he finds in his school learning. In many instances, the school simply reinforces attitudes already gained from the total environment, since a central purpose of the public school is to enable the young to learn how to be Americans. In fact, the teachers themselves share the tastes and values to be found in the rest of the society; the school and society in white middle class culture form one homogeneous community.

It is also necessary to repeat what has been said so often about the massive effects on the minds and attitudes of the younger generation from the single medium of television. Whatever else can be said about the television phenomenon, it is true that the flow of information, opinion, and value-forming images from this single source is a primary educational influence on the young and that from this source, along with the weekly magazines and paperback books, a supply of general information about the world and its happenings is provided on a scale greatly in excess of the amount communicated through formal instruction in the schools. The statistics most commonly used to illustrate this point are provided by the Reverend John M. Culkin of Fordham University: the average American child from preschool through to the end of high school has seen 15,000 hours of television, as compared to 10,000 hours of classroom time in the same period, and college students see 20 films for every book they read.

In part, this acounts for the rapid increase at an earlier age in the number of high school students who are sensitive to social questions ranging from the cultural habits of the hippy movement to the mistreatment of the Negro, and for the increased sophistication of a growing minority of college students and young political activists to the issues of domestic politics, war and peace, and world affairs in general. The formation of a youth culture with its own interests and values, separate from the older generation yet with influence on it, can be traced to some of the cultural effects of the television medium and the opening up of questions, ideas, and examples of human conduct which in former years were unavailable to the young because the medium did not then exist. For a variety of reasons, the power of the medium has been used as an instrument for cultural conditioning and the reinforcement of American ideological and social values rather than as a stimulus to fresh thought, social criticism, and cultural enlightenment.

In this context, other influences within education stem directly from the child's life with his parents, from their relation to each other, their attitude to the child, the emotional and cultural tone of the family life— all of this forming the cultural surrogate for his growing up. We now know enough about the early childhood years to know that the child's emotional set and his style of coping are derivatives of the emotional and social relation with one or both of the parents and are established, usually in a permanent way, by the age of 8 to 10. Although research conducted at Sarah Lawrence, at Bennington, and elsewhere shows that the values of college students do change under the influence of college teaching when the college considers the personal growth of students as a major concern, the political attitude and world outlook of American students are mainly the same as those of their parents. Other research, particularly of the kind carried out by Philip Jacob[4] and by Nevitt Sanford and the authors of *The American College*,[5] indicates that attendance at college has, except in the case of colleges with a "peculiar potency," very little influence on the values the students bring with them from the society.

Since it is the attitude taken toward the world which is decisive in what one learns to think and to know about it, it is with the creation of attitudes that the educator must be primarily concerned. By attitudes I do not mean agreement or disagreement with specific political or social doctrines or world views, but attitudes in support of rational enquiry versus dogma and prejudice, independent thinking versus acceptance of social norms, tolerance toward opposing views versus ethnocentrism, the achievement of a large view of world society versus a parochial view of one's own.

In considering the education of the teacher and his role in the society, it is therefore important to be reminded that during his childhood education the school or college teacher in America has been immersed in everybody's American culture, usually in the white middle class; that in about 70 percent of the cases the schoolteacher is a woman and, therefore, more likely, in this culture, to adapt to current social and political norms than to challenge them; and that public school teachers in America are regarded not as intellectual and social leaders, but as the carriers of the conventional wisdom under the direction of those elected to school boards and appointed to superintendencies who represent that wisdom. Otherwise they would be unlikely to be elected or appointed.

There is a sizable and convincing body of research which confirms the fact that whatever else may be taught within the American public schools, one major effect of school attendance is to create an acceptance of the existing social order, of the American world view and its attendant national and international policies. After a thoroughgoing and sensitive review of recent research in the field, John Patrick, research associate of the High

---

[4] Jacob, Philip E. *Changing Values in College*. New York: Harper & Brothers, 1957. 174 pp.

[5] Sanford, Nevitt, editor. *The American College*. New York: John Wiley & Sons, 1962. 1,084 pp.

School Curriculum Center in Government at Indiana University, has this to say in summary:

> Perhaps the most acute educational problem reflected by political socialization research is the proclivity of our schools to approach the task of political socialization in a one-sided manner, especially in schools serving mainly lower or working class children. The schools reinforce and develop strong, supportive attitudes toward state and nation. Most American children learn well the lessons of conforming to the socio-political *status quo*. Certainly the schools may contribute substantially to national strength and stability when they impart supportive political orientations. . . .

> However, certain consequences may flow from overemphasis upon conformity that are inconsistent with many of the professed objectives of American public schools and with certain democratic ideals. For example, overemphasis upon conformity appears to be associated with authoritarian school atmospheres where docile children are prized above active, deeply probing thinkers; where strict adherence to authoritative pronouncements is preferred over student inquiry into pressing, socio-political concerns; where strict obedience to rules is stressed to the exclusion of inquiry into the need for rules. This may contribute to some unanticipated and undesired consequences for adult political behavior such as alienation or cynicism, dispositions to passively accept authority, and tendencies to be intolerant of reasonable political dissent or non-conformity. Certainly social forces other than the school may contribute to these types of political behavior, such as the present quality of life in lower class homes and neighborhoods. But since the school's climate of opinion and educational atmosphere appear to be more influential in shaping political attitudes than does its formal programs of instruction, it is possible that an authoritarian school environment may subvert textbook and teacher prescriptions of democratic political values and that it may contribute to the hardening of political beliefs and to a close-minded resistance toward alternative or unorthodox points of view. . . .

> Another factor that may contribute to the ossification of political attitudes is that commitment to political beliefs in early childhood precedes knowledge of relevant political information, that early learning is based on emotional attachments rather than knowledge. Later cognitive learning often serves merely to reinforce these early commitments, to provide rational justification for a closed system of basic beliefs rather than reflective examination of tentatively held viewpoints.[6]

Although Mr. Patrick's comments focus on political attitudes and the socialization process, they are directly relevant to the problem of educating teachers and students in the field of world affairs. The findings of the present study confirm the fact that when education is considered as a total process, including, but expanding beyond, formal classroom instruction, the education of the American teacher is one which provides little opportunity for the introduction of alternative or unorthodox points of view either about America's position in the world or about the social and political attitudes of the people and governments of foreign countries. As a student, the future teacher is deliberately, and to a degree necessarily, taught to see the world and the world's affairs from an American point of view, and from the point

---

[6] Patrick, John. *Political Socialization of American Youth.* A review of research with implications for secondary school studies. Bloomington: High School Curriculum Center in Government, Indiana University, pp. 66-67. (Mimeo.)

Mr. Patrick cites 96 items of research findings and supplies a definitive bibliography of materials drawn from recent work in the field.

of view of one who accepts the American political and social system, as well as the ideology implicit in it, as a system of unquestioned superiority to any other. For the most part, when the character and structure of other systems are considered, they are considered in contrast to the worth of the American system.

It must also be remembered that the American teacher begins to be educated for his profession not just at the point of his admission to a teacher education program in a college or university, but in the elementary and secondary school and in the culture at large. He is subject to the same community pressures and value systems as anyone else, he moves through the same curriculum and the same school life as anyone else, and his conceptions of what education is, and what a teacher does and is, are images deeply embedded in his consciousness by the experience of being taught by the teachers in his school.

He then arrives at an institution for higher education, prepared for admission the day after he stops being a high school student and, in that sense, indistinguishable from a high school student, to undertake "cognitive learning (which) often serves merely to reinforce . . . early commitments." From my observations and enquiries, whatever commitments he may have had in his younger days, at the point of college entry he has not changed them in the direction of a wider concern for the world and its problems, not even in making a commitment to the vocation of the teacher, as I understand the meaning of these words. That is to say, he, or much more often she, has enrolled in a teacher education institution either because it is close to home and provides a fairly inexpensive education leading to a job after graduation—in teaching or in another field—or because teaching is a sensible and secure career if one has no burning desire to do anything else. For more than 60 percent of the women students in our research sample teaching was considered to be a career suitable for an interim period before marriage and a basis for employment security in the event of widowhood or during a later period when, with the family raised, it would be "something to do."

Once enrolled in a teacher education program, the student's curriculum and the methods of instruction, by textbooks, lectures, examinations, and grades, are essentially an extension of high school, with the same rewards and punishments, the same style of social life (which the high school copied earlier from the college), and the same culture-bound intellectual atmosphere. The education student arrives with almost no developed intellectual interests. The first two years of general education, as prescribed in the curriculum for certification, followed by an academic major, from four to six professional education courses, and practice teaching, usually in the senior year, leave him little room for electing courses either in foreign cultures, world affairs, or in any other field.

From the point of view of the student, not only is his college education substantially like that of high school in method, style, and content, but the professional education courses in college draw on materials from standard elementary and high school practices and curriculums with which the student is already familiar from having just gone through the schools himself. In addition, his practice teaching is carried on in schools almost exactly like the one that he attended, sometimes the actual one he did attend. The supervision of his teaching is conducted by a teacher very much like those by whom he has already been taught. In other words, he travels continually over the same familiar territory toward a destination close to where he started.

The International Content of the Curriculum

If we ask the question bluntly, To what extent are American teachers being prepared through their curriculum to understand and to teach about the nature of world society? the answer is, almost not at all.[7] Not more than 3 to 5 percent of all teachers, according to the best estimates presently available, have had in the course of their preparation to become teachers in the social sciences or any other area of the curriculum any formal study of cultures other than their own in the West, or have studied in a field which could properly be described as world affairs. This does not necessarily mean that they are ignorant of such knowledge, since it is possible to acquire it independently of the course system, or later on through in-service education, travel-study, summer institutes, and independent research. But it does mean that since, according to our findings, students who are preparing to become teachers seldom possess an initial interest in politics, world society, or foreign cultures, they are unlikely to develop such interest either on their own or through their curriculum of teacher preparation.

It would be useful to have, as the result of a national survey of all course offerings available to and elected by teacher candidates, exact information on a countrywide basis as to the content of the education of American teachers in non-Western cultures, world affairs, and international studies. However, despite the lack of such a survey, a sufficient amount of information exists, through the work of the research staff of Education and World Affairs and others in analyzing the undergraduate college curriculum in its international component, to make an informed and accurate judgment. Teacher candidates across the country take nearly all of their nonprofessional work in the regular departmental courses of the arts and science curriculum. As far as the content of their education is concerned, whatever is true for other undergraduates in general is true for teacher candidates, except that in their case the limitations in curricular content are more severe.

---

[7] Additional material having to do with curricular content is available in the EWA publications and other sources, particularly, *The University Looks Abroad; Education and World Affairs; Report on Program 1963-64; Coordinating International Programs and Activities at U.S. Colleges and Universities: A Directory; op. cit.* Introduction, p. 1 of Footnotes.

Also, *Teacher and Curriculum: Report of the Conference on American Education in a Revolutionary World,* U.S. National Committee for UNESCO, Washington, D.C.

Not more than 10 percent of American undergraduates, on graduation, have taken courses containing other than Western materials; 2 percent is approximately the amount of curricular time spent by high school students in studying cultures and societies outside the Western world. In many high schools there are no courses which deal in any way with world affairs or non-Western cultures. When that is transposed into its meaning for teacher candidates, the 10 percent of undergraduates with instruction in foreign affairs is reduced to well below 5 percent, due to the limited opportunity for electing courses outside the prescribed curriculum and the fact that in only two states are there requirements having to do with international or non Western affairs.[8]

The 1965 survey of the member institutions of AACTE carried out by the EWA Task Force on the professional schools of education showed that less than 20 percent of them offered education courses dealing with problems or materials outside the United States and that the courses which did exist were for the most part the result of effort by individual faculty members rather than through plans made by the school of education. This coincides with the findings of the present study: from our smaller sample, the percentage of schools or departments of education with international content in education courses was closer to 5 percent; those with overall plans for work in world affairs, a little over 2 percent.[9]

Another approach to an answer to the question of sheer curricular content available from teachers in the schools is to look at the number of courses and units of study in elementary schools and high schools which deal with non-Western and world materials and ask whether those who teach the ones which do exist have had any preparation to do so. Again, there is as yet no national survey to answer that question, although an answer of moderate accuracy can be given on the basis of what is already known. For example, Claude Phillips of Western Michigan University, in a study of the schools of one county in southern Michigan,[10] has found that the 69 high school social studies teachers who responded to his questionnaire were teaching 92 social studies courses, of which only 8 could be considered to have a world focus—1 in world geography, 6 in world history, and 1 in international relations.

Seventy-seven percent of the teachers said that they tried to incorporate materials dealing with the non-Western world in existing courses from time to time, although less than half of them had done formal study of any kind in relevant subjects. Of those who had, the study consisted of either one or two departmental courses devoted to a country or a continent. Five of the 69 teachers had had three or more courses which focused on non-Western cultures during their college training; only 9 had done such

[8] More detailed information about state requirements is included in Chapter IV "The Certification Question."

[9] *The Professional School and World Affairs: The School of Education,* a report from Education and World Affairs, p. 24.

[10] Phillips, Claude S., Jr. "World Affairs in Secondary Education." *Michigan Journal of Secondary Education,* Vol. 7, No. 1; Fall 1965.

work after leaving college. Nearly all of them felt that they were not actually prepared to teach subjects beyond those dealing with America and the Western countries.

Judging from the present state of the teacher education curriculum as seen in our research visits, the situation across the country is approximately that shown by Phillips' survey, with exceptions in a few institutions where students of declared interest in foreign affairs, including Peace Corps volunteers, have studied in the field in order to teach in high school. Phillips cites three present barriers to the broadening of the curriculum for teachers: the narrowness of the undergraduate curriculum in higher education, the continuing emphasis on the physical sciences both in high school and in college to the neglect of the social sciences, and the conservatism of school boards, college and high school administrators, professors, teachers, and parents who have been educated in the traditional narrow curriculum.

In trying to break down some of these barriers, Phillips' own institution has now included among its undergraduate requirements in general education one course in a non-Western culture; has developed an undergraduate minor in area studies, including Asia, Africa, Latin America, and Eastern Europe with approval from the certification officers of the Michigan State Board of Education; and has installed a master of arts degree program in international and area studies for students with a traditional background in the social sciences.

When the education of teachers is analyzed from the point of view of their opportunities for cultural and intellectual growth, new dimensions begin to emerge in the problem of extending the range of their knowledge and interest into the larger areas of world society. The problem begins in the fact that the teacher's range of possible experiences—intellectual, cultural, and social—is so severely limited by the circumstances of his education and his personal experience is so circumscribed by the social and cultural milieu in which his life is lived that involvement with the wider issues of international society, or even of his own society, is not natural to his temperament or to his outlook. He has not been asked or expected to become involved with wider issues or to see from a wider perspective, but only to learn what is taught by teachers who are older versions of himself and of what he will be someday, from texts which raise few fundamental questions.

From the time he began his own education to the time he begins to teach others, he has been locked into a curriculum and a culture of standard American proportions. He passes through agreed-upon procedures for becoming a teacher, and his development as a person of broad intellectual interests and a rich personal life has seldom been enhanced by these procedures. An additional irony lies in the fact that when he is introduced to courses in world history, in international relations, or in non-Western cultures, these, too, are taught in such a way that they seldom open up his mind to new perspectives or stimulate his thinking in new directions. The non-Western subject matter in the context of his curriculum for teacher preparation is regarded as more material to be covered, followed by more examinations to be passed. In his eyes, to include such subject matter in his education is not to open up a whole new image of what the world is like, but simply to add further items to the store of material available for passing on to his pupils when he becomes a teacher.

Some Underlying Causes of Neglect

It is not hard to see why this situation exists. The main reason lies in the fact that the education of teachers for service in the public schools has always been conducted in a local context and a poverty-stricken way outside the mainstream of the intellectual and social forces of contemporary history. We have never brought to the task of educating teachers the full power of the American intellect or more than a minimum of our social energies and economic resources. It has been an area of neglect, scandalous neglect, when compared to the energies and resources devoted to the development of the automobile, the refrigerator, television, highways, bombs, and space travel, or the education of scientists, engineers, fighter pilots, and astronauts.

It would be natural to assume, for example, that the colleges of liberal arts in America, whose origin lies in the intention of their founders to provide an education centered in moral values and religious faith and in an effort to develop graduates who in one way or another would propagate the faith, would have shown in the course of their development as secular institutions a continuing interest in preparing teachers for the schools and colleges. Through the work of their graduates as teachers, they would have been able to substitute for the former roles of their clergymen and convinced laymen the role of advocates and teachers of the values—secular, social, and cultural—as expressed in their traditional purposes as educational institutions.

This has not been the case. At a time when the normal schools and teachers colleges were struggling to develop programs to educate hundreds of new teachers, the liberal arts colleges were developing into all-purpose institutions in which the liberal arts and sciences were considered to be a preparation, not to teach, but to gain access to the social and intellectual prerequisites for entrance into the educated classes. The difference in social prestige between the teacher institutions and the liberal arts colleges has increased over the years, and the disinterest of the latter in the mission of teacher education has continued into the present. The irony is that while the curriculums and purpose of the liberal arts colleges have become more academic and less relevant to the needs of the student and his society, the students have in many cases been seeking a sense of purpose and relevance for their own education by becoming de facto teachers in the slums, in the rural areas, in foreign countries, and among themselves.

In the meantime, the country's central intellectual resources for what has now become known as the knowledge industry have been mobilized in a relatively few major universities, research institutes, graduate schools, professional schools, industrial research units, and government agencies with their research branches. Higher education, at what it considers to be its best, has become an instrument for producing manpower for purposes other than teaching. Yet the quality of higher education depends for its future on the quality of the teachers it produces—teachers for its own graduate schools, for its undergraduate colleges, aside from the teachers in whose hands rests the preparation of the oncoming generation of future college students now in the primary and secondary schools. One would assume that even in terms of the narrower interest of the university as an organized institution, the problem of developing new school and college teachers to serve its own needs would occupy a central place in university planning.

The contrary is true. There is at this moment no serious and continuing effort on the part of the universities to develop scholar-teachers for the undergraduate young and for the generation just behind them in the schools. Although there are a growing number of all-university committees on teacher education, concentration in planning and operation is still on the development of the research experts and Ph.D. specialists for the academic and institutional markets, leaving a teaching gap exactly in the middle of the whole educational system. When we look at the total quality of that system, it becomes clear that the achievements of the United States as a civilization and as a world power have been reached by the use of only a fraction of the latent intellectual resources within the population. The only way to bring this latent talent into full play is to develop thousands and thousands of teachers who know how to seek out that talent and to foster it, and first of all, in the colleges, to teach those who will do the teaching. When the problem is traced back far enough, it comes full circle, from early childhood education, through the years to college, to graduate school and back again, with everything interconnected, yet relying on the central pivot of the colleges and universities to make the system work. The colleges and universities are the breeding ground for teaching, yet they have not begun to create the conditions in which teaching and the teacher are honored and rewarded above all else, and in which scholarship, research, and teaching are linked together in the organic set of relationships they must have if the academic culture is to stimulate the best intellectual efforts of college students and the college faculty.

If we have not realized fully what a radical change in educational thinking and in the use of our national resources is now demanded by the new position of the United States in world society, this is understandable. We are less than 30 years away from the isolationism natural to the whole of American political thinking, and a little more than 10 years away from the chauvinism and xenophobia of the McCarthy period. It is worth noting that in a number of ways we have never left the McCarthy period. The main framework for policy decision and political alignments in the United States and abroad is still the dialectic of pro- and anti-communism. Ideas, persons, and countries are still measured in terms of their relationships within that frame of reference. Ideas and persons are still subject to suspicions of disloyalty to the country if they deviate in the direction of full-bodied internationalism on major issues of war and peace. During the years when the responsibility of the United States in world society has been making sharply increased demands for enlightened world understanding on the part of our leaders, teachers, and citizens alike, the cultural and political climate in the United States has not been at all congenial to the development of lively ideas for political education, either in world affairs or in liberal democracy.

That, too, can be understood. We have never had a tradition in the United States of broad political education in which a liberal or radical movement is taken for granted as a normal and legitimate part of the culture. The radical, no matter what he has been radical about, but especially the radical in politics, has always been suspect. In later life he may be revered—Norman Thomas, David Dubinsky, Sidney Hillman, Eugene Debs—but when he is young, active, challenging, controversial, and dissident, when he takes part in serious political and cultural movements, he is more often reviled than respected. When teachers have held political views even slightly at variance with the norms of popular consensus, they have been doubly suspect, since their role is considered to be that of Americanizing the young, not internationalizing or liberalizing them, or raising questions in their minds about the wisdom of the course of action pursued by their government in foreign affairs.

The years of rapid change in America's world position from isolation to world involvement were years in which educators at home, without a political tradition, without being accustomed even to thinking in political terms about their own place in the society, have been faced by the practical problems of expanding rapidly an inadequate educational system while at the same time reforming its content. So concentrated has been the attention given to the practical problems of funds, enrollment, buildings, personnel, and lobbying before the public to engineer consent for larger educational budgets that questions about the world and where it is going have seldom been raised among working educators. They have not been accustomed to thinking about the relation of education to the world, nor to any large framework of social or political thought. They have tended to do what they have been asked to do, by the government, by the public, by the foundations, by the state legislatures.

Reforming the science and mathematics curriculum in the 1950's, for example, was important, safe, praised, funded, and rewarded. It was, therefore, enthusiastically carried out. Meddling with issues in world affairs, reforming the social studies curriculum to make it more intellectually alive, politically relevant, and international was risky, open to criticism, unfunded, and, in many local situations, prohibited. What reform there was in the curriculum in world affairs was based on the principle of arming young Americans with ideas with which they could protect themselves against communism and could "strengthen the forces of democracy."

We have not yet begun to construct a philosophy for the development of new school curriculums in the social sciences and humanities free from the biases of American foreign policy, since the educators have not yet made a clear distinction between the content of knowledge considered as a body of material to aid in the process of Americanizing children and knowledge of world events and issues as a means of understanding America and oneself in a world perspective. Until that distinction is made and applied in curriculum reform, the teacher is unlikely to receive a preparation for teaching which will enable him to rise above the political environment in which his earlier beliefs were formed.

The Growth in Size

In the meantime, the American schools have grown to an extraordinary number and size, 25,000 school systems, 50 million pupils, and 2 million teachers, in response to the population growth, the demands of parents and citizens, and of powerful forces deep within the economic and social system. This growth has its roots in the fundamental needs of the communities and cities, and the local school boards and their schools are the American instruments for getting certain things done. Schoolteachers are the people to do them. It is only in recent years that there has been any direct relationship between the universities and the schools, and the relationship is still tenuous, even though most of the education of schoolteachers is conducted in college and university classrooms. The normal schools and later the teachers colleges were not invented by scholars—they were part of a citizens' movement to satisfy explicit educational needs, and they were linked directly to the society and to the schools, not to the universities. There has, therefore, been no public feeling that the elementary and secondary schools are intellectually or socially separate from the society. Parents have not considered the schools and teacher training institutions to be intellectual centers, but places where their children could be prepared to become useful Americans and could be given a chance to move ahead in their society. The present demands of the poor for education of a quality at least equivalent to that of the well-to-do is a continuation and a manifestation of that citizens' movement.

It is hard to remember that in most parts of the country, we are only 70 to 80 years away from the time when the idea was first accepted that teachers needed any particular kind of training lasting more than a month or two before they started work. With the drastic teacher shortage in so many American cities, we may be returning to what could be a refreshing new beginning of the old plan of learning to teach by teaching in the schools.

Less than 80 years ago, in September 1890, Joshua Crittenden Chilton, itinerant salesman of education from Michigan, bent on starting a training school for teachers somewhere in the United States, addressed the citizens of Denton, Texas, on that subject in the Denton courthouse square. After explaining the need for teacher training in Denton and in Texas and describing the Pestalozzi pedagogy, Chilton, who had dressed himself as an educator—long Prince Albert coat, full beard and moustache, and a tall silk hat—called on "all who believe in higher education and who want to see our state in the very front of intellectual as well as material progress" to help start the Texas Normal College and Teacher Training Institute. "Then," says the historian of the event, Professor James L. Rogers of North Texas State University, the institution which descended directly from Chilton's Institute, "with his high aspirations stated, the new president took his small staff and student body up the stairs over the B. J. Wilson hardware store and classes began."[11]

Since that time, when public schooling in Texas had existed for only six years and there was only one school in the state for training teachers, the citizens of Denton and Texas have continued their support of teacher education. But it was their movement, and they were the ones who had to decide whether they wanted to spend tax money to train teachers. What began as Chilton's private venture in persuasion, the idea of a man who held no college degree but had been to a normal school in Michigan, has now gone through stages of development similar to other institutions across the country, from normal school to teachers college, from teachers college to university—always justifying itself to the public by reference to the needs of the citizens for teachers and for education. North Texas State has now become a university of 16,000 students, graduating approximately 1,500 teachers a year, with a graduate student enrollment of nearly 3,000, of whom nearly 500 are doctoral candidates. What began as a movement in which teachers in and from the schools taught new teachers how to teach has become a movement in which faculty members in the colleges teach about teaching to students who have never taught. In a sense, it has been one long boot-strap operation, involving homemade boots and locally produced straps.

If the quality of intellectual effort is to some extent attenuated and if an interest in international affairs is not yet a major concern in the education of teachers, at North Texas State or elsewhere, this can best be regarded as a phase of social growth in a citizens' movement, rather than as a failure in the good intention of educators. The growth in size of the institutions of teacher education has produced problems common to such institutions, among them the problem of recruiting faculty members from outside the circle of professional educators and the creation of a curriculum for educating teachers which goes beyond the normal school and the teachers college. But the growth has come in response to the needs of citizens not unlike those who supported Chilton in the first place—the need for a place where the advantages formerly held by the well-to-do and the privileged could be obtained for those who had little money and little preparation for the higher learning.

[11] Rogers, James L. *The Story of North Texas*. Denton: North Texas State University, 1965.

It is also useful to remember that we can see in the history of the entire state college movement a direct and rapid journey back to the recent origins of teacher education. In the Pacific Northwest, the first settler who came to the present site of Western Washington State College in Bellingham arrived as recently as 1848; the first normal school started in 1896; the first B.A. degrees, marking the transition toward a teachers college, were awarded in 1933, with a change of name to Western Washington College of Education in 1937. By 1961, the shift to Western Washington State College was complete, with 23 departments and a continuing concern for educating teachers along with liberal arts students and those who would enter the other professions.

The speed of transition and the terms in which it was made are typical of the entire movement in teacher education. What is not as often recognized is the fact, demonstrated clearly in the case of Western Washington State (any one of hundreds of other institutions in Wisconsin, Connecticut, Massachusetts, or Michigan might serve in illustration), is the connection of the evolving teachers college both to the educational needs and interests of the state and its citizens and to the national interest as construed by the federal grant-makers and the foundations.

Some of the arithmetic of the connection at Western Washington State College is this: grants of $500,000 from the Ford Foundation for the graphic arts; $121,000 from the National Science Foundation for mathematics and the earth sciences; $2 million for a computer center; additional funds from various sources inside and outside the State of Washington for a speech and hearing clinic, a poverty program, a neutron generator, a Fresh Water Institute, and more than a dozen other projects in research and education. The College now has more than 6,000 students from its own state, 27 other states, and 13 foreign countries, all of whom have a chance to attend any of 50 major events in music and the arts each year and have a wide variety of curricular programs from which to choose, along with the curriculum for teachers, and of whom there are approximately 600 graduating each year in addition to nearly 100 teachers with the M.A. degree.

For the first time in this short transitional period, the education student is now placed in the middle of a variety of other students and in a situation in which his intellectual interests can be extended beyond anything that was formerly possible. It will take more years than have been available so far to find the ways in which the total environment of intellectual opportunity can be best used to the advantage of the education student. These ways are unlikely to develop until there is a great deal more clarity among the educators of teachers about the philosophy of education they wish to adopt. Having lost the basic insight of the rough and ready, practical and plain work of the normal school, the new transitional institutions need to return to the roots of their own tradition and to reestablish the principle that intellectual growth is a functional part of the process of learning to teach and that it is a *result* of teaching and learning, not a prerequisite for undertaking them.

There has been very little consciousness in the past that teachers should have more qualifications as members of a separate intellectual or scholarly community than anyone else who worked in town, read a lot, or liked to talk about books and foreign countries. In this country, although there are those who deplore it or deny it, there has never been an intellectual elite charged with the responsibility for running the country's cultural and educational life. Nor has education been considered to be the province of the intellectuals, elite or otherwise. It has been considered as a game anyone can play—The American Legion, the chambers of commerce, newspaper editors, crackpots, politicians, parents, admirals, clergymen, businessmen, assorted journalists, anyone with something to say.

In fact, since the subject of education has become a matter of constant and dominant public attention, a whole new breed of competent and informed critics has created itself among parents, public-spirited citizens, businessmen, members of the professions, and, above all, among the members of the press and public affairs division of the television and radio networks. There are 1,400 members in the 50 states of the National Committee for Support of the Public Schools, ranging from lawyers, labor leaders, doctors, and parents with considerable influence in their own communities to national figures like John Hersey, George Gallup, Omar Bradley, and the Committee chairman, Mrs. Eugene Meyer.

When one of the major weekly magazines or national newspapers turns its attention to educational issues, it can call upon a research staff of hundreds, along with reporters and writers who have followed closely the issues involved—teacher strikes, poverty programs, teacher education, the attitudes of high school students—and whose information, objectivity, and insight are in many ways of a higher quality than those of the professional educators whose work they are reviewing and reporting. A great deal of the time, the educators take their views and their information from what appears in the major magazines and television programs; while, conversely, those educators who wish to reach the teachers and educators, as well as the public, with their own views prefer to write for the mass magazines rather than for the publications designed for the teaching profession.

I find this a healthy and promising situation and do not see in it the sinister implications found by those critics of the mass culture who feel that the intrusion of the public into fields belonging to the intellectuals and professionals is dangerous to the future of the culture. Everyone *is* in it— the rioting Negro, the flaming segregationist, the anxious parent, the cultural critic, the practicing educator—and it would be dangerous public policy either to allow the teachers, as some have asserted of late, to claim the exclusive right to know what needs to be done with children and to be left alone to do it, or to allow any other sector of the total community, anti-intellectual or otherwise, to claim the right to settle policy for education in America.

However, the continuing open debate does raise certain problems, one of which is that if there is no sizable group of persons in the schools themselves who, by commitment, vocation, and the talent to go with it, take a serious interest in ideas and in the larger issues of American and world society, there is no place within the educational community, or in the experience of schoolchildren growing up, where fresh and relevant thinking in these matters is an area of continual and intense concern. Nor are there in the schools sufficient models of the active, enquiring, imaginative, large-minded scholar at work for the young to emulate. There are in the schools too few instances of man thinking and bearing witness to the power and delight of the intellect. There are mainly practitioners.

Added to this is the fact that the majority of those who enter programs of teacher education are from middle income and lower income groups, for whom entrance into the teaching profession is primarily a form of social and economic advance. They bring very few cultural and intellectual interests with them from the background of their own homes and schools. Since they enter institutions where learning to teach is considered mainly to be a matter of learning to handle children in classrooms with a standard syllabus, and since the academic subjects they have studied in college are studied in isolation from anything to do with teaching itself, they seldom have the opportunity to learn to understand what it means to be a scholar and a teacher in the full meaning of these words. What is missing is the idea of education as the liberation of oneself into new levels of intellect and emotion—education as a means of achieving new capacities and insights which can then become part of the stream of contributions made by the human race in the development of the arts and sciences, societies and civilizations. The present concept of teaching in America contains no call to lend oneself to great enterprises, to become *useful* in the larger sense.

Changes in American Society

In making these preliminary generalizations and the others which follow throughout the report, I have drawn on the results not only of the present study with its visits to the campuses and classrooms of the schools and colleges and the analysis of existing research and literature in the field, but of visits to foreign schools and universities, experimental work at Sarah Lawrence College, and the experience of teaching philosophy at, among other places, a Midwestern university to American undergraduates fresh from high school. There, whatever else they learned, they had learned to think in banalities and to allow unexamined assumptions and undefined concepts to flow freely through their minds unchecked by the process of critical or reflective thinking. I formed the simple conclusion then, at the beginning of my teaching, and not since contradicted by anything else, that to teach American undergraduates about the nature and dimension of the total world of which they are inhabitants, whether this be called world affairs, world history, philosophy, or political science, it is first necessary to develop in them an active state of enquiry into the meaning of what they learn and a commitment to go on enquiring and to act according to the results, no matter what the subject under study. This is a truism about all students, but particularly relevant when applied to their education as teachers.

As will be evident to the reader, I have conceived the present research into the education of teachers in the field of world affairs as an enquiry into education in its broad sense rather than as an analysis or survey of the technical problems of arranging teacher education programs and curriculums containing an international and intercultural content. These are, of course, central to the development of new educational methods and content for teachers in contemporary America, and I have dealt with them in ways which are, I believe, appropriate to the subject of the research. But the chief aim of the study is to find ways the education of teachers can be deepened and broadened and can become so serious and engrossing an enterprise to those who are involved in it and in the American culture at large that the American teacher may think of his task as nothing less than the improvement of the quality of life in American and world society. It is therefore impossible to deal directly with the problems of teaching and learning in the field of world affairs without first dealing with some of the more basic questions in the way American education is presently organized.

One difficulty immediately presents itself to an enquiry of this kind: The educational system and the society in which it exists will not stand still long enough to be clearly observed and accurately described. Since the study began, four factors have been introduced into the American society which affect deeply the character of its educational and social system and alter the perspective from which it can be observed.

The first of these is the sharp increase during these past two years in the commitments made by the United States to the war in Vietnam, a factor which has altered the national life in all its dimensions, nowhere more profoundly than in the educational system. The war is being fought with the bodies and minds of students from high school and college, along with students out of school entirely, and has reached far into the community and family life of the population, causing profound unrest within the intellectual community of the universities and among the students themselves, who question the policies of their government, ranging from its conscription for military service, its deferments, its expenditures for war, its pressures for acquiescence to the very policies most in question. It has also raised basic questions about the purposes of education itself and about priorities in the uses of our human resources on behalf of conflicting national interests and policies.

The second is the explosive and violent quality of life in the American inner cities, where conditions which have long required thoughtful and compassionate effort in education and social reconstruction have now become literally impossible. The pace of change and the degree of danger to the national welfare have now become so greatly out of balance with the progress of reform that many of the educational remedies and programs which, even one year ago, seemed adequate as a beginning have now in this short space of time become irrelevant and obsolete.

The third is the marked shift in the thinking of the younger generation about its place in American society and the educational system, in part a product of the other two factors, in part a product of a cultural shift through the communication system of a mass society which can now communicate with itself hourly, can expose its own problems and developments to the world minute by minute, and can bring the world into the American community day by day, week by week, and month by month on a scale never before known. The struggle between the blacks and the whites in America has now assumed a new phase of actual and potential violence which promises to defeat the normal procedures for maintaining public order. It has its parallel in struggles of greater violence between insurgents and counterinsurgents throughout the developing third world. For the first time there is now a cohesive movement within the younger generation of Negroes who have found an identity and a political base in the conception of pride of race and comradeship in rebellion. The younger generation, both white and black, now has its own sense of identification with the underprivileged of the world and with the insurgents of the third world who refuse to accept their place in a social order which they have no power to control. In one sense, this has broadened the conception of nationalism among a growing proportion of American youth to include a recognition of their national counterparts in other countries in the world. It has produced, indirectly, an internationalism of youth.

The effect of these rapid changes on those of us involved in the working areas of American education and, in particular, those of us concerned to find ways of relating the actions and ideas of educational systems to the world society in which they can play so great a role for good is to heighten the level of concern and to make more urgent the necessity for taking actions which can alleviate the increasing stress and the destructive tendencies in American life and international affairs. No matter what one's level of concern may have been in the past and no matter what one may have proposed or advocated as a solution to educational problems which have so clearly become worldwide, the needs and demands created by the events which press upon us make it imperative that we face the educational issues with a degree of seriousness and urgency which can match the urgency of the situation. If we are not to allow the speed of change to continue to outrun the provisions we are making to accommodate the change, we are going to have to do things in education over the next two years which we never dreamed we could or should do two short years ago.

A fourth factor which has been introduced into the educational system since the study began, at a level of significance different from the three I have described, is the passage of the International Education Act in October 1966 and the commitments it makes to the cause of internationalism in American culture and education. The philosophy on which the Act is based and the provisions it makes for putting that philosophy into effect change the framework in which education in America is to be conducted. We have never before had a statement from an American President or from Congress which aligned the American educational system with those of the rest of the world, nor one which outlined a course of action to create an international point of view within the schools, colleges, and universities of the United States. The legislation has not, as of now, had very much chance to influence the educational system itself, since the funds to carry out its provisions are still lacking. Luckily, the Act contains provisions for the use of funds already available in other government programs, and progress can be made in spite of the reluctance of Congress to put to work the money already authorized.

The Response of Educators

One way of reporting quickly the findings of the present study regarding the intellectual and social climate of the teacher education movement is to say that on few campuses did we find persons who recognized in specific ways the existence or significance of these changes in America's relation to the world. There was little discussion of the implications of the war for American society and its educational system, as well as little realization that what can only be called a Negro revolution was in progress, that deep-seated changes were occurring in the attitude of youth toward education and society, or that an International Education Act had been passed. It was as if the institutional structures and preoccupations of the educators of teachers had sealed off the reality of the very society they existed to serve.

The comment of a student in response to a question about the level of student interest in international affairs sums up one area of the findings of the study:

> Disregarding topical interest in Vietnam, most students have little or no interest in the outside world. By interest, I mean any kind of knowledge of and thought about world problems—peace, poverty, disease, economic status of many emerging and traditional nations. Again the influence of courses is small in the area of foreign cultures because even Western cultures are only touched on in government survey courses. Even these are taken by few who will enter the secondary education level.

Martha Darling—a former member of the staff in international affairs of the National Student Association who conducted a survey of student activities in world affairs in the Boston-Cambridge metropolitan area on behalf of the present study—to whom the above comment was made, adds the following:

> Nor are there major countervailing influences outside the classroom to stimulate interest. The majority of foreign students are reported to be few and quite Westernized and Americanized. International, political, economic, and moral issues seem in a way a little too serious for discussion—or irrelevant. More congenial are subjects like "How do you like the U.S.?" and the bits of information exchanged about national customs do not appear to be projected into an image of an international and interdependent community. . . . The education

students spend much of their course time with methods, measurements, and general educational mechanics. Their future charges seem to figure in their education courses more as objects of these methods rather than as the subject of the teaching process; more as identical models or types described in child psychology textbooks than as individuals with specific problems who are to be educated to live and function and contribute to a world which grows closer together. On the whole, the students in the academic majors seem to be more aware of the implications of the international and national scene for America and themselves.[12]

I have mentioned elsewhere the minority of student activists whose educational and political ideas are making a difference to the campus atmosphere. I should say at once that their numbers are comparatively small—perhaps 5 percent on the livelier campuses, none at all on others—and that to me the major problem in education and world affairs is the political lethargy of almost all the education students, matched and complemented by a similar lethargy on the part of their faculty members.

A vitally important theme has returned again and again to my mind as I have been reviewing the enormous power and possibility for good in our cultural resources—the new schools being built, the thousands and thousands of new students being added to the university rolls every year, the energies going into the poverty program, the National Teacher Corps, the Peace Corps, urban education, Project Head Start, job opportunity centers, the civil rights movement. It is the familiar theme: How can we turn the huge expenditures of intelligence, energy, and money being poured into the war in Southeast Asia in a new direction for peaceful reconstruction? We can now see evidence of a power undreamed of in any former period of American or world history. We have literally built whole new towns in Vietnam, taking sandy wastes and converting them into huge centers for service and supply, installing networks of roads, taking deserted coastlines and converting them into giant ports, converting jungles into airports, building an international transportation system.

The lesson, beyond all others, is very simple. When it comes to training, transporting, equipping, housing, and supplying vast numbers of Americans to accomplish a national purpose, whatever it may be, we have the capacity to do whatever we decide to do. Whatever else emerges from the present war, the scale of thought about what can be done in international education and peaceful reconstruction, if we decide to do it, has reached a proven magnitude which puts all previous scale of thought into obsolescence. We should be thinking, in our cultural and educational policies for internationalism, not of a few students here and a few teachers there, but of 25,000 to 50,000 student teachers sent abroad each year for cooperative learning with their foreign counterparts, thousands of fellowships for volunteers to the teaching profession and the human services, millions of dollars for the support of volunteers to help in the reconstruction of territories destroyed by war. The young men, Negroes and whites, who are fighting in numbers beyond anything we would have dreamed two years

[12] Report to Harold Taylor from Martha Darling, January 1966.

ago have the will and the idealism to turn their efforts toward reconstruction when that becomes our national policy.

A new kind of GI Bill at the conclusion of this war could divert these energies into the teaching and helping professions by providing subsidies for veterans to build on their experience in the villages with the people of Vietnam and, with new curriculums in the colleges and universities, preparing them for teaching and community development in Vietnam and Southeast Asia. If, as Secretary McNamara has pointed out, the Defense Department operates one of the largest educational programs in the world, let us take the skills and talents already developed within that system for peaceful use, for teaching, for social reconstruction.

As the months have gone by, we have already seen the colleges and universities become the source of new political thinking and social change in education and cultural affairs, with a new constituency of the young who have created their own leadership among themselves and have formed the basis for new political allegiances which run counter to those of the established national authorities—for education and for foreign policy. The break of the National Student Association with the Central Intelligence Agency was not only a political but a symbolic act. It marked the time when the younger generation broke with established government authority, when the students, through one of their major organizations, refused to accept the leadership, control, and policy of a government whose subsidies had determined the course of student policy in world affairs. From this point on, the political and social force of more than 6 million students and 450,000 faculty members constitutes a source of independent thought and action which will, in one way or another, affect the direction of American politics, education, and foreign policy. A wise and farsighted government will consider this to be a potent force for good. A negative and anxious government and educational leadership will ignore the existence and possibilities of this new constituency and will try to dampen its effects and to divert its attention into established channels.

Evidence that the liberal new thinking in international education exemplified by the passage of the International Education Act is in danger of such dampening is shown in the lack of Congressional support for the allocation of the necessary funds. A policy of internationalism in education cannot be carried out with the limited funds presently at the disposal of the colleges and universities, since in nearly every case they are already hard pressed to carry out the obligations of domestic programs to which they are already committed. As of the present writing, none of the funds in the total figure of $130 million for a two-year period authorized for the International Education Act in October 1966 has been appropriated. Unless the weight of financial support demanded by the terms of the Act and the demands of wise public policy are applied to the situation now, we will enter the 1970's farther behind than we have ever been, since we can count on the pace of increase in the need for a full program of international education to run even faster between now and then than it has in the past.

A Personal Note on Educational Theory

During the course of the present study, not only was I forced to consider these wider implications for education of the changes occurring inside America and in the relation of the United States to world problems, but I was confronted with the fact that to study education from the point of view of the education of teachers raises a different set of questions from those involved in the study of education as that term is generally used. Although I could find no basic distinction between the principles of education most applicable to the nurture of intellectual growth of all kinds and the principles applicable to students being educated to become teachers, I was continually made conscious of one very important educational difference—the difference betwen possessing knowledge and using it.

I had recognized this difference before and had thought about it, written about it, and was concerned about it, as any person involved in the study of philosophy must be, but I had never specifically applied it as a theory in the education of teachers. Put simply, the point is that to teach what you know is the most immediate way to find out what it is you know and whether you understand it and whether it is relevant, useful, interesting, important, accurate, or otherwise worthwhile. Every man has his own body of knowledge, made from the materials of his own biography, depending on where he was born and in what circumstances, on the variety of personal experiences he has undergone in his own and other cultures, and on the formal studies which the accidents of his academic history have provided for him.

My formal studies were mainly in philosophy, history, and literature of the West. I am thus the representative of a culture-bound education later corrected by confrontation and involvement with other cultures and their representatives. The formative experience in education which led to my present views was gained in the lively atmosphere of an American land-grant university and the even livelier atmosphere of an American experimental college, where the worth of an educational idea was continually on test and was judged by the degree to which it enhanced the intellectual and personal growth of persons for whom it was intended. As a student I carried out the academic tasks set before me in the Canadian and English systems of education, and I entered the profession of teaching without ever having learned to teach or having examined closely what it was that I knew which might be useful in the lives of others.

It was the first years of teaching philosophy to undergraduates in a relatively unselected student body at the University of Wisconsin that I learned, sometimes to my horror, the limits of my knowledge and the actual, usable content of the education I had received. Through teaching and through the teacher's necessity of meeting the educational needs of students from day to day, I learned what it was I needed to know in order to make what contribution I could to the culture of which I was a part. I also learned what it was I was most interested in. Until that kind of testing was administered daily in the classrooms of the University of Wisconsin, the body of knowledge which inadvertently was mine lay inert in my mind, certified by appropriate degrees, but uninvestigated and unchallenged by the demand that it be used within the culture.

My conclusions about education and about the kind of knowledge of most worth to the younger generation and to the culture at large have been formed almost entirely by the experience of teaching and by the experience of administering education at an experimental college where we tried continually to develop forms of organization which could involve the student in his own learning. The central idea, which has reaffirmed itself through the years, is that the best way to learn something is to teach it, that this applies to students as well as to teachers, that the way to teach teachers is to have them teach—themselves, each other, and children in the schools—and that the best kind of teacher is one who has had a variety of experiences outside the academic system and who teaches what he is most interested in and cares most about.

I must, therefore, confess to a strong practical bent in my thinking about education, one which leans more heavily on the value of direct experience with ideas, issues, people, and educative situations than on the regular apparatus of educational institutions. I hold to the central conviction that the scholar who divorces himself from teaching, who relies solely or principally on the insights and judgments of his professional colleagues, free from the necessity of justifying his scholarship in the context of its relevance, its intrinsic value, or its use in the lives of the young is likely to find himself wrapped in an academic cocoon inhibiting the growth of his mind and his scholarship. A book is an effort on the part of its author to express to others what it is he has found. It may be addressed to a special audience of those who already understand its terms of reference; but, unless he is able to make what he knows available in some measure and in some form to those who are not in his frame of reference, he suffers the fate of exclusion from his culture. A comparable fate awaits the novelist or the playwright who, having written from his own experience in the world, shuts himself up to write more, sees only other authors and writers, reads what each is saying about the other, and finds that he no longer has very much to say to the world, since the wellsprings of his experience have dried up. Either that, or he begins to write novels, plays, and critical pieces about other writers.

During the investigation of the state of teacher education, I found evidence that the limitations of personal experience in the lives of teachers and educators, imposed by the fact that they deal almost exclusively with each other within the institutions and environment of their profession, have an inhibiting effect on the scope of their educational imagination. I found this to be true in a personal way when, in writing about education and America, I discovered that to explain America and American education to those who are not Americans is one of the most direct ways to force oneself to come to terms with the content of one's own belief. This becomes necessary if an educator accepts the assignment, as was true in my case, to speak before the student bodies and faculty members of foreign universities about the philosophy of American education, or to discuss with foreign students and scholars issues in education and social change as they present themselves within American society.

I have, therefore, in this report, placed the central emphasis in the recommendations and proposals for change in the education of teachers in world affairs on the necessity of various forms of confrontation between the members of world cultures, rather than on the unilateral presentation through texts and curricular materials of ideas and facts drawn from the study of cultures. If one addresses a foreign audience about American education, it is necessary to start from scratch, assuming that apart from some elementary facts about the geography and national character of Americans, most of them mistaken, nothing very much is known about the American educational system or its aims. The experts in the audience have usually become experts by formal study rather than by direct experience within the American culture; and, whether in Moscow, Leningrad, Tehran, Djakarta, Athens, Tokyo, or Istanbul, the speaker is forced to return to the essentials of his own belief about his own culture and its educational system. In the case of addressing an American audience or teaching Americans about American education, it is useful to assume that they, too, are foreigners and that their society should be presented to them as if it belonged to someone else. The teacher who has never known what his society looks like to someone else can seldom see it as it truly is.

The Definition of World Affairs

With these preconceptions and presentiments, I was therefore not altogether surprised to discover when I began the study that the words I used to explain its nature meant something so different to the students and educators with whom I talked that, unless I took great care, I was almost certain to be misunderstood—I mean misunderstood about simple words like *student, teacher, educator, world affairs, curriculum, teacher education,* or the word *education* itself. The phrase "education of teachers in world affairs" meant to most others "teacher education" and courses in international relations and non-Western cultures. Non-Western culture was something studied as a counterpart to Western culture, teacher education meant something labeled, technical and quite specific, already classified, with an attitude adopted toward it. It was something you did in order to meet state certification requirements, while you studied the regular college courses in the academic departments. Various educators held various views about what was meant by international education itself. Among these were—

1. Courses in international relations, stressing the role of the United Nations, international organizations, and the business of governments in dealing with each other.

2. Courses in political science which stressed the relation of the Western democracies to the communist countries and the conflicts in ideology in post-colonial Africa and Asia—the political strategies involved in American foreign policy.

3. Courses in world history, world culture, and world geography, designed to broaden the scope of the student's general knowledge.

4. Area studies stressing the interrelation of the academic disciplines in exploring the history and characteristics of a given region of the world.

5. Comparative education, to explore the similarities and differences among national systems of education.

6. Special sequences of courses in foreign cultures, designed to prepare teachers to teach in a given area of the high school or college curriculum.

7. Courses in general education containing knowledge of foreign countries and their cultures outside the Western hemisphere.

8. World affairs courses emphasizing current events.

More often than not, no distinction was made between the need for such courses in the general education of prospective teachers and their use in the preparation of teachers who could themselves teach specific courses in international affairs, world history, etc., to elementary and high school students.

I found that teacher education was held in low regard by a large number of students and a considerable number of university faculty members, often with a formidable, if uninformed, disrespect. The negative attitude seemed to come in part from an unexamined assumption that "teacher education" was all one thing. It was what had been talked about and criticized in the public, it was what Admiral Rickover did not like, it was a standard program of professional courses, all of them unfortunately unavoidable. I can report as a primary fact that "teacher education," on the whole, is not highly regarded by most of those undergoing it, by those who stay out of it and hear about it from their friends, or by those who know little about it. When I turned from the interviews, meetings, conferences, and class visits with the students and professors to the literature of teacher education, I found almost exactly the same set of assumptions in the literature about the nature of the programs. I could see the reinforcing effect of documents from the educating profession on the practices of the schools and colleges. The documents reflect the practices, which then gain legitimacy from the documents. Again, teacher education is classified as one particular kind of education, defined by its own terms.

The tendency of schoolmen in search of guidance toward improvement of the schools is to review a kind of national checklist, of the sort provided by James Conant and others, of subjects, organizations, numbers of qualified personnel, costs, etc., and to measure themselves against a national agenda of the things they should have and the things they should be doing. I had the feeling that for many of those with whom I talked,

45

non-Western culture, if backed by sufficient authority, would be simply added to the obligatory list. There is thus a one-dimensional quality in the concepts which dominate the literature, the research topics, and the agenda of educational action and reform. The tendency is to think of education as a closed system, with no relation to the political, social, economic, or world context in which education operates. The educational system is assumed to have its own parts, students, teachers, administrators, curriculum, all of them organized within the system in such a way that each part can function at a certain level of efficiency.

The present aim of the professional educator, as I learned from deans of colleges of education, professors of education, and from the articles and books which they and other research scholars in the field have written, is to make education more professional, to raise the level and status of professional education as a discipline to that of the major graduate schools—law, medicine, architecture, or engineering. Although some faculty members of colleges and departments of education with whom I talked felt comfortable with the idea that the study of education could be usefully carried on as a central concern in the social sciences and the humanities, most believed that unless education were treated as a separate study and as the province of professional educators and students of education, its content would be misconstrued and its essential place in the curriculum would be lost. The teacher organizations and the professional educators together urge that teachers press for professional recognition and, with the accrediting and certifying agencies, urge that professional standards be applied to teacher education programs and to the performance of teachers in the schools.

Nor did I find a very different view in the documents, statements, and policies of the American Federation of Teachers, which, although militant and effective in political tactics for increased teachers' salaries and benefits, has no educational or social philosophy around which its members are organized. In common with the trade union movement in general, the teachers union is concerned primarily with economic advantage, and political considerations are relevant where organizing power is needed to achieve them. As far as teacher education and world affairs are concerned, there are no programs of broad consequence in effect among the union members, and it is fair to say that the American Federation of Teachers has no international education program and no present intention of creating one. I am not arguing here the legitimacy of union demands or of the organizational methods for improving the grossly inadequate salary scale of the American teacher. That scale is a matter of very great significance in classifying the teacher within the social and economic system and in stultifying the influence of teachers in social and political change. I wish, rather, to point out that teachers are union members of a particular kind and do not usually identify themselves with the interests or the ideology of the trade union movement. Nor does their membership alter the conception of professionalism which the union is concerned to foster. They wish to improve the status of their profession by increasing the economic and political power of the organization.

Within that professional framework, teacher education programs are designed to make certain that teachers can function within the existing system, can do what is required of them in their profession, and can make use of whatever methods and innovations are current in order to improve the effectiveness of teaching. This accounts in part for the current emphasis on innovation, most of it technical, having to do with programed learning, the use of television, electric typewriters, movable classrooms, computerized classrooms, team teaching, systems of reading, and so on. No matter what may be the merits of the innovations, effectiveness is measured almost entirely within the closed system by how rapidly and well the students learn the subjects they are taught, how well they meet the academic standards against which they are tested.

In this system, the most successful student also becomes a professional. If he is talented he learns the skills and habits sought by the system and its prize givers, who number in their ranks the sponsors of the National Merit Scholarship Awards, the Presidential Scholars, the donors of university and college scholarships, prizes, fellowships, and other awards. With high grades and academic aptitudes, the right student can earn financial reward, social approval, and a place in the professions and executive classes later on.

The best kind of teacher for working within this structure is therefore one who is skilled and experienced in teaching a subject in which he has become professionally competent, not one whose values lie outside the structure and who takes a serious interest in world events and issues. The teacher's rewards are based on his ability to prepare his students to meet the criteria of their success. He, therefore, prefers to teach bright students with academic aptitudes, and there is a good deal of jostling for position within a given school in which teachers of proven ability seek to acquire students with scholastic aptitudes, with the rest of the students often distributed to those who, for one reason or another, are less able to achieve success in teaching the subjects.

Prestige factors, of the kind which afflict the colleges and universities, then enter, where the highest prestige is reserved for those who teach graduate and postdoctoral students of proven talents. The average and below average freshmen are taught by the new, inexperienced, and less prestigious faculty members and by teaching assistants. These are drawn from the ranks of the less prestigious graduate students who, usually for economic reasons, teach because they are not subsidized completely by the graduate fellowships awarded to their higher-ranking fellow students. This means, among other things, that the genuinely professional student has all the advantages and the average student, comprising at least 90 percent of the high school and college student body, gets the least effective kind of teaching because he has not acquired sufficient academic skill to be recognized as a "good student."

The best administrator in the schools then turns out to be the one who is able to organize his school or college program so that the best curriculum is taught to well-motivated and able students by good professional teachers. The administrator's prestige rests on the same extrinsic criteria—in the case of the high school, the academic achievement produced by the student body and how many students go on to what colleges. For the colleges, the question is, What academic achievements are produced by the students there? and, How many of them go on to prestigious graduate schools? not, How many become lively and interesting teachers? I found in a number of institutions which were formerly teachers colleges and are now multi-purpose universities, as they prefer to be called, that faculty members were pleased to announce that many of their present students were *not* going to become teachers, having been so successful in their studies that they were going to graduate school in other fields.

I believe that this set of attitudes, so firmly fixed within the professional education establishment, toward teaching, toward students, and toward the aims of education, accounts in large part for the lack of initiative in the past among educators for tackling the social and economic issues in which educational intervention is so crucial—the problems of the ghetto, of the rural slums, of the impoverished and the neglected, and of the world order. The attention of the educators has been turned inward and directed to a set of questions which in the long run are technical and organizational, assuming that the student is a standard human entity, with individual differences measurable by educational devices, and that teaching is a standard process in which the teacher is defined by the functions he fulfills and not by the person he is. The *being* of the student and the teacher is, therefore, not a matter for educational concern. The main concern is in ensuring the adequacy of the professional skills which student and teacher can acquire.

The new demands of a changing society press upon the educational system from the outside, with a strength which is increasing daily, forcing changes in the educational system which it has not prepared itself to make. The social legislation of the Eighty-Eighth and Eighty-Ninth Congresses, with the sudden release of funds in amounts never before available for educational use, has so changed the external situation of the educable population that educational changes are happening outside the formal system of instruction designed by professional educators. This accounts for the fact that the educational approaches of Project Head Start, VISTA, the National Teacher Corps, and the Peace Corps are mainly the result of planning by a new group of government experts in the field of social welfare and social science, with cooperation from educators, rather than as initiatives taken from inside the colleges of education, most of which have been reluctant to change their ways, despite the demand for new approaches and new programs.

This also accounts for the fact that the concepts of direct social experience and direct action in social and cultural situations, or field work in education, are foreign to the basic construct of the standard educational pattern. That pattern in teacher education has been designed for the white middle class in a society of the moderately well-to-do, not for the variety of cultures and economic and social groups to which a democratic educational system must adapt itself.

One of the ways in which the pattern is reflected shows itself in the attitude to practice teaching, usually the only kind of practical experience for which the student teacher can acquire academic credit. Practice teaching is literally that: an assignment in practicing teaching in a classroom with assigned materials to practice with, including a roomful of children. For this reason, many young people with an interest in teaching have gone outside the regular system of teacher preparation to find their own way to where the educational realities are—in the lives of children who need tutoring, who need interesting adult companionship, who need recreational and social leadership and the chance to gain a personal identity.

Similarly, it accounts for the fact that the majority of Peace Corps members who want to teach abroad choose not to enter teacher preparation programs before volunteering and prefer to learn the art in their Peace Corps training and in their actual teaching assignment in a foreign country. The idea of learning to become a teacher by first becoming a person of rich and varied experience in the live situations of society is not one which fits easily into the thinking of the professionals. It explains in part the absence of a full-fledged program in teacher education which takes into account the richness of phenomena in world cultures and world society.

This brings me to the question of how the colleges and departments of education are related to the university and how policies about the education of teachers are developed there. There are distinctions to be made immediately among the various kinds of institutions where teachers are educated. Approximately 20 percent of the 200,000 certifiable elementary and secondary school teachers produced annually in some 1,200 institutions are from former teachers colleges now become general colleges and universities. The rest come from private and public liberal arts colleges, about 45 percent, and private and public universities, 35 percent. A small proportion of those starting to teach each year, 7 percent in the case of elementary and 10 percent in secondary school, take a master's degree before beginning.[13]

The Graduate School of Education

The graduate schools and departments of education in the major universities should be distinguished from the rest. The graduate school conception reflects a trend which has been growing over the past 20 years,

[13] Descriptions of the types of programs, numbers of teachers, requirements, etc., are contained in publications of the National Education Association, the National Commission on Teacher Education and Professional Standards, the U.S. Office of Education, and the American Association of Colleges for Teacher Education; particularly *Teacher Productivity—1966*, AACTE; National Education Association, Research Division, *Teacher Supply and Demand in Public Schools* (annual reports); *A Manual on Certification Requirements for School Personnel in the United States, 1967 Edition*, NCTEPS: All at 1201 - 16th St., N.W., Washington, D.C. 20036.

not only toward making the education of the educator more professional, but away from the idea that the function of the graduate school is to prepare teachers for service in the schools. The university faculty, some holding joint appointments in schools of education and university departments, have now assumed a more dominant role in planning for the education of teachers as an all-university function.

In general, they and the graduate school faculty believe that the best way to prepare teachers is to admit students with a regular B.A. degree to a graduate school M.A. program and to provide them with a year to a year and a half of combined school internship and graduate study in academic and professional subjects, yielding both the teaching certificate and the M.A. on graduation. The combination of these and other variations of the master of arts in teaching programs has recruited a new cross section of B.A. students, many of whom had not intended to become teachers during their undergraduate years, while diminishing the number of public school teachers prepared in the graduate schools. Until now, little has been done to include an international component in such programs, through either experience abroad or study at home.

The real thrust of the graduate schools of education is toward doctoral programs, designed to develop new kinds of school administrators and professional educators for the public school, for the departments and colleges of education, and for research institutes in curriculum and educational planning. The influx of federal funds for research and experiment in all phases of elementary and secondary education not only has created sharply increased demands for research talent and new kinds of organizational and professional personnel in the regional educational laboratories and community development work, but has made it possible for graduate schools of education, after years of financial starvation, to spend money on projects, research, and experiment which were impossible even to think about in former years.

The report of the Harvard Committee on the Graduate Study of Education,[14] although deliberately confined to the problems of Harvard, both sums up and indicates trends in contemporary university thinking about the role of the graduate schools of education. Theodore Sizer, dean of the Harvard Graduate School of Education, points out in his introduction to the report that schools of education have long been out of balance, owing to the tremendous pressures on them to produce the thousands of teachers necessary to man the schools.

> It is not that there are not enough persons in the field; indeed there are more degrees of every description granted in this country in education than in any other.[15] It is rather that there are not enough absolutely first-rate people,

[14] *Report of the Harvard Committee on the Graduate Study of Education.* Cambridge, Mass.: Harvard University Press, 1966. 125 pp.

[15] The fact that more degrees are granted in education than in any other field is beside the point. There are far from enough persons in the field, there are shortages in every sector, and the number of persons graduating in education, although large, is not within thousands of reaching the number of qualified teachers presently needed,

either academically or in terms of commitment, to move the field forward. Sadly, education classes in most universities are drawn from a low academic level of the student body, and from the best of this group (and from most of its males irrespective of quality) educational leadership is drawn. There are exceptions, of course; but the evidence of weak professional leadership and shoddy scholarship makes the general conclusion irrefutable. Service in the schools is low-status work; but it should not be. Scholarship on the problems of schooling is neglected, but it ought not to be. . . . The following report is, really, an affirmation that university schools of education can make a significant difference not only in supplying raw material for the nation's schools but also the significant ideas upon which education must rest.[16]

The report itself follows out the implications of Sizer's introductory remarks and is representative of both the method and content of policy making by university faculty members who are addressing the problems of education. After considering in turn the possibility of doing away with the School of Education, as at Yale, or turning it into a research institute, or reorganizing it on the basis of the regular academic disciplines, or using it exclusively for "the doctoral training of practitioners" or for model teacher preparation and service programs, the Committee came out for balance among the various scholarly and professional obligations of the School, for doing less work in preparing teachers through the M.A. and master of arts in teaching, and more work with doctoral candidates. In its argument for balance, the report is academic in the best, as well as the worst, sense of the term. That is, the Committee deals with the existing reality of the organization and resources of its university and the School and in an intelligent and thoughtful way seeks to find the best means of using these resources for improving the quality of research and professional preparation of the students attracted to the School. In so doing, it has called upon a cross section of the best informed and concerned persons in the country for their views and for information about the activities of the institutions with which they are connected.

At the same time, the Committee exhibits no passion; it introduces no large conceptions, no central ideas around which new patterns of thought might form, and presents no view of education except to say that—

Education is better conceived as an organizing perspective from which all problems of culture and learning may be viewed. To place the issues of professional practice within such a context is to relate it to the whole life of the university. The special task of a university school of education is to facilitate such relationship, and in so doing to benefit both practice and scholarship.[17]

In different words, the Committee is saying that it does not wish to own to a perspective according to which education, culture, and learning might be organized; anyone who wishes to do so can find his own organizing perspective, his own definition of education. The issues of education are to be related, not to the whole life of man, but to the life of the univer-

---

to say nothing of future needs. The dimensions of this problem are described on pp. 80-82 of the present report.

[16] *Ibid.*, p. vii.

[17] *Ibid.*, p. 72.

sity and its intellectual and professional concerns.[18] When one considers how narrow are the patterns of life in the academic and university community and how limiting the intellectual life there, it becomes clear that the aim of the American graduate school of education in shifting as it has toward a major commitment of the kind described by Harvard is to leave the world at large pretty much as it is, except for the influence which might be exerted on it by skilled professionals who bring intellectual acuity to bear on whatever problems their employers need help in solving.

There is no mention, in fact, of the world at all; no recognition of the changes in twentieth-century world society which demand reconsideration of the whole content and method of graduate, undergraduate, and public school education. The lack of explicit statement in the Harvard Committee report does not mean that reconsideration is not taking place or that individual faculty members and students are not taking initiatives in developing new conceptions of what is to be taught and what is to be done. Dean Sizer himself, for example, teaches a well-attended course in the comparative development of American, English, and Nigerian education. Robert Rosenthal has carried out important educational and research projects in the slum areas of Boston. Individual tutorial projects have involved students in the social and cultural problems of the ghetto. The Harvard-Radcliffe undergraduates have developed a rationale and a volunteer program for education with a world point of view.[19] The School itself, with the aid of government and foundation grants, is carrying on educational development and research projects in Venezuela, Colombia, Mexico, Tunis, and the Barbados, as well as a major curriculum-making project in Nigeria under a contract with AID.

But in the concept of education and society implicit and explicit in

---

[18] In explaining why the graduate school of education should emphasize doctoral study and thus produce "the greatest potential for fundamental and long-term influence upon the field of education," the report identifies the—

> Most challenging current problem of professional definition, namely, the problem of working out a productive combination of fundamental studies providing advanced training for a new variety of careers in education practice, all to be informed by intellectual values, technical proficiency, and clinical awareness. We have here a challenge to strengthen the power and raise the standards of the profession, as well as to improve the quality of the currently expanding educational endeavor, by training able and intellectual professionals for key posts in schools, communities, universities, industry, government, communications, planning, and research. . . . *Ibid.*, p. 24.

Here the aims of education are stated in a form which more clearly indicates the narrowness of the conception. The studies are to be informed by "intellectual values, technical proficiency and clinical awareness," all of them useful for training men and women to serve in key posts wherever they are needed, but not designed to develop men and women with a view of the world and of education which might help to enrich them both.

[19] *An Experiment in Education,* Radcliffe Government Association, Phillips Brooks House, Room 5159 Shepard Street, Cambridge, Mass. The student program, *Education for Action,* calls for a combination of educational study and teaching abroad and in rural and urban slums during two three-month summer periods, with appropriate studies on the campus during the regular terms.

the report, the world outside the university turns out to be only another element in the "organizing perspective," and the projects in foreign countries do not touch directly upon the lives and education and experience of those who will be teaching in the public schools, except as faculty members with foreign experience bring the elements of that experience to bear on the materials of the courses they teach. The conclusions reached by the Harvard Committee about the professional and academic prescriptions for work in graduate education coincide with those we found to be already drawn, or in the process of being drawn, by committees and faculty members of the graduate schools of education elsewhere in the country. In view of these common assumptions, it would be unusual for a school of education to concern itself with the development of an overall curriculum or program which was shaped according to a new conception of the nature of world culture and world society, or one which could assure an overall relevance to new philosophical, social, and political questions raised by the existence of what can only be called a world revolution. As far as education is concerned, the world continues to be one thing, the university another.

On the other hand, new opportunities for extending the range and depth of international understanding and experience on the part of professional educators lie in the specialized research institutes and academic departments of the universities where foreign cultures are dealt with—if only they can be linked to the educational issues and problems of the society itself. The situation at Harvard, as at Columbia and Stanford, presents a case in point. The Harvard Center for Studies in Education and Development is located in the Graduate School of Education, and its staff of scholars and experts in a variety of fields—economists, sociologists, statisticians, historians, mathematicians, administrators, educators, all with considerable experience in foreign service—carries out research and educational projects in Latin America, the Middle East, and Africa in the countries cited above. It is thus a valuable resource for the education of Harvard students of education who might otherwise not have access to teachers and scholars working so directly on the going problems of educational and social change in world society.

The experience of the members of the Harvard Center brings them close to agreement with one central point in the findings of this Report, that study and action having to do with the educational problems of the developing countries lead directly to a more sensitive awareness of the character and scope of similar problems in this country, or, conversely, research and action in the areas of educational and social change in the United States has a direct bearing on the development of educational ideas and attitudes within the wider context of a world system of education.

In the language of the *Annual Report* of the Harvard Center for 1966-67:

> Seminars and increasing interchange with faculty members outside [the Center] have resulted from the necessity for relating the Graduate School's overseas interests and capabilities to its domestic ones. This communication has

become increasingly important because of the growing realization that education problems are not primarily "foreign" and "domestic," but rather "common" and "critical" and differ more in place and time than in kind.

The Center's several involvements make possible a wider employment of the faculty's expertise in identifying and solving educational problems which plague the developing world. In addition, involvement provides an important perspective to our own domestic educational issues and a greater possibility for making contributions to education which extend well beyond our own borders.[20]

It is possible that in the future through centers of this kind—with an inflow of foreign students and teachers, returned Peace Corps volunteers, and others directly involved in field work and action research both in the United States and abroad and with the inclusion of graduate students as research and teaching assistants in the overseas projects—entire sectors of graduate schools of education can gain the advantage of wider experience in world education. What distinguishes centers of this kind from those in area studies and international relations is that they come at the problems of developing countries and world society from a concern to analyze and plan for educational and social development, and the kind of knowledge they put together and disseminate is of direct relevance to the educational growth of students of education. The centers are therefore capable, if the proper arrangements are made for linking their work to the rest of the curriculum in education, of expanding to an international dimension the interests, usable knowledge, and viewpoint of teachers and educators in the schools and in the colleges for teachers.

In the absence of centers or institutes of this kind, there are, of course, other ways of injecting a wider point of view into appropriate areas of the education curriculum. Too seldom do the schools of education consider the ways in which, without the support of foundation or government funds, existing budgets and programs can be converted to use as vehicles for international education. International programs most often occur in the universities when the interest of administrators and faculty coincides with the interest of the government, or of foundations working cooperatively with the government, in supporting special programs. At times during our visits to the campuses, it was hard to decide whether the programs were in effect because the government and foundations wanted them there or because they had developed through initiatives in the institutions themselves. It does not really matter in the long run which is true, as long as the interests truly coincide. But one thing is certain: The development of international programs in teacher education is, in comparative terms, so expensive that unless subsidies are provided from sources outside the present funds available to the colleges of education, it will be very difficult indeed to mount new international programs of substantial size and influence.

One frequent comment from administrators and directors of international programs in general was to the effect that if it were not for the

---

[20] Center for Studies in Education and Development, Graduate School of Education, Harvard University. *Annual Report, 1967.* Cambridge, Mass.: the Center, 1968 (In press).

Ford Foundation, the Carnegie Corporation, the government, and a limited number of other foundations, there would be practically no international programs on the campuses and that if that kind of support were withdrawn, many of the present programs would collapse. In the vocabulary of the initiates, the difference between hard and soft money—the latter being provided by grants, the former from regular university budgets—is crucial to long-range planning.

An Alternative Example

An example of the way an association with government programs can eventually affect the international education of teachers is to be found in the work of Ohio University in Athens, Ohio, over the past 10 years. Government and foundation subsidies made possible new international programs in the beginning, with consequent effect on the content of work in world affairs throughout the University as a whole. In 1961 and 1962, for instance, two groups of approximately 30 teachers from 17 countries came to the University, under the sponsorship of the International Teacher Development Program of the U.S. Office of Education and the Department of State, for three months of study and experience at the University and in the Ohio community. Their presence had the effect of drawing the attention of the College of Education to a variety of ideas in world education and served as a means of educating students and faculty at the College, aside from the education the visitors received in their turn. Three education programs—in Northern Nigeria, Western Nigeria, and South Vietnam —on contract with the Agency for International Development are under way at the University, which has also conducted Peace Corps training programs for the Cameroons.

The original initiatives which made the University a likely place for contracts and work of this kind came from the former dean of the College of Education, Frank Hamblin, and the president of the University, John Baker, whose successors, Gilford Crowell and Vernon Alden, have been zealous in the pursuit of international aims, both in the appointments they have made to the faculty and in the continuing initiatives they have taken in the development of projects and programs. These have ranged from a home improvement seminar and workshop for 14 home economists from Nigeria and Brazil to the establishment of a Southeast Asian Program and an African Studies Program with more than 20 course offerings in history, philosophy, government, the social sciences, languages, and the arts.

The College of Education has been closely involved in the work of the international programs and has more than 40 of its faculty members abroad and 32 presently teaching in the college who have had foreign interests and experience. Without setting down many details of the educational work of the College in Nigeria and South Vietnam, it may be sufficient to say that 10 secondary schools in the latter country are working on pilot projects with Ohio faculty members, curriculum materials have been worked out for both South Vietnam and Nigeria, where in-service teacher education programs have been started, and teacher training institutions have been or are being organized, in particular a new multipurpose teachers college in Kano, Northern Nigeria, which was started from scratch in 1963.

Having built this body of experience within the College faculty and program, the College has now begun to turn its attention directly to the way in which undergraduate and graduate students of education can extend the international range of their work and has proposed the establishment of an Institute of International Education in the College itself. The Institute would find ways of using the work overseas and the special competence of faculty members throughout the whole University to effect the education of teachers. The intention of the proposal, which is backed by the administration of the University as well as by the College of Education, is four-fold: (a) to make teachers more proficient in teaching about the world, (b) to develop educators with special competence to serve in educational projects abroad, (c) to prepare educators for positions in the United States which require a knowledge of the world's educational systems, and (d) to act as a study and research center for American and foreign teachers.

The kind of intention and program represented by the Institute of International Education proposal at Ohio University is characteristic of some of the work at Michigan State University and elsewhere, although in our visits to campuses during the study we could find in operation no satisfactory solution to the major problem of creating links between the study and experience of undergraduate and graduate students in education and the activities of colleges of education and their faculty members abroad. There are solutions to be found, some of them already suggested and carried out by the Peace Corps and by universities with AID and other contracts. Fuller discussion of that subject is to be found in Chapters II and IV of this report.

Some Analogies with the Professional Schools

In reviewing the work of graduate schools of education, I found it useful to consider some of the analogies inherent in their relations to other kinds of professional schools which, although operating in different areas of professional interest, share some of the same problems, including the problems of internationalizing the curriculum and introducing the component of practical experience as a central element in the professional training itself. The publication of the EWA series of studies of international education in the professional schools has drawn attention again to the basic fact that the role of the American professional—the doctor and public health administrator, the engineer, the lawyer, the agricultural expert, the business executive, the educator, the architect, among others—has taken on an international dimension by the very conditions of professional service, because "the functions they serve must be performed in all societies."[21]

---

[21] See introductory statement by William W. Marvel, president, Education and World Affairs, in *The Professional School and World Affairs*, "Introduction," published by Education and World Affairs.

The analogies to schools of education that appear most relevant are those found in architecture, for example—where the parallel between designing new environments and new educational systems is apparent and the inter-relationships are obvious—or in public administration, or in the law—with its necessary blend of the theoretical with the practical case-study approach —or, more particularly, medicine and public health, if education is considered to be a profession concerned with healing the diseases of ignorance, curing mental and intellectual deficiencies, enhancing emotional and social growth, and creating conditions for the optimum development of the human being.

I have often thought, as I have looked at the practices of the schools of education and the educators responsible for undergraduates, that if the medical analogy were taken seriously, educators are acting toward their students as if they were patients who, having come for treatment and having announced their physical symptoms and ill health, were told to go away and come back when their deficiencies were cured, that only then could they be admitted for treatment. Transposed into professional education, the analogy continues: the student of education is told that he must study academic subjects having little to do with the problems he will encounter in the lives of his students or their society, and, after at least three years of academic isolation from the life situation of those to whom he will minister, he is then allowed to see them, most often in the class-room (operating room or clinic), and to work with them (operate on them) as a way of learning his profession.

We can be thankful that at least the medical profession has begun to move in recent years in the direction of furnishing more direct experience with patients in the beginning years of medical training, and in the direction of research and education in the psychiatric and social aspects of medicine—combining in one program the study of mental and physical illness, the study of environmental effects on the human organism, and the consideration of educational and economic problems in the lives of those whom the profession serves. That is the direction in which the professional education of teachers must move if it is to remain relevant to the needs of contemporary world society.

Or, to put the issue in purely educational terms, the professional schools of education, both for undergraduates and for graduates, have moved toward the principle of isolating the student from direct experience with children, their parents, and the problems of the social order. In the meantime the needs of the children, the students of education, and the social order have all been creating demands in the opposite direction.

One of the most interesting documents in medical education, with several implications for the professional education of teachers, is the report of a special committee on curriculum of the Harvard Medical School issued in the spring of 1966.[22] The report reflects not only the views of the Harvard Committee, but a growing dissatisfaction among medical students and medical schools across the country that the curriculum is too rigidly organized, with insufficient freedom of choice among subjects for study, too little opportunity for taking care of patients in the earlier years of training, too little attention to maintaining the "motivation of most beginning students to help suffering humanity," too little attention to making "teaching the greatest of all educational experiences for the teacher."

Among the recommendations of the Committee are that, rather than postponing student experience with patients until the third year, students should begin in the first year to interview patients as part of the training program, that work in the behavioral and social sciences should supplement the work in biological science during the second year, that practical experience should be the emphasis of the third year, and that in the fourth year the students should choose courses, with the help of faculty advisers, from an elective curriculum covering all the divisions of the medical school offerings. "To teach the details before the motivation to learn them exists is pedagogy doomed to failure," says the report, in advocating fewer lectures and more time for small-group discussions and problem-solving exercises.

All of these recommendations apply with equal force to the professional school of education, and one could wish that among the educational planners in this field, at Harvard and elsewhere, there were more persons with the views and strength of educational conviction demonstrated by the medical staff of the Harvard Committee. Once professional education is considered from the point of view of the person who will use it and the person on whom it will be used, the argument for greatly increased flexibility in curriculum and an increased emphasis on the fusion of practical with theoretical studies is already made. The flexibility is necessary to accommodate the diverse talents and interests of those who are preparing to be teachers, including returning Peace Corps volunteers, foreign students, inexperienced high school graduates, those gifted in languages, mathematics, or literature, as well as those who are teaching the teachers— especially, in the context of the present study, those who have had experience abroad.

Too often the faculty member with foreign experience returns to his high school or college of education and, because of the rigidity of the curriculum, teaches standard courses in the present curriculum rather than developing new courses of his own which can use his international experience and talents to the best advantage of his students and of his own intellectual development. Too often the sheer existence of particular courses in the departmental system of the college of education demands that the courses be taught and that persons whose own training may not have

---

[22] "Report of the Subcommittee on Curriculum Planning, Harvard Medical School," May 1966; mimeographed, 23 pp. The continued reference to Harvard is not intentional, but made necessary by the fact, in this instance, that the Medical School Report states, more succinctly than any other, the point of view in reform which I am concerned to support.

prepared them for imaginative development of new course materials in the assigned area be simply put to work in order to fill the assignment. If we are to have interesting new work in international education or in anything else in the professional education of teachers, we will have to give serious and continuing attention to the intellectual interests of the individual faculty members and, through a vastly increased national subsidy for study and travel, turn them loose to develop new interests and new content for the courses now frozen into the teacher education curriculum.

Some Examples of International Programs in Graduate Schools of Education

The demonstration of what can be done when there is enough money to do it has been carried on almost exclusively in graduate schools of education which have agreed to prepare specialists who can carry out duties connected with government service abroad, in international organizations, professional research, and institution building in foreign countries. In general, the school of education becomes an agency under contract to produce certain kinds of professionals rather than an international center for the development of new modes of education and internationalism. Consequently, the effect of the subsidies for international education is seldom felt in the American undergraduate curriculum, in the preparation of teachers, or in the main body of graduate work in American education itself.

From the available examples, I choose three in illustration: Teachers College, Columbia University; Stanford University; and the University of Michigan.

Teachers College, Columbia University

Direct attention to international education at Teachers College began more than 10 years ago with the work of an All-College Committee on International Education, organized in 1956 to bring an international element into the education of Teachers College students, to prepare selected students and staff for work abroad, to provide educational services to other countries, and to organize fundamental research and publication in international, interdisciplinary education. A great deal has been accomplished since then, through several institutes and offices of the College, especially through the Institute for Education in Africa, which, among other things, has prepared 75 specialists and tutors for 27 different teachers colleges in Kenya, Tanzania, and Uganda and, since 1961, prepared 439 teachers for service in East Africa. An Afro-Anglo-American Program in Teacher Education was developed for a good deal of this work, under the auspices of the University of London Institute of Education, Teachers College, and 14 African institutes and university departments of education.

According to the latest available figures, for 1962-64, 63 percent of the 160 faculty members at Teachers College traveled abroad during that two-year period, 48 percent of them on one or more specific international assignments; 26 percent taught regular courses focusing on international subject matter; and 34 percent were involved in special activities and training programs having to do with international education. In 1966-67, approximately 400 of the 7,000 students were from foreign countries.

The most recent development at Teachers College has been the reorganization of the previous institutes and offices, with a new amalgam of programs in comparative and international education worked out in collaboration with Columbia University's School of International Affairs and the Regional Institutes of the Columbia Graduate School—in Africa, Latin America, and East Asia. A new doctorate in education has been arranged in the field of international educational development, for training and service in administration, curriculum, and teacher education abroad.

The other main sections of the international work at Teachers College are—

1. An Institute of International Studies, for research in education in Africa, Latin America, Asia, and industrial nations, with research projects ranging from a study of student unrest in Latin America to a policy study of teacher education in India.

2. An Office of Overseas Projects, organized for educational aid to Africa, Asia, and South America, supported by the Carnegie Corporation and AID, for work in teacher education in East Africa, Afghanistan, and Peru. Sample projects are the development of new administrative arrangements for education in Peru, reform of textbooks and examination systems in India, creation of 18 Peace Corps projects since 1961, and, since 1960, preparation of approximately 2,100 American teachers for service in Africa.

3. An Office of International Programs and Services, to deal with programs for foreign students, help incoming AID visitors carry out their missions, exchange programs for faculty and students, and work in international education within the departments of the College. One of the latter is a lively and important section in comparative education and provides one of only seven places in the United States where American and foreign students can enroll for serious and comprehensive research and study in the field.

As an indication of a trend found elsewhere in the graduate schools of education, the movement by Teachers College toward collaboration with the regular areas and regional studies sections of the University, and with the Columbia University School of International Affairs, is typical of a wish to combine the resources of the university faculty with the resources in the schools of education. Columbia's School of International Affairs, with its emphasis on extending the international dimension of the education of members of the professional and business community, can be an important element in the development of new patterns of graduate study for students of international education. Until now, however, the major contribution of Teachers College to international education has been in the provision of professionals for service abroad and in international organizations at home, rather than for the development of internationalist teachers for service in American schools.

Stanford University

A program for similar international careers in education, leading to a three-year Ph.D. degree and financed by the University and by foundation and government grants, has been in operation since 1954 in the International Development Education Center (SIDEC) of the Stanford University School of Education. The Center accepts candidates who already hold the M.A. degree and who have had two years of professional experience at home and two years abroad. There are no more than 40 students in the program at any one time: One half are Americans, the rest are from foreign countries. The level of their academic and professional achievement before coming to Stanford is high. They have served in ministries of education and of planning, colleges and universities, the Peace Corps, United Nations agencies, foundations, AID, and elsewhere. In addition to their concentrated study of the culture and language of a given area of the world, the students work in courses and research in the social sciences and professional education.

The presence of these experienced and talented students and of the internationally experienced faculty members who teach them creates a high potential for enlarging the international interests of the entire School, since education students may enroll in the advanced graduate courses in education and development required of all SIDEC candidates and since SIDEC faculty members serve on school committees and as advisers on doctoral programs in the school itself. On the other hand, I have found at Stanford, and elsewhere among the graduate schools of education, that when most of the faculty resources for international education are contained in research institutes, educational development centers, or area studies programs financed by foundation and government grants and when the attention of such centers is on specific programs for developing professional manpower for international service, the outreach of internationalism into the rest of the school and into the education of teachers for the schools and colleges is extremely limited.

In one sense, this is bound to be so. If you put your time, energy, and money into the education of professionals for international service and if you define your terms by recruiting only those who have already proven themselves both academically and professionally by at least five or six years of national and international experience, two things happen. The students you recruit for the program are interested in doing the things they came to do, not in extending the range of the Center's activity into other sections of the School of Education. The faculty members are chosen for their experience and knowledge in a given foreign culture, international development, the social science of internationalism. They are usually not interested in building new programs in international education for students who are not very closely related to their own major interests and those of the Center.

61

This does not mean, of course, that new developments may not change an original intent and commitment of manpower and funds. For my part, in observing what has been happening in the international sector of the graduate schools and colleges of education, I regret that so much of what is available within centers such as those at Stanford and at Harvard is not more widely shared and more influential in the day-to-day curriculum and planning of the School as a whole.

I feel a similar sense of regret in observing the absence of direct links between graduate schools of education and the undergraduate student bodies, especially at Stanford where so large a proportion of the undergraduates spend a year abroad in one of the seven Stanford overseas centers in European and Asian countries. This, combined with the fact that a higher percentage of seniors volunteer for the Peace Corps and are accepted from Stanford than from any other university, is both a tribute to the internationalism in the educational perspective of the undergraduates and an indication of a rich source of teaching talent for the field of world affairs.

One possibility would be to arrange a coordinated program of study, travel, teaching experience, and community work for students who, as undergraduates, are interested in foreign service and teaching, whether or not they wish to volunteer for the Peace Corps, with a special "master of arts in teaching" degree planned to take advantage of and to build on their undergraduate experience in overseas study and service. Another would be to take advantage of the fully developed programs of area studies in Asian, African, Latin American, Western European, Russian, and Eastern European regions that have been organized by the Stanford All-University Committee on International Studies and to work out both graduate and undergraduate curriculums for students interested in teaching who would carry out field work, practice teaching, and study of educational systems and problems overseas that were adapted to regional studies and study of education in the California communities and on the Stanford campus.

At the present time, a master of arts in teaching is available at Stanford to students who have already taken the teaching certificate and have had one or more years of teaching experience. Other curriculums of a fairly conventional kind are offered in a sequence that leads to teaching, administrative, and school service credentials, with special and very interesting work using video tape in microteaching—that is, intensive analysis and study of one's own teaching methods and practices as part of the program of practice teaching. However, there is not as yet any plan or program in which the preparation of public school, junior college, or college teachers is assured an international component or perspective. That is not to say that there cannot be nor will not be. The University is brimming with opportunities for just such developments.

University of Michigan

A quite different approach is taken at the University of Michigan, where the faculty of the School of Education states as policy that "the educator of the future must possess an international outlook, i.e., an understanding of society and education in other lands as well as the competence to work in the schools of one or more societies abroad. . . . Commitments to international studies are the concern of all departments and agencies of the School of Education."[23]

Consonant with this policy, specialists in foreign policy and foreign cultures have been appointed to the faculty in almost every field, and an International Education Project, supported by a grant of $200,000, has been designed to increase the teaching knowledge of the faculty in a variety of foreign cultures. For the past eight years, the School of Education has had an arrangement with the Universities of Sheffield and Keele in England, through which 180 undergraduate students, mostly juniors, have been exchanged, in addition to faculty members, 8 in all, who have spent an academic year at the University of Sheffield. Eight others have gone to New Delhi, Bombay, and Baroda for assignments of a year, in exchange with five professors from India each year at Ann Arbor.

The School has sponsored study tours to Mexico, Canada, Japan, and England, with undergraduates and graduate students working toward an M.A. degree; 200 have been involved. During the last three years, during the third term of the college year, the School has sent 140 seniors and graduate students to London for a six-week intensive study of the London school system. This program is to be expanded to other countries in the future. Plans are under way to develop yearlong exchanges involving foreign students at Michigan, as well as faculty members, with Baroda University in India, International Christian University in Tokyo, the American University in Beirut, and the new English universities of Brunel and Coleraine.

Although originally intending to develop a large number of exchanges with individual universities in other parts of the world, the planning of the School of Education has now shifted to the formation of a consortium of approximately 20 to 25 institutions across the country through which exchange programs are to be arranged on a regional basis with selected universities abroad. The budget, calculated for 25 centers, 1,000 American students, 25 American educators, 25 foreign staff members, and 125 foreign graduate students, would be approximately $1.5 million per year.

There are three characteristics of the Michigan program which are of special note:

1. Most of the projects in international education came as the result of initiatives by members of the education faculty over the past 10 years who have been planning a curriculum and programs in the international dimension, with most of the funds coming from university and local sources, rather than from government subsidy for AID programs or large foundation grants.

---

[23] *A Plan for the Development of the International Activities of the School of Education.* Claude A. Eggertsen, chairman of the Committee on International Education. Ann Arbor: University of Michigan, School of Education. (Mimeo.)

2. Although there is serious research and professional work done with graduate students, the largest proportion of international programs is for undergraduates who are becoming teachers in the public schools. There is no sharp separation between the graduate and undergraduate functions of the School of Education.

3. The collaboration of the School of Education with the various area study centers at the University of Michigan has come mainly from the initiative of the School of Education, which has made joint appointments with the centers as well as appointments of foreign educators and scholars to the School itself.

The Sources of Initiatives

In considering in general the work of the graduate schools of education in the international field, extending beyond these three brief references to examples, it becomes clear that the original impetus for making new programs has come from a combination of federal subsidies, usually through AID projects, foundation grants for advanced professional work of the kind illustrated at Stanford, and grants for area studies centers which have extended their course offerings to graduate and undergraduate students. The result has been, as is the case in other fields, that the major institutions with existing resources and capabilities have received the major grants, have built the strongest programs, and have worked most directly with government, foundation, and national education bodies in supplying the need for professional scholars and educators in the international area. The spread of new materials in foreign cultures and new courses in a wide range of international subjects throughout the entire curriculum in the major universities has come as a result of the subsidized institutes and centers and the presence on the campuses of qualified experts in foreign fields.

Beginning in 1956, when Michigan State appointed the first dean of international programs in the United States, the trend toward the development of such programs has grown until there are now executive officers—either deans, vice-presidents, coordinators, or directors of international programs—in 100 universities. In some instances, usually in the graduate departments, the progress toward a curriculum in which work in foreign cultures is integrated with the general curricular design has been extraordinary.

However, in very few instances has there been a serious effect on the actual content and style of the education of public school teachers, relatively few of whom are educated in graduate schools or in the universities where such graduate schools and international programs exist. Of the 40 institutions from which the largest number of secondary and elementary school teachers graduate each year, only 4, in the case of elementary school teachers, and 12, in the case of secondary school teachers, could be classified as universities in which substantial work is being carried on in the international field either in the school of education or in the graduate schools in general. As I have already pointed out, even in major universities with a generous supply of courses in the international area—languages, foreign studies, and world affairs—the standard program of teacher education allows little room for electives, arouses little interest in world issues, and involves a minimum of opportunity for enlarging the education student's view of the world.

Few people who are not directly involved in the work of educating teachers seem to understand that nearly all America's public school teachers are being educated either in the state colleges and institutions which were formerly teachers colleges, in the B.A. programs of state universities, or in four-year liberal arts colleges, public and private, where there are departments of education. Fewer people still, inside and outside the universities, seem to understand that the mere existence of prestigious graduate schools with special work in world affairs does not mean either that teachers have access to them or that their influence reaches into the school system, the undergraduate curriculum, teacher education, or the community. The teachers, I have observed, are the last people to be thought of where education is concerned. It is a trickle-down theory that once area studies, non-Western centers, international research, and the preparation of professionals for service overseas are established on a campus and in consorita of campuses, the word will trickle down to the teachers and eventually to the students in the schools. More often, nothing trickles, because the graduate center is sealed off both from the undergraduates and from other sections of the institution.

What is needed is a theory of a completely different kind, one that starts from a recognition of the educational needs of the children and their teachers in the schools and moves toward the invention of new educational plans and materials for meeting both, using the resources of the colleges and universities to fulfill the plans. It is a matter of making links between resources already available among experts in the university faculty and in specialized study centers, and the curriculums and teaching of the colleges of education and the public schools.

At the present time, since few of the faculty experts in foreign cultures and world affairs are interested in the schools or in their teachers, the initiatives will have to come from teachers and from *their* teachers in the colleges of education. Those who are now involved in making plans for the expansion of the international sector in teacher education have most often been motivated by firsthand recognition of present inadequacies as they have seen them in the teaching programs of the schools and the undergraduate curriculums.

An example can be drawn from the work of persons like Seymour Fersh, education director of the Asia Society, who, having taken his undergraduate and early graduate work in social studies at a teachers college, taught social studies in an American high school where his experience in teaching revealed serious gaps in the curriculum itself. After taking a doctorate in American history, Dr. Fersh began teaching in a teachers college in New Jersey, where a course in New Jersey history, but none in areas outside Western culture, was required of all social studies graduates.

This experience and a year's assignment on an education mission to India convinced Dr. Fersh that a great deal could and should be done to remove the parochialism of Asian and American systems of education, and he turned his interests and efforts toward the development of new programs in foreign cultures, particularly of Asia, for the education of American teachers and schoolchildren. Since then Dr. Fersh has written two texts for use in the schools—one on India for junior high schools, another on India and South Asia for senior high schools—along with pamphlets and articles for use by teachers in expanding their own knowledge of non-Western areas.

Dr. Fersh's work at the Asia Society consists mainly in the development and dissemination of annotated guides, bibliographies, and teaching materials in Asian affairs for the use of teachers and their students and in recruiting other scholars and educators to carry out similar projects. To do so, it is necessary to stay in touch with the best in contemporary scholarship in the field, while at the same time remaining close to the teaching and learning problems of the colleges of education and the public schools themselves. The point is that the work that Dr. Fersh and others like him are doing in Asian studies is no less scholarly or intellectually responsible than the work of those who are confined within the academic sanctity of the graduate study centers. It is a matter of using one's own scholarship to enable the teachers to improve theirs, and the particular virtue of the materials thus produced for students and teachers lies in the fact that it comes from scholars whose own experience has included not only a going relationship with the best work in the field but a direct acquaintance with the needs and conditions of the schools and of the institutions where teachers are educated.

In order to assess the degree of concern on the part of the universities for extending the dimension of teacher education in the international direction, and in order to know more about the way in which policies in this field are being made, we interviewed on each campus the faculty members of colleges and departments of education and members of the arts and science faculties. I found little of the intellectual hostility of one group toward the other that I had been led to expect by having heard so much in advance about the quarrel between the academics and the professionals. I found quite often an amused tolerance for the professionals on the part of the liberal arts faculty, and occasional signs of defensiveness on the part of the professionals.

But more than anything else among the liberal arts and science faculties, I found either a lack of serious interest in the problem of teaching and teacher education or a sense of certainty that these problems could be solved by fairly simple means. Put the students through a regular academic program with a major field of concentration, keep them away from education courses as much as possible, let them teach for a term, and they are ready to teach. This attitude was especially evident in our discussions with all-university committees on teacher education, which usually had a preponderance of liberal arts faculty in the representation.

After a series of 17 such meetings with university committees, I came to question the validity of the assumption behind their formation as the major group responsible for the education of teachers within the university. What this means in practice is that whereas in former years there was a central focus of attention by the teacher educators on the preparation of teachers, no matter how limited in scope that attention may have been, now the responsibility, when spread over an entire university, dilutes the attention as well as the responsibility. When everybody is responsible for everything, nobody is responsible for the core of the matter—that is, the continual and intensive effort to keep the education of teachers relevant to the cultural and intellectual demands of a rapidly changing society.

In attempting to correct a one-sided arrangement where teacher education was formerly the exclusive province of professional educators, the new arrangement now involves a group of people who are themselves more interested in the separate disciplines they represent and in making certain that students carry on work in these disciplines than they are in rethinking the entire problem of how best to develop interesting and internationally informed teachers for the schools.

The problem is wrongly construed by the separation between practice in the art of teaching and the content of the liberal arts, between a body of departmental subject matter to be assimilated and a set of practices and methods by which it is to be communicated to schoolchildren. As far as world affairs were concerned, most of the faculty members simply reported which of their courses were available if students wanted to elect them and what offerings in foreign languages and cultures were in the curriculum. I found that the university committees have failed even to question the premises on which their own teaching and system of instruction are based, at a time when undergraduate teaching has been denounced as an open scandal by scholars, critics, and students who have examined it in studies and experienced it in person. Membership in a university faculty and certified competence in a given academic discipline are no guarantee of educational insight or even of the capacity to teach or to understand what teaching means. Yet these are usually the criteria invoked to determine committee membership.

Over the past 20 years, the critics of teacher education, mainly from the universities, have concentrated their fire on the lack of preparation of teachers in subject matter fields, on the superficiality and redundancy of the instruction in methodology, and on the lack of intellectual content in the education courses. The reforms in teacher education have been responsive to these criticisms, but they have been responsive within the same narrow frame of reference as the criticisms. That is to say, the professionals have assumed that the academics are right: The way to produce better educated teachers is to have them take more academic courses, the way to improve professional education courses is to make them more academic. Accordingly, neither the academic man nor the professional educator has been giving concentrated attention to the practical arts of teaching and learning or to the relevance of what is learned to the actual world.

In many cases, this has reduced the college of education to impotence as far as taking action and making educational policy are concerned, since by definition the academic life of its students is in the hands of the arts and science faculty and educational policy is made largely by those who are not themselves educators of teachers and do not wish to be. The situation is worsened by the fact that, having turned over their students to others and having kept only the vocational side of the student's preparation for themselves, the colleges of education seldom even see their own students until the junior or senior year, after the necessities and duties of general education and the academic majors and minors have been fulfilled.

On the other hand, the students of education, who at least by declaration of intent are in college in order to become teachers, have no opportunity to be with children and to learn what it is like to be a teacher or to practice the art in any way, until three years after they enroll. This is to put the college of education into a situation comparable to that of a music school whose students are turned over to another institution for academic education for three years to be given courses in everything else but music and then are allowed to play an instrument and study music in their senior year.

It is also true that when an all-university committee makes the policy for teacher education, it brings with it the educational biases of the academic mind, a mind afflicted with the idea that only through academic study is anything of importance learned. The fallacy in this view is at the root of a great deal of bad education now being pressed upon the American undergraduate, especially when it fails to prepare him intellectually for taking part in the political and social movements so crucially important to the progress and improvement of education itself. The undergraduate curriculum of the universities has become the wasteland of the academy, at a time when this is exactly the territory which the fledgling teacher is ordered to traverse. What students need is not more subject matter of the kind they are now getting and in the way it is now given to them. What they need is a chance to put together a body of knowledge for themselves, on the basis of what they discover for themselves. They need to create something from the wellspring of their own actions, something about which they feel so deeply that they want to teach it to others. They need a chance to act on the world, not just to exist in it.

Although I would enjoy nothing more than to take the time and space here to describe, analyze, and decry the quality of teaching and content in the undergraduate curriculum of the American college and university, I have done this elsewhere, as have others, and I confine myself here to a brief repetition of what is generally known by students and other observers with direct experience of what has been going on in the colleges from day to day.

Having attended more than 70 classes of various kinds during the course of the present study—classes in education, the social sciences, and the humanities, from large lecture courses to discussion groups led by graduate assistants—I am prepared to say again that the system of lectures, examinations, grades, academic credits, and textbooks imprisons the student in an impossible situation in which his capacity for intellectual growth is inhibited, his imagination stunted, and his initiative impaired. Where there are occasional superb teachers, capable of turning the system to good use, the students are presented with a chance to learn, by example and precept, through admiration, respect, and delight. It matters less what may be the exact subject matter such persons teach—Western, non-Western, national, or international—than that they lead the student to a capacity for self-education by whatever means, that they lead the student to a commitment to use his intellect, his talent, and his personal resources to advance the level and extent of his own knowledge and that of the people around him.

What troubles me most is not merely the absence of powerful and enlightened teaching which can move and shake the younger generation into a new mood of intellectual and cultural concern, but that under the present circumstances the school, the college, and the university are losing all capacity to influence the lives and commitments of young people. The young seek, wherever they can find it, the kind of teaching which does have an effect on their lives, and if they cannot find it in the schools and colleges they will find it elsewhere.

As William Arrowsmith said in his rousing, devastating, and beautiful statement about teaching in America—

> If the university does not educate, others will. Education will pass, as it is passing now, to the artist, to the intellectual, to the gurus of the mass media, the charismatic charlatans and sages, and the whole immense range of secular and religious street-corner fakes and saints. . . . What matters is the integration of significant life and knowledge, of compassionate study and informed conduct.[24]

This is what matters to those students who have already begun to question the relevance of their education to the lives they hope to lead, to those who have already become involved in social action, who cannot stay tranquil while the big injustices perpetuate themselves. The path they can take into a larger understanding of the world and into an understanding of how best to act on it to secure its welfare does not lie through the orderly syllabus of a general education course, with or without a dash of foreign content. It lies through informed experience with the cultures which surround them in their own society. What the academic men do not understand is that to educate students to become teachers who understand the world and can teach honestly about it, it is first necessary for them to become sensitive to the character of their own lives in this particular society. Otherwise they have no way of understanding the nature of anyone else's

---

[24] Arrowsmith, William. *The Future of Teaching.* Address to the Annual Meeting of the American Council on Education, New Orleans, October 13, 1966. Washington, D.C.: American Council on Education, pp. 3, 8.

life. It is then like trying to explain modern art to someone who has never seen a modern painting.

I would, therefore, make one major generalization about the present state of teacher education, one which is implied by much that comes before and will come after. What is presently lacking among educators is a concern for the commitment the young are capable of making to teaching, not simply to a profession or a career, but as an act of devotion to the cause of learning and to the welfare of children. If they see around them in the colleges the cynicism of teachers who care little for the art of teaching, whose own true lives are lived elsewhere, or whose talents ill equip them for the task they have accepted, the young are unable to respond and unlikely to create their own conceptions of what it means to be a teacher. If they see in the four years ahead of them in college no large horizons, no anticipations of delight, no promise of an opening up of their lives, but only duties to be borne and trivial tasks to undertake, they are unlikely to find the inner energies through which to infuse their own education with a sense of purpose. The curriculum, whatever it is, must start with the intention of creating a situation in which the student can honestly commit himself to what he is asked to do, and what he is asked to do must in some way illuminate his understanding of what it means to be a teacher. His motivation for learning matters very much indeed, since it determines how he learns and whether he learns. Those who do not know how to arrange an education for teachers which makes them want to teach should not meddle with education.

Some Samples of Programs

It would be natural to expect that in the analysis of the kind of effort presently being made in institutions where teachers are being educated, the larger institutions, graduating from 1,000 to 2,000 certifiable teachers a year, would be more likely to possess the resources in faculty and educational initiative to move into the international education field. This did not prove to be the case. Sometimes the very size of the student body seems to prevent experiment or initiative of any kind, since standard curriculums designed for large numbers of students are regarded as unavoidable and necessary, and often the large number of faculty members, confined sectionally to their own departments, all of them busy getting their students through the requirements, seems to paralyze initiative of all kinds.

What made the difference in those cases where new work had begun in nonprestigious institutions[25] was the presence of a small group of faculty members, students, and one or more administrators who, as a result of their own interest in world issues and the education of teachers, had simply started programs of their own, with the permission of and, in some cases, the support of their institutions. It is encouraging to report that wherever

---

[25] I cannot think of a better word. I do not mean to divide institutions between those with and those without prestige, but to refer to the fact that those who do not already have what the grant-makers want can seldom obtain grants to get it.

we found serious interest in the reform of teacher education through adding a new cultural dimension to the experience of teachers, there was usually an interest in international education. Institutions which looked outward to the social issues of American life and were concerned to bring the forces of education to bear on them were prepared to look farther out to the issues in world society about which students should have knowledge and experience. The impact of the national concern for dealing with disadvantaged children through education has had the effect of inducing a greater concern for political and social issues of all kinds. Once education is conceived as a process of human development, and once the development of human resources for service in the society is considered to be a major function of the college of education, the attention of educators is likely to turn in the direction of international and world problems.

Some of the most valuable work, too little noticed in the past, has been going on in the smaller colleges of the Midwest, both private and public, usually through initiatives taken by local faculty members and administrators. In those cases where the American Association of Colleges for Teacher Education has involved administration and faculty members in even the limited ways made possible by a series of four-to-six-week travel-study projects abroad or by internships for foreign educators in American institutions, an appreciable difference can be seen in the institutional attitudes toward reform of education in the direction of internationalism.

Two examples are relevant:

Wilmington College, in Wilmington, Ohio, a private college of approximately 1,000 students, was designated by AACTE as one of 11 institutions to carry out pilot projects in international education, with a grant of $500, matched by $500 from the College. The money was to be used to bring visiting Fulbright scholars and foreign experts to the campus for short periods to teach in a number of areas—education, language, geography, history, political science. Through collaboration with other AACTE member institutions, with the Regional Council for International Education, centered at the University of Pittsburgh, and the Cincinnati Council on World Affairs, speakers and teachers in foreign studies have come to the campus, and Wilmington students and faculty have joined seminars on Africa, the Far East, and Latin America held nearby. As part of the pilot project, President James Read visited Kenya in 1964 and arranged for the assistant director of the Kenya Institute of Education, John Osogo, who is responsible for curriculum development in teacher education schools in Kenya, to spend six months at Wilmington as an administrative intern, visiting elementary and secondary schools, schools for special education, the Ohio State Board of Education, and other college campuses.

Other faculty members have taken study trips to Israel and to Egypt; students carry out independent study projects abroad as part of their four-year programs, in Latin America and in Europe; or students spend a junior year at the European-American Study Center in Basel, Switzerland, where the Center is supported by the Regional Council for International Education. The College has also begun an institutional affiliation with the University of Nicaragua aided by a grant of $1,000 from the U.S. Department of State to help with the exchange of tape recordings, books, curricular materials, as a prelude to more extensive exchange of students and faculty members in the future.

Among other items are included—

1. An eight-week travel-study project for 25 students to go to Africa for interviews with educational and political leaders, visits to schools and colleges, and two weeks in an African work camp.

2. Establishment of an International Education Center for American and foreign students, with discussions of educational systems, foreign cultures, world issues, etc.

3. A speaker's bureau on the campus for foreign students to speak to community groups and to college and school classes.

4. An international festival, now in its eighteenth year, brings artists, speakers, and art objects from foreign countries for a five-day celebration.

A contract has been signed for a Peace Corps project involving 80 students who will enter Wilmington College as freshmen, and combining a five-year degree of bachelor of arts with two-year Peace Corps service abroad, teaching and working in agricultural development. From my observations during a visit to the College, Wilmington provides an unusual example of the way in which a small institution with a serious interest in the education of teachers has, with extremely limited financial resources, injected a spirit of internationalism into its entire program. Further progress depends almost entirely on the provision of sufficient funds to extend the work already going on.

Earlham College in Richmond, Indiana, with 1,136 students in 1967, began 10 years ago to build into the four-year curriculum new work in foreign cultures; it was the view of the president and a small group of faculty members that the students should have a wider range of knowledge of the world than the usual courses in the liberal arts and sciences. Although the College does not specialize in the education of teachers, many of its graduates enter the field. The Earlham faculty designed a self-supporting study-abroad program which fitted the curriculum of the Richmond campus, by which students in groups of 15 to 25 go abroad for study in a summer and fall term, under the supervision of an Earlham faculty member. During the nine years of its operation, students have lived with families and studied in France, Italy, Germany, Austria, England, Denmark, Finland, the Soviet Union, Spain, Mexico, and Japan. The college has regular language programs in Spanish, French, German, Russian, and Japanese.

The Japanese development is especially interesting as an example of local initiative in foreign study. It has been done in partnership with

Antioch College, which has one of the most enterprising foreign-study programs in the country, and with the International Division of Waseda University in Tokyo. Earlham, without funds to appoint a complete new faculty, organized a long-range plan to develop the talents of faculty members already at the College and, over a period of annual programs, with seminars, visiting specialists, reading assignments, and independent research projects, ending with 10 weeks of study in Japan, has been able to install courses in Japanese culture ranging from the language itself to Japanese history, political science, art, music, drama, philosophy, and education. In addition, performances by foreign artists, discussion groups, lectures, convocations, and meetings, and annual institutes of foreign affairs deal with life in China, India, Japan, Malaysia, Indonesia, the Middle East, and Africa.

During a four-year period, the College was involved in the development of a comprehensive high school in Kenya on an AID contract and, at one point, as an independent project which they organized themselves, eight Earlham students spent a summer in a work camp to build and repair school buildings in a remote area of Kenya close to Tanzania. Again, it is clear that with limited funds and campus resources, the transposition of a small college, or a large one for that matter, from a local concern with a limited curriculum into an institution with the flavor of internationalism is not only possible but practicable.

The General Conditions

However, in most of the larger institutions we visited, the number of faculty members and administrators directly interested in the international education of teachers was relatively small and the programs seriously underdeveloped. It is natural that this should be the case when the collective faculty bodies are so little interested in educational issues, or in the education of teachers, or in political, social, and international issues as a whole. Few educators and fewer faculty members had read the literature available, from Education and World Affairs and elsewhere, on international education in the colleges and universities. Still fewer had applied the conclusions to be found in that literature to the possibilities for the education of teachers.

In general, the faculty members of the schools and departments of education were less interested in curriculum change, in an international or any other direction, than faculty members in the arts and sciences, and even there the interest was what could be called minimal. When I asked a group of 25 members of a college of education faculty if there had been any changes in the education curriculum to match the changes in world society, the question was asked, Why should there be?

One frequent result of campus visits was having to answer a flow of questions from faculty members and administrators about what was happening in the international education field, and what ideas and programs were in operation elsewhere. This was especially true of questions about the federal government, most of whose programs in international education and cultural affairs were little known on the campuses, including the work of Congress in preparing and passing the legislation of the International Education Act. There was little indication that the Act itself, with its implications for educational change, even when known, had been taken with the seriousness it deserves. Most of the questions about the new legislation and its provision for a Center for Educational Cooperation had to do with whether there were possibilities for grants to organize new programs and, if so, what form these programs should take in order to match the provisions of the Act.[26]

In tracing down the reason for the diffidence and lack of direct interest in university reform of teacher education and of undergraduate curriculums in an international direction, we found several main factors.

First, again the general lack of interest by university faculty members in educational reform of a serious kind, whether for teacher education or for undergraduates in general, but especially for teacher education. This seemed to be due simply to a preoccupation on the part of faculty members with their own careers within their own professional orbits and the pressures of keeping the present system going.

Second, the idea of general education is now so deeply embedded in the university curriculum and university thinking, the standard pattern of requirements for the first two years and for the B.A. degree so firmly fixed, that it is hard for anyone in the universities to think of other ways to spend the student's time during the first two and the last two years of college. Since the history of Western civilization in one or another of its versions is considered essential for all, that area of the curriculum is already preempted, with little room for other cultures. It is considered sufficient that courses in international relations, foreign cultures, foreign languages, and world affairs are offered by the departments as electives which education students can take along with everyone else. The fallacy lies in assuming that education students are interested in taking them or have any reason to take them as preparation for teaching in schools where there is very little demand for teachers with international qualifications.

Third, even where there are area studies programs and large research institutes in foreign affairs, these are designed for graduate students and for those undergraduates who intend going on to graduate school and into careers other than public school teaching. With the present disjunction between the graduate school and the undergraduate teaching programs, and the separation of the college or department of education from the main body of the liberal arts college, very little coordination or flexibility exists in arranging curriculums for teacher candidates.

Fourth, the teacher candidates, owing to the scholastic qualifications they submit for entrance to college, are much less likely to be the winners

---

[26] This situation may have changed somewhat since the above was written; the regional conferences arranged across the country by the Department of Health, Education, and Welfare have been reported to have had positive effects in arousing interests and in informing the colleges.

of scholarships or fellowships in the open university competition and in general have less money to spend on their education than other students. They are, therefore, less likely than others to take the initiative in trying for a junior year abroad or to vary in any way the pattern of curriculum which they know will deliver them safely into a teaching post at the end of four years. Consequently, they make few demands of their own for study in foreign affairs and go unnoticed by the faculty members in the field.

Fifth, the conception of study of foreign affairs and international relations held in the academic community is one which is essentially unrelated to the needs or interests of undergraduates, even when the undergraduates are interested in world society and its problems. The courses are constructed as background for an understanding of how scholars in world affairs deal with the problems in their field, not with the way men and women live their lives or with the way the conflicts of moral and political decision in American foreign policy are related to personal and cultural factors in American life. Grayson Kirk states the case for the conventional work in international studies in the following passage:

> It is necessary to consider just what a student of international relations attempts to do. His objectives are many and varied but most of them can be grouped under five main headings. These are: (1) analysis of the various forces which influence the foreign policies of the principal states of the world; (2) critical examination of the method which states use to carry on their business with each other, and the instrumentalities which they have established for that purpose; (3) assessment of contemporary economic, political and legal relations among states, and the trends which they reveal; (4) study of the means by which conflicts among states may be adjusted; and (5) consideration of the legal and moral principles which should govern intercourse among nations. . . . The focus must be on intergovernmental relations and all things which affect them.[27]

This focus on intergovernmental relations and all things which affect them provides very little interest to students, only a dreary procession of analyses, instrumentalities, trends in relations, and consideration of legal and moral principles presented by textbooks and lectures in the world affairs classes. Courses of this kind are generally of little value to the student who is becoming a teacher and who needs to gain a sense of the reality of life in another culture and of existing conflicts between ideas and ideologies and to learn something which he can teach to children.

Western and Non-Western Cultures

This indicates another extension of the problem of educating teachers —the consideration of what is already being taught to them. What are the courses in general education, including Western culture, not to mention non-Western affairs, intended to accomplish? What is the purpose of the study of foreign languages in the lives of students and teachers?

The study of a foreign language, if carried on in the context of the life and culture of the country whose language is learned, can be a serious

---

[27] Kirk, Grayson. *The Study of International Relations in American Colleges and Universities.* New York: Council on Foreign Relations, 1947. p. 8.

and enriching intellectual experience. It is an entry to a new world. When it is taught outside that context, as the preparation of a "language teacher" who is then employed to teach the language to students meeting "language requirements," it is a sterile exercise which adds nothing to the world dimension of the student's education or of American culture. If the language learned is never used either to talk with or to come to know the people who speak it, if it is never used to enjoy the pleasure of direct access to a foreign literature and culture, it is literally useless, except for gaining credits. It is like studying plumbing as a way of understanding oceanography.

Yet the study of foreign languages in the American school and in the education of the American teacher is usually carried on in isolation from the cultural context which gives such study its true meaning, and too often it is assumed that the mere addition of foreign languages to the curriculum is a blow struck for internationalism and against parochialism. Even in the Spanish-speaking areas of the United States, usually those poorest in economic and educational resources, the rich cultural heritage of the Spanish-speaking children is either eroded or ignored by an educational system which insists that the children speak English, while in nearby well-to-do schools for English-speaking students, learning to speak Spanish is an artificial exercise without a cultural base.

In a similar way it is assumed that requiring all students, as part of their curriculum in general education, to take a course in Western culture or Western civilization, usually a survey course in an anthology of famous books and authors, is a means of deepening their awareness of their own cultural heritage by relating it to its origins in European thought and culture. It then follows that the way to broaden the student's understanding of his wider heritage is to add a course in non-Western culture, through a policy of equal time for the rest of the world, a little of each for all.

What is actually needed is a radical revision in the conception of culture and in the conception of what truly educates. If we genuinely wanted our students and teachers to understand the nature of Western civilization and Western culture, or of world culture, we would immediately stop thinking of culture as entirely composed of what is set down in famous books, and we would begin to think of it as the way in which various peoples on the world's continents have set about coming to terms with the conditions of their lives, how they have organized their lives through their arts, politics, customs, religions, social systems, and personal values.

When we begin to do that, we find in the history of our own culture the roots of the world, roots so deep in the past and so intertwined that we can seen the world as one. Then we establish the continuity of our world in the West with the world anywhere, and we do not need to add units of non-Western culture to balance a parochialism which, if our teaching were sound and deep, would never have existed.

At one liberal arts college with an interest in educating teachers, I found an extreme case of the Western Culture syndrome during a series of all-college discussions of the reform of the present curriculum. In a lively meeting of the college curriculum committee, except for a physicist and a biologist present, to a man the faculty representatives, including one from the Education Department, assumed without question that what was needed for teacher preparation, as for anything else, was a program of the regular academic subjects in their proper order and that a required course in Western culture for four consecutive terms was *the* central integrating intellectual experience for every student.

Not only was there no response to the idea that this experience should be broadened to include other kinds of materials from other civilizations, but the flat statement was made and defended that all Americans had to cover the Western humanities in order to be considered educated men and women. The students, on the other hand, at subsequent meetings asserted stoutly that the four-term sequence was essential to their education, since it gave them the humanities as an antidote to science; and since the great works of the Western past were so much greater than anything in the present, the chronological sequence of Western thinkers was also necessary before the present or the outside world could be approached. The students refused the notion that a freshman student might be better off in beginning his education in literature with poetry by Robert Lowell or Andrei Voznesensky than with Homer. Their grounds were that Homer was a better poet and belonged to the Western classical tradition. No matter how I tried, I could not convince the students that a sensitivity to specific works of art, either in one's own or another culture, was the first essential to an understanding of art, in the past or the present. They preferred to stay with the standard Western classics, learned in the correct order.

There was also serious resistance to the notion that experience in society or in life had anything to do with the liberal arts. The liberal arts and life in the society must be kept separate. In their view, the real purpose of the liberal arts college was to take people out of society, since society is a corrupting influence. The humanities, they believed, must be kept separate from the social sciences, since the humanities deal with values and the social sciences are descriptive and deal with facts. Both faculty and students were thus opposed to the idea that direct experience in teaching children and in community action is a primary source of learning to recognize and to develop systems of values. Practice teaching was one thing, liberal arts and the humanities were another.

In a brilliant paper on this and related topics, Richard Morse makes the central point.

> Our non-Western specialists are important to us, not because they penetrate Oriental mysteries or predict Caribbean surprises but because they angle into subject matter freshly. They recognize no pecking order or compartmentalization of scholarly disciplines, no walls between Great Traditions and popular or folk-loric ones. This produces a good deal of cant about "integrated" and "inter-disciplinary" programs. But it also shows up our "Western" specialists as performing largely curatorial functions.

The real use of non-Western studies is in the emotional and intellectual shock they give. If this shock were now being provided by American studies— that is, if our students were experiencing their own culture as *foreign*—the situation would be propitious *ipso facto* for non-Western studies to find their proper curricular nest without elaborate strategies and apologies. To put it the other way, only when American culture is so experienced will we know that non-Western studies have found their nest.[28]

We have a right and a duty to make similar demands on the rest of the teacher's curriculum. The purpose of studying psychology, whether as a professional or liberal arts course, is to enrich the student's knowledge of the qualities and character of human nature. In this, the study of psychology is no different from the study of literature, philosophy, anthropology, or theatre. The idea that there is one kind of obligatory psychology which is necessary for the teacher to know before teaching and another kind of psychology (equally irrelevant as it is now taught) for liberalizing the college student is as absurd as it is harmful.

Even a quick summary of the content of psychology textbooks used in the instruction of teachers to teach must show that most of what is said is irrelevant, and what is not irrelevant is to some degree misleading. The basis for the study of psychology as far as teachers are concerned lies in the reality of the child and in what the future teacher can learn from being with children, helping them to learn, sympathetically, unobtrusively, and carefully taking account of who they are, how they behave, and what the problems are with which they need help. The psychology contained in the textbooks has little meaning to the student of teaching until he knows what the psychologist is talking about. The textbook is a substitute for experience when it should be a supplement and a guide to experience.[29]

Aside from the question of relevance, the content of the psychology courses presented to students who will teach is too narrow in its treatment of human nature. Not only do the texts reduce human nature to a series of banal traits, measurable characteristics, and scientific categories, but they do so on the basis of a fairly narrow conception of human nature, for example, the characteristics of the adolescent by which the adolescent is defined in terms of an abstract American of a certain age group whose characteristics are measurable and can be accurately described. Mankind is assumed to be an American. A course or text telling about the characteristics of an American adolescent may or may not be useful to the teacher or to anyone else, but it does not define the human being at a stage of his development, if by human we mean *human,* and not the local American product. A course in psychology designed to prepare students to teach or to inform the student about human nature would do both things at once and would draw upon the original sources of psychological insight and descriptive analyses of children and adolescents in a variety of cultures. It should

[28] Morse, Richard. *The Challenge of Foreign Area Studies,* in supplement to the Spring 1966 issue of *The Educational Record,* published by the American Council on Education, Washington, D.C.

[29] A more extended discussion of the texts and course material currently in use in education courses is to be found in Chapter 4, "The Certification Question."

not provide equivalents of the Gesell and Spock babybooks for the practical use of the teacher practitioner. The practical things are best learned in practice. The theories of psychology and the descriptive materials are best learned in relation to that practical experience.

I do not intend to go all the way around the curriculum in order to make this point in each instance. It is enough to say that if we are interested in enlarging the teacher's conception of the world through the kind of preparation we give him to teach, then there must be a radical shift in the content and approach now existing both in the professional courses in education he must take and in the courses in the liberal arts and sciences. The shift is necessary, not only for teachers, but for everyone else, since the question of the education of teachers is simply a testing point for the education of all those who are learning to enter the culture. College graduates, if they have been truly educated, should all have something to teach to someone wherever they may go. There is no more interesting subject than the philosophy of education, no more fascinating area of knowledge than the history of education, whether they be called professional subjects or by some other name. When they are taught to students who themselves intend to teach, they should be rich in the materials of the world, full of the sense of life, since they have to do with the way people struggle with ideas and conditions in order to make some kind of sense out of the conditions which surround them.

That is precisely the opposite of what general education courses deal with, and it is time that the mythology of general education be examined closely to see whether its myths are related to the educational realities. The idea of general education occupies a central place in all educational planning for the liberal arts and sciences and is now, more than anything else, an administrative convenience rather than a useful educational principle. I raise the question here, since in most of the curricular suggestions for the infusion of internationalism into the education of undergraduates, potential teachers and nonteachers alike, the proposal is to use these "traffic courses," that is, the courses through which all student course-taking traffic is directed, as the road to salvation. The general proposition is that since all students have to take two years of whatever is contained in the general education courses, that is the place to add some foreign and non-Western content. A similar argument is made for adding foreign studies to the other courses in the requirements for academic majors and minors, since they, too, are part of the traffic pattern.

Originally introduced in the 1940's and early 1950's as a national antidote to the disease of narrow and specialized courses and the fragmentation of a badly working elective system, the programs of general education have failed in their intention to develop broadly educated persons by confusing the idea of breadth of knowledge with the idea of an attenuated academic coverage of organized materials. The practical effect of introducing these programs has been once more to shift the emphasis away from the individual teacher and his creative imagination in developing his own courses, to a standardized set of materials in a curriculum made by others. When general education courses have failed, they have done so because an insufficient number of first-rate scholar-teachers with fully developed interests in teaching freshmen and sophomores have been available to conduct them. The rewards for the college teacher lie within the departmental system, with its specialized forms of scholarship which are more profitably applied to the preparation of students for graduate work in given fields. Few faculty members possessed of the conventional ambitions wish to throw in their lot with the inhabitants of a territory which grants no academic advancement and little intellectual stimulation.

As a countermeasure, the emphasis should be placed on the development and recruitment of scholar-teachers whose particular interests lie in the field of world affairs, foreign cultures, and international issues, preferably those who have had experience in study, teaching, and travel abroad and for whom the development of new courses in the field of their own interest would be a means of extending their own scholarship as well as the dimensions of knowledge for the freshmen and sophomores. In ascertaining that each student has had a broad exposure to the major fields of human knowledge, educators have failed to notice that the way to achieve a breadth of mind and a capacity for intellectual growth is to achieve a depth of knowledge in one or another sector of the available curriculum. Out of the study of a foreign culutre in depth comes an understanding of the breadth of variety in other cultures, that is to say, a breadth of mind. From study in depth comes a capacity to apply the experience of knowing a great deal about a few things to further study and exploration of what is not yet known. That is the road to liberal, rather than general, education.

The National Shortage of Teachers

One final dimension, the biggest dimension of all, must be added—the dimension of size in the number of teachers now required for the entire educational system. The problem is complex and far-reaching, more complex and farther reaching than is publicly recognized, even among those most directly concerned with the education of teachers. It has to do not merely with the annual provision of thousands of teachers for service in the public schools and with the continuing education of the approximately 2 million persons already teaching there, but with the question of who will teach the teachers and who will teach those who teach them. The question of who will teach an understanding of world society is subordinate to the question of who will teach at all.

Who will teach the 1.5 million students in the junior colleges and the additional 1 million students who are expected there in the next five years? From what source will come the presidents, deans, and academic leadership of this, the most rapidly expanding sector of American higher education, at a time when more than 300 four-year colleges and universities are already in search of presidents?

Who will teach the additional 4 million college students, among the 9 million predicted by the U.S. Office of Education for 1975?

President Johnson, in his message to Congress on education and health in February 1967, summed up part of the arithmetic when he presented the arguments for passage of the Education Professions Act of 1967.

> Our work to enrich education finds its focus in a single person: the classroom teacher. . . . Next year, more than 170,000 new teachers will be needed to replace uncertified teachers, to fill vacancies and to meet rising student enrollments. Moreover—
> —There are severe shortages of English, mathematics, science and elementary school teachers. (I might add to the President's list not only the shortage but the comparative *absence* of teachers of world affairs.)
> —More teachers are needed for our colleges and junior colleges.
> —Well trained administrators at all levels are critically needed.
> —New kinds of school personnel—such as teacher aides—are needed to help in the schools.
> —By 1975, the nation's schools will need nearly 2 million more teachers.
> To help meet this growing demand, the federal government has sponsored a number of programs to train and improve teachers. These programs, though they have been effective, have been too fragmented to achieve their full potential and too limited to meet many essential sectors of the teaching profession. . . .

The passage of the Education Professions Act will have a positive effect, but it is too limited a bill to help with more than part of the problem. The estimate is that by 1970 we will need to fill 35,000 new full-time teaching positions in the colleges and universities, with graduate schools now producing 21,000 Ph.D.'s a year, at least half of whom will enter nonteaching professions. Of the 75,000 students currently completing their preparation for teaching in the elementary schools, only 60,750 will actually assume teaching positions, and of the 166,400 students completing preparation to teach in the secondary schools, only 77,988 will begin teaching, leaving the schools far short, approximately 50,000, of the 170,000 needed for 1968.[30] This leaves aside the education of teachers for special assignments to disadvantaged children, those who can carry out educational research, counselors, social workers, subprofessionals, and specialists in reading and other fields.

But we must also ask, Who will then teach the rapidly increasing number of graduate students in the arts and sciences, medicine, law, architecture, engineering, social work, the performing arts, and the fine arts? Who will supervise the work of the increasing number of postdoctoral students drawn from every sector of the scientific and scholarly community?

These questions cry out for answers at a time when the entire array of social services in the United States and abroad is making new demands for educated men and women to deal with crucial areas of public welfare, the employment services, mental health, community development, race rela-

---

[30] Later figures, based on 1967 fall enrollments, would increase the shortage by a minimum of another 25,000.

tions, civil rights, poverty, urban planning, international agencies, and a dozen other fields.[31]

The kind of educated persons needed to man these posts on a national and international scale can come from no other source than the universities and colleges, particularly from those which have already taken a serious interest in education in its full dimension, universities where there are colleges, schools, and departments of education flexible enough to consider the idea that the teaching and the professions of the human services are closely intertwined. A new and broad definition of education, conceived as a means of aiding the process of human development in all its dimensions, is a first prerequisite for dealing with the new responsibilities placed on contemporary educators.

Until now the assumption has been continually made that we in America can do everything we want to do, all at the same time—fight a war in Asia, expand the social services, take the leadership in world affairs, solve the problem of poverty, give the Negro his due, increase the range of the creative arts, expand our cultural life, lift up the developing countries, extend the system of democracy, and build a great society—all with the same people, at a time when we have not paused long enough to educate more of them or to assess the finite resources of our present manpower. We seem to have forgotten that the existence of intelligent, skilled, enlightened, and highly educated persons is the primary base on which all of our plans, projects, and national welfare rest and that if we launch new projects entailing huge sums of new money in any one dimension of our national or international life, either in the military or any other sphere, we drain off our educated men and women, leaving the schools, the colleges, and the universities with the same problems they had before, but in greatly intensified form, without the resources in manpower and finances to solve them.

My earlier comments on the continuing neglect of teacher education throughout American educational history located the roots of that neglect in the preoccupation of the universities and their supporters with other

----

[31] Herman Niebuhr, Jr., director of the Center for Community Studies at Temple University, has discussed one part of this problem in a paper, *Training as an Agent of Institutional Change.*

The 1957 administrator (in the human services field) looked for adequate numbers of trained personnel at the professional level, for he still labored under the illusion that public assistance really should be populated by Master's level counselors; that an adequate number of psychoanalysts would solve the mental health problems of the nation; and that fully qualified Master teachers were the high road to the school's success. At least some of these illusions have washed away for the 1966 administrator. He still wants the graduate-level professionals, but he now knows that mass delivery of services takes place at another level. Yet there is no mechanism other than the College of Education for the preparation of human and community service personnel at the undergraduate level, and there are almost no nonprofessional preparatory programs at the high school level.

Training as an Agent of Institutional Change, prepared for a Conference on the Critical Need for Trained Personnel To Man the War on Poverty, July 1966, sponsored by the U.S. Office of Economic Opportunity; mimeographed.

matters, mainly research, scholarship, and professional services to various patrons other than the citizens and their school system. In spite of everything that is said about the new role of the university in America as the source of intellectual and social power for meeting the country's needs, there remains a disjunction between the major university as it functions and the deeper spiritual, social, and intellectual needs of the society it serves.

This disjunction reveals itself most clearly in the neglect of teaching. It is the imperviousness of the university to the needs of its own students, its institutional attitude toward the accumulation and dissemination of knowledge, its corporate character, its role in the knowledge industry—this is what arouses the antagonism, the criticism, and at times the contempt of observant and informed students who witness its character at close range. With the bulk of university energies reserved to meet the market for professional manpower, what energy remains is allocated in a diluted form to the education of students and to the development of teachers, for the public schools and for the colleges and universities themselves.

If the university were as seriously concerned with the creation and dissemination of knowledge of world affairs as it continues to claim to be, it would think of its students as subjects of primary and intensive concern, since they are the link between the university and its wider constituency in the total culture. The students are in fact the major agents of social and cultural change; they are the ones who can, if taught, take ideas out of the academy and transform them for use, through their lives within the society and within the professions and vocations which serve society, especially the profession of teaching. Otherwise, the ideas remain inert and unused, either inside or outside the academy. At the present time, the education of students is not being taken seriously, at precisely the time that they are beginning to take themselves seriously. What the universities ignore is that the only thing they do which could not be done just as easily elsewhere—research, publication, accumulation of knowledge, construction of libraries, laboratories, theatres—is teaching young people. The heart of the university is in its undergraduate college, and any university which bestows the bulk of its energies and favors on its professional schools is likely to find itself with no heart and nothing but an academic mind.

The answer to the question, Who will teach the teachers to be international? has to be sought within the present academic system.

Where are they and who are they?

First, the graduate school professors teach Ph.D. candidates in the graduate schools, who then become teachers in the undergraduate colleges and begin to move back up the hierarchy to teach in the graduate school. This leaves a shortage in the undergraduate college for potential teachers and nonteachers alike.

Second, the professors in the graduate schools of education concentrate on doctoral candidates, who presumably will teach the teachers in the schools of education. There is a shortage here of qualified persons trained in the social sciences and humanities rather than in the educational departments of the schools of education.

Third, the supervisors of practice teaching must be trained both in school teaching and in the disciplines related to education. There is a shortage here.

Fourth, the high school and elementary school teachers supervise the student teachers in their classrooms, provide advice and counsel, and occasionally run seminars for groups of teacher candidates. There is a shortage here, and many universities have serious difficulty in finding places in schools for their student teachers.

Fifth, there is a present shortage of teachers in the schools themselves, and, as indicated above, one which is bound to increase in the next two years unless something quite drastic is done.

Sixth, none of this includes the need for teachers to serve abroad, in increasing numbers if international plans and programs now contemplated are to be carried out.

At the same time, the pull of upward mobility in the teacher's career is constantly away from the public schools, and the combination of lower salaries and lower status for teachers in the schools, added to the proliferation of opportunities and demands for service farther up in the hierarchy, means that the most talented persons are the ones the schools lose first. When the universities recruit their faculty members, they not only seek them from each year's new group of Ph.D. graduates and from other universities, but from the most promising and talented faculty members in the state colleges which, with lower salaries to offer, then recruit from other state colleges and compete for the new Ph.D.'s. As the need for junior college faculty members and administrators increases, they are recruited from the state colleges, the colleges of education, and the high schools. In the competition for teaching talent, it is therefore difficult for all but the most devoted high school, junior college, and state college teachers to remain committed to service within their own institutions where they are needed most. It is as if everyone were looking over his shoulder to see where everyone else is going.

Some Points of Intervention

To change and improve the situation, there are certain points of necessary intervention. I am referring here not to international education for teachers, but to the basic problem of turning a national effort toward teaching itself.

In the first place the colleges and universities as a whole, particularly the liberal arts colleges, must face up to the responsibility they have shirked and turn major efforts into the development of teachers for every part of the educational system, starting with the improvement of the quality of teaching in their own institutions.

The colleges could reform their present curriculums and teaching methods to make the practice of teaching a normal part of the education of all their students. They could allocate at least 25 percent of their scholarship resources and loan funds for the recruitment and education of teaching candidates, bringing to their campuses for internships in teaching a nationally and internationally selected group of graduates with the B.A. degree, whose time would be divided equally between teaching undergraduates and studying toward an M.A. degree in the area of the curriculum in which they were teaching.

The study of education could be put where it properly belongs, not only in the colleges and departments of education, but as a regular component in the liberal arts curriculum, the social sciences, and the humanities; courses in the history of education would become as natural a part of the curriculum as physics or the conventional courses in the history of Europe. Comparative studies of educational systems, considered in the context of their economic and social setting, could become a normal part of the work in anthropology, sociology, political science, and economics.

The high schools could organize teacher curriculums in the junior and senior year with practice teaching and tutoring in the elementary schools by their own students, who could then be prepared to begin serious work in education in their freshman year in college.

The private schools could organize teacher preparation and education curriculums, with practice teaching by their students inside the school—seniors teaching freshmen—and in the neighborhood elementary schools.

Undergraduate social science and psychology students in the universities could study educational and teaching problems as a regular part of their course work in the liberal arts.

Graduate students in the universities could assist in teaching freshmen and high school students as part of their work in the social sciences and humanities, not merely as graduate assistants but as students of society through the study of schools in society.

In all these areas, foreign students, both graduate and undergraduate, could be enlisted to help in introducing new materials in foreign cultures into the stream of day-to-day teaching in the universities they attend and in nearby schools.

The graduate school of education is a major point of intervention, as the Harvard Committee on Graduate Studies in Education has pointed out. If the graduate schools in the arts and sciences concentrated on developing a new kind of practicing scholar with a serious commitment to the field of education, this could provide a main source of more and better teachers to teach the teachers. It is clear that, as of now, there are relatively few such people in the graduate schools whose entire attention is given to the education of teachers, and fewer still who have had either the experience abroad or the formal education to be able to teach in world affairs, foreign cultures, or international education. The most immediate way of remedying that situation is to make the relation between the college of education and the graduate faculty of the university much more direct, to make joint appointments of experts in foreign affairs, foreign cultures, and related fields, to plan joint curriculums with the other departments and divisions of the graduate faculty.

It should be perfectly possible to introduce a substantial component of the study of education into area studies programs already existing, so that graduate students of education could not only work with the existing materials of the social sciences and humanities available in area studies, but could combine that work with a central concern for the educational history and problems of the region under consideration. The major change to be made, however, is in the development of a serious commitment on the part of all the components of the graduate school, in education or out of it, to the education of teachers.

The State Colleges and Universities

In the meantime, the crucial point of intervention for change is in the institutions where most of the public school teachers are actually being educated—the state colleges and universities, former teachers colleges, the urban universities, the liberal arts colleges—where there is already a commitment to the education of teachers, especially in the state colleges, in which one out of every five students in the country is enrolled. The state colleges and the universities which have grown out of them have the advantage of being relatively free from a heavy concern with graduate education; many of them do not offer the Ph.D., and they have not yet had a chance to become fully set in their academic ways. It is, therefore, possible to develop a point of view within such institutions which links them directly to the problems of society, both national and international, and to the social and educational innovations represented by the National Teacher Corps, Head Start, VISTA, job opportunity centers, community action programs, and, in the world dimension, the Peace Corps and the wider extension of the land-grant conception of service to the needs of all citizens. Institutions of the size and character of Ohio University, with its connections to educational projects abroad; Southern Illinois University, with similar connections; Wayne State University, whose College of Education includes a Center for Teaching About Peace and War; Western Michigan University; and San Francisco State College are natural resources for the development of new concepts and programs which can concentrate on the education of teachers who consider the world to be their campus.

The smaller state colleges and universities have been the places most neglected in the consideration of major research and action grants for the expansion of international education. As in the case of federal and foundation grants for research in the natural sciences, the funds have gone to institutions already strong in their graduate work and already well situated in the accumulation of faculty members. Many of these state institutions have no resources of their own from which applications for grants, new international projects, and new ideas for education may come. In part this is because, as I have already pointed out, they have been so wrapped up in the problems of expanding their day-to-day work to educate the large number of students they already have that they do not possess the time, the energy, or the outreach necessary to gain the attention of granters.

Most state college administrators have not had wide experience in the world of grant-getting, from either foundations or the government, and are not as expert or as sophisticated as those with more experience and better connections. None of the language and area studies centers established with government subsidy under Title VI of the National Defense Education Act has been located in any of the 235 institutions of the American Association of State Colleges and Universities, even though these are the institutions which could make most use of them and which could have the most direct effect on the education of a large sector of the country's teachers. What is usually referred to as the humble origin of these institutions works against them when it should be working for them. Having sprung from the normal schools, from academies, teachers colleges, polytechnic colleges, agricultural schools, and seminaries, they are institutions where students and faculty members with experience in world affairs and knowledge of foreign cultures are most needed and can be put to the most direct use.

In a survey of the 191 members of the American Association of State Colleges and Universities in 1966, 36 replied that they had no non-Western courses, 96 replied that they did, and of the 96, 74 indicated that they had no overall coordinating committee for international education. Other evidence indicates that few of the 59 who did not reply offer courses outside the conventional Western subject matter. In other words, nearly half of the 191 institutions offered no opportunity to students to study the world outside the West. Only 10 percent of these institutions offered scholarships for foreign students; in the total of 625,000 students attending the member institutions in 1965, there were just 163 foreign students from non-Western regions on scholarships at 19 colleges.[32]

At other teacher education institutions visited during the study, we found that even where there were committees and administrators in programs of international education, some of them having to do with AID contracts, there was no effect on the education of teachers in the institution as a whole, and that the particular interests of particular students and faculty members in a foreign language or a foreign area were confined only to the section of the institution they inhabited, where the population was extremely small. It is not hard to understand why this should be so, in view of the lack of funds for increasing either the number of faculty or of students with an interest in world affairs and international politics and education.

The students, as has been noted, are quite unlikely to bring such interests with them when they come, the faculty are already embedded in a

[32] Harcleroad, Fred F., and Kilmartin, Alfred D. *International Education in the Developing State Colleges and Universities,* a report of a study conducted for the American Association of State Colleges and Universities, 1785 Massachusetts Avenue, N.W., Washington, D.C., November 1966. 42 pp.

curriculum which both is shaped by and shapes the state requirements for teaching certificates, the institutions are seldom reached by federal or foundation grants, and there is no visible place from which new energies in the formation of policies for international education can come. It is in the light of these considerations that the administration of the International Education Act can have the most important effects, provided it does not follow the policy so constantly found in the distribution of grants for new developments in these areas: that of putting the funds into existing "centers of excellence" and leaving the rest to gain what excellence they can on their own time and with their own money.

*   *   *

These are what I have found to be the main dimensions of the problem of educating American teachers in an understanding of the world at large and in gaining a knowledge of its cultures, social systems, people, and character. I think of the teacher's education, the whole of it—in world affairs, or art, or science—as a way of enriching the quality of his life, not as a way of preparing him to make a living by instructing children, running a school, or lecturing to young adults. The deepest criticism which can be made of the present system of teacher education is that it does not touch the life of its students, it does not arouse in them a delight in what they are doing, it does not engage them in action through which their own lives may be fulfilled. Its general effect is to tame their intellectual impulses and to fit them for duties in a school system.

I argue for a wider dimension of world thought and feeling in the education of teachers, for their sake first of all, then for the sake of the children and their schools, then for the sake of the improvement of the educational system and the country. That is the order in which it has to go. It is the quality and range of the teacher's mind and character which determine the degree of his influence and the form his influence will take. By working out ways in which his education may bring him face to face with cultures, ideas, values, facts, and people outside the range of his ordinary experience, we can make a difference in his life and in the quality of the gifts he brings to teaching. By so doing, and by giving enough teachers a chance to think in the bigger terms of world affairs and world issues, we should be able to enliven the entire educational system at a time it badly needs enlivening. Aside from anything else, that seems to me to be a good enough reason for introducing the world and its affairs into the education of American teachers.

Chapter 2. Colleges for Teachers

The art of teaching grew up in the schoolroom, out of inventiveness and sympathetic and concrete observation. . . .

William James
Talks to Teachers

What we need to do first in order to bring the American teacher into the mainstream of world culture and world affairs is to form a new concept of what a college for teachers should be. The question of how, through his education, the teacher can learn to understand world society and become sensitive to its character cannot be answered apart from the question of how his life, values, and intellectual qualities are affected by what the educators have him do.

If it were only a matter of deciding what courses not now being offered in the colleges should be added to the curriculum or of deciding how teachers can acquire new materials from foreign cultures for use in the curriculum of the public schools, there would be relatively few problems in deciding what should be done. The content of the total curriculum must obviously be broadened to include such new materials drawn from the cultures of the world. Important work to achieve that end is already being done in graduate schools and educational research centers (both here and abroad) and through UNESCO, educational organizations, foundations, government, and curriculum planning of all kinds.

But the problem does not end there; it merely begins. It begins with the quality, as well as the content, of the intellectual and personal experience available in and around the institutions in which teachers are presently being educated. It goes on from there to the question of, How can the teacher learn to create an intellectual and cultural life of his own? How can he move into the larger dimension of a world beyond the one to which his cultural origins are bound to confine him?

In looking for new kinds of institutional arrangements and contexts

89

for answers to these questions, I have returned to the old-fashioned idea of teachers colleges—or, to put it more accurately, colleges for teaching—and to the idea that learning to teach is the ultimate liberal art. I regret the mass movement of educators away from the idea of colleges for teachers and toward the multipurpose university. I would prefer to reform the multipurpose university rather than give up the central function it used to serve. The movement toward this kind of institution was an inevitable part of the growth of American higher education, and it does give both the institution and the student more room to move, both inside and outside the field of education. But in achieving greater flexibility, it is beginning to abandon its own heritage in favor of what seems to be academic respectability rather than intellectual or cultural vitality. In meeting all kinds of purposes, it tends to lose sight of the central purpose—the advancement of teaching, and therefore the advancement of learning.

I am strengthened in these convictions by the views of William James, whose ideas about education came not only from a genius for speculative thought but from a deep love of teaching and of the teacher's art. James broke many philosophical precedents, but among the most important was that the mind of a great scholar in philosophy and psychology should remain aloof from the practical problems of education and teaching. He was, in fact, the first philosopher after Emerson to concern himself directly with the problems of the teacher-scholar in reaching a wider audience of laymen and teachers than those ordinarily assembled in university classrooms. In 1892, he gave what he referred to as " a few public lectures on psychology to the Cambridge teachers" and later published these in one volume as *Talks to Teachers*.[1] In the first of these talks he was concerned with dispelling the "mystification" about psychology as a guide to the practice of teaching:

> I say, moreover, that you make a great, a very great, mistake if you think that psychology, being the science of the mind's laws, is something from which you can deduce definite programmes and schemes and methods of instruction for immediate schoolroom use. Psychology is a science, and teaching is an art; and sciences never generate arts directly out of themselves. An intermediary inventive mind must make the application, by using its originality. . . .
>
> The art of teaching [continues James] grew up in the schoolroom, out of inventiveness and sympathetic and concrete observation . . . in teaching, you must simply work your pupil into such a state of interest in what you are going to teach him that every other object of attention is banished from his mind; then reveal it to him so impressively that he will remember the occasion to his dying day; and finally fill him with devouring curiosity to know what the next steps in connection with the subject are . . . .[2]

Although few teachers can manage to do with their pupils all that James suggests, few could deny the two major premises on which his reasoning rests: (a) "the art of teaching grew up in the schoolroom, out of inventiveness and sympathetic and concrete observation" and (b) to

---

[1] James, William. *Talks to Teachers on Psychology and to Students on Some of Life's Ideals*. New York: W. W. Norton & Co., 1958.

[2] *Ibid.*, pp. 23, 24, 25.

apply the principles of education and psychology to teaching "an intermediary inventive mind must make the application, by using its originality."

These premises are basic to the construction of plans for improvement in the education of teachers. Present plans tend to ignore the fact that the art of teaching grew up and is growing up in the schools and in the American communities through a combination of inventiveness and concrete observation. Whatever may have been wrong with them, the teachers colleges had a fundamental and serious aim and were directly connected in the pursuit of that aim to the life of the community, the schools, the parents, and the practice of education. What was lacking was a direct connection with the major intellectual and cultural developments in contemporary society, for reasons inherent in the history of the citizens' movement from which the teachers colleges grew. They evolved *from* the normal schools rather than replacing them and were staffed mainly by practitioners of education rather than scholars with teaching experience or by teachers with a history of scholarship. Under the general American assumption that taking courses and getting degrees is the path to becoming educated, those who wished to take higher degrees and to enlarge the range of their knowledge and careers took courses from other practitioners. The "course taking" is still going on and accounts for the continuing criticism of teacher education by the university scholars, who are now joined by a growing number of serious students.

But the reform of the system is not served by deserting the heritage of the teachers college, nor by separating academic study from direct experience with teaching and learning in the communities and schools. The reform, as must always be the case in the long run, receives its impetus as well as its insights from the living situation of the society and the new demands the society has a right to make on the instruments for education designed to serve its needs. What seems to me to have happened is that with the shift of the center of gravity for teacher education from the actual problems of the school in society, the professional educators have lost touch with the roots of their primary talent and have tried, without a clear philosophy of education in mind, both to accommodate themselves to criticism and to emulate the academic habits of their critics.

The Academic Intelligence

In response to questions raised in conversation and correspondence during the study, a student at a large and academically sound Eastern urban university described the student teacher's academic environment in this way:

> The great mass of students at X University I see as middle class, rather conservative (meaning afraid to take risks or a stand about anything that might lead to remarks on a report card), provincial (their experience being limited to X University and its environs), and conformist. They are also nice, well meaning, and academically intelligent. I define academic intelligence as an intelligence brought to bear strictly on an academic problem raised in a course and related to

a grade. I saw little use of the intellect to explore and to clarify individual identity, the world, morality, philosophy, or the arts in relation to the individual. I saw little attempt at exploration of the problems of man and his world, of peace and technology, of the self within society. Certainly, there were students who were concerned with important problems; but, in general, I would say that their total number on the campus was small though at different times their impact varied; their impact on their friends was significant. World, moral, and esthetic problems were the concern of only a small minority.[3]

As the college programs for students preparing to be teachers have become more academic, and academic intelligence has become more highly prized than more useful forms of intellect, an increasing proportion of the student body has turned to forms of experience other than the academic for their own educational fulfillment. During the early 1960's some sought that experience in the civil rights movement, in which they learned to combine a concern for social justice with action programs for voter registration, demonstrations on behalf of the Negro, and, above all, with teaching—Negro history; constitutional rights; social structure; the arts; and elementary reading, writing, and mathematics—those who had little or no formal education.

The college students learned about education by teaching; and in the absence of textbooks, visual aids, classrooms, or previous instruction, they formed their own methods, prepared their own texts, and planned their own curriculums. Although some students dropped out of college and university to teach and work full time, most worked during the summertime. When these students returned to college in the fall, they had begun not only to understand the nature of their own society and to locate themselves in a social structure that was working in their favor, but they had learned an extraordinary amount about themselves and their education.

As the civil rights movement grew in size and strength on the college campuses during the early 1960's and as more and more students were caught up in education and action programs on behalf of the Negro, the student movement ranged beyond protest into action, beyond civil rights into international affairs and the issues of war and peace. Students who had worked in rural and urban slums found the courses in social science and humanities irrelevant to their own experiences. Having seen the effects of poverty and educational neglect on the lives of Americans and having become more sophisticated about what a society is and how it functions, they saw the world society in similar terms and began to make the connection between the causes of social conflict and injustice in America and the causes of social disorder and conflict in the world at large.

They also found that none of the issues that truly concerned them in national and world affairs were the subject of analysis, discussion, or treatment in the courses offered. Their dilemma was real. Either they subjected themselves to these courses in order to graduate, thus spending time and intellectual energy in ways inadequate to meet their genuine intellectual

---

[3] Letter to Harold Taylor—in study files.

and moral concerns, or they would have to drop out of college in order to become educated.

The way out of the dilemma for many of them was to create their own centers of intellectual and social action on the campuses, a way taken by the students in 1964 on the campus of the University of California in Berkeley. There, students who had had experience in direct social and political action in the civil rights movement, supported by those who felt a sense of outrage at the administrative rules governing their rights as citizens and students, engaged in organized action to change the rules and the educational system.

The effect the Berkeley events have had on other campuses has been recorded in a growing body of literature, and there now exists a substantial student movement concerned with the problems of educational and social reform, as well as with problems in international order. The teach-in as an instrument of protest combined with instruction was an invention of that student movement and a means of making international affairs a matter of serious concern to college students never before involved in such concerns. The disclosure that the Central Intelligence Agency had been covertly supporting the National Student Association (NSA) international programs of former years had the effect not only of shocking the educational community, but of increasing students' awareness of the importance of the role students have played, are playing, and can play in international affairs.

Coincident with the rise of a student movement of international scope and an interest in educational and social change came the impact of the social legislation of the Eighty-Eighth and Eighty-Ninth Congresses and the release of funds for educational improvement on a scale never before known in America. As far as college students were concerned, the main effect of this public welfare legislation was to give them a range of opportunity for service that matched their eagerness and willingness to take their education beyond the academic and into action.

Even before the legislation provided funds for new programs in which the educated young could become involved, 50,000 to 100,000 had already volunteered to tutor children in the rural and urban slums. This number has now increased to nearly 250,000 and has resulted in the formation of a student-run Tutorial Assistance Center, organized and administered by the National Student Association with a grant from the Office of Economic Opportunity. When the National Teacher Corps was first announced, 13,000 students applied for admission, and thousands more have served and are serving in VISTA, Project Head Start, job opportunity centers, youth projects, volunteer service at home and abroad, and in the Peace Corps.

The Student Movement Toward Autonomy

Outside the formal system of university education and of teacher education, a whole new body of young people have become involved in programs that put their intelligence and idealism to work for education.

They are learning to educate each other and the members of their society, either without formal university instruction or in programs of instruction directly related to the educational and social problems they are trying to solve. The citizens' movement has been renewed and has helped to create a new concept of the teachers college, a concept that goes back to the roots of learning and teaching as a function of direct experience with children, parents, and community problems.

In Brooklyn, New York, for example, a new kind of college sponsored by Pratt Institute and named The Central Brooklyn Neighborhood College has been established "because we feel that existing educational programs in Central Brooklyn do not prepare students for college and do not expose them to the variety of skills and professions open to them." Staffed by volunteers, many of them students, the school has no tuition fees, entrance requirements, tests, or grades. However, there is a great deal of tutoring and courses in poetry, dance, drama, Afro-American history, small-business operation, journalism, or in whatever area is of interest to the students. Headquarters are in a Brooklyn store-front, classes are held wherever there is space in the community, and a job placement bureau and an educational center are included as a part of the school. This is the ideal context for learning to teach. Since the volunteer teacher must make his own way by offering his own curriculum, he also has to learn a great deal more about what he is teaching. If he does not teach well, he is likely to be deserted by his students. The National Student Association has plans for a similar college to be staffed entirely by student volunteers, with a curriculum based on the tutorial system.

In the meantime, through the efforts of students who have volunteered to teach courses for and to each other, a movement inside and parallel to college programs of instruction and teacher education has been developing on approximately 90 campuses, from San Francisco State, Wayne State, and the University of Michigan to the City University of New York.

"Make your own course," says a poster distributed by the Committee on Participant Education at the University of California at Berkeley. "Is your interest history or chemistry? The war in Vietnam? Medieval literature and philosophy? A poetry workshop? The cultural effects of media? Are you willing to take responsibility for your education? All you need are ideas and a willingness to pursue them. The above are just examples of possible course subjects. The method of learning may range from individual study to seminars, from group research to regular classes. The teacher may be a faculty member, a grad student, or you! Credit (if you like) may be arranged through the Board of Educational Development. It's up to you."

The New Graduate Student

One of the unnoticed and unanalyzed developments in teacher education has been the graduate students' new interest in education, mainly in the social sciences and humanities in universities across the country. During their undergraduate years these students were involved in the civil rights movement, social protest, demonstrations, teaching, political action, and educational reform. Many of these students have moved into graduate schools—at Berkeley, Michigan, Wisconsin, San Francisco State, and elsewhere; have become graduate assistants in university courses; and have built their own education and graduate research around the issues and interests that engaged them during their undergraduate years. They are not career-minded in the usual academic sense, but are a new breed of politically sophisticated intellectuals, who while intending to build their careers on the campus are also seriously interested in effecting social and political change through their work as teachers and research scholars.

Many of them have been associated as undergraduates with the National Student Association and with Students for a Democratic Society (SDS), an organization which has provoked a great deal of negative comment and alarmed action from administrators on some campuses but which is one of the most intellectually alive and socially aware organizations in contemporary politics. SDS students have been militant in their protests against the war in Vietnam, as they have in their protests and action programs against the draft and against many other government policies.

Response to their campus activities has often been very much like the response of the Berkeley administrators and politicians to the activities of the Free Speech Movement on that campus: to resist their demands rather than try to understand their nature, to take administrative action rather than to deal with substantive issues. The students' actions have been considered by most educators not to be a demonstration of their serious interest in world affairs and education, but as irresponsible troublemaking. Not only do SDS chapters usually provide interesting political controversies and militant intellectual leadership within the student body, but they also often are the only source of such campus leadership. On many campuses we found only a small group of wistful students concerned that they had no issues to raise, protests to make, or international causes to support. One campus reported that the only issue that aroused collegewide concern was the question of wearing shorts to the dining room.

One of the centers of student action from which SDS first grew was the University of Michigan in Ann Arbor, where there has been for many years a tradition of liberal social thought and political action, partly due to the context of state politics in which militant unionism has its own political representation and partly due to the high-quality work going on there in the political and social sciences.[4] Students from Michigan, in the late 1950's and early 1960's, were active in the civil rights movement and in university reform, with a continuing series of criticisms and demands for educational change circulated on the campus through the university newspaper and among students with specific ideas on university education. In

---

[4] The Center for Conflict Resolution—staffed by University of Michigan faculty members interested in national and international problems ranging from race conflict to disarmament—has been a source of energy and talent to encourage the work of undergraduate and graduate students in world affairs.

their criticism and ideas about the mass university, they anticipated the Berkeley students and—through study groups, research papers, and campus political action—sought changes, some of which were made, in the conduct of university education and university policy.

Student Initiatives in Internationalism

One of the student-faculty groups formed during this period at Michigan was called the Association for Commitment to World Responsibility (ACWR). Along with a careful, detailed, and imaginative research study of the rationale, design, and feasibility of a united nations university, the Association also furnished some working papers on the idea of a student peace corps for service abroad. John F. Kennedy spoke at Ann Arbor during his Presidential campaign and urged students to make their own contribution to American society by volunteering from one to three years of their lives to public service needed by their country. Alan E. Guskin, a graduate student in social psychology and a member of the Association, became the leader of a group of students who urged the then-Senator Kennedy to make good on his speech by committing himself to the formation of a government organization that would give American youth a chance to serve the world wherever they were needed. It is generally agreed that Mr. Guskin and his friends were thus responsible for the fact that Kennedy made his famous "Peace Corps" speech in San Francisco in November of 1960 and that the speech took the form that it did.

When the Peace Corps began, Mr. Guskin and his wife, Judith Guskin, were among the first persons appointed to the staff in Washington. They returned to the Michigan campus in 1961 to join the Peace Corps volunteers being trained for service in Thailand, where they both served as instructors at Bangkok's Krungthrep University. They next took posts in the research and evaluation side of VISTA and are now working with the Florida State Migrant (farmworker) Program, of which Mr. Guskin is director.

I cite these facts about the students at Michigan and Mr. Guskin to illustrate what I mean by the importance of the undergraduate and graduate student in the development of educational programs. The ACWR studies were not done in regular courses of graduate or undergraduate work at Michigan, although in terms of their high quality of research they could have been. They were done as an expression of the serious interest, talent, and commitment of students involved in their own education.

Their research was not published in educational or social science journals, although, again, it could have been; it was distributed to interested and concerned people in public life, the universities, and politics. Through the research the students educated themselves and a good many others. As a part of a new and growing movement, these students represent a new kind of young scholar, one whose interest in education stems from a critical awareness of the weaknesses in his own and from the belief in the need for radical reform of the whole educational system. The career Mr.

Guskin has been following since 1960—into the educational system of a foreign country and now into projects of social and educational change in this country—is similar to those being followed by a growing percentage of others, whose talents have already developed to a maturity which, in many instances, is beyond that of the people who have been appointed to teach them and to supervise their research.

It is from these sources in the graduate schools that we are going to be able to recruit the world-minded college teachers we need for the reform of the undergraduate curriculum and for the creation of new teacher education programs in world affairs. In fact, even before graduation, a good many graduate students are ready to take full responsibility for teaching undergraduates who intend to become teachers and to coach them on individual study plans and field work. Rather than assigning this sort of graduate student to graduate assistant's work, colleges should invite them, on salary, to teach for one to two years with their peers and to direct their own and their students' research into educational questions and world affairs toward the preparation of new teaching materials. This could be done, for example, during the period of the undergraduate's practice teaching, with arrangements to try out some of the new materials dealing with world questions in the high school or elementary school to which the student teacher is assigned. This would greatly benefit the graduate student by linking his work directly to the public schools and would benefit the undergraduate and the college curriculum as well.

At present, a group of graduate and undergraduate students at Michigan, following in the tradition of ACWR and SDS on the campus, have formed the Radical Education Project to carry out an "independent education, research, and publication program . . . devoted to the cause of democratic radicalism and aspiring to the creation of a new left in America."[5] Over the past year, the Project has produced a series of student research papers on foreign and domestic policy, power politics, labor, community schools, the universities, and other topics (which are used by student and faculty groups on campuses in the Midwest), along with a series of study guides for students of political and social science. These have been used by faculty members to reorganize their own courses and by students to teach each other and to conduct their own seminars.

Among the topics on which the Project will be working during the coming year are the university and the military, college and university teaching as a profession, youth, the social sciences and social problems, disaffection in the United States, and contemporary educational theory and practice. Their work, related in varying degrees to direct political action, is matched in comparable form by other students on other campuses, both inside and outside the SDS organization.

The reason that American education has difficulty in taking advantage

---

[5] Radical Education Project. *Brief Report on the First Year's Activities of the Radical Education Project.* Ann Arbor, Mich.: the Project, 510 East William St., June 1967.

of such contributions to teaching and learning is that there has been little understanding among educators of the need for a radical student movement both in politics and in social change. Most educators are unaccustomed to the idea of student political action and student dissent, both on and off the campus. Thus, when it occurs they are ill prepared to deal with it except by looking for ways to muffle or repress it. Most educational administrators are more concerned about the effect of serious student political action on public opinion than they are about the validity of the action itself, more concerned to find channels for the control of dissent than to find ways in meeting the criticisms on which it is based.

Conservatism and the Social Sciences

Another source of educational conservatism in social thought and action lies in the organized academic society that functions within its own professional organizations, departments of the universities, and subcultures, particularly in the political and social sciences. The underlying causes for the remoteness of the academic subculture from public issues in social thought and social action, including its remoteness from the acting world of the student, have been described and analyzed elsewhere, particularly in Clark Kerr's Godkin Lectures at Harvard, *The Uses of the University*.[6]

I will not repeat the descriptions here, except to say that the subjects of research in the social and behavioral sciences are established more by academic convention and hierarchical leadership than by their relevance to the major issues confronting world society. Although the peace research movement has made some gains and the impact of social and economic problems produced by the protest movement of the Negro and the poor have turned more academic attention to the educational issues involved, the operating principles of the major academic bodies and organizations bear more resemblance to the American Medical Association than they do to the Society for the Psychological Study of Social Issues.

What I am concerned about here is the way in which the system of graduate education in the social sciences, particularly in sociology, anthropology, social psychology, and political science, can gain new momentum and new social direction from the energy flowing among the undergraduate education of activist students; graduate education relevant to the interests of young activists; and the going system of academic appointments, teaching, and educational organization. The process of change in the education of teachers to give it international social relevance will come from underneath, from the ferment produced among the socially conscious and intellectually aware members of the young generation who have formed their own groups and are carrying on their own action programs. It will come from the new high school and university constituency, which is creating its own style of politics and in some cases is supporting its own candidates for public office.

[6] Kerr, Clark. *The Uses of the University*. Cambridge, Mass.: Harvard University Press, 1963. p. 140.

In this connection, some signs of the effects of undergraduate and graduate school activists on the organized profession are already showing themselves, as in the case of the sociologists, who now include among their ranks some of the new generation of doctoral graduates whose intellectual interests are in social change and reconstruction. In conventional academic terms the academic and intellectual credentials of the new group are impeccable (as were those of most of the students in the Berkeley protest movement), and they have given a certain legitimacy, which in past years has been absent from respectable academic circles, to radical and liberal social thought. Having moved from the status of student to that of college teacher and research scholar without changing gears or changing sides, these young scholars have formed new groupings inside the profession of sociology and, among other things, occasionally turn their research talents in sociology to work on the sociology of the university community, with analyses and exposures of the process of power and change within the educational system.

Many of those who do so learned their trade outside the regular courses and research of the university graduate school through projects of the kind I have described at Michigan and elsewhere and are now in the process of making what was in former years a series of extracurricular ventures a regular part of the method and content of higher education. As yet, few of them have turned in the direction of international education and the social science of world development; but as their interest in the prevention of war and the achievement of creative social change increases, it is clear that more and more of them will concern themselves with world problems in an educational context. The listing of topics in work such as that of the Radical Education Project may soon become the listing of courses in university catalogs.

Students and the Teaching Profession

In the meantime, owing to the gap between the academic system and the reality of the world in which students live, most of the American student body, particularly those preparing to become teachers, remain politically inert and socially illiterate; while the small minority of student intellectuals and activists work out their own ways of expressing that dissent, ways that too often fail to achieve the genuine and valid goals of social change and educational reform with which most intelligent educators agree.

I know at firsthand what students who are trusted and encouraged in their efforts to think and act in radical terms can do in organizing political and social action projects that serve a serious purpose. For one thing, they learn that it is not enough simply to assert a view of one's own— either to have it considered as a radical view or to gain the assent of others to its validity. More than anything else, they learn to take things seriously and to understand the necessity of hard intellectual work in the formation of a point of view that can stand up under attack and make sense to those whom one is trying to persuade.

But it is in education itself that the students have most to offer to those who are willing to trust them and to give them the responsibility they deserve. In my view, the powerful social and intellectual force that exists within the new generation of students has been greatly underestimated, even by those educators who have taken the students seriously. Most educators and the public have tended to think of student activists and those concerned with civil rights and world affairs as a general nuisance, a motley group of radical dissidents, draft dodgers, or young rebels who will soon get over it.

On the contrary, what we have is a new and significant national asset. In fact, the core of the student movement is composed of a serious and informed body of young people who act out of a sense of personal commitment to each other and a sense of compassion for those who have been blocked from a place in society. They care very much about the quality of their own lives, are critical of the Philistine values of a television society, and are sensitive to the effects of their acts on the lives of others. They are responsible critics of the society and its educational system, and the best of them have a political sophistication and social energy in advance of that of many of those appointed to educate them. In short, by their work in society and their intellectual commitments, they have shown that they are already self-taught teachers.

But, as I conferred with hundreds of them during the course of the study, I found a curious paradox. The motivations and interests that caused them to confront directly the problems of world society and of American life are exactly those that turn them away from the teaching profession. Within their ideas, their talents, and their social idealism lies a formidable force for educational change of exactly the kind the country has been calling for. Yet most of them do not intend to be teachers.

When asked, they give two reasons for this. They refuse to spend what they believe to be wasteful time in taking education courses that do not have serious intellectual content or relevance to their own experience as teachers and tutors. They want to work out their own methods and curriculums directly with children and teachers in and out of school with such help as they can get from educators who welcome their questions. They then say that even if properly certified and installed in a teaching post, they would not be able to teach about the world with any sense of integrity because the system—the school board, the principal, the other teachers, and the community—has a set pattern of political, social, and educational attitudes to which they have to conform, which would cause them to lose their personal identity and their fulfillment as teachers.

To all of which I have replied, then how do you hope to reform either the society or its educational system if you refuse to act either in or for its educational institutions? I have usually won the argument but lost the candidate.

Until we create programs in the undergraduate and graduate colleges of education that can speak to the concerns of these students and give them the satisfaction of learning to act in the world and of using their lives in a cause that has meaning for them, we will not tempt the most promising of them into the teaching profession. We have been going about it backwards. While we should have been creating an education that could enlist their energies, we have, instead, been organizing a system that bores them to death and asks too little of them.

Education for Students

In the institutions visited during the present study, we seldom came in touch with educational plans based on the idea of involving the students in teaching and learning, of evoking the kind of enthusiasm for teaching that the students have begun to generate among themselves without benefit of required curriculums or instruction. Yet here is the primary resource of talent and intellectual energy upon which programs for the education of teachers should be based. I need not repeat again the truism, now so widely circulated, that the present system of higher education puts the student almost entirely in a passive role. The young activists refuse to stay in that role; they challenge it on all sides but find themselves frustrated in their desire to act within the framework of existing institutions, especially those designed for the education of teachers. That is why they are forming their own enclaves inside the institutions and are gaining their direct experience with teaching and learning in the real situations of their society outside the colleges.

If, under these circumstances, we analyze the resources for change in the style and content of teacher education, we find within the younger generation a flow of energy and a body of ideas that are now available for use within the colleges in a way unknown in previous periods of educational history. The collective faculty body is conservative in character, as all collective bodies are eventually bound to be, and is tied to certain preconceptions about the organization of knowledge and instruction into departmental categories. Yet these collective faculty bodies, through their committees and departments, control educational policy. The administration is in the hands of administrators whose major responsibilities are for the most part noneducational; they administer policies agreed upon by the bureaucracy of the faculty. Their major educational power lies in the funds they can obtain for particular projects and in the appointments they make to the academic sector of the institution, although even here their authority is limited by the faculty procedures governing appointments, both administrative and academic. The existence of a lively and enterprising body of students varying in size and quality from campus to campus and interested in improving the quality of their education and their society is, in my judgment, the main potential for improving the quality of teaching and learning in the institutions of higher education.

What I wish to propose is the concept of a college for teachers deliberately designed to enlist the energies of its students in teaching and learning—in a sense, a students' college, where the students would be asked to teach children, themselves, and each other. The practice of teaching by the students would be continual, since instruction would be carried on through independent study, joint research projects, seminars, discussions, field work, study guides, experience with children, community development work, and study abroad. The classroom would be conceived as the place to which the student brings the fruits of his own efforts to learn and to teach, the place to receive help and instruction in what he is learning at the hands of his teacher. His motivation for learning then becomes an integral part of his preparation to become a teacher. He wants to learn in order to teach, just as a musician wants to play his instrument in order to be heard. Then the problem of learning how to learn and learning how to teach can be seen as two parts of the same process.

The Conversion of Colleges

A college or university that took the education of teachers seriously, a true college for teachers, would take the world as its campus and move the world into its curriculum and into the life of its students. It would be an example of how liberal education can best be conducted, since it would treat the liberal arts as a body of knowledge and experience to be used in the lives of its students and, through them, in the lives of the coming generation. It would act as an institution primarily devoted to the education of students, whether or not they were all to become teachers; those who did not enter the profession would have had the very great advantage of having learned how to create their own education out of the materials at hand.

A college of this kind would be a staging ground for expeditions into the world, a central place where through study in the arts and sciences the student could prepare himself to understand what he will find beyond the campus and how to continue to learn wherever he goes. The time spent on the campus would be a time for doing the things that can best be done there, or can *only* be done there—in the science laboratory, the library, the art studio, the dance studio, the theater, the classroom. The time spent off the campus would continue the student's education in a variety of settings through a mixture of teaching, community service, field study, writing, social research, work with children. The student would be considered an intern in his society, learning from the experience it has to give him. He would be testing for himself whether the things he was learning—through the books, lectures, ideas, values, and the instruction of his teachers—squared with the facts as he saw them in his own experience. In preparing himself to be a teacher, he would possess a central motive for learning, since everything he learned would be in some way relevant to its future use. Like the poet, he would think of his total experience as enriching and deepening the practice of his art.

In fact, preparing to become a teacher is like preparing to become a poet. The preparation begins in a decision to become something, a commitment made about one's own life and the purpose in it. Then every available kind of human experience for the teacher or the poet becomes a source of learning. Everything becomes a possible source of knowledge, a means of extending the boundaries of one's imagination, sensibility, and intellect, a way of extending and of deepening the original commitment. In the case of the poet, the ultimate expression of that commitment is in the lines he writes. In the case of the teacher, the expression is found in what he leaves in the lives of others.

The Peace Corps as a Teachers College

What are the practical applications and possibilities of the concept of a college for teachers deliberately designed to enlist the energies of its students in teaching and learning? The most immediate application has already been made in the development of the Peace Corps. Although it did not start that way, the Peace Corps is a teachers college in world affairs, where the combination of practical experience in teaching and immersion in and knowledge of a foreign culture is a preparation for the volunteer to teach in the schools and colleges of the United States. It is not the whole of a preparation, but it can be, once the two years of Peace Corps service is made an integral part of a five-year undergraduate or three-year master of arts program in a cooperating college or university. An experimental five-year program has already started at Western Michigan University, at Wilmington College in Ohio, and elsewhere; and the possibilities of Peace Corps service with a three-year graduate degree in education are wide open for experiment.

At the Conference on World Education Harris Wofford said:

We have seen the Peace Corps right from the beginning as a kind of university in dispersion, and some of us have even thought it was a model for a new kind of education which, although it has been tried by many people around the world and in America, had never taken the sort of quantum jump it was possible for us to take when we started our program in Washington. I would like to describe the Peace Corps today as a teachers college, since all Peace Corps volunteers in one way or another are teachers. Half of them literally go to teach in classrooms, the other half are out teaching in the community—birth control, agricultural extension, public health, community development.

What is the novelty?

First, we were and are a new source of teachers as well as a source for new teachers. Not many of the volunteers had ever thought of teaching before they joined the Peace Corps. The largest proportion of the volunteers are liberal arts graduates. Many of those who are exposed to teaching in the Peace Corps decide that that is what they want to do with their lives, or with the next part of their lives, and many more would decide that way if we had better opportunities for them to teach in challenging situations when they come home.

We have been trying to find new ways of learning to teach, above all by *teaching*. . . . The division between teacher and student is blurred because the definition of a good Peace Corps volunteer includes possession of the spirit of learning. If the volunteer does not have the learning spirit, that fact is going to be discovered in the difficult assignment in which he is engaged. People are going to sense that he has come to do good against them. In the Peace Corps you have to learn from those you teach, you have to learn by doing, and it is not only learning by doing, but learning by going. Migration, people on the move, going into a radically new setting, with the possibility of trading the old life for a new one—this is part of the energy and motivation in the Peace Corps kind of education, just as it was for those who migrated to Israel or, in earlier days, to America.[7]

The Impact of the Peace Corps on Education

In retrospect, the Peace Corps can be seen not only as one of the most important developments in American foreign policy during the postwar period, but as a crucially important contribution to the development of American education. It would not have been even remotely possible to have mounted in 1960 an international teacher education program involving 14,000 persons a year in 50 countries supported by millions of dollars through the resources, either intellectual or financial, of the American colleges and universities. Yet that is the program that was mounted by the government.

Since the beginning months of the Peace Corps in 1961—when no one, either in the Peace Corps or the universities, was very clear about how best to train volunteers for service abroad—a body of knowledge and experience in education has been accumulating in the Peace Corps through its research and evaluation and through the ideas the volunteers themselves have brought into the program. Each year of operation has been a test of the validity of the political, social, and educational principles on which it is based, a test applied by the Congress, by the governments and people of the countries in which it has operated, by the American public, by the educational institutions, and by the Peace Corps staff and volunteers themselves. The fact that the Peace Corps has grown in strength and educational maturity during its six years of existence is a tribute to the quality of its volunteers, the quality of its administration, but perhaps most of all to the validity of the principles on which it rests.

One of these principles has gone largely unnoticed: the principle of self-correction leading to continuous change. The Peace Corps selects

---

[7] The Conference on World Education, held at Warrenton, Virginia, December 9-11, 1966, was convened in connection with the present study, and the proceedings have been published by the American Association of Colleges for Teacher Education: *Conference on World Education.* (Edited by Harold Taylor.) Washington, D.C. $1.50. 58 pp.

The full text of Mr. Wofford's statement will be found in the Conference proceedings, along with statements by others on teacher education, world affairs, and international education. Mr. Wofford, a member of the Advisory Committee for the present project, was associated with the Peace Corps from its beginning and served as director for Ethiopia and as an associate director in Washington before leaving in February 1967 to become president of the State University of New York in Old Westbury. There, Mr. Wofford is at work designing a college with the help of students and a number of interested educators, scheduled to open with an experimental program involving 100 students in 1968.

highly qualified, well-educated, and intelligent young people; gives them an unusual degree of responsibility and freedom to carry out a complicated and highly significant set of tasks; and then relies on their judgment, criticism, evaluation, and talents for the continuous operation of the program. This means that, unlike most educational organizations, corrections within the educational system are the direct responsibility of those who are undergoing the education. The experience of the volunteers, who would be called "students" in other circumstances, is the basis for planning the educational program itself.

The organization, therefore, learns incomparably more about itself as it functions from day to day than any other kind of educational institution. Aside from the views expressed by foreign officials, Congressmen, educators, and even its own staff, approximately 7,000 two-year graduates emerge each year, all of them with ideas of what can and should be done, all of them with access to the administration of the program, even to the point of being recruited into the instructional and administrative staff. It takes several generations of students, even in the experimental colleges, for educational institutions to change. In the traditional institutions it takes forever. In the Peace Corps, the change happens year by year, both in the shaping of Peace Corps goals and in the operation of its programs.

However, even though the Peace Corps has grown fast and learned much, it has found itself in an odd situation. On the one hand, it has become—without having set out to be and still without being recognized as such—a powerful educational institution, powerful in the outreach of its programs into the world, powerful in the effects it has had on those who have entered its service, sophisticated in the knowledge it has accumulated about education in action. As a contractor for educational services, it began by asking educators to set up the training programs for the volunteers. The programs that resulted were almost entirely a projection of the academic conventions, with all the deficiencies and weaknesses inherent in the conventions.

Having seen the programs in operation and having learned through research and the direct testimony of reliable witnesses about the irrelevance of many of these programs, the Peace Corps could only conclude that there must be some better way and that they would have to take the initiative in finding it. On the other hand, the Peace Corps had not been asked by Congress to build an educational institution but to send Americans abroad to be helpful; and although the officers had become educators by default, as well as by interest and concern, they could not very well start a Peace Corps university. What they could do, and what they did, was to furnish a critique of conventional education out of the materials of their own history and to establish a working relationship with educators in colleges and universities where there were people who understood their educational problems and responded to their style of educating.

After a meeting with a group of such educators in July of 1965[8] to discuss the future of the Peace Corps educational programs, a Task Force was appointed to work out plans for what might be done. The report of the Task Force, dated February of 1966,[9] is a document of serious importance for American education and of particular importance and relevance to the present study. The conclusions of the report are based on the idea that preparation for Peace Corps service should not be looked upon as short-term training, but as a full process that begins in school and college, is intensified in full-time training before the volunteer goes overseas, and reaches its climax in the two years of service and in what follows after. Getting ready for service in the Peace Corps and then engaging in its service are in themselves an education which prepares the volunteer to continue his education and his life at a higher level than he would otherwise.

The recommendations of the Task Force for the full-time training programs held that the training schedule should include only a very few lectures by academic experts; should leave a great deal of time for individual study, research, and seminars with returned volunteers and foreign participants; and should include "considerable periods of community action, practice teaching, or other work—in radically unfamiliar environments; in slums or rural areas or Job Corps camps in the mainland United States, in other cultures such as Puerto Rico, the Virgin Islands, the State of Hawaii, Mexico, Quebec, or Israel or in the host countries themselves—with some programs taking place entirely in these locations."[10]

The report calls for the use of foreign students and returned volunteers and others from the host country to be full members of the faculty for the training programs and states that rather than separate courses in the conventional disciplines, the curriculum should include the study of problems in American and foreign societies on a comparative basis. More than anything else, the report called for the continuing involvement of colleges and universities with the Peace Corps, including some responsibility for the continuing education of the volunteers overseas and on their return to America. The beginning of preparation for educational and community service abroad should lie in the entire program in high school and college—through work with foreign students and returned volunteers, through the study of foreign languages and foreign cultures, through field experience in teaching and community action. The person who serves America abroad, in other words, should be an example of the best that

---

[8] *The Peace Corps in an Educating Society.* Excerpts from a discussion at the Brookings Institution. July 22, 1965. Dr. James Dixon, chairman. Peace Corps, Washington, D.C. 64 pp.

[9] U.S. Peace Corps. *Peace Corps Education Task Force Report.* Washington, D.C.: the Corps, February 1966. (See also, *Peace Corps Education Task Force Discussion Papers* by Sister Jacqueline Grennan, Rev. Theodore Hesburgh, John R. Seeley, and David Riesman; and *The Future of the Peace Corps* by Harris Wofford. Annals of the American Academy of Political and Social Science, May 1966.)

[10] *Op. cit.*

the whole system of American society and American education can produce. While serving America abroad, such persons are also becoming better prepared to serve America at home.

A New Framework for the Education of Teachers

Looked at as a design for the education of teachers in the field of world affairs, the Task Force recommendations, many of which have been and are being carried out, provide a new framework for education applicable equally to the Peace Corps and to colleges and universities. By a kind of historical accident, including some of the political events preceding and following President Kennedy's election to office, the country has been presented with a national and international instrument for educating teachers, an idea which had not been contemplated by educators in the form of a Peace Corps, but which has now taken a place in the forefront of experiment and change in American higher education. In one great sweep, it has reformulated a philosophy of education whose roots lie deep within the history of American democratic thought, has linked it and American society to the going concerns of contemporary world society, and has developed workable methods backed by Congressional funds for putting the ideas into practice. In doing so, it has involved colleges, universities, and other components of the educational system in a national and international endeavor of high purpose and serious significance.

Here is the structure, considered not as the Peace Corps *per se,* but as an instrument for the education of teachers:

1. An organization and a staff in Washington, supported by Congress and the executive branch, with enough funds for educating approximately 7,000 teachers in world affairs each year

2. A national recruitment program for teachers, which produces approximately 44,000 applicants a year

3. An enlightened selection process, continuing throughout the training program, which chooses approximately 7,000 qualified persons annually for foreign service

4. Provision of two years of foreign teaching experience and study abroad, preceded by a training period that varies from three months to two years, sometimes three, and that could be fully integrated with a four- or five-year college program

5. Administrative connections with foreign educational institutions, governments, and individuals in 46 countries, in addition to connections with American government representatives in those countries

6. Direct connections with students, teachers, and community workers around the world; connections with similar domestic and international programs abroad

7. An approach to education that gives a wide degree of freedom and responsibility to the student and relies on the energies, talents, and

resources of the volunteer to create new forms of education and service, according to existing needs

8. A structure of motivation that stresses the satisfaction of service rather than material rewards or status and provides compelling reasons for the study of foreign languages, foreign cultures, the liberal arts, and world society, both as a means of entry into new areas of experience and as a means of preparing oneself to serve others as a teacher

9. A contractual agency for the development of new programs for the education of teachers in world affairs.

Considered in terms of this structure as an educational instrument, apart from its relation to American foreign policy, the Peace Corps provides the best available model now in existence for the education of teachers in the field of world affairs.

There is already a sufficient body of research on the content of experience and the educational results of Peace Corps training and service to identify the place it occupies in the American educational system as a whole.[11] The emphasis in the research findings is on the way in which entrance into an alien culture by those committed to aiding its growth and welfare creates certain educational demands and requires certain personal attributes for the successful completion of the mission undertaken. Success is measured by how well the alien culture is served by the volunteer; the volunteer's intelligence is measured by the degree and quality of use he makes of it in ministering to the educational needs of the community he serves and must understand.

Accordingly, the rules of the educational game are changed, and academic intelligence must be fused with social sensitivity; ability in the teacher must include cultural proficiency and a capacity to tolerate ambiguities, paradoxes, and uncertainties and to undertake educational initiatives. These are qualities not often sought in their students by those who teach teachers, nor are they introduced as primary concepts in the thinking of those who plan for the education of teachers. Yet they are qualities crucial to any serious understanding by students of cultural differences and world affairs. Throughout this chapter and the Report as a whole, I have for this reason stressed continually the concepts of cultural immersion, social sensitivity, and cultural empathy in the education of teachers. I have argued that no matter what the teacher's specialty, from non-Western cultures to mathematics, and no matter what population of students the teacher is teaching—poor, rich, black or white, ghetto or suburbs, foreign or native—experience within a culture other than one's own is an essential

---

[11] One of the best of the recent research publications is *Cultural Frontiers of the Peace Corps* (edited by Robert B. Textor of the School of Education at Stanford University), which contains chapters by university scholars associated with the Peace Corps and by returned volunteers on problems, results, and implications of Peace Corps work in 13 countries. In addition to its own reports, the book contains a useful bibliography of other research. Published by M.I.T. Press, Cambridge, Mass., with a foreword by Margaret Mead. 363 pp.

ingredient in the development of teacher-scholars able to deal with the ongoing demands of teaching in America.

The evidence piles up that when the student teacher and the teacher in service have had the advantage of work in community development and in teaching within the context of the aims and practices of the Peace Corps, marked gains become visible in the teaching capacity and cultural proficiency of the participants. Ever since the psychologists and anthropologists began to turn their attention to the cultural and psychological implications of educational systems, the relation between cultural and intellectual factors in intelligence and human skill has been a central item of enquiry. But that relationship has not found its way into the working areas of educational reform. In the specific matter of education in world affairs, the establishment of the Peace Corps as an instrument of American foreign policy and cultural diffusion marks a turning point in both the theory and practice of teacher education. It has demonstrated in action the effect of cultural immersion on the growth and development of the teacher.

The Lessons of the Peace Corps

The intention of the Peace Corps, stated in the original Peace Corps Act, is to create and promote understanding of other cultures, values, and ideas on the part of the volunteers. Not to possess such understanding would make it impossible for the volunteer to achieve the objectives for which the Peace Corps was established. Partly through the selection process by which cultural sensitivity, or at least a capacity for such sensitivity, is a determining factor in the admission of candidates to the program, partly through the content of the training curriculums, and mainly through the actual two-year experience of working one's way through the problems of adapting intelligently to another culture, the achievement of cultural proficiency has been a distinguishing characteristic of the vast majority of those who have completed their Peace Corps service. The possession of this attribute is closely related to the idea of democratic man, at home with every kind and condition of human being, and is central to the ethos of a democratic society. Having to cope with people and situations, often in a hierarchical or feudal society with attitudes repugnant to one's own, and to carry through an educational or social mission in circumstances hostile to one's own sense of how things should be done is a direct means of coming to terms with oneself and learning to sustain integrity while accomplishing the task.

The lesson for the educator of teachers is simply that the development of this kind of proficiency and quality of character, whether to be used in foreign service, in teaching in the American ghetto, or in acting as an American citizen, is best achieved by making it one of the major criteria by which a teacher and his work are judged, along with "knowing his subject," and being able to teach it to others.

Considered in this and other dimensions, there are five certain educational results that can be listed in the achievements of the Peace Corps, each of which has serious implications for the theory and practice of teacher education.

1. Experimental programs in short-term preparation for teaching should concentrate on those factors that directly relate to the service to be undertaken. The social, economic, political, and cultural characteristics of the society in which one is to serve as a teacher are of the first importance in curriculum planning for teacher preparation; and the way to learn about them is by direct experience combined with fresh materials and documents in the literature of social science and the humanities, with emphasis on the role of the student in collecting his own knowledge and putting it into useable condition. That is what has given the successful Peace Corps training programs their strength.

2. Willingness to give to the student teacher responsibility for independent action and decision and for individual initiative and autonomy in style and content of teaching and learning is a necessary element in the development of capable teachers, when teaching is conceived as cultural diffusion and developing useable talents, knowledge, and skills in those being taught. The success of the Peace Corps volunteer, since it is measured by how much he contributes to the personal and social welfare of those he has been asked to help, depends in large measure on the imagination and initiative he is willing and able to take. His own feeling of accomplishment is, therefore, a necessary ingredient in the measurement of that success, just as it is a necessary component in the educational program that precedes his period of service. Since he is a volunteer, since he is in the program by commitment and choice, he invests himself in the success of his own efforts and in the success of the program itself and the aims it is designed to serve.

In helping the volunteer to adapt to future situations that both he and his teachers know will be relatively unstructured, his preparation for service must give him experience in dealing with a variety of unstructured problems, for which he must find his own solutions. On the other hand, since some of his duties abroad may be quite specifically structured—he may teach a specific and highly organized syllabus or serve in a government post with clearly circumscribed duties—he must learn how to take the initiative and contribute his talent within a precise frame of reference.

The lesson here for the education of teachers is obvious. The motivation for learning depends on the commitment of those who enter a career of teaching, and the strength of both the commitment and the motivation depends on the opportunity the entrant is given to serve the cause to which he is committed. Unless he feels that what he is asked to do in his education gives him genuine responsibility and preparation for further responsibility ahead, his motivation is weakened, even destroyed.

3. As was the case in the development of military crash programs for language training during World War II, the Peace Corps has developed

110

a high degree of sophistication in short-term intensive periods (300-400 hours) of language instruction and has a great deal to contribute to teacher education in this field. Since the ability to work in the language of the host country is essential for the objectives of the program, there is a direct, self-evident, and strong relation between learning the language and using it, with a consequent strong learner motivation usually lacking in the conventional college language courses.

Additional strength is given by the fact that language instruction is often conducted by teams of host-country natives, who are eager to serve as instructors, and by the fact that the cultural content of the rest of the training program is so closely linked to the concepts and linguistic patterns of the language itself. Students in programs of this kind can see, sometimes for the first time, the intricate and subtle connections between language and cultural characteristics.

Faced with the problem of providing instruction in languages for which no previous texts and materials had been prepared, the Peace Corps called upon expert linguists for the kind of analysis modern linguistics can now provide and then built new and effective materials, methods, and programs that can be transposed into college curriculums whenever they are needed.[12] In this they can be helped by the returned volunteers, many of whom have become interested in language training and language teaching through their own experience in the field. The body of experience and knowledge is available to those language teachers, linguists, and educators who wish to make use of it.

4. Through the appointment of country representatives to supervise the programs in the host country, the Peace Corps has developed a new breed of foreign service officer whose duties have in a large sense to do with education and social change, rather than with conventional diplo-matic representation. Additional appointments of associate representatives, usually former Peace Corps volunteers, make it possible to continue the education of the volunteers through seminars, consultations, and informal research projects while they are in service. For those representatives who have had research experience in the social sciences and university teaching experience before appointment, an interesting new form of continuing education becomes possible, with direct relation between the foreign service and the universities from which the volunteers have come.

This means that the education of teachers in world affairs could begin with the appointment of faculty members on American campuses to serve for a year at a time on Peace Corps missions abroad to coordinate the continuing education and practice teaching of the volunteers with the work they have done before service and will do when they return home. Over a period of five years it would thus be possible to build up a sizable cadre of professional educators who are equally at home in the educational life of their own country and that of a foreign culture. At that point we will

---

[12] The Peace Corps now provides instruction in 120 languages, many of which were unknown in this country before the Peace Corps began to teach them.

begin to have the leadership we need but do not now have in this kind of teacher education.

5. The policy of the Peace Corps in appointing to its staff in Washington and abroad young volunteers who show themselves particularly qualified for the work, regardless of their age or place in the academic or Peace Corps hierarchy, has implications for an improved use of teaching and educational talent among the teacher candidates on American campuses. Most of the appointment policies in the colleges of education and the colleges and universities in general involve a slow and sometimes painful series of apprenticeships by graduate students who are faced with a long series of academic requirements, many of them irrelevant to their intellectual or educational interests. The application of the Peace Corps policy to American campuses would result in teaching appointments that were made from the ranks of those with the talent and knowledge, regardless of their academic status and age.

* * *

The sum of these five attributes can have wide consequence for the development of a new body of teaching talent in the United States over the next 10 years, which is exactly when this development is most needed if we are to extend the international dimension of the curriculum and of teaching in the American schools and colleges. There are now 18,000 returned volunteers; by 1970 there will be 50,000; by 1980 there may be as many as 200,000. Just as we have found in the past that the flow into our educational system of Fulbright scholars who have studied in foreign countries has given us the nucleus of talent for research and teaching in the colleges and universities, we will find in the future that the return of Peace Corps volunteers into the public schools and colleges as teachers, community workers, and scholars will give us the nucleus of leadership ideas for expanding the whole concept of international education.

The difficulty at the moment is, as I point out in a subsequent chapter,[13] that the educational system has not yet adapted itself to the importance of collaboration with the returning volunteers or with the Peace Corps itself in such an expansion. There is not yet a full realization on the part of educators that what started as a Peace Corps has become an educational movement with a record of tangible results in producing new teachers and agents of social change.

Some Extensions of the Idea of Voluntary Service Abroad

A whole new variety of Peace Corps arrangements can be adapted to the existing schedules and curriculums of colleges and universities. One pattern is the 15-month arrangement: The volunteer begins with one summer of Peace Corps training on a campus. Foreign teachers and students are recruited from host countries in an exchange Peace Corps

---

[13] *See* Chapter IV: The Certification Question.

role, along with returned volunteers with experience in the host country and selected experts from American college faculties, to lead seminars and supervise student research. This is followed by a year of college work, usually the senior year, which includes practice teaching or community involvement and a planned curriculum of studies in a foreign culture, language, and related disciplines. Then the volunteer has a final summer of training in a cultural setting close to the one to which he will go, in some cases the host country itself. An example of this pattern can be drawn from a Dartmouth program, in which the volunteers spent the first summer in a training program at Dartmouth and the second in French Canada, with their senior year in between, before going to French Africa for their two years of Peace Corps service.

What this suggests for the regular, or non-Peace Corps, teacher education program is to recruit foreign students already in this country, along with returned Peace Corps volunteers and faculty members with foreign experience, into a summer term for sophomore and junior student teachers similar to that of the Peace Corps training. Follow this with a college year in a specially designed curriculum that includes practice teaching, using some of the materials drawn from the previous summer program. Then include a second summer term spent abroad—through arrangements of the kind that can be made by the Experiment in International Living, Operation Crossroads, Africa, or the American Friends Service Committee—for study, community service, and practice teaching, ending with the teacher's certificate and the B.A. degree.

In other words, we can apply the pattern of the Peace Corps experience apart from the two years of service abroad to speed up, improve, and intensify the education of the teacher for service in this country. Through its administrative organization, the Peace Corps can serve to help recruit the teaching talent for such projects from the ranks of its own volunteers and their counterparts abroad, to teach American teachers in special campus programs of the kind demonstrated by the Peace Corps model.

Beyond the 15-month approach is the possibility of a full five-year B.A. program that mixes the methods already described with two years in a planned curriculum of studies in a foreign culture and language— along with the regular academic subjects and practice teaching—then two years of Peace Corps service overseas, followed by a final year on the campus and the award of the teaching certificate and the B.A. degree at the end of that time. Western Michigan University has already begun a similar program, as have Franconia College in New Hampshire and Wilmington College in Ohio.

One obstacle to the spread of the Peace Corps "degree" lies in the fact that the host countries need volunteers with skills and maturity more developed than those possessed by American college juniors and seniors. It is possible that as these experiments continue, there could be a mixture of summer terms in training programs during four years of college, followed by a final term in the host country and two years of service. Practice teaching and study abroad would be supervised by Peace Corps personnel or by an American faculty member who would travel abroad for that purpose. A six-year M.A. degree and a teaching certificate would be awarded at the end.

There are, of course, dozens of untried variations around the central idea. One could imagine a program in which the student who wished to become a teacher through the route of the Peace Corps could work out as a freshman an individually planned curriculum, in which community work, practice teaching, assignment to a Peace Corps summer term (either in this country or abroad), and study of foreign language and the culture of the country of assignment, along with the regular college subjects, would prepare the student to take the B.A. degree with his teaching certificate. He then would go abroad fully prepared for his assignment.

Or, one could start at the other end with the B.A. volunteer who has had either a 15- or 3-month training program before service. It is possible to arrange a relationship between the volunteer and a sponsoring college through which the volunteer would use his teaching experience abroad as a focal point for the study of the culture and educational system of the host country, would send back reports of his work to a faculty member at the home college, would receive recommendations about his teaching ability from educators in the host country assigned to work with him, and would receive the teaching certificate and consideration for a teaching appointment to a school on his return to the United States.

As the Peace Corps continues to develop, it is clear that certain of the host countries will extend their present requests for volunteers to include those with special skills in technology, medicine, agriculture, and other fields, rather than for those with a general B.A. degree. It is also clear that collaboration of colleges and universities can evolve curriculums designed to produce those skills along with the B.A. degree. The Wilmington College Peace Corps B.A., for example, includes work in agriculture. The facilities of the college experimental farm and the talents of the faculty in this field are used to teach certain courses without diminishing the regular requirements of the students' liberal education.

In other colleges, the interest of the liberal arts college in developing teachers would not necessarily be deflected by including summer programs for study and work in medical or technological fields. The need for teachers with technical skill and knowledge to serve in the vocational schools and the junior colleges in America is growing by leaps and bounds. A three-year M.A. degree related to the two years of teaching and service in the Peace Corps—with training before, during, and after the service overseas—would be an ideal preparation for a new kind of teacher with experience in world affairs who would work in the junior colleges, the high schools, and social welfare posts. Other possibilities exist for doctoral candidates. For them, a three- or four-year doctorate in education coordinated with Peace Corps service would be ideal.

When the comprehensive, all-year-round Peace Corps education centers begin to operate on college campuses and carry on a continuous series of training and education programs, there can be a new kind of association with members of the faculty where the centers are located. Not only will it be possible to appoint faculty members from foreign countries to work in the center with foreign students and returned volunteers, but faculty members not presently associated with the Peace Corps can be recruited for teaching at home and working with volunteers abroad.

That is to say, faculty members who have had a hand in preparing the volunteer for teaching or community duties would remain in touch with the volunteer through correspondence; could supervise research and study projects; and could go abroad on assignment to lead seminars, help the volunteers with their teaching, or serve on the Peace Corps staff. Their assignments abroad could last for two years, during a summer, or for a sabbatical, as part of their college's contract with the Peace Corps. The host countries are now asking for volunteers with more skill and experience than the present young B.A. graduates; in some cases, the countries are actually asking for professional agriculturalists, engineers, medical technicians, and so forth.

At the same time there is an obvious need for the continuing education of the young volunteers while they are in service, both in getting help in their teaching and in having a chance to talk to and work with a person who could help supervise a research project. The research project might be collecting case studies of children and families in the community where the volunteer is serving or preparing new texts for elementary school children, using incidents and narrative from the volunteer's experience. This would make it necessary to increase the number of people sent abroad to supervise various parts of the Peace Corps program. Some of these people—called "volunteer leaders" by the Peace Corps—could become a new kind of traveling professor, one who as a tutor, adviser, teacher, scholar, and educator would go where needed to do what was needed.

If and when this happens, we will have a full chance, through collaboration with the Peace Corps, to build the education of teachers directly into the curriculum of the colleges, since faculty members, appointed because of their special qualifications and interests in world education, teaching, and community service, will be able to gather around themselves more and more students whose interest in world affairs will grow as they discover the range of studies and experience open to them in Peace Corps teaching and service abroad.[14] At the present time there are few incentives to persuade students to come into teaching programs in world affairs. The idea that signing up to become a teacher is a promise

---

[14] The University of Missouri has already begun an M.A. program in community development that includes Peace Corps training and supervision (by Missouri faculty members) of the volunteer in the field. Michigan State University has an M.A. in teaching which is built around Peace Corps service, both before and after the student goes abroad.

of honest-to-God adventure, undertaken in foreign countries, with serious and interesting people, is one that has not yet been introduced to the American student, but now can be, more and more often, both in the Peace Corps and outside it.

The existence of close collaboration between the Peace Corps and the colleges, especially those with continuing Peace Corps centers, will have the effect of pushing the liberal arts colleges toward more concern with teaching teachers and with the liberal tasks of working on the social problems of American society, since these are the concern of the Peace Corps. In teacher education institutions it will raise the level of concern for the liberal arts and sciences since the quality of study of foreign cultures and languages, the direct relation between studies in social science and the problems of the society, is a necessary element in the preparation of Peace Corps volunteers. The work of the college or university in teacher preparation for service abroad, when carried on in collaboration with the Peace Corps, will be scrutinized and judged by people outside the field of education who care about good teaching and international education but are not in the grip of the academic and professional criteria which tend to warp the judgment of the professional educator.

My hope is that with the extraordinary apparatus the Peace Corps now has for raising the level of teacher education, its officers will not make the conventional mistake of combining forces only with colleges and universities that already have the resources and the prestige to produce the support the Peace Corps wants and that they will not turn away from teacher education institutions, which may not have exactly what is needed at the moment but which, in the long run, are the basis on which reform and improvement of teacher education rests.

An illustration of what I have in mind can be drawn from the experience of Northern Illinois University, DeKalb, Illinois. Near the beginning of its transition from a teachers college to a university, Northern Illinois contracted to prepare the first group of Peace Corps volunteers for service in Malaysia. At that time, like most of its counterparts elsewhere in the country, the University had little concern with problems in world affairs, either in the development of curriculums or in the preparation of teachers and others for whom knowledge of a foreign culture or language would be a prelude to a career in international education.

The necessity of carrying out the recruitment program for staff to train the volunteers for Malaysia, the necessity of developing a Malaysian training program for which there were no precedents, and the success of the first efforts in putting well-trained volunteers into the field meant that a body of interest and personnel was collected on the campus, out of which grew new programs for Malaysia and other countries in Southeast Asia. Thus, it was both possible and natural to launch a Southeast Asia studies program for undergraduates as well as graduates and to staff it in part with former volunteers who returned to Northern Illinois for graduate work based on their service overseas. The University now has an institutional commitment to education in world affairs and the basis on which to build a full international curriculum in the future. There is no reason why other institutions of similar size and educational history should not move in this direction either on their own or in collaboration with the Peace Corps and other universities, agencies, and organizations on a national or international basis.

When the actual effects of involvement with the Peace Corps begin to show themselves on more campuses through returned volunteers studying there, through cooperative programs with the Peace Corps itself, or through the general infiltration of the idea that teaching is a rugged profession that separates the men from the boys, the idea of the teacher as an employee of the school board—neuter, passive, accepting, and unaware of the larger issues of the world—is going to change radically.

There is no real distinction to be made between work in community development and work in teaching. They are both forms of teaching. That is not commonly known in America, where we separate everything. The difference lies only in the possession of certain kinds of information and skill, none of which is difficult to acquire if you are interested in acquiring it. That is one of the most important contributions the Peace Corps has made to the study of international affairs. International affairs, considered as the manipulation of ideas, rhetoric, and situations by governments, is one thing; it is studied incessantly in colleges. But international affairs as the effect of certain conditions in which various nation-states find themselves, and the change in those conditions by persons who deliberately educate themselves to change them, is a different kind of thing. This is the area in which the Peace Corps has chosen to operate; again, not so much by original design but by the ideas of those who collected themselves and were collected around the original idea. What I mean to say here is said directly by Frank Mankiewicz, former director of the Latin American Peace Corps program, in describing the problems in Latin America with which the volunteer is asked to deal:

> A lower-class man in Latin America believes that he himself is powerless, and his neighbors are powerless, to do anything about their environment. People talk about themselves as abandoned or forgotten. They have lost the belief that they can accomplish anything for themselves. There are exceptions here and there in countries which have undergone some kind of premature revolution. But in most countries, although elections are held and a democratic façade is maintained, elections have often been only a contest to determine which group of upper-class partisans will control the country.
>
> Into that situation we are asked to put Peace Corps volunteers. Community Development is essentially a revolutionary process, consisting of helping these outsiders to get in. Our job is to give them an awareness of where the tools are to enable them to assert their political power. The only reason that groups take a part in the political, social, and economic life of their country is because they are noticed and taken account of.[15]

The parallel between the situation among the poor in Latin America

---

[15] Quoted by Andrew Kopkind in "Peace Corps' Daring New Look," *New Republic*, February 5, 1966; p. 17.

and in the United States is obvious, but it is seldom made real to the American student or teacher. International relations and world affairs are not taught that way. During visits to colleges and universities situated near the rural and urban poor, I often heard from faculty members the difficulties in finding places for practice teaching; there weren't enough schools to go around. I would then find out later that often the Spanish-American, Negro, or white poor in nearby areas were almost completely neglected by the colleges of education, either because they did not consider the poorer schools suitable for learning to teach or because the students were not interested in preparing themselves to teach that sector of the population. It seemed not to have occurred to them that tutoring the children of the poor after school or working with them in recreation or the arts in the evenings or on weekends or showing them how to make a playground out of vacant lots or helping their parents form educational committees is a form of teaching and learning that is in some ways more important than learning to work in the classroom.

What the Peace Corps volunteer, the VISTA worker, the inner-city tutor, and the National Teacher Corps member have learned is that teaching and community development are part of the same profession and that as soon as you begin to become involved in the lives of the children in the slum school, you would have to be fairly obtuse not to see the connection between the problems of the child and his total situation in society: "They have lost their belief that they can accomplish anything for themselves. . . . Our job is to give them an awareness of where the tools are to enable them to assert their political power." It is because the Peace Corps has tried, through its educational programs, to bring its volunteers directly in touch with the reality of the foreign culture that these programs are of such significance in the reform of teacher education. By breaking down the distinction between something called "world society" and the society of the United States, by giving a living demonstration through the training and service abroad of the connection between the problems, cultures, and societies of the world, the Peace Corps is providing a genuine international education.

One of the most interesting of the experiments of the Peace Corps in training its volunteers[16] is an example that has many lessons for the reform of the American system of teacher education. Although it was designed to prepare volunteers to teach in Nigeria, this experimental program could be put into effect, with or without the Peace Corps and with or without Nigeria. The program was arranged under contract from the Peace Corps by Educational Services Incorporated (ESI), the organization started by Professor Jerrold Zacharias and others to invent new curriculums in the sciences and that has since taken up a wide range of experimental work in the social sciences and the humanities.

---

[16] A full account of the experiment is contained in the proceedings of the Conference on World Education (see note 7). Roger Landrum, director of the project, described how it was run and answered questions about details.

The contracting system should also be considered as an important contribution by the Peace Corps to the field of educational experiment. As used, that system allows for a much greater range of experiment outside the academy than most colleges and universities are capable of allowing, owing to the nature of the commitments colleges and universities are bound to make in the appointments to the faculty for the training programs. The Peace Corps style calls for faculty membership, not in terms of degrees held and academic position, but in terms of usefulness and relevance to the project. By contracting with Educational Services, Inc., and arranging with its officers to allow a free hand to the director, Roger Landrum, in the appointments to the faculty and the design of the program, the Peace Corps gained use of the backlog of experience and research in curriculum of ESI and, at the same time, kept the situation open for full experiment in applying new methods and curriculum content to the training program.

Mr. Landrum, who had served as a Peace Corps teacher in Nigeria and then in the Peace Corps administration in Washington, was responsible for training 90 teachers in mathematics, science, and English to work in Nigerian secondary schools. He recruited a staff of returned volunteers and Nigerian nationals for work in the language and culture and called upon others from the universities as they were needed. To give the volunteers direct experience in the problems of a culture other than their own, the program went to Roxbury, the Negro ghetto area of Boston, where the volunteers found rooms in Negro homes in the area, held "environmental seminars" on the problems of the Roxbury community, did practice teaching in the Roxbury schools, studied the Nigerian language and culture, and immersed themselves in the issues and concerns of the Roxbury community while seeking ways in which an understanding of that community could be related to the issues, facts, and values of Nigerian society. The program ended with a week of seminars, discussions, and meetings of the whole group of 90 at Franconia College in New Hampshire.

The staff and the volunteers, under the direction of Mr. Landrum, had most of the responsibility for planning the program itself, which emphasized the fact that once the volunteers were in service in Nigeria, they would be responsible for adapting themselves to new conditions there which, although unlike those of Roxbury, would be easier to understand once the habit of responsible adaptation had been established by the Roxbury experience.

The success of the Roxbury program as far as the aims of the Peace Corps are concerned will be measured by how well the volunteers function in their work in Nigeria. For the purposes of the present study, the success of the three-month program can be measured by how well the students learned to teach and to serve their assigned Nigerian school and community, the degree to which they became committed to teaching as a fulfillment of their own talents and as a profession, and the amount of knowledge they acquired in the language and culture of a foreign country.

The sum of this then must be judged in comparison with an equivalent amount of time and energy devoted to the conventional three months of courses on a college campus.

Leaving aside the two years of teaching experience which the volunteers will have had before their cycle of Peace Corps service is complete (that, too, should be counted as part of their educational preparation for teaching in the United States), it seems to me that the three months spent in Roxbury is vastly superior to any of the conventional teacher education programs or patterns in operation for the education of teachers in the field of world affairs.

International Education at Home

This suggests the application of the idea by colleges of education across the country. Under modified circumstances, they could place 50 to 100 student teachers for one semester of their senior year in Watts in Los Angeles, Hough in Cleveland, Harlem in New York, the central city in Newark, or smaller groups in the Spanish-American communities of the Southwest. Instruction would involve the help of foreign students, returned Peace Corps volunteers, and exchange Peace Corps students and teachers from foreign countries, under the supervision of faculty members from the college of education.

Seminars on college campuses could be led by selected foreign students and teachers, especially recruited for that purpose. These seminars would feature the study of foreign cultures in relation to their educational systems and would involve field work in the neighboring communities and schools where social, personal, and educational problems were most pressing. Or, returning to a basic idea in the Peace Corps Task Force report, the foreign cultures already existing within the United States and neighboring countries—French Canada, Spanish-speaking America, Puerto Rico, Mexico, the Virgin Islands, Indian communities, Negro communities— should be considered cultural resources for the education of teachers in world affairs, not simply as deprived areas in which poor people live.

One promising area of development in the exchange of student teachers interested in world affairs lies in direct collaboration with the British. British problems in education and community development have reached a state of some degree of crisis in dealing with the race problem in the urban areas of England, where the influx of colored immigrants from the Commonwealth has sometimes raised the level of tension between the white population and the new arrivals to the breaking point. In this situation, there would be considerable advantage to both the Americans and the British in organizing cooperative programs by which young British volunteers, both colored and white, who are being prepared to become teachers or community workers in Great Britain could join with their American counterparts in educational and community programs sponsored by American colleges of education in our major cities.

Over the past year, more than 1,000 British university students have been brought to this country under the sponsorship of the National Student Association for a summer of work and travel designed to acquaint them with America. If suitable arrangements could be made to shift the emphasis of this program to the areas of social development and social conflict in the educational system of the American inner cities, teams of British and American students could engage in teaching and community projects designed to find ways of coping with both the British and the American problems.

The Qualities of Cultural Learning

Some of these ideas are already at work in the programs of VISTA, the National Teacher Corps, and the various kinds of educational patterns developed through the poverty program. Yet they have never been connected by the colleges of education to a concern with world affairs or to the idea of recruiting into the teaching profession the young activists who are already concerned with social issues and world problems and who find few ways in which these concerns can be turned to social use within the profession itself. In comments on the use of the Roxbury model as a basis for further experiment, Michael Rossman says the following:

> Programs in which young teachers are given freedom to evolve their own teaching relations, when they are left free to explore, involve much more time and energy per student and are much more effective. Thrust under a standard load of courses, students can't put these to work, let alone explore further. But a teacher in a Roxbury-style program would have half-time classes, roughly, which would in turn permit him to take on a group of students with whom he could explore relationships at some depth.
>
> More and more, young teachers complain about not being able to enter their students' lives in a broad enough fashion. Ideally, the hybrid role of teacher-community worker would enable a teacher to know the families of his students, and to work with them: thus, to work with the child in and on his entire environment.
>
> This in turn would enormously broaden the spectrum of possible ways the teacher could involve his students in learning situations suited to them. The sensitivity of both components of his role would be or could be increased.
>
> The Roxbury model has a different kind of academic component, and with good reason: the usual academic experience tends to impede engagement, constrict the sense of the possible, and prevent the development of autonomous skills. A variation of the Roxbury model might be used to change the nature of the academic experience directly, rather than by outside example.[17]

Another way of looking at the extension of the Roxbury example into other forms is to ask, Where would the teachers and the students for such programs come from? or to ask the broader question, What are the sources for new teachers among young people already interested in social issues and world affairs, and what are the resources for teaching them in

---

[17] Memorandum to Harold Taylor—in study files. Among other assignments, Mr. Rossman studied the Roxbury program in some detail and spent the final week with the staff and students at Franconia College. His detailed reports of his findings are among the records of the present study.

121

the unconventional situations that are suggested? We have some clue to the numbers when we consider the number of those already engaged in comparable projects and add them to those who have indicated that they want to be.

In the potential for recruitment of students, we can count approximately 250,000 who have already been serving as volunteers in tutorial programs and community work around the country; to these we can add a good proportion of the 44,000 Peace Corps applicants each year, only 7,000 of whom can be selected, along with the 7,000 volunteers who return each year from abroad; in addition we can count the 13,000 applicants for the National Teacher Corps, only 1,200 of whom are in the program; the 15,000 applicants for VISTA, of whom 4,000 are in service; 20,000 now working as teachers in Project Head Start; 5,000 members of Students for a Democratic Society; perhaps 10,000 members of the National Student Association campus branches interested in educational reform, social problems, and world issues; 10,000 students associated with religious organizations, the equivalent of the American Friends Service Committee and the youth groups of the denominations. This would provide, at rough estimate, 375,000 young people who, in one way or another, already have the kind of interest for work in the human services that would indicate the need for programs of the kind described. The point is that except for the Peace Corps, VISTA, and various parts of the poverty program—all of them *outside* the colleges of education, or, as in the case of the National Teacher Corps, brought in from outside—there are scarcely any arrangements now being offered to some of the country's most interesting and talented students, arrangements that can give them a sense of adventure and provide them with the kind of education they are seeking and that they genuinely need.

It is obvious that the Peace Corps alone cannot produce all the teachers with foreign experience that the country must have to staff its schools in the future. What it can do is to provide the machinery and the prototypes for a vastly enlarged program of teacher education through its returned volunteers' involvement in the American teaching system. Once in it in sufficient numbers, they will recruit their own Peace Corps successors, those who will volunteer for Peace Corps service with the intention of teaching when they return. This will demand initiative from the colleges and universities in inventing programs in graduate education built upon the talents and experience that the volunteers bring with them when they return, rather than dealing in a grudging way with the matter of granting academic and certification credit to those who wish to teach.[18]

The Role of Colleges for Education

In fact it demands an entirely new role for the colleges and departments of education as a whole. Presently, the colleges of education must

[18] *See* Chapter IV: The Certification Question.

take their own initiatives without waiting for all-university committees and collective faculty bodies to deal with the key issues. The colleges of education must make their own alliances abroad, as a few have already done; invent their own programs; recruit their own scholars and students, foreign experts, artists, scientists interested in curriculum, sociologists, and anthropologists interested in education; and prepare themselves to teach a much more varied student body of social activists, young poets, composers, internationalists, political scientists, and students interested in foreign service.

If they are to retain the title "colleges of education" they must make good on the claim implicit in it and take the leadership in educational reform in the universities and schools by joining forces with those students who have begun their reforms through protest and social action and have now turned, hundreds of them, to the development of educational programs of their own. This would immediately make the colleges of education the allies of the students I have described, nearly 350,000 of them, and allies of the teachers and intellectuals in this country and abroad who seriously want to reform education, teaching, and society, but have few places to go in order to fulfill their concerns. If the colleges of education arrange their programs imaginatively, the best students will beat a path to their door.

No area in the entire field of education is more open and interesting than that of world affairs, if only because in a college for teachers of the kind I have described it offers the student the wide-ranging and tangier experience of getting out to the world, of traveling, of seeing with his own eyes, of having responsibilities of his own to prepare himself for service, abroad or at home. In this, both the colleges of education and the students have the backing of the U.S. Congress in the International Education Act, which specifically calls for the improvement of undergraduate and graduate education in its international dimension. Although the legislation contains no specific provisions for the education of teachers, it is obvious that the provisions for work in the graduate and undergraduate field must be applied to teacher preparation, otherwise the rest of the legislation makes no sense.

Suppose, in the worst situation, the appropriations from Congress of the funds necessary for carrying out the International Education Act are not granted. Even if they are not, and especially if they are, initiatives from the colleges of education are absolutely essential. The new Center for Educational Cooperation and the entire U.S. Office of Education, no matter what its appropriations may be, are powerless to act unless there is a surge of energy and enthusiasm from the teacher education institutions to take on the tasks implicit in the legislation. The stage in government thinking represented by the International Education Act, and the President's message that introduced it, is far in advance of the present stage of planning by the educators. It is time now to close the gap. We can close it by making use of every available organization, public and private, outside or inside the colleges and schools—the state departments of education; the agencies of government, from AID to the Office of Overseas Schools; the voluntary organizations; student organizations; teachers organizations; citizens' groups—to further the cause of an international education for teachers.

An Idea for the Use of Existing Resources

I present one basic proposition upon which a sizable amount of educational strategy can be built in developing international programs for teachers. The proposition is this:

Wherever there is in existence an organization, private or public, with the slightest interest in international affairs and education, or the slightest possibility that it may become interested, efforts should be made to turn its resources toward the education of teachers. Rather than deploring the fact that too little time, money, and attention are available for educating teachers and citizens to understand the nature of the contemporary world, rather than turning constantly to foundations, government agencies, and organizations that include the name "international" in their titles, departments, and functions, we should be inciting the whole array of American cultural institutions to turn their attention to what should be presented to them as the major need in the whole of world society—the education of teachers.

If we broaden the definition of *teaching* and *teacher* to include all those, in whatever capacity they serve, who are capable of exerting cultural, moral, and intellectual influence, we extend our range of international interest all the way from poets to engineers, doctors to dancers, scientists to philosophers, teachers to students. We gain a new frame of reference for the work of teacher education by the simple device of extending the definition of *teaching* to include the exercise of cultural influence and the definition of *world affairs* to include the interrelationship of the world's people and their ideas. We deliberately take advantage of the ambiguity in the term *education* itself, a term widely used to describe whatever is carried on to develop new attitudes on the part of present individuals in society toward certain goals of the society—as in educating the public to understand foreign policy or in educating children to become good citizens. An international film festival can then be perceived as an educational instrument for internationalism. It brings together ideas, experiences, realities, and people possessed of a full variety of differences and expresses the variety of the world and its values. Yet it also reveals the essential unity of mankind in the imaginative representation of elements in the universals of human experience. The unifying effect is gained through an aesthetic experience shared on a world scale.

An international congress in sociology, biology, geophysics, theater, water supply, public health, or engineering is a means of educating members of the world community, including teachers, to understand each other once they assemble themselves around common interests. The fact that these common interests do exist is the greatest single factor that we have in the continuing struggle to bring the world together and to build new institutional and cultural forms in an international order.

The range of organizations with international potential for teacher education moves all the way from the obvious ones of UNESCO, WHO, the International Association of Universities, the newly forming groups of scholars in the World Academy of Art and Science, and Universities and the Quest for Peace to the Camp Fire Girls (who have the beginnings of an international program), the Home Economics Association (whose member institutions provide upwards of 400 home economics graduates a year for services overseas in the Peace Corps), and World University Service (which for years has had a serious influence in internationalizing the thinking and attitude of American college students). We simply ask the question, How can programs in the education of teachers be made a functional part of the work of organizations that already have budgets, staff, and a general intention of serving as an "educational" organization?

The answers in each case may differ, but the intention remains constant. The UN Association, through its student branches with their leaders, could organize summer travel-study projects for student teachers who could spend two months in Africa with their African counterparts on an English-teaching workshop project; UN Association summer institutes could be established similar to those of the Workshop of Nations in San Francisco for foreign and American students of education. The Rotary Club could extend its international fellowship program to include teaching fellowships for college juniors and seniors. The American Association of University Women could organize a project for women college students interested in teaching, to travel abroad and study specific topics in the education and status of women. State education associations could arrange teachers workshops in foreign countries for association members as part of the preparation of reports and discussions at their annual meetings. The Society for Medical Technologists could organize study tours to investigate public health problems in developing countries in which teachers from American medical schools could be helpful. In other words, wherever there is an organization, use it for the international education of teachers and of students preparing to be teachers.

The World Confederation of Organizations of the Teaching Profession

The most wide-ranging international network of organizations of teachers is the World Confederation of Organizations of the Teaching Profession (1330 Massachusetts Avenue, N.W., Washington, D.C.) with 151 national teacher groups from 95 countries, representing a total membership of 5 million teachers. An Assembly of Delegates is held once a year, attended by approximately 500 leaders of teachers organizations, with an agenda which gives the delegates a chance to exchange ideas and to develop programs for their own countries. Among these are regional meetings and seminars on topics ranging from teaching science in the Asian elementary schools (Manila, December 1964) to the status of the teaching profession (Niamey, Niger, September 1963) and a seminar on the role of teachers in nation building (Tunis, March 1967). Two publications, *Echo* and a quarterly *Education Panorama,* serve as a means of reporting the work of the national organizations to each other and of exchanging ideas and information about educational programs on an international scale. An interesting series of books on "Man Through His Arts," sponsored by the Confederation and supported by UNESCO, which can be obtained from the New York Graphic Society, Greenwich, Connecticut, gives substance to the UNESCO project on the "Mutual Appreciation of Eastern and Western Cultural Values."

A council on the education of teachers operates within the Confederation and has obvious possibilities for carrying out programs in international teacher education which, if funds were forthcoming, could do many of the things recommended in the present Report. The difficulty lies, as is so often the case in international education, in the stringency of the budget making for other than national education systems at a time when nearly every country in the world is in trouble with its own expanding needs for education and the education budget has to fight its way against other national priorities. There is not yet a powerful constituency in the international field to support the idea that international education is a matter of high priority for all national systems.

On the other hand, as far as American teachers are concerned, the range of existing budgets, both personal and public, within the colleges of education, the universities, the state departments of education (as in the example of New York State), the foundations, and the federal programs is broad enough to make it possible that American initiatives for organizing study-travel projects, visits by foreign students and educators, and research and practice teaching projects here and abroad could stimulate new activity through the Confederation and its existing set of world connections. Here is a structure ready for international use on a much larger scale than any other in the field of teacher education. It remains to see what more can be done.

The Example of the National Science Foundation

In this connection, I commend to the attention of my colleagues in teacher education the sixteenth annual report of the National Science Foundation[19] which, in the expenditure of $466 million on behalf of the sciences, mainly in American colleges and universities, has created a model for the wise use of public funds in support of the cause of useful knowl-

---

[19] National Science Foundation. *Report for the Fiscal Year Ended June 30, 1966.* Washington, D.C.: U.S. Government Printing Office.

edge. The custom among many educators has been either to lament or otherwise view with alarm the fact that enormous expenditures of federal and private funds have been poured into the support of the sciences and technologies and that, in comparison, the expenditures for basic research and activity in education, the humanities, and the social sciences in the colleges and universities have been small and insignificant.

The basic postulates of many of those who analyze the shift to science of financial resources and intellectual manpower in the universities have been that the course of university education has been directed more by the availability and use of funds for research and education in science and technology than by wise educational policy in planning a rich variety of curriculum and research in the humane arts and services. These postulates have validity. That is what has happened. The needs of the military, of industry, and of a technological society, and the political and economic power that they have at their disposal to make certain that the needs are filled, have thrown the entire educational system out of balance.

But I suggest that we set aside those considerations for the moment and recognize what enormous power for the education of teachers and for internationalism lies in the existing structure of science and technology and all its spreading educational branches. We tend to forget that while the President has a body of scientific advisers at his elbow for consultation on major questions of public policy from disarmament to allocation of natural resources, he also has a strong body of equivalent advisers and an $11 billion budget to go with them in the U.S. Department of Health, Education, and Welfare.

Because of what could be called a deep misunderstanding of the nature of science in relation to other forms of knowledge, American educators tend to classify science as a separate academic discipline, contrasted both in form and in content with the humanities and the arts. In part, the definition is accurate. Science, as presently organized within the curriculum, *is* a separate discipline. It suffers by being so classified.

The spirit of science, which is another thing altogether, is humanistic, universal, international; it belongs with the arts and the humanities as a moral and intellectual force, asserting the claims for the use of the intellect in resolving human questions and in inculcating the habit of and the desire for truth. In this it is the ally and friend of the arts, perhaps the greatest ally and friend they have, since it teaches a fundamental respect for the mind and for the fruits of intellectual enquiry without which no society can grow from an anonymous collection of a mass of men into a genuine civilization.

With this in mind, I return to the sixteenth annual report of the National Science Foundation and suggest that it be read with an eye to the ways in which the Foundation has taken initiatives, and can take even more, in the education of teachers in the field of world affairs. I am here defining *world affairs* in the terms I have used throughout this Report, not merely as the flow of political and diplomatic events, but as the cultural and social process of the world society.

In the first place it will be evident that the term *science* is much more inclusive than is usually supposed among educators, and it may come as a surprise to some to learn that more than $12 million of Foundation funds have been allocated to the social sciences—$3,840,093, for example, to anthropology; $3,589,142 to sociology and social psychology; and $1,009,861 to the history and philosophy of science. It may come as another surprise to educators that education is a social science and that if one wished to conduct a piece of research in international education, the qualifications of a sociologist or social psychologist may be exactly those that would add most to the research results and that could very well be put to work on these problems under the auspices of the National Science Foundation. As the Foundation report says, in its succinct style, "The social sciences seek to explore the nature of man and to understand individual and group behavior. Because the social sciences are still less well developed than the natural sciences, the potential for new ideas, new techniques, and new paths of enquiry is very great.[20]

But more than this, there is no sharp delineation of the field of intellectual enquiry to be made between the environmental and biological sciences and the social sciences, properly conceived, since all three are parts of the study of man in his environment. What is to be found, for example, through enquiry in the field of cultural geography is directly related to what can be found in its complementary field of environmental biology, physiological processes, and psychobiology. It is the separation that does the damage. The separation is only necessary to delineate areas in the organization of knowledge into manageable parts, not to separate the total enquiry into forms of intellectual discipline. While we continue to need to know specific and special things about physiological structure and processes, the oceans, the deserts, and the sky, the concern of the educator must lie in a total understanding of the interrelationships between them as these relationships center themselves in human consciousness and affect human growth and awareness of the larger world.

Therefore, when we turn to the matter of educating teachers, we should be concerned not so much with the fact that they are teachers of science, but with the fact that they are learning to teach one of the greatest bodies of knowledge that the human mind has ever put together and that their purpose in teaching it is to enlarge their pupils' understanding of the world, not to give them the information through which they can progress to other science courses. Consider, for example, a statement in the National Science Foundation report on the relation of science to human problems. Noting that scientific and engineering progress has created problems that the natural sciences cannot solve by themselves, the report states:

Solutions to the problem of poverty . . . lie in a combination of scientific

---

[20] *Ibid.*, p. 7.

and social developments. These cannot be produced on order. . . . As social scientists search for a deeper understanding of the interactions between man and his environment, they strive for increasing precision in their data. They, like other scientists, have two basic ways of approaching their material—they may observe an existing situation, or they may set up a model experimental situation. Studies of existing situations help show how man actually behaves under conditions that the scientists cannot control. Model situations permit social scientists to vary conditions and find out how individuals and groups react to the variations. Both types of study are necessary and both have produced results of interest and significance.[21]

If ever there were a description of the way in which sound educational research should be carried out, it lies in this brief passage. The best work which has been done in the field of education as an instrument of cultural and social change has been the result of applying these two phases of the work of social science to the problems of poverty—by examining what exists, by setting up various models through educational innovations and experiments to see what can be done through new hypotheses and programs. An extension of this basic approach to the whole field of education would consider the school and the college as experimental models for the development of new forms of human growth and intellectual advance. The curriculum, the community life, the social organization, the lines of authority, the emotional content, and the entire ecology of the school and college in society would become the central focus for serious research and experiment in creating new kinds of development in the education of teachers to an awareness of their world.

Comparative Cultures

An example is at hand in the National Science Foundation report itself, with reference to the work of Urie Bronfenbrenner of Cornell University, who has been studying, under Foundation auspices, child-rearing practices in different cultures and "their effects on two aspects of the child's value system: (a) The extent to which he aligns himself with the values of peers versus those of adults; and (b) the extent to which these value orientations are maintained or modified in response to social pressure from either adults or peers. Comparative studies have been conducted among preadolescents in the United States, England, Switzerland, the USSR, and West Germany."[22]

The significance of this kind of research for international education is obvious, and a wide range of suggestions for further research in these and other areas of world culture flows from the work of Bronfenbrenner and others who, should they become engaged in the education of teachers, would add significantly both to the curriculum of internationalism in education courses and to the methods by which the education students are taught.

---

[21] *Ibid.*, p. 10.

[22] *Ibid.*, p. 11.

Other studies cited in the Foundation report on the problems of food gathering in primitive societies, biology and the medical sciences, and the effectiveness of language in communication have serious implications for the development of new curriculums in the elementary school, where the new knowledge provided by the biological and social scientist can teach children how basic human needs are satisfied through a variety of local methods around the world with which they can compare the methods of their own society. The lyrical title of one international project sponsored by the Foundation, International Years of the Quiet Sun, suggests other projects equally appropriate to the aims of the Foundation, including International Years of the Quiet or Unquiet Child.

In teacher education itself, the work of the Foundation in science education could very well serve as a general model for educators of how progress might best be made in raising the level of teaching talent in world affairs. The goals of science education, as stated by the Foundation, include improving the public's understanding of science, improving subject matter competence at every level of the educational system, and increasing the scientific knowledge and experience of high school students and college undergraduates. Most educators are familiar with the fact that the new developments in science curriculums have come from the amalgamation of the talents of university scientists and those of experienced science teachers, in order to inject new knowledge from contemporary science more directly into the materials offered to the public schools and their teachers.

This approach, with its obvious virtues, has only just begun in the most tentative of forms within the field of world affairs and teacher education, partly because the funds have not been available on the same scale as those for the natural sciences, but mainly because the initiatives have not been taken either by university scholars or by educators. I recommend the language of the report once more, this time to describe the coordinated way in which the problem should be tackled if education in world affairs for teachers is to receive the radical improvement it must have:

> Faculty-centered activities are directed toward three major groups: college science teachers whose initial preparation was once adequate, but whose teaching effectiveness has been eroded by years of classroom work unrelieved by adequate refresher training; those who were never adequately prepared for their present duties; and those whose preparation for their major duties is adequate, but who are assigned to collateral teaching in subspecialties in which they are not fully qualified.[23]

That pretty well summarizes the problems of raising the level of teaching in the other sectors of the curriculum and in the world affairs sector in general, except that in the latter case the evidence is that rarely has the initial preparation been adequate, and teaching about world affairs has almost always been collateral as well as subspecial.

The methods by which the Foundation has approached its problem of teacher education have been to organize institutes, both full-time and

---

[23] *Ibid.*, p. 97.

summer projects for teachers financed with grants; conferences; research projects; and pilot models in undergraduate colleges. In 1966, 43,400 secondary school teachers of science and mathematics were given study opportunities in 851 Foundation-supported projects, or about 20 percent of all the science and mathematics teachers through grades 7 to 12 in the country. In addition, nearly $38 million was spent for precollege teacher education activities for more than 48,000 participants, including four special projects to improve the education of the teachers of teachers, of which one was designed to help a state department of education in the development of in-service work for elementary school teachers.

What I am suggesting in this re-reading of the Foundation report is that to accomplish the results in the field of world affairs that I believe most educators, including the scientists, would agree are of even more crucial importance to science education, we are going to have to attack the problem with a degree of intensity and intelligence and an amount of money equal to that now dispensed on education in science. But I am also suggesting, in view of my general argument for using all existing organizations and resources to accomplish the purposes, that the National Science Foundation itself has a large role to play, both on its own and in conjunction with the work of the Center for Educational Cooperation, when it is established in the U.S. Department of Health, Education, and Welfare. The role the Foundation plays will depend, in large part, on the initiative educators take in asking for its support and in making proposals for ways in which it can function on behalf of international education. It is worth noting that even the Foundation college teacher projects, in an area fully recognized by teacher educators as a crucial one for teacher improvement, were awarded on the basis of only 207 proposals for teacher institutes from colleges out of the more than 1,000 specifically eligible to apply.

It is generally agreed that science has its own universal language and that in many ways international cooperation among natural scientists is easier to arrange than cooperation among social scientists, since the latter have always to take account of the politically explosive nature of the materials with which they deal. My proposal is that the forms of cooperation already open to the natural sciences, armed with their own particular advantages, should be extended more and more widely into the international community.

For example, should a college of education concern itself with the teaching of elementary school science on an international scale, it should be able to count on a sympathetic hearing from the National Science Foundation for a grant that would enable it to establish an international center of research and education on its own campus, with field work abroad. Student teachers from foreign countries supported by AID or Fulbright-Hays travel grants or young teachers with a year or two of experience in teaching science would come to work at such a center in curriculum development, not only teaching methods and materials but also examining cultural and social factors in education through seminars in world affairs, international problems, and the development of internationalism as an educational and political concept.

The Elementary Science Advisory Center at the University of Colorado in Boulder, established under the leadership of Professor David Hawkins in collaboration with Educational Services Incorporated (now the Education Development Center) and the U.S. Office of Education, is a most congenial setting for an international project of this kind. Professor Hawkins, as a philosopher of science with a deep interest in education and the development of science teaching, brings to the work of the Center a broad point of view in international culture and represents the kind of university scholar whose own work in philosophy brings him in touch with contemporary developments in many other fields. Through the focus of effort on creating new science curriculums for the world's children, it would be perfectly natural for that rare combination of university research, undergraduate teaching, educational research, and teacher education to come together in a form of internationalism based on common interests among persons of different cultures.

The Smithsonian Institution

It is useful in this connection to look at the Smithsonian Institution as one of our major national resources for the development of teachers with an international point of view, since the nature of the Institution's work in the past fits it admirably for an extension of this dimension in the future. Already there are teams of researchers affiliated with the Smithsonian at work in anthropology in Brazil, Mexico, Greece, Turkey, Burma, and Iran, as well as on archaeological problems in the United States, making clear—

> The processes by which human groups respond to, adjust to, or break down under the impact of sudden overwhelming changes imposed from outside sources, by providing information on such processes in primitive tribes subjected to such changes. [The work] permits analysis of languages, ideas, concepts, and attitudes that lie behind the more visible and material segments of rapidly disappearing cultures.[24]

Under the heading of "urgent anthropology," the Smithsonian Office of Education and Training intends to collaborate in an international effort to recover ethnological data while it still remains available, by training ethnographers both here and abroad, cooperating internationally with anthropologists, preparing guides and manuals, and so forth. The opportunities for building a system of international teacher education into this kind of research await only the extension of present efforts by the award of fellowships, travel funds, and other aids to teachers in the social sciences and humanities.

---

[24]Smithsonian Institution, Office of Education and Training. *1967-68 Smithsonian Research Opportunities: Fine Arts, History, Science.* Washington, D.C.: the Institution, 1966. 153 pp.

The same set of extensions can be made throughout the other fields with which the Smithsonian Institution is concerned, in fine arts, history, and science, particularly in ecology and the study of ecosystems through the Institution's Office of Ecology, where problems in population biology and population dynamics can furnish the setting for educational studies related to the evolution of societies.

Oceanography provides another field in which the Smithsonian has already taken initiatives which could be turned in the direction of teacher education on an international scale; a full variety of American research resources and agencies, from the National Aeronautics and Space Administration to the Lamont Geological Observatory, are cooperating through the Smithsonian in a program with wide implications for the future of education in those sciences connected with the study of oceans and the ocean floor. Enterprising educators with an interest in teacher education could give the same kind of reading to the Smithsonian Institution reports already recommended in the case of the National Science Foundation. Out of such review and consideration of available resources could come new plans of benefit to all concerned.

The progress of the Education Development Center from a primary interest in the reform of the American science curriculum into the field of the social sciences and humanities demonstrates not only the close relationship between the natural and social sciences that can be established when they are considered in the light of problems in curriculum making and teaching, but the way in which such problems can be intelligently attacked when university scholars and schoolteachers put their heads together in the solution of common problems. The American Association for the Advancement of Science is another agency of great potential in teacher education. In other words, since science already has the support of the funding agencies and the educating community, let us rejoice in that good fortune and share it with the sponsors of teacher education wherever they may be.

Chapter 3. International Experience Abroad and at Home

> I think in terms of the wider consequences of a particular event, no longer only of its effects upon me or upon a scattering of people close to me. A world issue has meaning in space and time.
>
> Po Chong Mar
> Student
> World College Pilot Project, 1963

If it were possible for every American student preparing to become a teacher to spend one to two years abroad in teaching, study, and community service—preferably in Asian, Latin American, or African countries—we would, in a short term of years, have in the American schools and colleges a student curriculum and intellectual life enlivened and broadened by an international dimension. As U Thant put it, the time may be close at hand, perhaps by 1970, when people everywhere "will consider that one or two years of work for the cause of development either in a far-away country or in a depressed area of his own community, is a normal part of one's education."[1] The opportunity for teachers in America to undertake this kind of service abroad or in the "foreign" cultures at home is far greater than that of any other country in the world, far greater than American educators have as yet realized.

We obviously cannot send all U.S. student teachers abroad each year, but we can plan in a realistic way over the next two years to place 25,000 to 50,000 students each year in teacher-community-service posts abroad and at home. It should become natural to think of service, teaching, and study abroad as a regular part of the teacher's preparation for his profession. One of the major reasons it has not become natural to think this way sooner, aside from the recency of a broad national interest in world affairs, is the meager financial support we have been giving to teachers and their

---

[1] U Thant. *University Service*. Washington, D.C.: Division of National Voluntary Service Programs, Peace Corps.

education in the past. Our magazines and newspapers are full of accounts of the millions of Americans who travel abroad each year, the 1.5 million Americans living in 130 countries, the comparative ease and modest expense in such travel; but we have never applied the idea of spending money to enhance the possibilities of travel and study for teachers, either inside or outside the United States. And, apart from teacher education itself, 59,000 students and 17,550 teachers went abroad in the summer of 1967.

There are colleges—including the public colleges of California and, more recently, of New York State—which are beginning to see that study and experience in foreign countries can be arranged for only a little more in expense than an equivalent year in the United States. Yet the ideas for such study have not been applied to the education of teachers. The junior year abroad, for example, which started as a year for liberal arts students who could afford it, has never been used as an instrument in teacher education. The AACTE study-travel projects for college adminis- trators arranged in cooperation with AID are the first small beginning in the use of foreign travel to acquaint administrators of teacher education institutions with problems of world education. It is not too much to hope that a large percentage of student teachers (at least 25,000) can have such experience through a variety of possible programs from eight weeks to a year in duration and that the rest can have comparable experience within the boundaries of the United States.

Three Levels of Intensity

In purely educational terms, within the system of teacher education there is a descending scale of vividness and intensity of experience for those learning to teach and who need to understand the reality of a culture other than their own. The first degree of intensity can only be reached by directly participating in the life of another culture, by living in it for at least a year, by teaching and by carrying out common tasks with members of its communities, by learning the language, and by working directly with other teachers and the parents of children in the schools. The figures I have used throughout this Report as the potential number of student teachers or teachers who could spend part of their education abroad are from 25,000 to 50,000. The figures are based on analysis of existing programs, including the fact that 35,000 students are already abroad under junior-year-abroad arrangements. Many pioneer projects are already under way under the auspices of Operation Crossroads, the Experiment in International Living,[2] World University Service, Inter- national Voluntary Service, the Council on Student Travel, church groups, community service organizations, and educational organizations.

---

[2] The possibility of the use of the approach of the Experiment in International Living on a broad scale in cooperation with the colleges is discussed on pp. 188-90, Chapter III.

Many of these organizations have long experience in the field and a network of relationships with government and community representatives interested in exchange and cooperation in teaching and travel-study programs. A teacher education component could be built into their work by increasing the number of national teacher fellowships, college scholarships, foundation allocations, and individual and community supporting subsidies, which would vastly increase the mobility of teacher candidates and teachers in the course of their education.

The experience of Operation Crossroads in Africa, the World University Service, the Experiment in International Living, and the colleges has shown that short, intensive summer travel-study and work projects often have a dramatic effect in creating new attitudes and a new awareness of world problems on the part of the student and teacher. The short-term experience is often enough to start a chain of consequences lasting an educational lifetime. In those instances where colleges have incorporated such experiences—as at the University of Michigan College of Education and at Antioch College—into their educational programs in American subcultures or in foreign cultures, the immediacy of the cultural experience broadens the student's conception of the world in which he lives.

This kind of field work can also be added to the high school. For example, Hudson High School, Hudson, Ohio, has conducted two-week travel-study projects in the United States (by bus). It is experimenting with a semester abroad in the United States for its senior class. With the introduction of short periods or semesters of nonresident field work (as at Beloit College or at the Justin Morrill College of Michigan State University[3]) and the growing number of intersemester field projects in the liberal arts colleges, a new opportunity is opened up for the enlargement of experience for the teacher. It remains to make these opportunities directly and regularly available as a normal part of the education of teachers.

The Second Level

The next level of educational effectiveness below that of immersion in a foreign culture is direct contact with members of those cultures, in a situation in which Americans and the foreign students or teachers can learn from each other. This can be arranged through summer institutes in the United States resembling Peace Corps training projects. Foreign students and teachers would be invited to these institutes to serve as the main body of instructors. There could be concentration on one country: the Philippines, for example, whose present connections with the Peace Corps would make the recruitment of the instructional staff relatively simple. Other examples are Nigeria and Ethiopia, which have similar connections.

One of the most important sources of new teaching talent lies in the new Exchange Peace Corps project, or Volunteers to America, which,

[3] See the description of Justin Morrill College, pp. 186-88.

although recommended by President Johnson, was eliminated from proposed Peace Corps legislation in favor of a two-year pilot project for 200 volunteers supervised by the Bureau of Educational and Cultural Affairs of the U.S. State Department. Sixty-four men and women from 12 countries in Africa, Asia, and Latin America are now in this country and have had training in Brattleboro, Vermont, in Boston, and in Los Angeles before being assigned to those elementary and secondary schools and communities across the country who have asked for them and who will pay a share of the costs of their services. Some volunteers will work in VISTA-style programs with their American counterparts; others will teach in elementary and high school classrooms and will not only add their knowledge and talents to the American educational system, but will use the experience acquired in this country when they return home.

Aside from anything else, Volunteers to America illustrates the way in which existing government programs can combine resources in funds and personnel to support new projects in international education. In this case, the Fulbright-Hays Act of 1961 supplies the funds for training, travel in the United States, and administrative costs; the foreign governments supply the travel to the U.S. and return; the schools and agencies receiving help from the volunteers supply the rest. But the most important thing about the new program is that it marks a beginning in the whole process of linking this country's educational system directly to those of foreign countries.

We have had visiting teachers before through cultural and educational exchanges sponsored by the government and private agencies, but we have never had a national program (similar to our own National Teacher Corps and Peace Corps) that explicitly declares the need and significance of the contribution that students, teachers, and community workers can make to the improvement of American education and social welfare. Forty more volunteers will come early in 1968, with more to come when the first year of the program shows its results.

Members of this project, if it can be expanded in size to a scale at least approximating that of the President's request for 5,000 visitors, can make a crucial difference to the quality of American teaching and learning in foreign cultures and world affairs. Volunteers could be recruited in teams with foreign students already in this country for special summer institutes in world affairs, where issues in international politics and culture could be studied in depth by multilateral teams that included Americans.[4] New curricular materials, films, videotapes, texts, translations of literature, and presentations in the arts of foreign cultures could be prepared by the visitors and ourselves. The whole problem of world poverty and social change could be examined in the context of field work by the visitors and their American co-workers in the inner cities and impoverished rural areas of the United States, with consequent benefit to the visitors and to the American social system.

---

[4] See the example of Nations Incorporated, Chapter III, pp. 163-64.

Individual colleges, should they wish to develop foreign area studies for teachers, could select foreign students from among those already here and could recruit experienced as well as inexperienced teacher-students coming to this country to do graduate work in education. Connections with such student teachers could be made through members of college of education faculties serving abroad on AID missions, our cultural affairs officers abroad, the Peace Corps, and private organizations like the International Secretariat for Volunteer Service or the Experiment in International Living. Once the visiting student teachers arrived, they could work in partnership with American undergraduate and graduate student teachers to develop new materials in foreign cultures for experimental use in the schools here and to study the educational problems of the countries from which the visitors come. This could also be combined, in certain cases, with community work of the VISTA and Project Head Start kind to internationalize our own domestic programs of educational and social amelioration.

American teachers with experience abroad, returned Peace Corps volunteers, AID consultants, and others could join with selected foreign students in this country to develop new curricular ideas and materials, possibly through translations of foreign literary works, texts used in foreign countries, paintings and sculpture, and new texts written jointly by the American and foreign student teachers as a project in the college of education. Students going abroad for their teaching experience could also undertake photographic essays, research in curriculum, or film making, which could be studied before going overseas. The fruits of this could then furnish the beginning of original film libraries for experimental use in American schools in collaboration with the foreign visitors.

The Third Level

At the next level of intensity and effectiveness would come the regular courses in non-Western culture taught by American professors who had studied abroad or who had gained competence in the field through study at home in the various graduate programs provided, such as the international program of the State Department of Education in New York. Under the influence of the general education movement (whose advocates argue that the courses now offered in Western civilization should be supplemented by courses in the cultures of the East), these courses, as at Western Michigan University, can become part of the general education requirements for teachers. The reservations expressed on this approach in an earlier chapter should be repeated here, in the light of the possibilities for a richer and more direct experience with the foreign culture, which can be planned in place of the usual course offerings.

The farther we get from direct experience with the foreign culture and its representatives, the less likely it is that the student will gain a genuine sense of the reality of the culture he is studying. For example, if courses in non-Western culture are to be added to the general education requirements for teachers, it would be much sounder pedagogy to invent them from original materials in collaboration with visiting teachers and students from abroad than to offer them, as is contemplated at Western Michigan, to 5,000 students through lectures by American academic experts—televised and taped for reuse—and through texts drawn from standard sources. If television is to be used, would it not be much wiser to encourage American students and teachers abroad to make original films and foreign students and teachers to make such films through their joint resources on the American campuses, than to rely on the lecture system staffed by experts and fitted into the mechanical system of the regular general education programs? Would it not be possible to staff the entire course with foreign graduate students who were themselves preparing to become teachers, under the supervision of foreign-educated American faculty members?

The use of films and television tapes of all kinds for the study of foreign cultures is still a relatively undeveloped area in teacher education, although progress has been made in experiments at Stanford and at Antioch College, where student teachers have a chance to see immediately what their own teaching is like through the use of television taping of classes, which includes playback and discussion of the experience while the class is still fresh in the mind of the student teacher. There are, of course, documentary films of foreign cultures and some superb foreign films that, like Satyajit Ray's fine series on Indian life, can become a central part of the curriculum in undergraduate and graduate education. But the relatively unexplored territory lies in student film making, where the idea of the photographic essay is extended into the preparation of scripts (made by students together), calling upon children, parents, other students, storekeepers, policemen, and teachers to act out their parts in real-life situations.

Student Film Making

Many purposes can be served at once in student film making. Students must construct a plan for the script and scenario, which calls for a far deeper understanding of the social and personal situations which they are to document than, for example, writing an essay on the problems of the three-year-old or the school system of Watts. The film assignment tests the imaginative resources of the makers in deciding what pictures to take of what, who the people are who would best express the film's ideas, what is the central point of the film itself, and in what setting the participants are to be placed.

Although the purpose is not necessarily to create a work of art, but rather to photograph an idea, a situation, or a reality, the components of a work of art exist when the film maker is asked to undertake the presentation of a given subject. The participants, or "actors" in the film, have an unusual opportunity for self-expression or for the preparation of

139

what one would say in a given scene to present accurately what life is like in the situation being photographed. We have had enough experience in children's theater to know that when children are asked to make up their own plays and to act in them, they gain a degree of insight into the arts seldom possible for them simply by watching other people perform in plays. In those student films that document social and cultural situations, research is necessary as a central component of the film making, along with critical review of the results by other class members who are also studying the problems and issues treated by the film.

It is not hard to think of a strong program of student film making on issues and problems in American culture and education as part of their education as teachers. Students could make films on the Indian, the Spanish-American, the Negro, the Puerto Rican, the Chinese-American, the American small town, or on whatever topic whose treatment would illuminate their experience of the culture. Students could also build up a library of film materials for use in their own college of education classes. In connection with foreign study, students who had had experience in the use of the movie camera could include as part of their research and teaching experience abroad the preparation of documentary filmstrips or moving pictures for use in the college of education back home. Or, in courses like the one proposed at Western Michigan University, the student who had returned with his films from abroad could, in conjunction with assistance from foreign students, discuss the content of his film essay with the students of the non-Western culture with which the film deals.

In the absence of an opportunity to go abroad oneself, such films and discussion would serve the many purposes already described, including that of sharpening the reality and immediacy of the concepts of the American nontraveling student, who must rely on books, lectures, seminars, and art to gain a knowledge of the foreign culture. Using closed-circuit television to show such films makes much more sense than using the system simply to transmit a lecture by an academic expert. It becomes a live medium for the transmission of direct experience and, since it transmits the ideas of students, is less likely to keep the formal relationship of an academic lecture. The student's questions will flow more easily, since he is not questioning the information and knowledge of a professor, but the ideas and presentation of other students about whose work he can be perfectly candid.

The experimental work carried on by Professor T. H. McKinney, director of the field study program at Justin Morrill College, Michigan State University, has broken some new ground in this form of student film and television production. A great deal of what he has been doing can be applied directly to the international education of teachers. For example, as a regular part of his work in teaching, Professor McKinney arranges for taped interviews and speeches of campus visitors, such as Martin Luther King, Sargent Shriver, Hubert Humphrey, James Farmer, Paul Douglas, and Eli Ginzberg. He then uses these tapes in his classes in social science. The interviews, which usually include one or two other faculty members, are the beginning point of class discussions led by the students themselves. Students are also encouraged to conduct their own interviews with other faculty members, visitors, and each other for use in their own discussions.

In a more formal application of the idea, Professor McKinney arranges for 10 hours of videotape, a producer-director to handle technical problems, and a studio for four hours each week for the use of a class of 46 students. The students are divided into three groups, each of which spends five weeks to prepare television presentations and mimeographs materials related to topics drawn from the texts in the course. The results are shown to the class as a whole during the last four weeks. Among the other educational advantages derived by the students are the experience and knowledge the students gain in interviewing, preparing materials for themselves, and leading discussions. It affords Professor McKinney the opportunity to supervise the learning and teaching, that is to say, the education, of students in seven different groups, with the aid of two faculty colleagues. The possibilities for the extension of this experimental work into the field of world affairs and foreign study are interesting and obvious: They involve the use of foreign visitors, foreign students, and local faculty members with foreign experience and training. They also involve the preparation of symposia, documentaries, and filmstrips based on materials the student teachers can collect abroad, as a specific part of their work in preparation to teach their fellow students when they return.

A Summary of Possibilities

It may be useful at this point to sum up briefly the variety of initiatives at all three of these levels that could be taken by colleges and universities and by colleges of education in collaboration with the Peace Corps, Volunteers to America, and other agencies and organizations in developing new educational programs in world affairs for teachers.

Previous sections of this chapter have emphasized ways in which the colleges and universities can join with the Peace Corps in training volunteers for foreign service while achieving their own objectives in the education of teachers. The other way around the question becomes, How can the colleges take advantage of the experience and organization of the Peace Corps and other agencies to develop new programs of their own in the international education of teachers?

First, and above all, the colleges of education should meet squarely the need for graduate work that can be adapted to the valuable experience, training, and knowledge the Peace Corps volunteer brings with him on his return to this country. More than 50 percent of those who return wish to enter the teaching field; most of these wish to go on into graduate work before beginning their teaching. The conventional graduate programs in the arts and sciences and in education are usually incapable of adjusting either to the particular kind of qualifications that the returned volunteer brings or to the goals he wishes to meet. This is also true to some degree of those VISTA workers who have completed their year of service.

The usual graduate education seems too tame and irrelevant to those who have been out in the world and have been using their knowledge for teaching and social action. This will mean scrapping many of the formal requirements of conventional graduate programs in education and planning individual projects and curriculums that allow a great deal of responsibility for their nature and content to the graduate student himself. This would be especially valuable both to the college and the student if it could be arranged with small groups of returned Peace Corps volunteers from the same foreign area, so that they could work together in seminars and take responsibility for building new curriculums for trial in the schools in collaboration with the regular teachers. A multiplying effect could be achieved if a given college made a point of recruiting returning volunteers to its campus, since the development of new school curriculum projects and the extension of work in foreign cultures for which the volunteers would take responsibility are the means by which the ideas, knowledge, and attitudes of other students and teachers would be affected. The volunteers would stimulate new interest in teaching, in world affairs, and in foreign cultures. One of the most important things a college of education could do to extend its work in world affairs would be to appoint a group of a dozen returned Peace Corps volunteers as instructors, tutors, and research workers in the education of teachers, either through graduate fellowships or full subsidy for teaching appointments. Those who have worked with returned volunteers in Peace Corps training programs can testify that those who have been selected for such work from the hundreds of qualified candidates are competent, interesting, and vigorous young educators with a will to get things done.

The irony is that both the Peace Corps and the National Teacher Corps, which combine forces so admirably in meeting new educational needs, should have emerged not from the initiatives of the colleges of education, but from government efforts to increase the scope and application of its foreign and domestic policies. An additional irony is that of all the new programs designed to deal directly with the problem of developing new talent for coping with inner-city problems, the National Teacher Corps has had the most uncertain Congressional history, with more cliff-hanger rescues from oblivion than almost any other piece of social legislation. One way of putting the question squarely would be to ask, Which two methods would be more likely to give a richer quality of experience and education for the American teacher: staying in college for four or five years within the regular professional and academic teacher education programs without practical experience in the slums? Or serving in the Peace Corps abroad and the National Teacher Corps at home?

Returned Volunteers as Instructors

Second, the colleges of education could build a program around Peace Corps talent by inventing some new forms of yearlong Peace Corps preparation programs for teaching abroad.

1. A qualified faculty member could be designated as the director of a small Peace Corps program of possibly 15 to 20 students who wish to train for Peace Corps service in a designated country or area. Six returned Peace Corps volunteers from that area could be invited to join the project while taking a master of arts degree over a period of 18 months to two years. Approximately one third of their time during the first semester would be spent in studies having to do with the foreign area in which they have carried out their service and in studies related to it in work with appropriate members of the arts faculty. Another third of their time would be spent in Peace Corps instruction, with three to four students assigned to each. The returnee would tutor, lead seminars in educational and social problems of the country to which the students would be going, and assist in individual language study for those whom he was tutoring. The final third of his time would be spent in the study of American education with a member of the faculty, with field work in a local school.

Over the 18-month period the allocation of time and study would shift while the responsibility for the Peace Corps training would continue. The graduate student would carry out practice teaching in a local school, using the materials of the country in which he had served along with the studies he had completed over the previous semester to organize a semester of instruction in the school, for either a full class or part of a class.

During the summer semester, the M.A. candidate could serve full-time with foreign students and teachers on the instructional staff at a summer institute for Peace Corps volunteers. During the next six months, his work with the Peace Corps program would taper off, and he would concentrate on his teaching in the school and his study in the appropriate section of the curriculum identified with the country in which he had served. This would give him a full chance to make use of what he brought to the graduate school both for the training of future Peace Corps volunteers and for learning to teach in the area of his interests.

2. A variation of the master of arts in teaching could be arranged that would follow the standard model except that after two years of foreign service for the returned Peace Corps volunteer, his first summer seminar would be balanced between practice teaching in a school one half of each day and afternoon seminars and study in the materials of the foreign culture in which he had served. The purpose of this is to prepare him for teaching in this area during the year of internship which would follow. During the period of internship in an American school, he might carry out a comparative study of the educational problems of the American school and those of the schools in the country in which he had served. After

his internship during the second summer of work he would return to the practice teaching for half of each day and the continuation of preparation of curriculum and teaching through study with experts in the area of his concern.

3. The returned volunteer could simply be put in the hands of a faculty member designated to advise all returned Peace Corps, M.A. candidates. Special arrangements would be made for individually planned curriculums that would prepare the student to build on his previous knowledge, to add to it in whatever ways seemed appropriate to him and to his adviser. American education could be studied in individual research projects in connection with practice teaching rather than by courses, or in seminars arranged for several Peace Corps returnees who teach in the same school system. The latter could be done also in combination with the former.

4. For those interested in teaching in junior college, a three-year doctorate program for returned volunteers could be arranged, again individually planned to take account of the volunteer's previous experience and including research, seminars, and practice teaching, both in the college of education and in a local junior college, if one were available. A candidate might be asked to conduct a community development project of his own over a three- to six-month period and be made responsible for recruiting his own staff from other students of education and from the community. A full report on the research and its results would be part of the doctoral obligations, the community development projects would be a substitute for the doctoral thesis, and the research report would in fact be the thesis.

5. A three-year M.A. program could be arranged for the B.A. student who wished to qualify for the Peace Corps or similar service. The student would spend six months of his senior year in a specially arranged preparatory program in language and study of the country of assignment, instructed by returned Peace Corpsmen and others, followed by two years of service during which the student would remain connected with the college of education through correspondence and research supervision by faculty at the home base, or possibly by Peace Corps personnel abroad. This program would end with six months of combination study and practice teaching on the home campus.

6. A four-year Peace Corps doctoral program could be devised from a mixture of 4 and 5, in which junior college or undergraduate college teaching and special work in a foreign area in the humanities, social sciences, and language would lead to an appointment either in the public schools or in college teaching. The two years of service abroad would be an integral part of the study and research project, which would serve as the thesis subject. This program is analogous to that of the Ph.D. in cultural anthropology, which includes one or two years of field work as a section of the doctorate.

Non-Peace Corps Projects

Third, the undergraduate colleges and the colleges of education could develop plans for Peace Corps-style programs, whether or not the graduates intended to serve in the Peace Corps.

1. The assumption here would be that students entering the teaching field—as part of their first two years, summer terms, and field of major studies—would concentrate on one area of the world, learn the language appropriate to it, carry out field work for at least one or two semesters in community development projects and teaching, travel abroad for study, and, if possible, practice teach from one semester to a full year. The tutoring of children would begin in the freshman year and continue until graduation. This would be an appropriate program for students interested in teaching and in the Peace Corps, but who did not wish to commit themselves until college graduation.

2. By taking advantage of the presence of foreign students and others, who could be recruited either from their home countries or through the exchange Peace Corps, undergraduates could develop informal as well as in-school teaching projects about foreign countries for children in the arts, literature, and philosophy. They could teach children to dance, act, and sing in Indonesian, African, or Japanese style; to act in translations of foreign plays; and to read in the literature of another culture. This again could be carried out most effectively in collaboration with foreign students, exchange Peace Corps volunteers, and faculty members recruited for a Peace Corps center on the campus.

3. What could be called "world affairs centers" could be established in the colleges of education specifically to bring together in new study programs returned Peace Corps volunteers and foreign students who would be brought to this country on the recommendation of the volunteers themselves. That is to say, the Peace Corps volunteer would recommend such persons, who would then apply to the world affairs center in a given institution and would work in partnership with their American counterparts and others at what would be a new kind of world studies program. A qualified American student would act as a tutor for his foreign counterpart.

World Centers at Home and Regional Centers Abroad

One of the most intriguing ideas which keeps rising spontaneously in a variety of places is the idea of regional world centers for the development of educated talent to administer to the social, technological, and human needs of every region of the world.[5] I have discussed this elsewhere in this Report—in part through the ideas suggested by the World

[5] See: Zweig, Michael. *The Idea of a World University.* (Edited by Harold Taylor.) Carbondale: Southern Illinois University Press, 1967. The Appendix contains a listing of institutions and proposals for institutions that approximate or might become world centers of education.

Conference on Water, from which came the U.S. proposal to establish such centers with the help of American money and scientific resources. The idea also emerges in several of the reports issued by Education and World Affairs on the role of American professional schools in international education, particularly in the report on medicine and public health.[6] In that document, the proposal is made for establishing regional "staff colleges" around the world, where "research, planning, and seminar-type training activities would bring together professionals in medicine, public health, engineering, agriculture, education, and public administration. Students and faculty in these diverse professions might design mutually cooperative plans and programs for the utilization of what will remain into the next century inadequate human and material resources to deal with the needs of the world."

The report cites the National Institute of Health Administration and Education near New Delhi as an appropriate model and suggests links to the United Nations or a voluntary world federation of professional schools. It also cites the example of the School of Public Health of the University of North Carolina, which has contracted with the Peace Corps for training volunteers and professional help in this country to serve the rural areas of Malawi. The volunteers work in teams of two Americans and one Malawian in testing for and treating tuberculosis. The School of Public Health receives the benefit of field experience for its students in broad community health problems, and the faculty of the School receives invaluable experience in research and practice by dealing with the organizational and administrative problems of public health in a foreign setting. New contributions to research in tuberculosis will undoubtedly be made by work in a physical and psychosocial environment different from that of the United States, and "documented experience has been gained in teaching (and learning about the use of) intelligent but nonprofessional health workers to perform specific functions, under strict professional supervision, which were formerly considered to be professional in nature."[7] The implication in this approach for the field of education is obvious.

In his article *A Healing Diplomacy*[8] William D. Lotspeich, who was formerly on the faculty of the University of Rochester Medical School and is now executive secretary of The American Friends Service Committee, proposes a similar plan. Dr. Lotspeich says:

> I visualize a regional cooperative center for graduate training in the medical sciences. In sub-Sahara Africa, for instance, there are six or so medical schools that could cooperate in this venture. The center might be located in one of the participating schools with a good nucleus of African staff and facilities that could be easily expanded. This staff would be supplemented by a mobile pool of scientists from other countries.

---

[6] Committee on the Professional School and World Affairs. *Report of the Task Force on Medicine and Public Health.* New York: Education and World Affairs, 1967.

[7] *Ibid.*, p. 83.

[8] Lotspeich, William D. "A Healing Diplomacy." *Saturday Review.* July 1, 1967. p. 45.

146

The scientists would come for periods ranging from one month to a year, depending on availability. Students, drawn from medical students in the participating schools, would include a year to two years of study and research in their regular programs, returning to their work as teachers of medical science, public health, or the practice of medicine in posts awaiting them at home.

If we were to broaden the concept of the healing arts to include education, community development, social planning and research, early childhood, family needs, and home economics, we would designate a central place to education, knowing that without the continuing spread of practical and theoretical knowledge of how to cope with the total problem of creating a congenial environment for the world's people, from birth to old age, we are not going to be able to make use of those scientific and technological discoveries that the Western world possesses in such profusion. Unless the cultural development of each of the world's countries keeps pace with its technical and economic programs, the peoples of the world will be unable to make use of the tools available to them for human betterment.

As Dr. Lotspeich points out in reference to Africa, the major causes of sickness and death in that region are infectious and parasitic diseases and malnutrition—

> all readily controlled by well-known public health and therapeutic measures now standard practice in the highly developed countries. Magnificent as are the efforts of agencies such as WHO, UNICEF, and FAO, these do not represent a long-term solution to the chronic problems of health and over-population that plague the under-developed world. These countries must create their own institutions to train the medical and para-medical personnel who can then plan and sustain their own apparatus of public health.[9]

The Brain Drain

By reference to the forbidding concept of the "brain drain," we in the United States are continually made conscious of the fact that in the process of educating foreign students, too often the countries whose students come to us lose some of the most important talent they need for the solution of their own development problems. In addition, many graduates of foreign schools also are attracted to the United States. As the Education and World Affairs Task Force on Professional Education in Medicine and Public Health points out, "The richest nation in the world, it [the United States] has depended on foreign medical schools for the education of 49,300 of its 302,600 practising physicians (as of December 31, 1966) and is licensing foreign graduates at the rate of 1,500 per year."[10]

The following sentences from the Task Force report could be cited

---

[9] *Ibid.*, p. 46.

[10] "The Medical School and World Affairs." *The Professional School and World Affairs.* Report of the Task Force on Medicine and Public Health. New York: Education and World Affairs, 1967. p. 50.

with equal relevance as applicable to schools of education, if the words "schools of education" were substituted for "medical schools."

> The international content of the curriculum in most U.S. medical schools is very limited indeed, and most physicians in this country have little concept of health problems in the rest of the world. This situation will not be improved by mere curriculum manipulation, but only by *involvement* of faculty and students in much larger numbers in programs abroad and in work in this country with students and physicians whom they have also seen in their own setting.[11]

The solution does not lie in forbidding foreign students from finding ways in which their own talents can best be used, in the United States or abroad. It lies in working cooperatively with foreign governments and international agencies to provide the educational help they need in the countries and regions where it is needed and in creating the conditions in the home countries that make it possible to use to the full the talents of those who have been educated abroad. It is possible to find only partial solutions to this problem by educating foreign students in this country or even through bilateral exchanges.

Through our AID educational assistance we have done, and are doing, some useful projects in institution building abroad. But in the next 10 years, if a philosophy of internationalism as proclaimed in the International Education Act is to be basic to our foreign policy, that assistance must be given more and more through international and regional projects in which American initiative and funds can and should be central but which are aimed at pooling our resources with others in multinational ways. The initiatives must be transferred away from ourselves and into the hands of those who are able to take them because we and others have helped them to gain experience in doing so. Otherwise, the integrity of our political and social intent will continue to be questioned on the grounds that it has to do more with gaining political allies in the world power structure than with helping the world to solve its own problems.

Or, to put it more positively, our major effort must be to build into the institutional structure of the world community a truly international point of view of the kind generated by such projects as the International Geophysical Year, the Pugwash Conferences, the Water Conference, UNICEF, and the work of the UN agencies. Bilateral projects of AID and other public and private agencies have short-term advantages. For one thing, they skip the interminable negotiations and political complexities of organizing any project at all through a multiplicity of governments. But the long-run and basic disadvantage is that they fail to blend the variety of national interests, our own included, into the new forms of internationalism the world must have if it is to create a stable world order. Fortunately, we are in a situation in which it *is* possible to take the initiative in beginning any number of useful international projects, provided we set about it by calling upon the cooperation of colleagues in education and public service abroad in carrying out projects that are clearly in their interest.

[11] *Ibid.*, p. 51.

148

The International Secretariat for Volunteer Service (ISVS)

The most striking example of the development of this kind of international idea into new institutional form, one that has direct relevance to the possibility of establishing regional world centers for teacher education in the human services, is the International Secretariat for Volunteer Service (ISVS), which has offices in Manila, The Hague, and Washington, D.C.[12] The Secretariat is sponsored by 49 governments involved in one or another kind of volunteer service in development projects of Peace Corps style either at home or abroad and is an outcome of the International Conference on Human Skills held in Puerto Rico in October 1962 to deal with the problem of developing trained manpower for work in technical assistance programs around the world.

My interest in ISVS for the purposes of the present Report lies not only in its contribution to the international technical assistance movement but in the promise it gives of finding some new ways to bring the new world generation of youth in touch with each other. It can provide, in realistic terms, a series of practical situations in which international relations are established on the most solid of all foundations—the experience of persons from a variety of national, cultural, and political origins who work together on common tasks of human service to which they are committed. Out of that can come the organization of a body of precedent and a body of literature on the theory and practice of international cooperation. By literature, I mean not only research materials in the social and natural sciences, but poems, novels, short stories, and plays written about new persons in new situations that have never been written about before, literature about people who for the most part have lived unnoticed lives in cultures largely illiterate.

Since 1963, ISVS has served as the center of organization, information, research, and planning for the member countries; and since that time Australia, Austria, Belgium, Canada, Denmark, France, Germany, Israel, Japan, the Netherlands, New Zealand, Norway, the Philippines, Sweden, Switzerland, the United Kingdom, and the United States have either started or expanded programs, most of which are administered by private agencies with experience in the field, for volunteers in service abroad. In 1962 there were many private voluntary organizations sponsoring volunteers in technical assistance; less than 5,000 volunteers had any kind of government backing. In 1967, over 50 governments were supporting more than 100,000 volunteers in programs of national development in their own countries and general assistance overseas. At the March 1967 World Assembly in New Delhi—sponsored by ISVS and preceded by regional preparatory conferences held in 1966 in Paris, Lima, Addis Ababa, Bangkok, and Cotonou—plans were made for the future development of

[12] A series of documents and publications describing the Secretariat is available from the International Secretariat for Volunteer Service, 1424 Sixteenth St., N.W., Washington, D.C. 20036.

volunteer projects and their integration into national development programs.

There are now, including the U.S. Peace Corps, over 19,000 volunteers from 18 countries serving abroad in 95 states and territories of Africa, Asia, and Latin America; and it is clear that the idea will continue to spread and its programs to expand into other countries. In addition, there are projects, similar to those of VISTA, in which volunteers are working in their own countries: Over 17,000 young people are involved in domestic volunteer projects in 18 countries of North and South America, Asia, and Africa. A third category of service consists of programs of basic education and training, similar to those of our Job Corps, for unemployable youth who learn while doing useful projects in public works. In Ethiopia a year of service in a rural development program as teacher or social worker is required for the university degree. Elsewhere, as in Israel and Iran, the program is linked to national service, in which the civilian components in education combine with the development of skills necessary for the armed forces.

A World Organization

As an international institution, ISVS is a natural beginning point for a world organization in the education of teachers in world affairs. It already has a highly significant reason for existing and a high cause to serve in providing an organization and research center for the recruitment and education of a new and untapped sector of talent in the world's youth—those who wish to serve the cause of human betterment. It exists for the strongest of reasons—that it is deeply needed, and the needs it serves will continue to grow. It has practical solutions to offer, both on the way in which youth can be trained to serve and on the way their service can best be used. It brings together at its regional world assemblies, in its daily work, and in its staff a cross-section of people from around the world who are engaged in the human services and whose ideas about education, social change, and economic development are grounded in experience and enriched by contact with the world's other cultures. It furnishes both personal and institutional links between the educators, teachers, government officials, technologists, intellectuals, and social planners of 43 countries.

From this base, and continuing with its present task, the Secretariat could, if its member countries agreed, extend its work into the development of world regional centers for the education and training of volunteers from a number of countries to serve abroad as teams of teachers and community developers in whatever capacity they were needed. Regional education and research centers could be established in Asia, Africa, Latin America, the United States, and elsewhere and could be staffed by selected teachers with experience in community development and teaching in previous programs, along with university faculty members, UN personnel, and others specifically interested in world education and community development.

The centers would be attended by volunteers from a number of countries who would be trained as teachers, medical technologists, or in whatever field their assignments indicated. This would mean the beginning of a new kind of curriculum and program for teachers, one that would have many implications for the future involvement of national educational systems with each other. If the regional center were in Nairobi, for example, half the volunteers could be recruited from Kenyan universities, secondary schools, and technical institutes and the other half from Israel, the United States, England, Peru, Iran, Thailand, Vietnam, and France. Their training would be followed by service as teachers in Kenya. The relationship between the Kenyan educational system and those of the countries represented at the center could easily be made a direct one. A Kenyan student teacher could return with a volunteer to his home country for volunteer service there in teaching as a part of his continuing education to become a teacher in Kenya.

There could also be two- and three-month summer camps in international education where volunteers returning from their foreign service could work together, spending half their time teaching youth of the country where the camp is located and the other half studying problems in world affairs through seminars, discussions, and research that drew upon their experience in the volunteer service. As the report of the Government of Kenya Plan, 1964-1970, points out, in developing countries "the government is aware that the great energies of youth, if constructively channeled, could become a vital force in the development of the country. Large numbers of young men who are keen to contribute to the task of nation-building find themselves unemployed, unable to contribute and frustrated by their idleness." In Zambia, thousands of young people are unemployed "because they have received only sufficient education to make them dissatisfied with the subsistence economy of the rural areas but have been given no training in the skills which will enable them to become cash crop farmers. Great numbers have migrated to the towns where they live on the charity of their friends and relations. Many of them played their part in the political struggle of the last few years and now look to the new government in the hope that their past efforts will be rewarded. Zambia's new government faces a 'crisis of expectation'."[13]

The Idea of a World College

These are exactly the problems inherent in the social changes now happening in the developed countries to an extent equal to those in the undeveloped. Practical experience in dealing with them in Africa, Asia, or Latin America by graduate students, teachers, and a multinational group of U.N. and university experts would provide a rich educational program for those involved in it, especially if it were combined with research and

[13] Quoted by Y. Benron in *Camp Oriented Volunteer Training.* Secretariat Experience Exchange Report. Washington, D.C.: International Secretariat for Volunteer Service.

educational planning of the kind which the International Secretariat has already been carrying on. The United States could very well serve to experiment with some pilot projects designed in this way in this country, with invitations to volunteers from countries in the International Secretariat membership to join them for a summer term, possibly with field work in Detroit, San Francisco, or Appalachia.

As the curriculum developed through such centers and pilot projects, and the number of direct relationships between governments, educational systems, teachers, and students increased, the curriculum itself would broaden and deepen its international and cultural dimension by the personal contributions of the students and teachers involved. This was one of the most successful results of the pilot project in a World College carried out during the summer of 1963 on a campus in Long Island with a student body drawn from 22 United Nations countries, an international faculty, and a curriculum devoted to the development of student and faculty research projects on problems in world affairs.[14]

Each student worked independently and in groups with students from the other countries on topics ranging from the formation of a world youth movement (in which a Communist student from Rumania, who later went to serve in the Rumanian UN delegation, and a student leader from Malaya worked together) to the effects of international trade on the politics of Indonesia. Each student and faculty member wrote an autobiographical account of the content and character of his own education and what he considered to be its strengths and weaknesses as the basis for further research on problems in the construction of an international curriculum, and as a basis for the actual discussions of education and world affairs that made up the content of the seminars and symposia through which the College did its teaching.

In most instances there were no available texts that dealt with the problems in world affairs with which the curriculum was concerned, and the faculty members and students substituted for such texts written materials of their own which were mimeographed and distributed, as well as original documents from the United Nations, their own national governments, international organizations, and elsewhere. For example, one major section of study had to do with the control of nuclear weapons and the development of the test ban treaty, which was in the process of negotiation at that time. The text of the treaty was used as the basis for analysis of the problem, along with materials from the Geneva disarmament conference introduced by Arthur Lall, who came as a faculty member to the College directly from his work as head of the Indian delegation to the 18-nation disarmament negotiations in Geneva.

Since many of the countries represented in Geneva were also represented in the College, students were able to identify with the positions taken by their own governments as revealed in the documents and to

---

[14] A brief account of the World College experiment is contained in *The Idea of a World University*, pp. 169-183. See note 5.

explain those positions in relation to political and cultural factors in their home country. At the same time they were free to criticize the positions where they felt criticism was needed, since they were members of a college that was devoted to studying and finding solutions to world problems, not to defending or attacking the correctness of national positions taken by governments. The cumulative body of research papers from the 22 students and five faculty members form a basis of materials which, had the experiment continued to its next phase with an additional group of students, would have made the beginning of a new and original library to which subsequent students and faculty would have contributed their own share of research and documents.

In other words, both the curriculum of the World College and the body of knowledge on which it was based emerged together from the content of knowledge and creative talent of the faculty and the students. It was completely international in the sense that it used the ideas and point of view of every nation represented at the College to come to terms with the problems of world society. There was no confrontation between East and West; in a college as completely international as this one the distinction was obliterated by the variety of nationalities and political points of view represented in the student body and faculty.

Had it been possible to combine with the serious intellectual and cultural activities of the experiment some practical work in teaching and community development in cooperation with American students and teachers, the World College would have become the forerunner of the kind of regional world center I am suggesting could be organized by the International Secretariat for Volunteer Service. If the participating governments were asked to choose for attendance at such a center students who had given evidence of leadership among students in their home countries and who were expected to enter their country's service in teaching and in related fields on their return, this would guarantee the existence of a common set of interests and concerns among them. To study world problems together would be for all of them an immediate way to learn to understand the size and character of those problems and to learn to look at them from a truly international point of view. It would furnish some of the links we need to put this generation of youth in touch with itself.

The curriculum of the regional center could extend itself into the arts and could be designed to prepare volunteers not only to help with the variety of technical assistance and public health missions typical of the work of volunteers, but to teach the dances, painting, sculpture, plays, poetry, music, and literature of their own culture. Here the use of tape recorders and films and, eventually on a larger scale, radio and television with the benefit of broadcasts from world communication satellites would make a significant difference in the ability of the members of one culture to understand and enjoy the arts of another.

The social and educational problems of the United States and the West are worldwide—poverty, rural and urban; the undereducation of large sectors of the population; the uneven character of the social progress of one region as against other sectors and regions of the society; and the necessity of assessing and meeting the needs of the new generation of youth. These are the problems that determine the common interest we educators and teachers in the West have with those in other countries. It is time to concentrate on these areas of common interest rather than to continue to divide ourselves up into categories as historians, mathematicians, elementary school teachers, postdoctoral scholars. The new areas of subject matter that can link the world together are not only the conventional ones recognized by scholars and teachers everywhere, but the new combination of knowledge of all kinds that creates itself as it is used. This in the largest sense may be called education, by which is meant teaching people to make use of the resources of science, technology, the arts, and the intellect for the collective and personal good of the human race.

A United Nations Teacher Corps

During the course of the work with members of the UN Secretariat and delegations and of the Society of Friends in planning the World College pilot project of 1963, I discovered that many had a serious interest in the possibility of creating an "international teacher corps," which might be supported by the United Nations, with direct connections to the UN Institute for Training and Research and the Economic and Social Council. Since that time, an interest similar to that developed by the International Secretariat for Volunteer Service has continued among members of the United Nations and other internationalists. One way of furthering that interest would be to expand the work of UNICEF in the field of teacher education.

Since 1961, UNICEF, in collaboration with UNESCO, has been supplying equipment for teacher education institutions and elementary schools connected with them in nearly 50 developing countries—typewriters, scientific apparatus, library books, mimeographing machines, and other items—in addition to carrying on some in-service training for teachers. The assignments of professional educators from around the world for the latter have been made by UNESCO; and since the work of UNICEF is supported in part by the host countries where UNICEF projects are in operation, there is already present in that body a truly international apparatus for education with interconnections between ministries of education, international educational organizations, and foreign educators on a worldwide rather than a unilateral or bilateral basis.

It is thus possible that through UNICEF a United Nations volunteer teacher corps could be established, with volunteers recruited on a worldwide basis among students near the completion of their preparation as teachers, among graduate students interested in educational service abroad, and among young teachers at the beginning of their careers in teaching. The purpose of the corps would be fourfold: (a) to expand the kind of technical help now given by UNICEF to countries needing it, (b) to extend that help into the education of teachers in internationalism, and (c) to provide opportunities for student teachers, on the one hand, to immerse themselves in the educational system of a culture other than their own and on the other, to provide such assistance as the student teachers are capable of giving to the children and educational system of the country to which they were assigned. The assignment could be for two years, after which the corps member would return to his own country to complete his education and to begin, or resume, his teaching career.

Nominations of candidates for the corps could be made to UNICEF by the participating countries, assignments to teacher education institutions and allied schools could be made by the host countries, and in certain cases programs of research and curriculum building might be worked out jointly among teacher education institutions in various countries. Costs for the corps could be shared by UNICEF, the host country, and the cooperating teacher education institutions. Because UNICEF is already working with UNESCO and is in touch with the major world organizations of teachers and with a variety of educational institutions around the world, the task of communication and organization could be shared by a sizable number of persons and groups interested in internationalism in the education of teachers.

There is no doubt that the contribution that the members of an international corps of this kind could make to world education would be direct and invaluable. Teacher education institutions everywhere would benefit from the opportunity to work with highly qualified student nationals of other countries on educational problems common to them all. Assistance in teaching in areas of the school curriculum where talent is not fully available—in science, mathematics, foreign languages, comparative education, history and the social sciences, agriculture, public health, and other fields—could be supplied by the presence of the corps members. In cooperating with UNICEF, educational institutions would find new means of making connections with each other through a strong and widely admired international organization whose central purpose is to help the world's children through whatever means possible.

World Education Centers on American Campuses

Turning back to the possibilities for the international education of teachers on American campuses, I would now like to cite some examples of what can and should be done both through individual faculty initiative and through collective faculty action in organizing a new kind of world affairs center at colleges and universities. One example is provided by the work of Stewart E. Fraser at George Peabody College for Teachers in Nashville, Tennessee. Dr. Fraser is director of the International Center and professor of international and comparative education at the College. The Center is his own creation and was established three years ago with practically no money and no staff, which to a certain extent can be put down as educational advantages since without funds, grants, or other emoluments, there are likely to be no restrictions on the ideas around which the program forms, no elaborate conditions to conform to, and no committees and all-university bodies to clear, approve, and otherwise modify programs that should be given a chance to be tested in action. Without staff, one is then forced to look into present resources. In Dr. Fraser's case these were the doctoral students in international and comparative education at Peabody; approximately one third of the 20 of them were from foreign countries, the rest were American.

Dr. Fraser's ideas for extending the concept of international education into residential international centers have grown from the raw experience of establishing the Center and in many respects parallel the main recommendations of this section of the Report. The concept also contains parts of the "world urban teaching center" idea proposed for San Francisco State College. Having noted the fact that international residential centers for foreign students seldom make use of the resources of the students or of residence in developing international education programs, Dr. Fraser proposes that American campuses consider the establishment of what he calls "residential academic centers for international education," where the training of teachers, educators, specialists, and research scholars to work in overseas development tasks would be part of the program, along with the study of international, comparative, and developmental education for use in teaching in the United States.[15] Dr. Fraser points out that—

> International Houses in America, with multi-universities in their neighborhood, cater to all faculties and all disciplines. Their cohesiveness is nurtured primarily through social and residential, rather than through professional affiliations or contacts. The concept of a residential center devoted *solely* to exploring the common problems of education throughout the world and developing both specialists and strategists to overcome them is different when contrasted to the goals of traditional international houses. The involvement of social scientists jointly viewing the theme of developmental education in a residential community setting cuts across many of the traditional boundaries that have risen between academics, educators, and those concerned with the training of teachers. A residential center devoted to the study of the "accelerating and inhibiting factors" in international education offers a framework for cohesive study that the customary international houses cannot and do not necessarily wish to offer.

There are elements in Dr. Fraser's proposal similar to those in operation at the Center for Educational Development in the Harvard School of Graduate Education and the Center at Stanford, except that Dr. Fraser proposes a direct relationship among (a) the tasks and personnel involved in international teacher education and research, (b) the international center, and (c) the other intellectual resources of the university or universities, in the region where the center is established. In addition to regular

---

[15] Dr. Fraser's ideas for the centers are developed in two papers: (a) "Residential Academic Centers for International Education: A Proposal for their Establishment in the United States." *Peabody Journal of Education.* March 1966 and (b) "Some Aspects of University Cooperation in International Education." *School and Society.* April 16-30, 1966. pp. 234-238, 240, 242, and 244. For additional ideas on international educational exchange, see Fraser, Stewart E., editor. *Government Policy and International Education.* New York: John Wiley & Sons, 1965.

degree programs, the residential center for international training would offer cultural and orientation services for Americans going abroad to teach, to advise, or to do research. One third to one half of the residents would be Americans, the rest would be from a cross-section of countries. The residents would be mainly graduate students, who would be available not only in seminars within their own ranks for cooperative research and study, but for teaching in the local school and community programs.

The emphasis would be on intellectual and cultural exchange between various cultural groups already committed to working in international and developmental education, and on acting as a focal point for research in the extension and improvement of the international curriculum in American public schools. Visiting educators from other American institutions could come for limited periods of work in a congenial international setting to use the documentary and resource materials of the center. Dr. Fraser, whose thinking also parallels that of the New York State University Center in Planting Fields and that of the proposed Institute of International Education in the College of Education at Ohio University, has in mind the use of all the disciplines of the social sciences in furnishing the manpower and materials for a continuing interchange of international ideas between faculty members and students of this and other countries. Collaboration with the Peace Corps and with other government programs, particularly those of the Center for Educational Cooperation, would follow naturally as an operational offshoot of the basic idea.

Through consultation and cooperation with the Peace Corps and other agencies, colleges of education could establish educational centers for summer programs, work camps, hostels, and so forth in foreign countries to which their students would be sent. Peace Corps personnel, both volunteers and supervising staff, could help in study and work programs designed for teachers.

Colleges of education, in collaboration with other parts of the university, could organize student research projects on problems in food production, birth control, technology, and medicine, which could be carried out with the help of Peace Corps volunteers while they were abroad, other volunteers when they returned, and the faculty and student body of the sponsoring institution. Coincident with this might be a program of volunteer professors who would agree to go with a group of a dozen students for a half-year to a year to work in countries where arrangements might be made by the Peace Corps in connection with the centers suggested in Dr. Fraser's proposal.

Aside from the establishment of formal programs, one of the most effective ways of giving the teacher education candidate the kind of foreign experience he needs would be to send abroad on an individual basis a promising student teacher to one of the regional centers conducted by various American universities for a semester or a year. Or an arrangement could be made with the East-West Center and the University of Hawaii for an integrated program of Asian studies carried on over a three- to six-month period for a selected group of juniors or seniors in a teacher education plan. Or, if there were world affairs centers of the kind described above, a student could be sent for one semester to study at another college where there is a world affairs center, preferably one staffed by returned Peace Corps volunteers, foreign students, and others who are directly interested in education and teachers.

One simple device that could be used within the United States or by any college abroad is to send a qualified faculty member and 15 students to a community in the United States or in a foreign country selected in collaboration with the Peace Corps or other appropriate organizations. The faculty member would supervise individual study, teaching, and community development projects for one semester or two. Each of the students would prepare research papers, curricular materials, and so forth. A monograph or a research report on the project might also be written by the faculty member. The work abroad would be coordinated with the course requirements and previous studies and experiences of the students in the program.

Cooperating Organizations

As noted above, there are a large number of private agencies and international organizations that could be of use in making some of the arrangements described aside from those already in the field, like the American Friends Service Committee or the American Field Service or the American Council of Voluntary Agencies for Foreign Service, Inc. Forty-one agencies have direct connections with governmental, intergovernmental, and international organizations through the Council committee. Problems in migration and refugee work, health, technical assistance, and food resources are dealt with and, should colleges be interested in working with such committees in connection with teacher education, some relationships might be established there. The Council works in more than 100 countries and includes self-help and community development, as well as educational, medical, and agricultural projects.

To put it in the terms suggested earlier in the Report, this would mean the use of all existing organizations and institutions, national and international, as far as is practicable, to contribute to the education of teachers and to build a component of teacher education into every kind of existing program where there is an opportunity to do so.

Some Examples

The International Institute for Educational Planning in Paris has identified 99 international, regional, and national organizations in the field of research and training in educational planning. Undergraduate and graduate students of education from the United States and elsewhere could travel to other countries for joint research and comparative studies with other students and teachers, using the facilities of appropriate organizations in making the arrangements.

The Association of Overseas Educators, with headquarters in Wiesbaden, Germany, and Washington, D. C., has a potential membership of 30,000 persons who have had overseas teaching experience, with a present membership of 300. The Association has local chapters throughout the United States; runs a lecture program; sponsors cultural relations seminars and foreign student and teacher welcoming and orientation projects; supplies a newsletter; and has a Foundation for Educational Exchange for research, publication, and education on questions having to do with teaching in world affairs.

There is a body of experience within the membership that should be fully used in the education of teachers, both for those in preparation and those already in service. In collaboration with other organizations—for example, the National Education Association Teach Corps and the World Confederation of Organizations of the Teaching Profession—the Association could conduct a wide range of research and action programs in teaching through (a) autobiographical accounts and research findings of experience overseas for use in education courses, (b) the spread of information about overseas opportunities for American teachers, (c) special seminars and training programs for students interested in foreign service, (d) organization of yearlong seminars in foreign cultures with six- to eight-week travel-study trips during the summer, (e) research in curricular materials based on the members' foreign experience and relationships abroad, (f) exchange programs with schools where members have taught, (g) development of one- and two-year projects for service abroad—for which the school system grants special leave and special inducements for recruiting foreign service teachers—planned by the school system specifically to enlarge and deepen its curriculum in world affairs, and (h) full use of the experience of the returned teacher in school and community education. National planning would include putting selected returnees to work in a variety of schools other than their own, along with projects in curricular development conducted jointly by colleges of education and nearby school systems.

The study centers already established abroad by American universities could add a strong component of teacher education and research to their present programs for graduate students and the undergraduate junior year abroad.

The International Secretariat for Volunteer Service could set in motion programs of teacher education in which students and teachers from many countries could find ways of working together on problems common to the rural and urban areas of each of their countries.[16]

A system of sister institutions abroad where American colleges exchanged students and teachers to teach in each other's classes and to work together in learning more about each other's culture could include regional grouping of American colleges with international centers established at the sister institutions. An American faculty member might take 10 to 12 of his

---

[16] See Chapter III, p. 191.

own students with him to the sister institution for a semester or a year for practice teaching and educational study.

The variations of matching projects and organizations are very nearly endless, even without the wide range of possible new programs in international education that could be sponsored by UNESCO.

Foreign Students as Teachers

If we return to the matter of cultural power possessed by the United States and the use of the United States as a continental center for teacher education, it is clear that in the 100,000 students and 10,000 scholars who come here to study each year (nearly a quarter of all those who go to the rest of the world combined), we have a great resource for the development of a broad concept of international education. The present number is only a fraction of the total number of foreign students, in education and every other field, who would come to the United States if given a chance and the small amount of money needed to make it possible. The percentage of the total student body in America represented by foreign students is less than the percentage they represent in many other countries.

That is, 1.7 percent of the students in U.S. colleges and universities are from foreign countries, which puts us eighth on the list of leaders in the field—far behind Austria (20.4 percent), the United Kingdom (11.4 percent), France (10 percent), and Canada (6.3 percent). In some U.S. colleges and universities there are no foreign students at all; in many there are so few that their presence makes little difference to the texture of the institutional life; and in most cases where they are present in larger numbers, little is done to give them a chance to teach what they know either about their own country or about subjects they have previously studied. On one campus where there were nearly 500 foreign students, I discovered that they had formed national or regional groupings (particularly the Arabs, Africans, and Asians), that they held their own national meetings, and that their experiences in America with invitations to talk to the local Rotary Club or the Kiwanis or the Association of University Women and invitations to dinner in local homes tended to make them more self-consciously and sometimes aggressively nationalist than they were when they first arrived.

A cultural policy adequate to the present situation would call for acceptance of the idea that foreign students and teachers in the United States are a major resource for the development of a wider understanding of world affairs on the part of Americans and that every effort should be made to involve them in teaching here, especially in relation to the education of American teachers. The visitors are also crucial to an understanding of American aims, attitudes, and ideas in the part of the world from which they come and to which they will return.

At present, the attitude of American schools and colleges toward foreign students has been to consider them as a category of "foreign students," people who are not American and who have a particular set of problems in adjustment to American education and American society. There is no doubt that they do have special problems because they are inexperienced in dealing with unfamiliar situations in a society about which they know comparatively little. But the services in counseling and the general management of their lives, on and off the campus, are only one part of the practical aspect of their education and are aimed at induction into the culture rather than at the full development of their intellectual and personal resources.

It is also true that not all of them possess the personal and intellectual resources appropriate for the education of their fellow students or that their interest in coming to the United States extends beyond a wish to receive particular kinds of training in a given field. The point is that in developing a national policy of internationalism and in using public funds to achieve international ends in relation to a broad and enlightened foreign policy, the recruitment of student teachers, educators of teachers, and others who are involved in the educational systems of their own countries is a far more important item on our educational agenda than most of the others on which we are now concentrating.

This is not only a matter of supplying the funds—from foundations, government, and existing university budgets—with which to bring more teachers and student teachers into the American education system (a minimum of 25,000 additional students from 50 to 60 countries would be a suitable beginning), but of seeking out students already here and giving the opportunity to those most qualified to teach and learn in partnership with Americans, inside and outside the institutions of education.

The Ogontz Plan

An example of what private initiative can do is shown by a group of Philadelphia citizens who started the Ogontz Plan for Mutual International Education, in which qualified foreign students at the University of Pennsylvania and other universities in Philadelphia have been recruited to teach in the Philadelphia public schools. The purpose of the Plan as stated by its sponsors, International House in Philadelphia and Carl Stenzler, chairman of the Ogontz Plan Committee, is "to add to existing school curriculums a greater emphasis on the international humanities; the objective study of other peoples and cultures, by bringing into the schools . . . foreign students who identify with world peoples about whom we know too little . . . and to broaden the perspective of foreign students so that they will be better able to understand the United States."[17]

Five students representing five different parts of the world come to a given school for a half day a week for three weeks to present classes on foreign cultures carefully prepared with advance consultation with the local teacher. These student teachers are paid from the regular school budget for substitute teachers. Beginning in 1962 with one school and five

---

[17] Ogontz Plan for Mutual International Education. Sponsored by International House of Philadelphia, 140 N. Fifteenth St., Philadelphia, Pa. 19102. Carl Stenzler, chairman.

student teachers from Liberia, India, Turkey, Sweden, and Japan, the program has grown until in 1966-67, 142 foreign visitors from 51 countries (110 graduate students, 13 undergraduates, 9 professionals, 10 wives of foreign students) from 19 universities and colleges in the Philadelphia area have worked with 14,000 pupils in 50 elementary and secondary schools in 19 school districts in seven counties and three states.

Not only has the program successfully brought about a direct awareness of foreign cultures to the children in the participating schools, but it has effectively helped the foreign student to become involved directly with educational problems and American values. In addition, through relations with the other teachers in the schools and with the parents of the children, the foreign students have become enmeshed in the community life of the area; and their ideas and points of view have been a source of mutual education in the adult society of which they might otherwise not have been a part. A variety of extensions of the idea are possible—for example, trips by teams of foreign and American students to outlying areas for symposia and teaching, community forums, college seminars, adult extension classes, television programs, and discussion of films about foreign countries.

There is no reason why the Ogontz Plan could not be used nationally as a model for U.S. communities everywhere, nor why programs comparable to it could not be sponsored by colleges of education which might import selected foreign students to join in practice teaching programs already under way, nor why the Plan could not become the basis for new policies in the recruitment of foreign students through government funds to establish direct relationships with teacher education institutions abroad. The question of how to inject the element of a world perspective into the American educational system could then receive a direct answer without our having to wait to influence the curriculums of colleges and universities and educate a generation of new teachers, while leaving the present teachers, nearly two million of them, untouched by the ideas available to them in the resources of our foreign student population.

Volunteers to America

A similar approach to undergraduate teaching in the colleges, particularly in education, would give us necessary help in exactly the places where it is needed most. The experimental program now being conducted by the U.S. State Department in the Volunteers to America project, in which 200 teachers and community workers from abroad are joining their American counterparts this year and next in community development projects around the United States, can break ground in establishing a new cultural policy in the relation of the United States to the world, particularly if the philosophy of genuine teaching exchange can be extended throughout the entire American educational system.

A limited experiment that will also prove useful in testing out the idea lies in the group of six foreign students who are working in the National Teacher Corps. Although the number is too small to produce definitive conclusions, it is clear already that (a) for the foreign student the Teacher

Corps involvement with American community problems and the people who are having them is an important experience in understanding the values and content of American culture, (b) for the Americans who are working with the visitors—including fellow students, teachers, children, and the community participants—the effect is to achieve a comradeship with and an understanding of persons whose own national background is completely different from their own, and (c) the idea of the common interest of all countries in helping to teach those who need teaching most does introduce a world concept into the thinking of those who are in the Teacher Corps together. Similar reports have come from the foreign students who have worked with the VISTA program.

Nations Incorporated

Another model for cooperative effort among community organizations, universities, schools, and foreign students is found in a project organized by a group of internationally minded citizens in the Bay Area of San Francisco under the title Nations Incorporated. Financial support has come from local foundations, businesses, and individual donors.[18] The work is concentrated in a Summer Workshop of Nations, now completing its sixth year, to which high school juniors and seniors are invited for three-week sessions of intensive study, lectures, seminars, and conversations, led by selected foreign students who are doing graduate work in California universities or elsewhere and aided by visiting scholars who have special knowledge to add to the work in the Africa, Asia, Latin America, and Middle East areas. Robert Scalapino, then chairman of the Department of Political Science at the University of California at Berkeley, was responsible for bringing university resources to bear on the organization of the first workshops.

The Workshop of 1967 was held at a conference center in La Honda, near San Francisco, with 100 high school students divided into study groups of approximately 25, according to the country and area of their particular interest. Each had a staff of two foreign instructors and one American classroom teacher, who served as moderator. The design of the Workshop is one that aims to involve the students in a serious consideration of the cultural, political, religious, economic, and educational problems of the countries chosen for study, and to give them a sense of immediacy of the foreign cultures and their people by bringing them closely in touch with young graduate students from abroad, whose knowledge of their own society and its problems is personal and direct as well as scholarly. During the evenings, special lecturers in related topics are introduced to speak on the arts, foreign policy, and education, along with films and special sessions on careers in world affairs, the Peace Corps, and the problems of world society.

One of the most important attributes of the Workshop of Nations and of Nations Incorporated lies in their reach into the existing educational

---

[18] Nations Incorporated. Franklyn M. Barnett, executive director, 2428 Hillside, Berkeley, California.

and community life of California and the possibility that it might extend into a series of similar projects across the country. Largely through the enthusiasm of a 16-year-old student who attended the 1965 Workshop, a similar project was organized in Ithaca, New York, by William Lowe, assistant dean of the College of Education at Cornell University, for the summer of 1966 in collaboration with the assistant superintendent of schools and a committee of citizens in the Ithaca community.

The first International Workshop in Ithaca was attended by 16 high school students, and, with a design similar to the California program, the second was held in 1967 with a focus on Latin America at both of the two-week sessions. The instructors were graduate students from Central and South America studying in a wide range of disciplines at Cornell. North American public school teachers were also involved, including the director, a history teacher from a local high school. Additional lectures, seminars, and demonstrations were provided by the faculties of Ithaca College and Cornell University. All the educative agencies in the area have cooperated, with financial help from individuals, businesses, service clubs, children's groups, units of Cornell, and the Center for International Programs and Services of the New York State Education Department.

The implications of this kind of project for the education of teachers in world affairs are clear and have already begun to work themselves out in California. There, initiatives have been taken by the director, Franklyn Barnett, and Dean T. Reller, of the School of Education at the University of California, for proposed cooperation with local school systems for teachers workshops, in which in-service credit is awarded for weekend conferences and continuing seminars. Having foreign participants share equal status with their American colleagues and teachers not only makes use of a neglected resource for the development of a serious and informed interest in world affairs on the part of teachers and students, but provides the opportunity for the foreign participants to engage in a much more direct relationship with American educators and each other in dealing with common interests and problems. Some of the same effects obtained in the pilot project for a World College[19] have occurred in the Workshop of Nations— the intermingling of ideas and points of view from a variety of foreign participants who have usually not had an opportunity to work closely with one another, either at home or in the United States.

But, above all, it is again the sense of immediacy of access to the foreign culture as seen through the eyes of its representatives that makes this approach to the education of teachers so important as an experiment both in educating the educators and their students and in making an impact on the community at large. Films of the Workshop in session, as well as television tapes of selected speakers and sessions, have been made for use in local schools and on local television stations; plans are also under way for the student participants in the summer programs to serve as teachers' aides when they return to their schools in order to bring the materials developed

---

[19] Described on pp. 151-54.

during the summer into regular school classes. A combination of this approach with that of the Ogontz plan—the use of foreign students as teachers in the schools themselves—in collaboration with the student aides and the teachers who have served in the special summer workshops suggests itself as an extension of the work presently going on.

Mr. Barnett has already investigated the possibilities of this kind of extension through conferences with educators at nearby universities and through suggestions that the universities, through their departments and colleges of education, develop their own programs in collaboration with "foreign area studies" centers and allied departments where foreign students could be most helpful. "I believe," says Mr. Barnett, "that the problem is essentially one of finding a mechanism to work within existing structures." Some of these structures include not only the state system of education in California, but the Center for Educational Cooperation in Washington, the U.S. Office of Education, the regional center of Projects to Advance Creativity in Education of the San Mateo County Department of Education, and the American Association of Colleges for Teacher Education. The operating center could be in a department or college of education, where one person could be appointed to act as director of international programs and could call upon foreign students and scholars as well as members of area studies centers in university faculties.

Overseas Schools

Coupled with this kind of community project are the possibilities of (a) using the foreign study centers of American universities as a base for teacher education projects and (b) collaborating with the American overseas schools where internships, practice teaching, and curriculum making can be carried out in ways comparable to those in effect at the American School in Guatemala, which cooperates with the Memphis City School System and the State Board of Education of Tennessee.[20]

The best pattern for individual colleges to follow in beginning such projects is found in a modest experiment started by the State University in Plattsburgh, New York, which has sent two student teachers to the American School in Tunisia, along with a faculty member from the Glens Falls High School, who had supervised the work of the students during the year and had previously served with the School. Even in relatively undeveloped American or international schools abroad, arrangements could be made for a college of education or university to send a faculty member, interested in comparative education and foreign cultures, and several students for a year of internship, practice teaching, and research.

The supervising faculty member would be responsible for placing the students in a given school or in a nearby area and for supervising the students' research, language training, and other learning activities—such as the study of education, community development, family life, child rearing,

---

[20] See Chapter IV, pp. 238-39.

value systems, or teaching problems. At the same time, as an assistant teacher, the student would make a contribution to the school and to the community. Under optimum circumstances, the student teacher while based at the school would also explore the community, social structure, history, and educational problems of the host country.

What has already been said about the way in which a Peace Corps volunteer can relate his Peace Corps work to his preparation as a teacher would be applicable to student teachers sent from a given institution in the United States to work in one of the American-sponsored overseas schools. There are 132 such schools in 80 countries, which enroll 28,000 American children as well as 22,000 others from 100 countries; and their combined resources can contribute importantly to the international dimension of teacher education in the United States. Among the stated purposes for the support given to the schools through the Office of Overseas Schools of the Bureau of Administration in the U.S. State Department is that of increasing mutual understanding between the people of the United States and the people of other countries by maintaining the schools as demonstration centers for American educational philosophy and methods.

This is difficult to do in many of the schools where there are shortages of funds and staff and often a lack of clarity as to what American educational philosophy amounts to. President Johnson's February 2, 1966, message to Congress in proposing the International Education Act helped to establish one element in what might be called an official international philosophy for American education when he said, "International education cannot be the work of one country. It is the responsibility and promise of all nations. It calls for free exchange and full collaboration. We expect to receive as much as we give, to learn as well as to teach." In referring to the Overseas Schools, the President added that they are a rich resource for helping to carry out the provisions of the Act and for providing "close contact with students and teachers of the host country."

Among the resources the Overseas Schools afford for the education of teachers and the extension of international education in general are the following:

• Nearly 1,500 foreign teachers and professionals from 56 different countries are employed in the schools.

• Local citizens serve with Americans on more than half of the schools' governing boards.

• Students in most of the schools can take regular courses of study in the local language and culture.

• In nearly all schools, non-American students take English language instruction.

• In a number of the larger schools, special materials have been developed in language and area studies—course outlines, tapes, filmstrips, films, and so forth.

166

• There are open opportunities for exchange of students, faculty, and school board members.

• Many of the local educators in the host countries visit the schools to learn how they operate, and there is a broad range of projects in which local educators could cooperate in the development of joint international curriculums and research.

• Many of the local teachers take in-service courses in extension work with American institutions.

• Hundreds of American teachers and supervisors are serving overseas in the schools on either short- or long-term contracts.[21]

The Office of Overseas Schools wants to improve the quality of teaching and education in these schools and invites cooperation with colleges of education in the development of new projects in teacher education abroad. The schools could, under the right circumstances and with the proper financial support, become genuine international centers for research and teacher education and could extend their present, limited forms of binational internationalism into a world dimension. They could, for example, carry further the implications of the new international syllabi developed by the International Schools Examination Syndicate in Geneva and the UNESCO Associated Schools project in Education for International Understanding and Cooperation, aside from starting new projects of their own.

Although I have visited only a few of the overseas schools and can write from only a limited experience of their direct operations, that experience and the testimony of others leads me to say that the internationalism of the schools is seldom carried very far. The character of the schools is essentially American—a suburban, white, middle class school transposed into a foreign setting, with nationals from the host country entering what amounts to an American curriculum with all its parochialism, strengths, and weaknesses. The governing board of American members, American faculty, and American parents combines to create a cultural surrogate in many ways antithetical to a spirit of internationalism—one with noticeable pressures, even in as international a setting as the International School in Geneva, for a curriculum and instructional approach as much like an American school as possible.

Yet the potential is there, as the above listing of resources would indicate, and it remains for educators in this country to create the imaginative projects through which the schools can make full use of their privileged situation. One beginning has been made by the American Association of Colleges for Teacher Education in cooperation with the U.S. Department of State in pairing seven teacher education institutions with seven selected

---

[21]See: Leubke, Paul T. *American-Sponsored Overseas Schools: A Rich Resource for International Education.* Washington, D.C.: International Educational and Cultural Exchange, U.S. Advisory Commission on International and Cultural Affairs, Summer issue, 1966.

schools in all parts of the world, with help in the recruitment of staff, visits to the schools by educational experts, teacher exchange, and curriculum development. These activities have been mainly for the purpose of strengthening the existing schools rather than stretching the scope of their work in world affairs. A project also exists for pairing selected overseas schools with selected American school systems. Foreign teachers are brought to this country for experience and training, and American teachers work abroad in social studies and foreign languages.

Aside from the usual things done by way of exchange of teachers and materials and the use of local educational resources and community life for field study and curriculum development, there are some variations to consider on the theme of undergraduate and graduate teacher education work abroad. Among these is the possibility of regular junior-year-abroad programs, in which undergraduate student teachers would serve as tutors, teachers' aides, and assistant teachers while carrying on study and research in the language, culture, and school system of the host country. The presence of a succession of lively, young college students interested in foreign cultures and in teaching would have a marked effect on the quality of the education offered. If the concept were agreed upon that each school is a center for the development of international education and a true demonstration of the philosophy of American education in action, we would have exactly what we need to extend the work of preparing American teachers in world affairs, in addition to improving the education of the children and teachers overseas.

There are good possibilities for doing this with new M.A. programs sponsored by colleges of education. Such programs would include three months of preparation in the United States, a year of research study and practice teaching abroad, and then return to the home campus for a final semester with individually planned work based on the year's experience. The M.A. candidate—or in a comparable plan, the doctoral candidate—could use the materials gathered in the foreign country for the content of a new course or courses he would teach on his return to the United States or as the basis for a research study in fulfillment of his doctoral requirements. Programs of this kind not only would be valuable to the college of education and to the overseas school, but would add a new range to the career possibilities for students with the B.A. degree for whom a year abroad would be a way of opening up new areas of interest in the teaching profession—possibly with a view to a career in educational administration abroad—while developing a new and satisfying alternative to some of the dead material in present graduate programs.

To free the overseas schools from some of the restrictions on their international growth, it should not be too hard to make arrangements through American college admissions officers to work with the overseas schools to encourage new work by their students in the foreign cultures they are living in. This would simply mean revising the academic requirements that already do so much to prevent curricular experiment in the

American high schools. The fact that a student applying for admission to college was educated abroad should be considered a point in favor of that student's admission to an American university, not a defect in his record because he does not present a conventional set of credits. It should be a rule that the American student educated abroad who does *not* show a knowledge of the culture and language of the country in which he has resided has less chance of admission to an American university than those who can demonstrate such knowledge.

A Comprehensive Plan for the Overseas Schools

A comprehensive plan for doing something about the international education of American teachers and the overseas schools at the same time is under consideration by a colloquium of persons and groups drawn from several state systems of education, the Office of Overseas Schools, the Kettering Foundation, and the State University of New York. I would like to use the example of the plan, whether or not it ever goes into effect in its entirety, to illustrate the possibilities in taking a systems approach to the whole problem of the use of existing resources for improving the international education of teachers. That approach demands that the planner not merely invent a new plan to achieve a given end, but that he analyze the various interconnections that are already made or could be made among existing institutions and organizations.

Before describing the plan for the use of the overseas schools on a national and international basis, I must first describe what I have found to be the most complete statewide organization of a state university system to achieve an international dimension in higher education, teacher education, and everything else—the program of the State University of New York. I have referred to this in the chapter on the certification question, where initiatives by state departments of education are described. Here I wish to describe the overall plan for international education in the State University of New York.

After the decision was made that the state university system should be internationalized, an administrative center was established in 1966 on university property in Planting Fields, Oyster Bay, New York, with the name Center for International Studies and World Affairs of the State University of New York. The Center is the administrative arm of an overall plan for international education, which has its operations in the 58 colleges and universities of the state; it is part of the central administration of the state system, whose headquarters are in Albany. Glenn Olds acts as university dean of the Center and has a staff of five directors to deal with international services and contracts, international faculty and student exchange, international librarianship resources and information, and an international center for conferences, research, curriculum development, and teacher education.

The implications of the new program are extraordinarily far-reaching. The assumptions on which it rests are that (a) the study of the world's cultures should be an integral part of the liberal education of every student in the state system, (b) personal experience in the culture of another country is an essential element in learning to understand that culture, and (c) this kind of experience should be made available to qualified students in the state regardless of their economic means.

The University of California has an Overseas Program with some of the elements of the New York State plan included. Students from the 18 state colleges of California are eligible for a year abroad, arranged by the Office of International Programs, for study in France, Germany, Italy, Japan, Spain, Sweden, and Taiwan. The assignments are made to foreign universities by the Overseas Program office at a cost of from $1,500 to $3,000 per student, most of whom obtain National Defense Education Act loans and private or government scholarships. During the present year, 265 students are abroad, all but 40 of them in Europe. A total of 786 have taken part in the program since it began in 1963. Again, there are no specific plans for teacher education built into the project, although it is possible to do so on an individual basis depending on the student, his faculty supervision on his campus, and the arrangements possible with the university faculty members abroad.

The International Studies and World Affairs Center of the State University of New York

Although these assumptions about equality of opportunity in study abroad are generally acceptable to American educators, they are seldom used as the basis for complete university programs. However, the International Studies and World Affairs Center of the State University of New York does take these assumptions as a basis, with the following proposed operations supervised by the various directors:

Liaison will be established between the University of the State of New York and international agencies, including the United Nations, the ministries of education of foreign countries, the American embassies and binational centers abroad, universities overseas, international libraries, museums and scientific research institutes. Through such liaison, the practical arrangements for research, teaching, study, and service will be made.

Faculty members from the state system of education will come to the Center for short periods of intensive study in foreign cultures, international affairs, and world education; and a comprehensive program for increasing the competence of the faculty in foreign cultures will be administered, to include faculty experience abroad, seminars, conferences, and independent study both at the Center and on home campuses in New York State.

Students and faculty members in a variety of disciplines, particularly in education, will come to the Center for study of world culture in seminars with foreign students and scholars and American experts.

Seven regional centers will be established overseas in Western Europe, the Middle East, Latin America, Eastern Europe, Africa, Southeast Asia, the Far East. The work of the regional centers will be to administer the programs for students and faculty members, both for research and study in a given region. For example, the Western Europe Regional Center will be in Paris, where the staff will work out plans for 400 students in 1967-68 for 17 different study programs in Western Europe in collaboration with the universities there.

The faculty and student resources of the 58 institutions of higher education in New York State will be surveyed with the view to making full use of the particular skills and talents of students and faculty in the various institutions for aid to the developing countries.

Arrangements will be made for the exchange of faculty members who have special knowledge and experience in foreign cultures between the institutions of New York State, with concentration of various area-studies programs in designated universities.

New programs will be organized to make possible direct experience of students in foreign cultures in cooperation with the Peace Corps, the United Nations, the State Department and other agencies with international interests.[22]

It will be clear that the implications of the new Center for the education of teachers are serious and important. Not only is the curriculum of the state university system to be enriched by the inclusion of a sufficient amount of work in foreign cultures to make certain that student teachers have an opportunity to study in the field, but the opportunity for service abroad, the mobility of students and faculty members between one New York State campus and another, and the availability of the International Studies and World Affairs Center for special international work in collaboration with foreign students and teachers will provide a stream of new ideas for further extension of the program. Within five to ten years, this should have a marked effect on the world dimension of education in the New York State University system, on the quality of the teaching staff in the public schools, and on the scope of the public school curriculum throughout the state. Once the International Studies and World Affairs Center begins to operate fully, it should also have a marked effect on national and international conceptions of what can be accomplished in world education.

A System of Interconnections

An indication of these possibilities can be seen in the proposal discussed at the Center for the use of the overseas schools in connection with teacher education, so that students may receive part of their education abroad in one of 76 of the present schools. The plan calls for cooperation with 39 experimental schools in 20 states designated by the Kettering Foundation for research, exchange of students and faculty members, and teacher education, as well as nine colleges for teachers whose campus schools are part of the experimental group. Faculty members from the overseas schools would come to teach at one of the nine colleges and would also work in the experimental schools attached to them. Faculty members from these institutions would go abroad to work with student teachers at one of the overseas schools and would act as liaison among the International Studies and World Affairs Center, the overseas schools, and the state systems of education.

In its beginning, there would be 300 student teachers involved, 150 would be American and 150 would be from other countries. As a regular part of his preparation to teach, the American student would go abroad,

---

[22] Description of International Studies and World Affairs Center, Planting Fields, N.Y. (mimeo.)

probably in his junior year, to do practice teaching and to study the foreign language and culture as well as the educational problems of the host country. He would use his experience abroad as the basis for further study and preparation to teach when he returned home. The foreign students would prepare themselves to teach in their own countries after a year spent in one of the 39 experimental schools.

Funds for the support of the project would come from federal and state governments and from foundations, possibly the Kettering Foundation, which has been active in the planning. One of the most important results of the plan, aside from starting up some new conceptions of how the American educational system can extend itself into the international community, will be that the overseas schools will have the advantage of the presence of a group of students and faculty members whose interest is in studying the culture of the country being visited and in constructing new curriculums for use in the host school as well as in the school and college at home. It is hoped that the overseas schools could also establish relationships with universities nearby, so that not only will there be a binational approach to the development of school curriculums, but an opportunity to develop multinational programs through collaboration with faculty members in the foreign universities.

Organizations and Consortia

The approach also suggests ways in which the regional college groups and consortia among the colleges and universities can combine their resources in making further extensions of the foreign study centers they have begun to establish. The Great Lakes Colleges Association consists of a consortium of 12 Midwestern colleges and universities (20,000 undergraduates altogether), which have agreed to pool their resources and work out educational programs among themselves and, in the case of the international sector, have begun overseas study centers in Latin America, the Near East, and Japan. They too have taken a systems approach and have looked for existing organizations and programs that could be integrated with their own, among them the Peace Corps, the National Defense Education Act centers for area studies, scholarship grants for foreign students, and fellowship grants for faculty members. Although their attention has not been turned specifically to teacher education, and the number of students involved is not large—22 students in Beirut, 25 in Tokyo, 40 in Bogota—the implications for the future are clear.

For example, one outcome has been a seminar in 1965 in Yugoslavia, arranged for 15 students and four faculty members from the Association, through cooperation among the University of Ljubljana, the U.S. Department of State, the American Embassy in Belgrade, the Johnson Foundation, and the Great Lakes College Association. The combined experience of the 12 colleges in the international field has also given access to programs in Africa: Earlham College has worked with AID in starting a comprehensive school in Kenya; Oberlin has a Peace Corps project for French-speaking

Africa; Kalamazoo has sent students to the University of Sierra Leone; Antioch and DePauw students have gone to African universities; and faculty members, under Association grants, have gone to several African countries for research and study. Funds for support of the Association have come from college budgets, foundations, and U.S. Office of Education grants for particular projects. The Association has had considerable success in the education of college teachers for its member institutions through an intern program and, should it turn its attention more directly to teacher education for the public schools, could expand that dimension of its work. In the meantime, in the true meaning of the word, the member colleges of the Association have become to some degree "internationalized."

A similar grouping of 38 institutions in Ohio, West Virginia, and Pennsylvania—the Regional Council for International Education—has given support to faculty, students, and institutions in increasing their work in area studies, foreign cultures, and languages. Although not specifically related to public school teaching nor as fully involved in overseas work as the Great Lakes Association, the Council gives seminars for faculty members; brings foreign scholars in residence; arranges programs for foreign students; runs a European-American study center in Basel, Switzerland; and can give help to its member institutions in arranging connections with universities abroad. It is supported by foundation grants and has developed and administered programs for AID, the Department of State, the Department of Agriculture, the Institute of International Education, and other organizations. Again, if there were specific ideas forthcoming from member institutions in teacher education, the machinery of the Council could be used to aid in carrying them out.

Two other organizations whose business it is to work directly with school systems and teacher preparation programs have serious potential for the expansion of international education—the Western Interstate Commission for Higher Education, with headquarters in Boulder, Colorado, and the Eight-State Project in Designing Education for the Future, with headquarters in Denver. The Western Interstate Commission has 13 Western states in its membership, with three commissioners appointed by the governor of each state to serve on the Commission "to look for and suggest to the states ways in which regional cooperation or effective statewide planning could create new opportunities for Western students, improve educational programs, and assure the best use of available funds." The Commission is supported by $15,000 annual appropriations from each member state and by foundation grants combined with grants from the Public Health Service, the National Institute of Mental Health, and other government agencies, including the Office of Education.

In looking and suggesting, the interest of the Commission is in undergraduate training for the helping services—mental health, nursing, medical education, and similar areas not usually central to the concerns of the educators of teachers. The undergraduate education program for the helping services has the ring of internationalism in its intent: "to provide for the

173

development of model programs of education for the helping services at the undergraduate level and thus to attack the shortage of trained manpower in the West." All that would be required to shift into international gear would be to substitute the word *world* for *West* at the conclusion of this sentence and to transfer the meaning of *West* from its reference to the Western United States to the Western world, which could include the Southwestern world of Latin America.

The intention of the Commission coincides directly with the need for new forms of teacher education, here and abroad, that function in the areas of cultural and social change rather than in conventional curriculums and syllabi. Robert Kroepsch is executive director of the Commission. Following his attendance at the Conference on World Education, a phase of the present study, he suggested four areas in which his organization and others like it could function in international education:

(1) Increasing the international or world affairs component in the preparation of elementary and secondary school teachers in Western colleges and universities

(2) "Internationalizing" faculty members in our Western colleges and universities, most of whom have had very limited education and experience in other cultures, particularly non-European cultures[23]

(3) Assisting Western colleges and universities to improve their foreign programs through the exchange of information and knowledge of practice, particularly with regard to AID and Peace Corps programs, other contracts, and foreign study programs for their own students

(4) Assisting Western colleges and universities in improving the manner in which they "handle" foreign students who come to their campuses, so that their own academic community can benefit to a higher degree from the presence of these nationals from other countries and cultures.[24]

It would be possible in all these ways to set in motion a series of international ideas and projects within the 13 states which could result in exchange among the member states of selected foreign students who are studying in this country to become teachers and to plan new projects through an interstate committee on world education. These could include teams of American and foreign students who would work together in the home countries of the foreign nationals as a regular part of a one- or two-year sequence, with summer sessions in the United States and abroad that the Experiment in International Living and the World University Service, for example, could help organize. Long-term programs could be planned with help from AID and the Center for Educational Cooperation.

Similar programs could be advanced by the Denver-based Eight-State Project in Designing Education for the Future, which until now has not dealt specifically with the international side of the future. The direct relation that the Eight-State Project staff has with the state departments of education, with the colleges of education, and with the school systems in

---

[23] This could begin with field experience in the indigenous nonwhite, non-English speaking cultures of the Western United States.

[24] Letter from Dr. Robert Kroepsch (in study files).

the Western states and the national outreach that the Project has already demonstrated in the choice of experts and scholars in the educational field for its research papers and conferences could be used to good advantage, particularly in collaboration with the Western Interstate Commission, owing to their common geographical location and regional interests.

The International Baccalaureate

One of the forces at work to develop a new kind of international school in the United States and abroad lies in the unnoticed sector of family life among the international community of scientists, scholars, administrators, businessmen, diplomats, and other professionals. When invited to accept posts abroad with organizations like UNESCO, WHO, the UN Secretariat, the European Organization for Nuclear Research, or commercial and financial firms, those with families have a natural and serious concern for the education of their children and in some cases make stipulations about good educational facilities, school curriculums, and good teachers a condition of their acceptance of overseas assignments. Out of these needs have grown a number of international schools—aside from the American overseas schools already described—in Great Britain, Chile, Denmark, West Germany, Ghana, India, Iran, Lebanon, Switzerland, the United States, and other countries. Two of the largest schools are in Geneva (1,500 students) and in New York, where the UN School now has more than 600 children from 68 countries.

For schools of this kind, a set of new educational problems immediately arises: on the one hand, to meet the educational requirements of a sound education with a truly international flavor applicable to all young persons in the modern world and, at the same time, to present an education that will prepare most of the students for admission to an institution of higher education in their home country. That means meeting the demands of national university entrance requirements without sacrificing the breadth and depth of the international curriculum in the schools themselves and without concentrating excessively on the academic specialities of any one kind of examination or national system.

The International Schools Examination Syndicate was organized in Geneva in 1964, with funds from the Twentieth Century Fund and the Ford Foundation and the support of UNESCO, to see what could be done by way of constructing examinations that could be applied to a number of national university systems simultaneously based on an international syllabus of the subjects required by most countries. At a conference held in Sèvres, France, in February 1967 and attended by educational administrators and members of examination boards from 10 countries, a general structure of international examinations and syllabi was approved; and plans were made for a six-year experiment from 1970 to 1976 with a group of 500 students each year drawn from groups in various international schools in Europe, Latin America, and the United States. Following two years of previous discussion and research, there was general agreement at the Sèvres conference that the aims of an international curriculum for the last two years of secondary school should include—

1. The general development of the powers of the mind rather than the acquisition and temporary retention of an encyclopedic range of information.
2. The development of those skills necessary to enable the student to profit from a university course.
3. Sufficient experience in chosen limited fields to enable the student to start specialized work at the university.
4. The development of at least a limited acquaintance with the contemporary world and an international outlook.[25]

As will be evident, the aims are stated in minimal terms, in view of the particular elite clientele the international schools are designed to serve, but they do furnish a beginning to what may develop into a larger conception of what international education can be.

There are obviously some very serious problems in making a curriculum and a set of examinations that can satisfy even these aims without restricting them by the entrance examinations required in the European universities. There are also some equally obvious problems in the recruitment of teachers who have the facility in foreign languages and the depth of scholarship to be able to deal with an international curriculum at the level of seriousness required by the experiment. The title International Schools Examination Syndicate is somewhat misleading as a description of the work of the educators involved, since the development of examinations is merely the motivating impulse behind a far larger educational experiment —that of developing a new kind of education in the liberal arts and sciences that is truly international. In view of the difficulties inherent in the task and of the conservatism prevalent among educators in general and European educators in particular, it is a tribute to the determination and imagination of the educators in the Syndicate that they have been able to produce outlines of syllabi and a structure for examining that satisfies the requirements and interests of 10 national systems of education. To meet the problem of teacher recruitment and teacher education, the Syndicate is developing a series of Teacher's Guides—to be written by present teachers in international schools—that, together with bibliographies and library grants, will help the schools and the other teachers to teach the new courses.

But more than anything else, the Syndicate project will provide one of the most interesting laboratories yet in existence for research and experiment into the content of contemporary knowledge relevant and necessary for the modern educated person and, at the same time, investigate the concept of education itself in its application to the lives of late adolescents born and raised in a variety of cultural, social, and economic circumstances. Not all the children of foreign nationals living abroad have had an elementary school education at home that would satisfy the requirements of admission to a European, American, or British high school or one that would make it

---

[25] The International Baccalaureate, International Schools Examination Syndicate; 37 Route de la Copite, 1223 Cologny, Geneva, Switzerland. p. 8.

possible for them to keep up the pace in a curriculum concentrating on university preparation. This turns the educator toward the question of the establishment of comprehensive high school on a world scale and, for the Syndicate project, provides the opportunity for research and enquiry into the question as to who is educable and in what terms.

Should a fully international school concentrate only on the preparation of high school students to go on to university? What can be done to rescue intelligent children with inadequate elementary school education from the oblivion to which they might be condemned by lack of further education suited to their talents? What can be done, or should be done, to enrich the purely academic curriculum of the international preparatory school with allied and complementary forms of education in the creative arts, community development, and preparation for the human services? What is the relation of independent study, laboratory and field work, and student-initiated projects to the conventional academic methods of texts and bibliography, lectures, recitation, and so forth? What use can and should be made of new materials drawn from films, television tapes, records, and other technical devices? By what means can the students in a fully international setting learn to understand each other's culture, politics, and social ideas? How can an international school best serve as a center for the education of internationally minded teachers?

Although at the present time the educators in the experiment have their hands full simply in developing the new courses and the examinations to go with them, they are conscious of the possibilities of what might result from the present beginning and have noted some topics for research related to the examinations themselves. These include enquiry into the validity of various kinds of testing other than that of written examinations; assessment of the relevance of the kind of education usually offered in the last two years of high school to the concepts, skills, and information actually used by the students after they go to the university; and comparative study of the content of education in the last two years of high school in European and American schools.

It would be possible, for example, to try out the new international curriculums in a variety of American and European schools, as well as elsewhere around the world, and to find out whether or not a unified approach to the study of the sciences, philosophy, mathematics, and other fields could make it possible for teachers everywhere in the world to agree on certain common elements in the content of education both for those who are not likely to go on to the universities and those who are. The Syndicate intends to organize a central research unit in one university and to develop particular projects in collaboration with other universities and schools.

Examinations and syllabi are being prepared in philosophy, history, classics, foreign languages, geography, economics, physics, biology, and mathematics. The preliminary statements about what the syllabi will contain give a clue to some interesting developments in curriculum making in which American teachers could join, even without direct connection to an

177

international school. For example, in the statment of aims of the biology course, the following ideas appear:

> An education in biology should lead to a respect for all forms of life, springing from a deeper understanding of man and his place in nature, his effects on other organisms, and their effects on him. Biologists are in a unique position to call the attention of students to the position of man in the world, being able to provide insights into the problems facing man that the more traditional ways of studying human societies (e.g., from historical, political, and economic viewpoints) cannot.

In philosophy:

> The purpose of the proposed course is to require the students to reflect on a certain number of themes at the period when what they have learned in other subjects has raised important questions in their minds. . . . More than any other subject it is important here to avoid *ex cathedra* courses; as far as possible, the basis should be the personal experience of the student, in the light of which he can diagnose problems, understand their scope, and study them against the background of the thoughts of different authors.

In geography:

> The inclusion of geography within the syllabus of an international school is justified on three grounds: in being a science of observation and in ensuing the development of a pupil's power of discrimination and correlation lies its main educative value. It is, further, the ideal subject for synthesizing most school subjects, a bridge between the future. Finally, and of immediate importance, is the contribution it can make towards international understanding, and it is this aspect of geography which justifies its inclusion in the group of "human sciences." The study of geography should be centered around a study of the relationships between man and his environment, and the physical aspects of the subject must not be given more weight than the human.[26]

It is possible that through cooperative research and teacher education programs in the United States and with a research center located at the UN School in New York (this school is a member of the experimental group in the 1970-76 project), the work in Geneva and in other countries with interested teachers and students could stimulate new international curriculums in the arts and sciences in a variety of U.S. schools and colleges of education.

The UNESCO Project in Education for International Understanding

The UNESCO Project in Education for International Understanding and Cooperation, initiated in 1953, furnished its first report of findings in 1965.[27] The report indicates that a growing number of institutions around the world have a commitment to work in curricular reform and experimental work in extending the range of student involvement in world affairs. The Project began with 33 schools in 15 countries, each of which was to devise its own programs and to carry them out in whatever ways seemed best to the teachers, who were asked to select one of three themes or areas of study: the rights of women; other countries, peoples, and cultures; or

---

[26] International Baccalaureate Syllabuses, *ibid.*

[27] UNESCO. *International Understanding at School: An Account of Progress in UNESCO's Associated School Project.* Paris: UNESCO, 1965. p. 22.

178

the principles of human rights. By the time the report of the Project was issued in 1965, the number of schools involved had risen to more than 300, of which 55 were institutions for teacher education in 43 countries of Africa, Asia, the Middle East, Europe, Latin America, and North America, institutions encompassing a wide range of cultural traditions, stages of development, and economic and political systems.

In addition to the work of supplying materials—booklets, posters, film-strips, bibliographies, and so forth—the UNESCO Secretariat arranged, in cooperation with the members of the Project, a series of regional confer-ences, meetings, and seminars in Europe, Latin America, Asia, and the Middle East. A full international meeting to sum up results after 10 years of work was held in Paris in 1963. Aside from the general stir in the schools involved in the Project and the specific programs that developed from the initial stages into what, in some cases, were important reforms in school and teacher education curriculums, national organizations in several countries took up the idea and extended it throughout their own educational systems. For example, in India, which began with nine schools and 13 teacher training institutions, the Indian National Commission for UNESCO started a nationwide project on the same lines as the parent experiment; by 1964, 350 secondary schools and teacher institutions were involved in workshops for teachers in world affairs to prepare new materials and syllabi and to circulate available information which the Secretariat in Paris had been collecting over the years.

This has made it possible for the Project to expand in ways that promise additional expansion in the future and indicate that when the Center for Educational Cooperation under the International Education Act begins its operations in Washington, D. C., there are a good many prece-dents and existing intercountry connections that can link the American schools to a large number of educators and institutions around the world. In the modest terms of the UNESCO report, the results so far have "led to the development of a great variety of examples of activities which can be carried out by the ordinary school or teacher training institution and which are therefore of general education significance" and have demonstrated that "not only is it possible to teach for international understanding without overloading or disrupting the school programme but that such teaching enriches the content and increases the impact of school subjects."

For further details about the kinds of activities undertaken in the schools associated with the project, I refer the reader to the UNESCO report. From conversations with teachers and administrators for overseas schools involved, I gathered that the main impulse toward reform of existing curriculums in the international dimension came from the feeling that teachers in local schools were linked together with teachers around the world in carrying out a common task, each making his own contribution to the total result.

The impact on teacher education has not yet reached a similar level of significance, although some progress has been made. At a regional seminar held in Hamburg in 1958, at which teacher education was a key point in the agenda, it was agreed that the study of the "techniques of education for international understanding should find a place in the professional training of all teaching students and that the methods and programmes developed from this work should be used by the students in their periods of practice teaching in demonstration schools."[28]

In Belgium, Ceylon, and Spain, where this idea has been taken seriously, students have in fact carried out such work in their practice teaching periods. Graduate students in Ceylon have started projects of this kind in different parts of the country, maintaining contact with their colleges of education by reporting to them on progress and receiving guidance and sample materials in exchange. What remains for Americans, both through the American UNESCO Commission and through AACTE and other organizations, is to circulate the ideas and materials to the colleges of education and to organize similar projects in the spirit and approach of the original undertaking.

Internationalism and Access to Higher Education

The close connection between examinations and curriculums in the schools and colleges and the even closer connection between examination systems and the development and maintenance of social classes within each society make the concept of educational testing one of the most important ideas in the entire field of international education. As may be apparent throughout this Report, my own views of the conventional examination system, with its ties to sterile methods of instruction and obsolete curriculums, are that it is a naive and coarse-grained way of dealing with human talent. When one considers that almost the entire world's educational system uses the examination as a screening device in the selection of those who will receive the benefits of further education, further, that is, than the first five to eight grades of school, it is possible to argue that a thorough analysis of the relation of social inequality to educational methods, including the use of conventional examinations as a device for the selection of educable talent, is the most important place that anyone could start in a review of the problems of world education.

A pioneer study in this field, carried out by Frank Bowles, now adviser on international education to the Ford Foundation, was organized in 1959 by the Joint UNESCO-International Association of Universities research program through an international commission of educational experts representing a variety of world regions and educational systems. It was the first time that a systematic effort had ever been made to join together a cross-section of educational systems throughout the world in mutual efforts by educators and scholars to focus attention on one major problem of concern to all. The results of the research,[29] published in 1963 after two years of

---

[28] *Ibid.,* p. 40.

[29] *Access to Higher Education,* Volume 1, the International Study of University Admissions, Bowles, Frank. UNESCO and the International Association of Universities, International Document Service. New York: Columbia University Press, 1963. p. 212.

field work, conferences, and study by Dr. Bowles and his staff from 1960 to 1962, furnish the basis for the consideration of nearly every major problem in international education and in planning for education on a world scale in the future. If taken seriously by educators in the United States and elsewhere, the conclusions reached and the educational issues raised could be used as the materials for a continuing effort in educational reform in institutions of higher education everywhere in the world.

The core of Dr. Bowles' findings is contained in his statement of five hypotheses about worldwide admissions programs:

> The problem of admission to higher education is only superficially administrative. At base it is educational, rooted in the purposes and goals of the educational community. If the result of the study is stated as a finding that the present admissions process is educationally inadequate, an entire set of new approaches to the problem is uncovered. These may be presented as five hypotheses to be tested against the established facts of the workings of the process:
>
> 1. The annual entry into higher education represents not more than one third—and in some countries as few as one tenth—of the students of superior ability who start the admissions process with the intention of preparing for higher education. The other two thirds of the group are eliminated by present methods of examination and selection.
>
> 2. Much of the elimination even in countries with well-developed educational systems is the result of social inequalities which take the form of financial barriers to continue the education, particularly in the secondary schools.
>
> 3. The present programmes of preparation for higher education are educationally inadequate as evidenced by high rates of failure to complete higher education programmes after entry.
>
> 4. Current methods of selection make insufficient use of secondary school information about the intellectual capacities and interests of individual students.
>
> 5. The facilities and programme offerings of higher education are incapable of satisfying the existing demands for entrance to higher education by properly qualified students. At their present rates of development the inadequacy ten years hence may well be frightening.[30]

The implications of these hypotheses for the education of teachers add to the sense of urgency felt by educators who have looked at the problem of aid to developing countries through the improvement of their educational systems. The Bowles study raises new questions about world education at some of its most important points, including the problem of part-time professors in institutions of higher education in the developing countries; the limitation of entry into the teaching profession at universities controlled by those who have a professional interest in limiting access to teaching; the inadequacy and low status of teacher training institutions in nearly every country in the world; and the intricate interconnection between higher education and the secondary and elementary schools, between education and the political, social, and economic forces in each society.

In his discussion of the expansion of the world's educational oppor-

---

[30] *Ibid.*, pp. 30-31.

tunities, Dr. Bowles sets the problem in its American and world dimension when he says—

> In operation, higher education has before it two choices for discharging [its] responsibilities. One method widely employed but now being modified is to control student entrance by examinations, a type of control ordinarily operated through a series of eliminations. Another method is to control student entrance through advice based on the student's performance, judgments of student abilities, and expressions of student preference—in short, control through orientation or guidance.[31]

Dr. Bowles proposes an emphasis on the second alternative—revision both of admissions and curricular policy to bring to all young people in elementary, secondary school, and after education that combines the two crucial elements—the ability to perform useful tasks and the ability to understand oneself in the context of cultural, intellectual, political, and historical traditions of world society. Future studies of international education will have to take into account the findings of the Bowles research, both as a method of collaboration among teachers within the worldwide educational community and as a means of focusing attention on the key issues in social, political, economic, and educational development.

Some Examples Drawn from American Colleges

There are colleges in America that have developed educational strategies consonant with the main recommendations of this Report and which can serve as examples of what is being done and of what can be done. The strategy begins when a college takes the students and their education as the primary purpose of its program and gives them responsibility and freedom to teach themselves and each other and to share in the planning for their own education and in learning how to teach. They learn to teach by teaching. The strategy moves from there to the idea that if you want teachers with a large and generous view of the world—prepared to understand it, act in it, and teach about it—you must give them a chance to experience the world at firsthand, or as close to firsthand as it is humanly possible to arrange, and to find ways of coping with it in their own terms. You must then accept the fact that the curriculum comes out of the teachers and their experience and character; teachers do not come out of the curriculum. What comes out of the curriculum is people who have taken courses, not people prepared to give them.

I therefore return to the idea that the college for students who will be teachers is a staging ground for expeditions, a planning center for an education that can and should take place all over the world whether or not the teacher ever intends to teach something called world affairs, world history, or international relations. How far into the world the student can get depends on the local circumstances—his own initiative, his previous education, his temperament, but above all, the attitudes and ideas of the institution he is attending. If he has the misfortune to be in a college that simply

---

[31] *Ibid.,* p. 168.

grinds out graduates through courses, he may never know that there is anything else than what he sees around him and learns from his courses. On the other hand, if a college turns its attention to how the student can move into the world in order to use it for learning purposes, then he is twice blessed, since he is taught what he needs to know on his campus by what is given to him by his teachers and he can learn to use it in his life as he practices teaching, that is to say, goes to Ethiopia or to the Philippines or to Watts to practice what he can do to help children and others to learn what they need to learn.

Antioch College

The problem then becomes one of making use of the world outside the college for educational purposes, using it to stimulate serious intellectual activity while teaching the student to collect his own knowledge in some coordinated form. The example of Antioch College in Yellow Springs, Ohio, is a case in point. The present phase of the educational history of Antioch springs from a time when, in 1920, President Arthur E. Morgan established the pattern of the work-study program as a central component in the Antioch plan of education in the belief—shared by John Dewey, the founders of Bennington College, and other experimental institutions—that work experience, whether or not related to a particular sequence of academic studies on the campus, is a prime educational factor in the life of the student. From that time to this, the conception of off-campus education at Antioch has grown both in size and sophistication and is so woven into the fabric of the Antioch curriculum that it has acquired an imaginative and efficient administrative staff and a set of direct connections with the institutional life of the United States and of a large number of foreign countries. Of the 1,800 students enrolled, approximately half are in residence in Yellow Springs at any one time; the rest are working in a variety of ways in occupations ranging from the factory to government service to teaching. More than 250 go abroad for 12 to 15 months in study programs and jobs arranged through six regional centers in Mexico, France, Germany, Italy, Japan, and Lebanon and through individual arrangements made with foreign universities in 20 other countries.

The College is essentially a college for students, with full student participation in educational policy making and administration. Although it is not a teachers college, a fairly large proportion of the undergraduates become teachers, approximately 225 of the 1,800 students, who combine their studies on the campus with field work in education. At least half of the teachers have had experience abroad by the time they graduate. They meet the Ohio certification requirements through work with teachers from the regular college faculty, in courses that do not suffer from the usual student criticism of education courses because of their relevance to the student's experience and needs. In fact, one of the main courses in psychology for Antioch undergraduates is an education course which meets the state requirements and is elected by more students interested in psychology than any other course in the College.

As far as preparation in world affairs is concerned, there is no specific undergraduate program that links the offerings in Asian studies, the Chinese and Japanese languages, and other work in foreign cultures to the education of teachers. However, through the College's affiliation with the Great Lakes College Association and the Peace Corps, students who are becoming teachers may, and often do, undertake study abroad in Japan, Latin America, Africa, and elsewhere. The College has also organized an 18-month international work-study program for foreign teachers, mainly from Western Europe, who come to the Antioch campus for three months of seminars in American culture and education, followed by three months of work experience in schools, school camps, outdoor education centers, and social service projects; two months as staff members of summer camps; and then a regular paid teaching post in the field of their competence in an American school. Each participant pays his roundtrip transportation to and from Yellow Springs and is able to finance the 18-month period from the income supplied by his teaching post. The broad extension of this idea by colleges of education throughout the United States would bring many more foreign teachers from many more countries into the middle of the American educational system—without the expenditure of large sums and with great benefit to all concerned.

In addition, Antioch conducts a 10-week advance training program for Peace Corps volunteers who will serve in Colombia in urban and rural teaching and community development. The volunteers work on the campus in Colombian area studies, the Spanish language, American institutions, world ideological conflict, public health, and vocational subjects related to sports and the elements of agriculture. Those going to rural areas gain practical experience in agriculture, home economics, nutrition, and community development through field work in Ohio; those going to urban posts are assigned to field training in community development and urban renewal projects in Dayton and elsewhere. Most of the instruction is conducted in seminars and field work, with the help of young Colombians and Peace Corps returnees brought to the campus for that purpose. At the end of the 10 weeks, the volunteers return to their own campuses to complete their senior year and to continue their work in Spanish, Colombian culture, and service projects with a final training period in extension of the work of the previous summer, either in the United States or in Colombia. The connection of this to the possibilities for teacher education, as described in a previous section of this Report, are obvious.

It is in the Antioch-Putney Graduate School of Education that some of the most significant advances have been made in this style of teacher education. More than one half of the 120 graduate students are returned Peace Corps volunteers who are given the opportunity to use their previous experience and knowledge in constructing a study program for themselves at the School.

The year of the master of arts program begins either at the School headquarters in Putney, Vermont, or on the campus in Yellow Springs with interviews through which the student works out an individual program for the year and decides on a major independent study project around which his curriculum will be planned. Two months are spent in residence in the beginning term. The full resources of the campus are available to the students, who work in courses relevant to their study plan; hold seminars with selected professors and visitors; take field trips to local schools and agencies; and, if they have not taught before, carry out practice teaching in local schools.

The next term is spent in internship, teaching three quarters of the time at inner-city schools in Philadelphia, Baltimore, Washington, D.C., or Green County, Ohio, where work in community development, school teaching, academic study, field experience, and individual research combine to furnish a rich educational content for the succeeding two-month period of study either in Putney or in Yellow Springs.

The variety of student experiences over the year—from field trips to the United Nations to two weeks in Southern Appalachia, from study in Sartre and Camus to research on the Kashmir problem or the power structure of a Vermont community—is greater than any I have seen in any program of graduate education. Yet in concentrating on the central matter of the relation of those experiences to the development of the student as a teacher, the variety is of a kind that remains relevant to the intellectual and personal growth of those who are learning to be teachers. They are teaching each other, themselves, and children in the schools while creating a body of knowledge for use when they begin their full careers as teachers. By substituting foreign internships for the American in the case of students who have not studied abroad, the program can be made international. By continuing the education of the returned Peace Corps students in ways appropriate to their previous education and experience, the international component is already included for the rest. Since the Experiment in International Living headquarters is also in Putney, arrangements for internships abroad are comparatively simple to make.

I have presented the work of Antioch College in such detail in order to underscore the fact that once an attitude toward education and teaching is built into the institutional habits and administrative structure of a college, it becomes possible to use an enormous range of outside agencies, institutions, and organizations to further the education of students who are becoming teachers. In no other college connected with the study did I find such an amount of educational energy combined with practical arrangements for finding ways to use the world outside the college to further the intellectual and personal growth of the students, nor more ideas in education that could be easily adapted to the education of teachers in world affairs. If colleges of education were to adopt a plan of action similar to this and to build a structure of curriculum and field work designed in similar ways, the possibilities for the enrichment of teacher education in its international dimension would be increased by at least 100 percent.

Justin Morrill College

Justin Morrill College at Michigan State University is a different kind of example. Its existence contradicts one part of a generalization I have been making throughout the Report—that initiative for new kinds of education is not coming from the collective faculty bodies—but it confirms another part, that when initiative does come, it comes from a few people who get up their own ideas, not from the official policy committees. The College was "suggested, investigated, debated, approved, planned, and opened" in less than a year, in 1965. It is established as a inner college, eventually to enroll 1,200 students. The students live in the residence halls of the University. The curriculum is in the liberal arts and sciences, which allows its faculty members (who are regular members of the University faculty) to each courses in their own area of interest and which encourages students to carry on independent study. My reason for citing the College here is to show how large universities and the state colleges can organize an international dimension to their curriculum, release new ideas from the faculty, give more freedom and personal responsibility to the students, and do it all within the framework of a large institution. It remains to make more specific the relationship between a college of this kind and the preparation of teachers.

The students at Justin Morrill College are based there for work in the arts and humanities, the social and natural sciences, foreign language study, foreign study *or* independent field study in the U.S., and a senior seminar. The rest of their work, including enrollment in a major field, is in the University at large. The College is an experimental institution in the sense that it will continue to revise and experiment with the courses and the elements in the program from year to year as more experience is gained, and it intends to involve the students in the planning and revising. For those students who wish to follow the prescriptions, the Michigan teaching certificate is available with the B.A. degree.

The international flavor of the College is introduced—

• By the requirement of a full year of intensive foreign language study.

• By the international content of courses in the humanities and social science taught by faculty members with international interests, a good many of whom have had foreign experience.

• By the inclusion of foreign students in the residence arrangements.

• By the inclusion of all-college lectures by foreign scholars in the curriculum and by their membership in the regular faculty.

• By an optional requirement for a term of field study in the United States or in a foreign country.

Out of the 535 students enrolled in the College in 1967, 220 or 42 percent will have had at least one term abroad by the end of the College's first two years of operation. An effort is made to place students who go abroad in homes and community projects through which they can come to know the foreign culture at firsthand, with the possibility of a more extended foreign experience later in the college years. In this way, both the motivation and the educational justification for the intensive language study of the first year becomes clear to the student, and the possibility of genuine use of the language and the term overseas is vastly increased by the formal inclusion of both in the curriculum.

In addition, the flexibility in the system makes it possible for a student interested in teaching to plan for the kind of independent study, study and teaching abroad, and elective courses in foreign area studies that would give him the educational range he needs to enter the teaching profession with a knowledge of world affairs. The foreign study is divided into French-speaking programs in France, Morocco, Switzerland, Belgium, and French-Canada; a Spanish-speaking program in Spain, Colombia, and Peru; and Russian-speaking in a Soviet seminar tour and a Leningrad-based project, which includes six weeks of classes at the University of Leningrad followed by three weeks at a binational camp. The cost to the student ranges from $400 to $500 for the places closest by to $1,000 to $1,400 for the more distant. Loans and scholarships are available to the students. Most of the arrangements for study and community projects are made in cooperation with the Experiment in International Living.

It is possible that once the College gains more experience with the ways in which foreign projects can be made an integral part of the education of prospective teachers, liaison with the Michigan State College of Education, the many area studies centers on the Michigan State campus, and the dozens of faculty members on that campus who have various kinds of overseas assignments could result in a much greater variety and intensity of work in international education than is now being carried out. The main thing is that the framework is there, and that is what makes the Justin Morrill idea so adaptable to other institutions, including the colleges of education.

For example, within the present pattern at Justin Morrill, a careful selection of foreign students combined with returned Peace Corps volunteers could add college tutors, seminar leaders, and instructors who would begin experiments in student-organized seminars and projects, which could then be developed (off the campus in the field study term) into community development projects in teaching and organizing in the industrial cities of Michigan and the Midwest.

Similarly, foreign students and their American counterparts could do comparative studies of the educational problems of American and foreign cities, small towns, and villages by organizing two-year projects that would alternate study at Justin Morrill with field work in the United States and abroad. Since there are already 900 foreign students from 89 countries at the University, the possibility of recruiting Michigan State foreign students to help with the Justin Morrill teaching and project planning is clear, particularly since at this point the teaching talents of the foreign students, as far as the Michigan undergraduates are concerned, remain relatively unexplored.

Also relatively unexplored is the possibility of using the variety of international projects in which the University is engaged to support research and study by graduate as well as undergraduate students of education. I have been speculating, without knowing the difficulties involved, on what it would be like if each Michigan State faculty member abroad made himself responsible for at least three to five graduate or undergraduate students for placement and supervision in a learning situation either in connection with whatever might be the project which took him overseas or in some aspect of educational or community development in the area of his assignment. Other speculations entail the possibility that students themselves could be asked to devise projects that could be included in the general framework of Michigan State missions, could be tied directly to the College of Education, to the area studies centers on the East Lansing campus, and could send a mature graduate student with five undergraduates to one of the places where Michigan State holds contracts. Whether Justin Morrill College is the right center for developing such ideas is another question. But at least for the 1,200 undergraduates at the College there will be room, and perhaps even time, for speculation about what else can be done in linking the world to the campus and in creating a genuine international community at the College itself.

The College has already begun experimental work in the use of student teachers for courses in sociology through undergraduate discussion leaders and a member of the faculty who serves as senior scholar or roving supervisor for the student discussion groups. The point of view expressed by the faculty members who have planned this program is to develop the unused teaching talent of the students and to call upon their intellectual resourcefulness to find out for themselves the things they need to know. It would remain only to bring into their work on equal terms the exchange Peace Corps and foreign students who wish to join them in work having to do with international affairs and foreign cultures.

The Experiment in International Living

The example of Justin Morrill College as a planning base for the use of the Michigan State campus, the communities and schools nearby, and foreign countries as resources for the education of their students suggests another set of uses for international organizations whose business is not necessarily to educate teachers, or even students, but whose structural arrangements are such that they could be helpful to the educators of teachers. I am thinking particularly of the Experiment in International Living, which began 35 years ago as a small band of dedicated people who wished to apply the simple principle of bringing people into each other's homes and communities as a means of creating a better understanding between countries. The Experiment has now become a paraeducational

188

institution with connections throughout the world and a body of experience in conducting education that goes far beyond that found on most college campuses.

In one sense, the Experiment serves as a service organization: it places individuals and groups in one part of the world or another or provides, through contracts, parts of educational programs carried on by other institutions and organizations. In another sense, it serves as a source of ideas and energies that flow from a philosophy of education on which the Experiment is based; and, like the Peace Corps (with which it has had affiliations from the time the Peace Corps began), it has a very important educational function without having established its own formal institutions. The exception is the case of the Experiment's School for International Training, which alternates, over a 15-month period, study at the School in Brattleboro, Vermont, with placement in international organizations in various parts of the world.

Such is the skill and organizational talent within the Experiment that it would be quite feasible for any college of education interested in a program for teachers in international education to turn over a group of students for 12 to 18 months and trust the Experiment to turn them back again in a condition suitable for teaching with an international point of view in the American school system. What still seems unusual to most educators of teachers in the use of a varied set of experiences for preparing students to teach is a comparatively simple affair to the staff of the Experiment.

They concentrate on three essentials: (a) putting people together in living situations in which the relations between them have a full chance to become established at a serious personal level, (b) giving people access to the knowledge and information they need for the purposes for which the knowledge will be used, (c) providing common tasks—work projects, community development, joint research, independent study, teaching—in which the persons concerned can unite in a common effort. They propose no grand theory of education, they simply go ahead with the most direct way of making it possible for people to learn and to teach themselves whatever it is they need to know. Since 1961 they have trained 1,265 Peace Corps volunteers for service in 16 countries in skills ranging from rural public health, primary education, urban development, and school construction to credit unions and cooperatives. Since 1932, the Experiment has placed 22,991 persons in homes and communities around the world and 17,781 in this country, for a total of 40,772 persons. In one year, 1965-66, the Experiment dealt with 52 different groups from 24 different countries on every continent—468 persons in all, who came to the United States to learn at firsthand about their counterparts in engineering, the Girl Scouts, teaching, political science, student leadership, medicine, and other fields.

It will be obvious that the body of knowledge collected on the question of what to do to satisfy the interests and educational needs of teachers in world affairs would go much beyond the resources of most large univer-

189

sities and could be of very great importance—as it has proved to be in the case of Justin Morrill College—in institutions without large international program staffs of their own. When asked point-blank if the goal of 25,000 teachers and student teachers abroad each year would be a reasonable increase above the 18,000 American students now studying in 68 foreign countries, Gordon Boyce, president of the Experiment, immediately replied in the affirmative and mentioned several centers where numbers could be greatly increased, such as the University of Algiers (1 hour and 20 minutes by air from Paris) for the study of French and Arabic. It has an international student population ranging from Arabs to French and from Bulgarians to Chinese.

A plan by which several colleges of education in a given region of the United States combine forces with the Experiment to make a program of American and foreign study for periods of six months to a year would make available a whole variety of new plans, programs, and student placements beyond any yet contemplated, even by the Experiment.

Internationalism at San Francisco State College

During the course of the study I have had the opportunity to work in some detail with the faculty and administration of the College of Education at San Francisco State College on several ideas in international education that have relevance to colleges of education elsewhere. One of the central characteristics of San Francisco State College lies in its full acceptance of the fact that it is an urban institution with a student body composed of the full variety of the population whose needs it serves, from the young men and women who hold full-time or part-time jobs to the older men and women who wish to resume their education and to prepare for new careers. Since the late 1940's and early 1950's the School of Education has been involved in community education and in student field experience in community problems, ranging from juvenile delinquents and the educationally underprivileged to the relation of education to social and cultural change. In recent years, the approach to local and state problems has been transposed into a concern for international education by a natural process through which these problems have been seen as an integral part of the common concern of cities and rural areas in the world at large.

In consequence, not only has there been a rich and varied curriculum of cross-cultural and international studies available to undergraduates, both inside and outside the School of Education, but the College has involved itself directly in educational missions in West Africa, Brazil, India, Thailand, Liberia, Japan, Sweden, and Iran through AID and the Peace Corps, missions that have had an impact on the thinking and curricular developments on the San Francisco campus. Approximately one third of the faculty of the School of Education either have studied abroad or have served in international education programs abroad; and interdisciplinary and cross-cultural approaches to research, teaching, and learning have become central to the institutional development of the College as a whole.

For example, the School of Education has produced special programs of preparation for teachers to serve in the inner city with a cross-cultural nursery school project, an Upward Bound project, and a demonstration teacher education project for a suburb with pockets of cultural and educational deprivation. It also has held NDEA summer workshops for teachers of the culturally deprived. Through an urban studies center, which offers an undergraduate major for students in the School of Behavioral and Social Sciences, it has developed new curricular patterns that have a direct relation to the need for fresh thinking and action in coping with the educational problems of the expanding population of the inner cities of the United States.

The World Urban Teaching Center

Through a series of meetings, analyses, and working memoranda prepared by faculty members of the School of Education and bearing directly on the subject of the present study, the elements of a new and promising approach to the education of teachers in world affairs and world problems began to emerge and to form themselves into an idea that describes itself in the working title, World Urban Teaching Center. In the language of one such memorandum—

> Among educators interested in the international implications of education the realization is growing rapidly that professional and technical assistance must be channeled in ways that help nations to help themselves; that improvement in the qualitative aspects of life within nations depends fundamentally upon human development. . . . This means educational reform, innovation, and extension of educational opportunity, in ways relevant to a particular culture and its severest problems; they reside in problems of health, nutrition, human understanding, conflict or alienation born of affluence. . . . Recent experience in the international education field, including the AID programs, Crossroads Africa, the Peace Corps, student exchanges, and others, is helping us to see that in helping educate others we educate ourselves and learn much from other nations, that in contributing to the economic and social well-being of nations less fully developed, our own well-being as a nation is maintained and improved.[32]

The idea that the development of programs of international education on American campuses, combined with faculty and student service abroad, is a major benefit to the enrichment of American education and social well-being is one which reverses the usual rationale for American international involvement. It confirms one of the major findings of the present study, that the introduction of the international component raises the level of aspiration, interest, and commitment of American student teachers and faculty members. The corollary idea that within the American city we have in microcosm the problems of the world's cities suggests an immediate way in which American education can be linked directly to world systems of

---

[32] McKenna, Bernard, and Smith, Robert. *The Need To Strengthen the Resources of Higher Education Through Programs for International Education and Education for World Affairs.* San Francisco: School of Education, San Francisco State College, November 1966. (Memorandum) See also Taylor, Harold. *Draft Proposal for a World Urban Teaching Center.* April 1966. (Mimeo.)

191

education by concentration on common urban problems by multinational groups of students and teachers who would come together in regional world centers, as suggested elsewhere, for cooperative research, action, field experience, and curricular development.

The Rationale

There are three major propositions on which the concept of a World Urban Teaching Center rests.

1. The world's political, economic, cultural, and social power is centered in the world's cities, which over the past 25 years have experienced an enormous immigration of families and persons (usually uneducated, poor, and untrained) from the rural areas and a sharp increase in educational, political, and economic problems. In the case of the developing countries in Asia, Africa, and Latin America, the major political power and the major social developments, in some cases produced by revolution and insurrection, have centered in the cities. Many governments have only to control the political and social instruments of one or two major cities to control the entire country.

2. The world's major intellectual and political community is gathered together in the cities. The greatest forces toward internationalism, cosmopolitanism, and cultural and social power of the world are concentrated in the major capitals.

3. The world's cities have developed a large array of common problems—ranging from transportation to water pollution, health services, and housing and education—that can and must be solved by the most intense efforts in education, social planning, and economic reform. The solution of these problems is not only crucial to the welfare of those who live in the present cities, from Calcutta to Djakarta, Nairobi to New York, but is crucial to world peace and stability. The frustrations of the urban peoples, their rapidly rising expectations for which the means of fulfillment does not yet exist, breed isolation, aggression, distortion of perception, and political anarchy. In their power of destruction and potential unmanageability, they pose the kind of severe internal problems which disrupt the lives of whole nations and spread the elements of disaster far beyond the city limits into the politics of the world.

The Possibilities at San Francisco State College

These propositions furnish part of the ground for a continuing discussion conducted by members of the San Francisco State College faculty during the academic year 1966-67. That discussion called upon the experience and conclusions of the Department of Interdisciplinary Studies in Education, which had already taken action to authorize staff members of the School to explore with other departments in the School and in the College as a whole to work out ways of increasing all-College work in international education.

192

In what follows, I wish to report some aspects of the discussions with the San Francisco group as an example of the way in which fresh thinking for international education and the education of teachers has developed and can develop within a given institutional setting, with the major initiative coming from the School of Education within the institution. In doing so, I do not wish to invade the privacy of the College or to suggest commitments and planned programs that do not in fact exist. That is a matter for the School, the College, and its administrative officers and governing bodies to determine. What I have to say about the possibilities and merits of the ideas involved is the outcome of the research study and is applicable to institutions as various in character as Wayne State University, Southern Illinois University, and Temple University, where similar discussions were carried on.

San Francisco State College, as previously noted, has had experience with AID missions abroad; the most important assignment that the College is now responsible for is a nine-year project in developing a modern school system in Monrovia, Liberia. The School of Education—one of the five institutions in the country that graduate the largest number of qualified teachers annually—for 15 years has had direct relations with most of the elementary and secondary schools within a radius of 25 miles of the campus and with more than 100 youth and health service agencies of the metropolitan area of San Francisco. From 2,000 to 3,000 students have been involved in related field experience each year. With Ford Foundation and National Institute of Mental Health funds, it has in the past worked on programs of teaching internships and programs for mental health education. As a result of these and other projects at the College, faculty and administrative personnel with interests in cross-cultural and international education have been added to the staff over the years and furnish the manpower and cumulative experience on which further advances can be made in the international field.

Briefly, the plan for a World Urban Teaching Center would involve support by the federal government and foundations, possibly through the International Education Act at the time funds are granted for the development of undergraduate centers as provided by the Act. Selected students recruited from abroad, possibly in collaboration with the Volunteers to America project now under way, would join with other foreign students preparing to become teachers who are already in the United States. The selection would include (a) students who had had one to three years of experience in teaching and education in their own countries and (b) graduate students mature enough to be able to take part in seminars and tutorial sessions, for which they would be mainly responsible.

Faculty members from universities and teacher education institutions abroad would be invited to the Center for joint research and field experience on a multinational basis with their colleagues in San Francisco. Research could be done not only on the social, economic, and educational problems of the city, but on world curriculums; textbooks that could be used

in various countries for a variety of age groups; new collections of translations of world literature; and the mental and physical health aspects of
education, including nutrition, medical technology, housing, school construction, social work, and other areas, depending on the interests of the
San Francisco faculty and the interests of the visitor.

Modes of Cooperation

The method of teaching and learning would be consonant with the
approach of much of the work of the School of Education and would
include teams of foreign and American students working together in reverse
Peace Corps style in community development and practice teaching in San
Francisco schools and neighborhoods. In other instances, students and
teachers from abroad interested in rural problems, agriculture, public
health, and rural development could do field work in the rural areas of
California in connection with the department of agriculture programs,
possibly in new programs that might be developed at Chico State College
where the rural setting and teacher education interests could combine to
furnish an extension of the Center's work in San Francisco.

Opportunities for interdisciplinary research and program development
are clear. Just as the tutorial movement among college students teaching
children in the slums has brought the contemporary student in touch with
the housing, employment, educational, and racial problems of life in the
inner city, field work done by students of anthropology, sociology, social
psychology, and political science in teams with foreign students would
enrich the total curriculum and aid the foreign student to understand these
problems in the context of his own culture. This form of operational
research, unfamiliar to most foreign students and teachers, would give both
to them and to the Americans who worked with them a chance to develop
a greater degree of sophistication and sensitivity in finding solutions to the
educational problems of the urban communities.

For example, in the Liberian project at San Francisco State, 10 to 15
qualified students who had previously studied the language and culture are
assigned to go with faculty members to Liberia on a work-study basis for
periods from three months to a year as a regular part of their teacher preparation. Similarly, in education projects on Vietnam—which are carried out
by Ohio University, Athens, Ohio, and by Southern Illinois University,
Carbondale, Illinois—education students are attached to faculty members in
the overseas mission, with faculty members and students from Vietnam
imported into the teaching and educational programs of the practice teaching and laboratory schools in and around Athens and Carbondale.

In connection with the curriculum and research in social science and
education, the visiting members of the Center could work in multinational
seminars on problems related to economic and social development, peace
and war, disarmament, and conflict of ideologies. Through the seminars
they would have the opportunity, so very difficult to come by, to confront
persons, ideas, and attitudes that spring from the experience of people

194

unlike themselves, people who have been educated and conditioned by their own particular national culture. The Center could, in some sense, become an intellectual counterpart to the United Nations, except that its purpose would be not to settle political conflicts but to understand their setting in the cultural and educational conditions of world society.

The Community and Internationalism

The effect of a World Center on the college or university in which it was located and on the community surrounding the college would be to increase markedly the awareness of the students, faculty, and community that we in America share with the citizens of other countries a set of life problems connected with living together in the cities and that we also share the means of helping to solve them. The thrust of these problems into the consciousness of Americans and the response of the foreign student and teacher to experiences that he has shared with his American counterpart would lift the usual education available to the foreign visitor—which is one-sided at best—to a level of internationalism unavailable by any other means.

In Calcutta, for example, the problem of the destitutes who crowd the streets has never been directly dealt with since it is generally assumed that there is nothing to be done about them and certainly nothing to be done through education. Whether or not a visiting student or teacher would return home to Calcutta from San Francisco armed with new knowledge and experience that could remedy Calcutta's educational and economic problems, he would at the very least have had an insight into the ways in which such remedies can possibly be found and into the principle implicit in the San Francisco program. It is the responsibility of colleges, cities, and states to try to find such remedies. On our side, at the very least, we would have had the benefit of another pair of hands, another trained intelligence, and another point of view in working on the question of how to improve urban education in San Francisco.

The Student Contribution

The students at San Francisco State College have a considerable amount of educational talent to contribute to international education through the spontaneity and vigor of their efforts at educational reform. One area for which they have taken responsibility has resulted in the formation of an Experimental College staffed and taught by students to each other, in courses of their own making and their own choosing. There were approximately 1,000 students enrolled in 90 such student-taught courses in 1966-67. During the visits for this study, I conferred with the student leaders most active in the experiment, since I had followed the work of the student body in previous years and had known something of the origin of their ideas.

As was the case on other campuses, the students found the idea of working actively in the field of teacher education or of world affairs (in the sense in which these terms are used among educators) to be alien to their central interests. The Experimental College had grown out of a combination of interest in education aroused by the student tutorial movement and dissatisfaction with existing courses and methods of instruction. It is a tribute to the imagination and good sense of both the College students and faculty that the answer the students found to their own questions on how to improve undergraduate education was to invent programs of their own, a good many of which earn academic credit toward the B.A. degree when led by invited faculty members.

In doing so, the students hit upon content and methods of instruction that were quite close to those which would have been suggested by progressive educators in the experimental colleges, although the students developed their programs not on a knowledge of the theory and practice of progressive education but simply on what they decided they wanted to do. In so doing they made the obvious connection in many of the courses they designed between experience in the community—in the arts, in teaching children, and in dealing with juvenile delinquents or racial tensions—and the research literature, readings, and discussions related to the live experience.

Yet when asked if they intended, through the Experimental College, to do something new and fresh about the education of teachers, they replied that that would deflect them from the interests that had brought them into the formation of their College in the first place. I pointed out that in many ways they had already formed a college for teachers by turning their own students loose to teach each other and that as they went along they would find that the students able to sustain the interest of their fellows for an entire semester would have to have at least more skill and talent for teaching than the members of their classes. This they admitted, and they cited instances in which the classes disintegrated because of failures by the student teachers.

When I asked about the relation between their College and the School of Education and whether or not many of their student teachers intended to take teaching certificates and enter the profession, the answer was "no." In the discussion that followed, I discovered that they were not aware that, like themselves, the School of Education offered a sizable number of courses which used practical experience in the community as an integral part of the method of instruction and of meeting certification requirements.

When we turned to the topic of world affairs and the education of teachers, I found that it was even harder for them to make the relation between teacher education and world affairs than it was to see the relevance of teaching to courses in education. This may have been because they did not think of the Vietnam issue—or American foreign policy issues in general—as related to the regular educational program of the College, but as issues on which they had strong feelings, which they demonstrated on the campus by meetings, teach-ins, speeches, and other means.

Students and World Affairs

In other words, these students were without a doubt leaders in educational reform on the campus, but they thought of themselves as persons actively engaged in carrying on education itself rather than trying to develop a new system of education for teachers, or even for students, in the context of the College as a whole. I believe that the contribution they have made, not merely to the enrichment of the intellectual and social environment at San Francisco State but to the development of projects similar to their own on other campuses, is a serious and important one. It is the basis for one set of answers to the drastic need for reform of undergraduate teaching and the education of teachers.

If into their situation it were possible to inject a group of foreign students who would work with them in joint projects of educational change, practice teaching, seminars, and research, their own education and social thinking would unavoidably move in a much wider international direction. We discussed the possibility of a World Student Center with connections both to a World Urban Teaching Center at the College and to the East-West Center in Honolulu. This, they agreed, would be an important development for students at the College and should be included in visible form by physical arrangements for such a Center for 40 to 50 foreign students in the new student center now being planned for construction. But their interest lay in the extension of the student role in educational policy making on the campus and in conducting their own College—not in developing new programs either in teacher education or international affairs. Although the situation varies from campus to campus, this is true of most of the leadership among the student bodies where educational reform has become a live issue.

If, in one form or another, the World Urban Teaching Center could be established at San Francisco State College and/or elsewhere, it would serve as the basis for further international developments—both in the direction of regional world centers linked together through common interests in problems of the kind discussed here and through the serious need for more and more teachers, students, and knowledge of teaching everywhere in the world. A center of this kind established at New York University and linked to the educational, social, and public service agencies of New York City—including the United Nations and the dozens of international and national organizations concerned with teaching—would have a stimulating effect on the whole city and on the extension of present programs of international affairs into the school system itself. Whatever problems other cities may have, New York City has more of them (and usually more serious ones, especially in the educational sector). The city could do with a great deal of help from abroad, and could very well make more educational use of the presence in its institutions of higher education of the 9,000 foreign students currently enrolled.

What a World Urban Teaching Center Might Achieve

Although San Francisco State College can not be considered typical of other colleges where teachers are prepared, either in the cities or elsewhere, were its work in international education to move in the direction indicated by the preliminary planning for a world center of this kind, it could have a serious effect on the thinking and planning of other colleges with similar interests. Under the heading "What a World Urban Teaching Center Might Achieve" the faculty group at San Francisco has said in an excerpt from a paper prepared for discussion among interested colleagues: [33]

Such a Center, sustained by the School of Education, the College, and the metropolitan areas they serve, should be able to—

1. Provide improved strategies for teaching and learning in large urban centers of the world.

2. Contribute to cooperative relations among cities and nations of the world and the reduction of destructive conflict, as a result of a direct intellectual and working association among emerging educational leaders from major urban centers of the world.

3. Provide direct assistance both here and abroad to urban school systems, colleges, and universities in program development relevant to varying cultures and urban settings.

4. Deepen the self-awareness of urban educators as they confront the stubborn problems of urban education both here and in other national settings.

5. Broaden perspectives of teachers, supervisory personnel, and college professors on the educational process specifically, and cultural studies generally.

6. Capitalize more fully on the contributions of international students in improving the scholarly and qualitative aspects of college campus life.

7. Improve ways of relating the world and insights of students and scholars to those from other nations in college and university settings.

8. Develop more functional approaches which lead to programs for guest students and faculty that will enable them to cope more effectively with their professional roles in their own cultures.

9. Develop a learning resources center in cooperation with our library, its materials and publications to be placed at the service of participating nations, educational institutions, metropolitan centers, and professionals involved in urban education.

10. Strengthen the competence of our own college faculty in the crucial areas of intercultural and international education as well as in urban education and world affairs.

11. Prepare nationals from a number of countries to work more effectively in educational programs in nations other than their own.

12. Contribute to a fabric of international associations and communications and a common fund of experience among educators that goes beyond national interests and experience.

13. Work to develop a model center for developing and testing cross cultural approaches to educational problems of a related nature which are challenging many nations.

---

[33] Hansen, R.; McKenna, B.; Simpson, R.; Smith, R.; and Webb, L. "Toward a World Urban Teaching Center at San Francisco State College: A Working Paper." San Francisco: School of Education, San Francisco State College, November 7, 1966.

The idea of World Urban Teaching Centers, or their counterparts in rural centers modeled on the Justin Morrill and Antioch plans, can be transferred intact or in parts to other institutions here and abroad. Certainly the American urban universities are in an ideal position to serve as central agencies for international urban problems. The fact that urban studies centers in American universities are already growing in numbers and in size makes the inclusion of an international educational component in their future work a natural part of their growing influence and usefulness. They have already influenced the thinking of city planners abroad. It remains now to turn their attention toward world education.

Chapter 4.　The Certification Question

> I believe that all reforms which rest simply upon the enactment of law, or the threatening of certain penalties, or upon changes in mechanical or outward arrangements, are transitory and futile.
>
> John Dewey
> *Reconstruction in Philosophy*

Among educators in recent years there has been a growing amount of discussion and a fair degree of controversy about the certification of teachers. I have never been able to take the question of certification with the high seriousness it commands among many, both critics and proponents. Instead, I have held the oversimplified view that the philosophy, history, psychology, principles, methods, or foundations of education, whatever a course may be called, if it has to do with education, it can by that reason be one of the most useful, fascinating, and intellectually stimulating undertakings in the whole university curriculum. I also hold the ordinary view that the test of the worth of a teacher lies in his demonstrated ability to teach from a body of knowledge and experience he has fully made his own, not from the number of courses he has taken in a certification program.

Now that I have studied the question in far greater detail during the present research, I hold the same oversimplified views, although more strongly than before. After visiting a full array of classes in education, it seems to me that the main problem in certification is inherent in the emptiness, irrelevance, and redundancy of so many of the education courses, not primarily in the rigidity of the requirements. I believe that it is up to the colleges of education to use the responsibility that is already theirs to modify and enrich the content of the work they ask their students to do. They and the state departments of education must see to it that the requirements are minimal in number, maximal in relevance, and administered with a degree of flexibility not sufficiently apparent at present among the certifiers.

I would also like to see everyone in education spend a great deal less time discussing certification requirements and all the rules about them and free themselves for more time to raise questions about what they should be doing to make education interesting and engrossing to those undergoing it. Certification is a bookkeeping problem and should be treated that way. Yet it now involves hundreds of people whose talents could find better use than in holding endless discussions, conferences, and management sessions about standard setting, coordination, units of credit, and the rest of it in the interlocking agencies of the state legislature, the state boards of education, the national and regional accrediting bodies, the National Council for the Accreditation of Teacher Education, the National Association of State Directors of Teacher Education and Certification, and the National Commission on Teacher Education and Professional Standards, among a good many others.

There is something about certification and licensure which, once it becomes ingrained in the consciousness of those who think in its terms, has the effect of narrowing the range of educational discussion into a set of details essentially unrelated to education itself. Like all modes of regulation, it comes at the subject it regulates in an essentially negative mood—it demands observance rather than inciting fresh action. It can therefore be used equally well as an alibi for the acquiescent or a club for the stern, a challenge for the rebel or a defense of the status quo.

The fallacy in taking the whole apparatus of licensure so seriously is that education itself is already too formally conceived. What we need is not more rules and administration but more excitement and display of intellectual energy. The less concentration there is on the eternal ordering of requirements, both inside and outside the schools and colleges, the more attention can be given to the process and content of education itself. Otherwise, education soon becomes a series of structures designed to hold prearranged content. Like the teacher-proof curriculum, it produces the student-proof certificate.

The most definitive analysis of the system by which teachers are granted certificates has been made by James Conant in *The Education of American Teachers.*[1] In his judgment, the state departments, with their close connections to the professional education associations and the professional educators, exercise so tight a grip on certification requirements, and therefore on the pattern of teacher education, that Mr. Conant not only considered this to be the central problem in the education of teachers, but urged the removal of the responsibility for certification from the state departments to the individual colleges and universities where teachers are prepared.[2]

---

[1] Conant, James B. *The Education of American Teachers.* New York: McGraw-Hill Book Co., 1963. 275 pp.

[2] According to the replies of the state departments of education in 1964 and 1967 in responding to a National Education Association research question, the responsibility was already in the hands of the colleges since 40 states reported the use of some kind of approved-program approach by which the state departments accept for certification as teachers those recommended by the college in programs previously agreed upon by the college and the state department.

The effect of Mr. Conant's criticisms and recommendations, along with previous and subsequent discussions of the impact of accrediting agencies, state requirements, and the whole problem of bureaucracy in teacher education, has been to assign a heavy degree of responsibility for the obstruction of new programs of teacher education to the inhibiting effect of the requirements themselves and the agencies that insist on them. The popular way of saying it is to complain that Albert Einstein would not be allowed to teach physics in the high school or even in the third grade; he would not have met the certification requirements or taken the proper courses. Each of us can submit his own horror stories. They are many and they are true. But the point is that there are specific ways in which the regulations can be changed, and that is what we should be talking about.

Another effect of Mr. Conant's book, and of the seriousness with which it has been taken in the public discussion of the education of teachers, has been to concentrate attention on requirements in general and on the structure of the curriculum—number of credit hours, sequence of studies, minimum standards, major and minor fields—rather than on its content; on the need for release of teacher education from the restrictions of the bureaucracy, rather than on the way in which the bureaucracies and agencies of education can work for improvement in the quality and breadth of education in general. What I would like to do in this section of the Report is to see how the bureaucracies can best use their resources in educating teachers. No matter what else can be said about them as a massive establishment, the agencies of federal, state, and local governments, along with the educational associations and private organizations, are composed of people working at educational problems—some of which are regulatory, others administrative and responsive to policies set elsewhere. The growth of bureaucracy is a necessary outcome of the massive spread of popular education; and this being the case, ways must be found to use its size and strength on behalf of wise and enlightened policies.

Where the Problem Is

The requirements for teacher certification are administered by state departments of education. But that is a comparatively simple matter. The crucial point is that the requirements themselves are developed and formulated mostly by deans, departmental chairmen, and professors of education in the teacher education institutions and that the requirements are heavily influenced by a variety of educational organizations, each with its own pressures for courses and credits in given disciplines—chemistry, health education, English, mathematics, and others. The state department is often in the role of referee rather than combatant; in many cases it needs protection rather than attack.

If the present requirements are standing in the way of educational programs that could develop in teachers an awareness of the world in its

202

larger dimensions, then something should be done about them and some changes should be made. Conversely, if changes in the requirements would make a positive difference in encouraging new work of an international kind, then they should be made for that reason. I started the present analysis by trying to see the character of whatever inhibitions now exist and to find out what initiatives have been taken or could be taken for developing programs likely to produce teachers with a world dimension to their thinking.

It seemed to me that it would be useful, in addition to studying the certification literature, to have a direct response from the state certification officers to some specific questions about Peace Corps volunteers and that their responses would be useful in assessing what should be done, if anything, about revision of requirements. The case of the Peace Corps volunteer is a good testing point for bureaucratic rigidities, since the teaching experience abroad is of a two-year duration and the initial selection of the volunteer is very carefully done. Only one out of six to eight applicants is chosen for training, in contrast with almost automatic acceptance of applicants for teacher education programs. Eventual selection of the Peace Corps volunteer who goes overseas is made over the course of several months of intensive training and observation, during which 10 to 25 percent of the candidates are dropped. In addition, the returned volunteer has usually had not only two years of teaching disadvantaged children, but experience in direct work with parents, principals, and community problems as well as with his pupils. Any regulations applying to a volunteer with these qualifications would certainly apply doubly to others with foreign experience.

A Survey of State Requirements

To learn what I could about the attitudes and programs involved in certification, I wrote to the certification officers in each of the states to explain the study and to ask three questions. I made one of the questions specifically on the state department's attitude about certification toward Peace Corps, VISTA, and field experience to focus attention on the certification problems involved. The questions were these:

1. Have you made any changes in the teacher certification requirements to allow credit for service in the Peace Corps, VISTA, tutorial programs, and other forms of practical teaching experience? The reason I ask is that I am recommending that teachers be educated by direct experience with social issues and problems, both in the U.S. and abroad. Many who agree with me about the importance of this kind of experience tell me that it is an impractical idea since the state certification requirements would prevent the award of credit for anything but the regular academic and professional courses. What would be your own response to this kind of problem?

2. In *The Education of American Teachers* Mr. Conant criticized

the state certification provisions as a major obstacle in the reform of teacher education. Do you feel that the requirements in your state prevent experiments and new developments that otherwise would be happening in the colleges and universities?

3. Do you see any special trends in teacher education in your state? In the direction of more interest in foreign affairs and world issues, for example? Has your department interested itself in any projects to increase the international emphasis?

The replies ranged from a simple "no," written in the margin by the side of questions 1 and 2, with the notation, "We do not control the teacher training program in our state colleges" to some serious and thoughtful letters from state directors who discussed the problem, enclosed further information, and presented their own views.

According to the replies, the only state which unequivocally accepts Peace Corps experience in teaching abroad as a qualification for receiving a certificate to teach in the United States is California, where in 1965 the legislature passed enabling legislation to make this mandatory. The language of the education code[3] is as follows:

> Notwithstanding any other provision of this code to the contrary, the minimum requirements for the standard teacher credential with a specialization in elementary teaching, secondary teaching, or junior college teaching may be met by compliance with all of the following:
>
> (a) Four years or its equivalent of university or college education.
>
> (b) A baccalaureate degree or higher degree from an institution approved by State Board of Education.
>
> (c) A major and a minor, one of which shall be in an academic subject matter and one of which may be in a nonacademic subject matter area normally taught in the public schools.
>
> (d) Certification by the institution that the applicant has satisfactorily completed all academic subject matter courses which he would otherwise have had to complete to be issued a standard teacher credential with the specified specialization applied for.
>
> (e) Certification by the director of the Peace Corps of the United States that the applicant has satisfactorily completed not less than eighteen (18) months in the Peace Corps assignment in a foreign country, during which time fifty percent (50%) or more of the duties consisted of teaching resident children or adults of the foreign country.
>
> An applicant meeting the requirements of this section shall not be required to complete any education or methodology courses or meet any other requirement relating to education or training.

A further addition to the education code allows for the waiver of student teaching requirements for administrative, supervisory, and counseling certificates if the candidates have had certain kinds of field experience as part of an approved program of an "experimental, exploratory, or pilot program of preparation for such a credential."

The most frequent response to the question about field experience was that although no specific changes had been made in certification

---

[3] Statutes of 1965, State of California, Department of Education. Chapter 1473.

requirements to accommodate returned Peace Corps volunteers, VISTA workers, or others, the certification officers believed that present arrangements for temporary certificates and the ability of the universities and colleges of education to grant credit for what they considered to be appropriate teaching and professional experience give qualified persons the opportunity to become teachers without too much trouble. Except in a few isolated cases, I found no unwillingness among state officers to consider the problem seriously or to look for ways in which practical experience in the field could be given credit. Since the academic faculty usually resist the notion that direct cultural and social experience, i.e., that anything outside formal classroom teaching, has educational value, this point of view is usually reflected in the state regulations.

A typical and fair reply on this point from one of the moderate conservatives reads as follows:

> We have not made any changes in the certification rules in the State of .... to allow credit for service in the Peace Corps, VISTA, and other programs of this type. Certainly we are not disinterested in teachers having experience with social issues and problems, both in the United States and abroad. We do feel, however, that this type of experience does not make up for the specific kind of preparation the teacher should have to teach children in the public school setting in this country and that if this type of experience is to be substituted as part of the teacher's educational program, some basis should be worked out for identifying what kind and how much of such preparation can be accepted with gain, and without loss, to the teacher education program generally.

Eleven states grant temporary certificates to returned Peace Corps volunteers under certain circumstances—Kentucky, Maryland, Mississippi, Montana, New York, Oregon, Pennsylvania, South Dakota, Texas, Vermont, Washington.

Nine states and the District of Columbia allow Peace Corps teaching experience as a substitute for the student teaching part of the professional requirements: Alaska, Hawaii, Maine, Maryland, Nebraska, New York, North Carolina, Puerto Rico, Rhode Island.

Five states have a policy of review in individual cases: Hawaii, New Jersey, Utah, Washington, Wisconsin.

Four states give partial credit toward either the renewal of the certificate or toward a permanent certificate: Michigan, North Carolina, Pennsylvania, Vermont. New Mexico reports the beginning of adjustments in its provisions in cooperation with the University of New Mexico. Colorado State College in Greeley, Colorado, with the state department's approval and encouragement, enrolls returned Peace Corps volunteers who have degrees and foreign teaching experience in a summer of professional study followed by a one-year internship at half-pay under supervision. If all goes well, they are recommended for certification at the end of the three-semester program.

A 1964 survey by the New York State Education Department found that 28 states grant "some sort of credit for overseas experience. Such experience must in general be related to the individual's teaching field.

In some cases, this credit is only for renewal of teaching certificates; in others, overseas experience may be used in lieu of student teaching or other professional experience."[4]

The most common procedure for dealing with Peace Corps returnees and other special cases of people who have had field experience abroad or in this country is to have the candidate enroll in an accredited teacher training program. Once in the program, the candidate's experience in the Peace Corps or elsewhere can be evaluated by the faculty or administration, and allowance toward certification requirements can be made on an individual basis. Most of the replies emphasized that the individual institutions could do most of what they wanted to do under the present regulations, provided the teacher education programs were carefully conceived and backed by the appropriate faculty and administration approval at the college or university. Although state department officers might regret the fact that college authorities were backward in granting credits to students and teachers with foreign experience, they felt powerless to do anything but accept the recommendations for grants of credit as these were made by the colleges. An Eastern-state certification officer writes, "We approve teacher education programs that deviate markedly from the minimum certification regulations. These programs are designed by creative teacher educators. We encourage this."

The problem of how foreign experience can properly be evaluated came up again and again in the replies. When you have the students with you in a classroom or you watch them teach children in a local school, you have a better idea of what they are actually doing. Although some certification officers expressed doubt about field experience of all kinds, most felt that a reasonable evaluation could be worked out by the teacher education institutions themselves. As one officer reported:

> The State Department of Education is not an operational agency comparable to a college and the evaluation of individual experiences poses problems difficult to handle in the mass numbers that must be handled by a very limited staff. Possibly the matter of evaluating individual experiences falls more upon the colleges that traditionally have evaluated educational programs and experiences completed before or during attendance of the student at their institution.

A typical and vigorous statement, placing the responsibility on the colleges and universities, came from one officer who said:

> The belief that state certification requirements are the main obstacle to educational progress is so deep-seated that any attempt to show the fallacy of this reasoning gives the appearance of defending "lichen-covered requirements." . . . If we have certification requirements which are not desirable, the leaders in . . . . colleges and universities are at fault. Certification requirements in . . . . are determined by an Advisory Council which has been in existence since 1940. If our regulations are too exacting, the blame can be placed on college representatives who dominate the membership. The State Department of Education has three votes on a Council composed of 43 members.

---

[4] The State Department of Education, The University of the State of New York. *American Education in a Revolutionary World: The Role of the States.* Albany: the Department, 1964. p. 15.

Some Special Arrangements

The most enterprising state department of education as far as the returning Peace Corps volunteers are concerned is New York State, which deals with them in three complementary ways.

1. A liaison officer appointed by the state visits the major training centers of the Peace Corps so he can be in a position to decide on the credit to be given in the professional education courses designed to prepare the Peace Corps volunteers for teaching.

2. The State Department of Education organized a statewide conference in New York City in August 1966, at which 100 returned volunteers were put in touch with school superintendents. The result was that 50 volunteers were appointed to teach in public schools in the state. A 1967 conference was also held.

3. It is a practice of the State Department to allow "solid teaching experience" in the United States or abroad to take the place of the regular student teaching, and the Department is now working on programs for evaluating that experience through the College Proficiency Examination Center, which is now operating in 20 locations throughout the state.

Other colleges of education, working with their state departments of certification, have organized special programs for returned volunteers. These programs usually involve an internship during which the candidate can earn a salary while in preparation and can take professional courses as needed. As of early 1967 there were 23 such programs around the country.

In addition, 17 school systems (mainly in the East), in cooperation with state departments of education, have shown a special interest in recruiting returned Peace Corps volunteers for teaching service precisely because of their foreign experience. One of them, the Cardozo Program in Washington, D.C., was organized especially to recruit and prepare the returnees for service in the school.

Among other special arrangements are the following:

• Western Michigan University has an experimental teacher training program, accepted by the state department in collaboration with the Peace Corps in Michigan, by which candidates may credit 12 semester hours for the three-month Peace Corps training program toward a degree at Western Michigan University. Field work and independent study abroad are also credited toward the degree.

• North Carolina will credit Peace Corps experience by adding increments to a teacher's salary rating.

• Vermont allows special certificate privileges for returning Peace Corps volunteers.

• Washington has flexible arrangements for temporary certificates. Provision for individual cases is handled in the office of the superintendent of public instruction.

• The North Dakota state legislature, which has the final say on requirements for the certification of teachers, includes a section in its legislation expressly enabling teacher education institutions to experiment with programs of their own, which could include those organized for Peace Corps returnees if the North Dakota institutions wished to do so. Michigan has similar legislation.

General Conclusions

On the basis of the findings the following general conclusions can be drawn:

1. While there has been no inclination among the states to grant blanket credit toward teacher certification for practical experience in teaching in foreign schools by Peace Corps volunteers or others, there has been a general acceptance of the validity of requests for such recognition.

2. Through either the "approved program," by which within certain limits the individual institutions can take responsibility for certifying that teachers have met state requirements, or through flexible administration of present requirements by the state officers, Peace Corps returnees and others with foreign teaching experience can receive in most states academic recognition for their work abroad.

3. The state officers and most professional educators assume that some actual experience of teaching in the American schools and some knowledge of the history and philosophy of American education is a necessary prerequisite for certification, no matter what other kinds of experience a teacher candidate may have had.

4. There has not yet been any general tendency for certification agencies to take the initiative in changing the requirements in order to encourage new work in the international sector.

5. The certification officers do not believe that state requirements are blocking educational progress, but that the colleges and universities do their own blocking by the way they deal with their own requirements.

The Negative Influence

After reviewing the situation on the campuses and talking with faculty members and students in the colleges of education and the arts and science divisions, I found that in their minds there *is* a problem and that a large proportion of university people, both students and faculty, consider state requirements to be both excessive and inhibiting. On the one hand, certification officers say that their regulations represent the views of educators and that if changes are needed, they can be made through the regular process of developing new programs in the colleges. "To some of us," says one certification officer, "it seems that 'the education department won't allow it' is a convenient excuse."

On the other hand, students and faculty members, especially those from the arts and science divisions, believe that the combination of the rules made by state legislatures, the accrediting and certification associations, and the state departments of education present a major inhibition to the development of new forms of international education as well as other kinds of preparation for teachers. What seems to me to be closest to the truth is that when serious efforts are made by men of independent mind and informed judgment in the universities and in the colleges and departments of education to carry out programs of whose value they are deeply convinced, the state requirements, whatever they may be, do not prevent the programs from being put into effect.

The main problem is that of developing institutional backing within the universities for new ideas, of developing initiatives among the educators themselves, which can then form the basis for changes in requirements where changes are needed. Even in the State of California—where the state legislature has taken an excessive role in regulating teacher education—the variation among individual institutions in the quality and character of their programs is still the most important factor in determining what happens to students. A semester in international education spent in foreign experience and accredited by a given college or university is acceptable under state requirements. As one member of an education faculty in a Midwestern university put it, "I can certify students of mine from the Peace Corps or from Mississippi if they have had practical teaching experience outside the regular system. If they satisfy the requirements of my courses, and if I honestly think that their practical experience is the equivalent of the requirements set by the state, the state approves."

The difficulty, described elsewhere in this Report, lies in the reluctance of the educators who work within the system of the universities and colleges of education to allow change and innovation to become a regular part of their educational planning. That is why educators of more liberal persuasion have found more satisfaction in working with VISTA, Head Start, and National Teacher Corps projects than with programs initiated by the formal procedures of the universities and colleges. For the same reason, the innovations developed by volunteer students in tutoring children in the inner cities are much more satisfying to the students than the regular programs in which they would enroll were they to take the regular certification courses.

As far as the international dimension is concerned, the overriding consideration in every situation is the need for faculty members who have a full degree of knowledge of non-Western countries and a high degree of motivation for doing something with it in the education of teachers. Whenever there are faculty members with appropriate qualifications or wherever there are programs in operation to develop such faculty members, things begin to move. This is also true of students, even those who have had as short an experience abroad as a summer with the Experiment in International Living or with the Friends Service Committee and, of course, particularly those who have had a longer experience with the International

Voluntary Service or the Peace Corps. When such students come together on the same campus with faculty members with international interests and experience, new ideas for curricular change are generated by their mutual efforts.

The Education Courses

To obtain more direct access to the facts of the certification problem and its attendant controversies in the matter of "liberal" as against "professional" courses, practice teaching, and the study of methods, we visited a cross-section of classes in the liberal arts and in education courses. In connection with these visits, I made a brief survey of the texts commonly used in the preparation of teachers through education courses. Since the purpose of the visits and the review of texts and methods of instruction was to examine the realities and possibilities of education in world affairs, rather than to analyze the entire problem of education courses in relation to certification requirements, the research results are not intended to give a definitive answer to questions that have received much fuller treatment elsewhere, more particularly in Mr. Conant's studies. The conclusions of our study are based on a modest and incomplete sample of some 61 class visits and a survey of 45 typical texts in use in education courses themselves.

Although the requirements for professional education courses, general education courses, practice teaching, an academic major, and methods courses vary greatly among types of institutions (both for elementary and secondary school preparation), the teacher education programs in our sample ask for 50 to 65 semester hours in general education, 10 to 25 hours in a major field, 15 to 30 hours in education courses, 12 to 30 hours in methods courses, and 8 to 14 hours in practice teaching. The variations in quality of teaching in the education courses were staggering and ranged from methods courses—which, since they were related to direct experience of students with children in school and the community, were vibrant and full of interesting educational ideas and practical content—to courses that were obviously a waste of time for everyone concerned. Unfortunately, I must report that the latter kind predominated.

I do not wish to join in the general denunciation of education and methods courses, except to say that in most of those we visited and in most of the texts reviewed I found little intellectual nourishment and little practical help in becoming a good teacher. The heart of the matter lies in giving the student who intends to become a teacher a direct experience in teaching children early in his preparation, preferably in high school, and certainly not later than the freshman year in college, so that the study of the methods and content of education as a discipline and a body of knowledge can give him something to which he can respond from his own experience. He needs to study education, but as he studies he needs to practice it. Otherwise, it is simply like teaching a boy to play basketball by showing him charts of plays.

The education courses as a whole were—as is so commonly reported by critics among the student body, the faculty, and outside observers—

intellectually sterile and largely irrelevant to the needs of students and to their preparation as informed teachers and educators. In one class the 150 students (mostly juniors) and I spent the 50 minutes in a desultory discussion of a one-half page of mimeographed description of the question of teacher shortages (the entire reading assignment for the day). The professor's intention seemed to be to reassure the class that jobs would be awaiting them after they graduated, although there were variations in the need for high school mathematics teachers as against general teachers for elementary school. That is literally all we learned that day.

In another class of 30 elementary school candidates, we spent 15 minutes listening to the professor tell us how to teach first graders to fold a letter and to indent the first paragraph. In another of a mixed group of 100 students, the professor raced through a description of existentialism, scholasticism, and pragmatism, one after the other in 50 minutes, with references to two or three philosophers representative of each as he went. He paused at intervals to allow the note-takers to catch up with him.

One of the most interesting and stimulating classes of all those visited in the liberal arts *or* education was in methods of education. The two hour class contained 40 students of various ages, each of whom had been conducting field work on the problem of the high school dropout. At the beginning the class listened to a 20-minute taped interview with a dropout. This interview had been conducted by a student who, with two other students, was responsible for presenting a three-quarter-hour symposium on the subject of the dropout by using the case materials collected.

The rest of the time consisted of class reports and discussion by the students of their own experiences, and critical evaluation of the methods each had found in progress in the schools and cases studied. The teacher remained in the background of the circle of students, occasionally raised her own questions, made certain that certain points were developed, and counted on the momentum generated by the students themselves to develop the ideas and theories with a sufficient degree of clarity.

The tragedy is that in a field as rich in intellectual content and aesthetic experience as education, so little is done to enrich the lives of the students with ideas and modes of knowledge drawn from history, philosophy, anthropology, sociology, literature, and the creative arts. To be involved in one or another kind of education, formal or informal, is the universal experience of man; and the study of education is the study of every question of importance in philosophy and history, from the question of how should one's life be lived to the question of how things came to be as they are. To study a school is to study the entire culture of man in one of its particular manifestations. To prepare oneself to become a teacher is to undertake a process of personal development and cultural growth that includes the added dimension of learning how to translate what one knows into a form that can make it available to others.

Yet, when general education courses offer surveys and brief descriptions of elements of knowledge from the academic disciplines, when history is taught and education is taught by the use of lectures and texts that are one long series of topic sentences and subheadings about things with no intrinsic interest or importance, one can see why so many teachers entering the service of the schools carry with them no serious intellectual interests of their own and so often have learned nothing more than a technique for the use of similar materials and texts adapted to the age group of the children they are teaching.

In the course of visiting the classes and reviewing the texts, I came to a clearer understanding of what are the operating mechanisms which keep the system of teacher education at its present level of achievement. It is not only the interlocking forces of custom and habit that join together the state departments of education, the colleges of education, the accrediting and certification agencies, and the practices of the schools. It is a particular and dominating conception of what knowledge is and how it must be organized and communicated. That conception is based on a typical confusion between knowledge and information, that is, the known facts about a given subject are assumed to form themselves into a body of knowledge which can then be communicated in an organized way.

Once this idea is accepted, the rest of the system—from textbooks to audiovisual aids, to semester hours of this and that, to practice teaching and methods courses—logically follows. What the system actually does is to eliminate the teacher as "an intermediary inventive mind." Although I can align myself with Mr. Conant in his concern to locate the center of professional work in education in the practice of teaching and to make colleges and universities fully responsible for certifying that their graduates have demonstrated a clear ability to teach and a mastery of a subject or subjects, I do not believe that any system of clinical professors, supervising teachers, and practice teaching in the classroom, unless it springs from a different theory of knowledge, is likely to do much more than continue the same deadly attitude to knowledge as an organized body of information.

Let me cite an example. A reputable text with selected readings in learning theory drawn from respectable educational sources introduces the student to an excerpt in the psychology of education with the following note:

> This description of the learning process is taken from a study by a national committee of the relation between learning and instructional process. After suggesting a definition of learning, the authors outline the structure of the learning process in a simplified schematic diagram, discuss its interpretation, and indicate the key processive concepts which they believe to be useful in understanding the characteristics of change in learning.

Most of what I mean is included in this short example. There can be no quarrel with the accuracy of the description. It *was* a description of the learning process written by a committee; and the authors, whose personal character was lost in the committee prose, did exactly what the note, with its own banal vocabulary, said they did. But the result of it all is a flat and tiresome presentation of something that could not possibly evoke any degree of student interest in learning about the learning process.

The style of the note is exactly the style of the academic lecturer; it tells the student in summary form what it is he is about to hear, then tells him. Then, as is usually the case in the textbooks and anthologies, it asks questions about the topics already described. Most of what is taught to undergraduate students in and out of education courses is organized according to this style of pedagogy. This is what I mean when I say that all the parts of the system, from lecturer to text to examination to grade to award of credit, are coherent.

Another side of the same pedagogy turns up in the constant use of anthologies and readings in the courses in introduction to education—which as far as the title of the course is concerned opens up a full opportunity to include anything that seems important to the teacher. I mean by this that an introduction to education could be one of the best and most valuable courses in the whole of higher learning if only it were taught with a degree of understanding and knowledge appropriate to its title. It could include the study in depth of children in the neighborhood; it could include tutoring children and college students; it could include novels and plays; it could include a study of childrearing and education in French Canada, Mexico, Poland, or Bali.

Yet the anthologies and introductory texts are arranged in the conventional sets of topics familiar to all colleges of education—without reference to readings in foreign literature or culture, as if there were only one content to the whole of education. Even the anthologies that contain a suitable variety of topics and writers should only be used, if at all, as reference books to be read over a period of a week or so and to be consulted for figures, topics, and information. I came across articles of my own in several of the anthologies and was astonished to find that even those seemed not very interesting to me and thus, I would imagine, not very interesting to the students either, especially since these articles had been written in other contexts and for other purposes, only some of which were served by their repetition in so different a context.

In any case, short pieces classified under topics and administered to students week by week cannot provide the nourishment they need nor the impetus to further thought. The whole procedure does not allow the student to put together a body of knowledge and a set of experiences that can give him an intellectual life and a style of his own. It does not call upon the best that is in him, but rather only on those peripheral human abilities that have to do with following a given pattern, chart, or guide to the communication of a stated and prescribed form of information.

The Education Texts

"Are you ready for the most interesting, the most satisfying, the most thrilling of your educational experiences thus far?" trills the opening sentence of a text on student teaching in the secondary school. Another text begins, " 'This semester I'm doing my student teaching.' What does the foregoing statement mean to you? Have you thought through the term *student teacher?* What abilities, skills, and understanding should you possess?" On the next page a student is reported as saying, "Well, this is it. This is the time when I go out and see if all the things they taught me in the past three years are true. What is it like out there?" Later, the text warns about possible problems the teacher will face: "One of the major weaknesses among student teachers is that they have spent four years in a university where they were subject to a great deal of front-of-the-class lecturing. Many student teachers assume this same technique when they begin teaching."

After describing what schools are like, a third text, widely used, produces the usual checklist of teachers' attributes for the student to consider and among the items raises the following questions:

> Is your hair neatly arranged, free from dandruff, frequently washed?
> Are your nails carefully manicured and your skin free from blemishes?
> Do you have an upright posture and a free-swinging walk?"

Other texts, with their own lists, ask the student teacher to decide whether he has the appropriate personality for the classroom and to rate himself and other teachers on such questions as personality, sparkle, drive, vitality, warmth, and radiation. Another defines the teacher as "one who stimulates and directs learning activities." Another provides the information that "the modern library usually is housed in an attractive, well-constructed building; and it is so organized that readers can meet their needs effectively and with as little lost motion as possible."

As I read the texts I could recognize the tone of voice and the feel of the classrooms in the education courses I had visited—the treatment of college students as if they, too, were elementary and high school children to be spoken to and encouraged with sparkle, warmth, friendliness, and well-combed hair. I could also see in the conflicting internal evidence of the texts—like the one that warned students about carrying over a front-of-the-class lecturing style—the other tone that warned the student that he was about to be thrilled by meeting real children. I could see in the example of the student who declared that he was about to go out to see if what he had been told all these years was true that even the practical implications of what was being said in the college classrooms were not examined or related either to a theory or to the practice of teacher education.

When I turned to the classes and to the texts on the philosophy of education and on the introduction to education, I found different but comparable materials. In one of the latter classes and its text I found the following topics, all included within 15 pages that the students had been asked to read:

> The Advance of Science and Technology
> Impact of Industrialization
> Growth of Nationalism
> Consequences of Imperialism

214

Effects of Militarism
Uses of Propaganda
Tragedy of the "Great War"
Failure of the League of Nations
Rise of Dictatorships and Totalitarian States
World War II and the United Nations
The Threat of Russian Communism
Challenge to Education

I leave to the reader the task of working out how much space in the text was devoted to each of these huge topics.

In a text in the philosophy of education I found the counterpart to several of the courses I attended. In a chapter of 19 pages there were short statements on free will, the nature of man, the meaning of metaphysics, and a description of the philosophy of education from Plato to Aquinas. Later in the book we students were told, "Impatient with scholastic thought, Sir Francis Bacon urged men to discard the idols of thought and begin anew by careful empirical observation of data and the treatment of these data by an inductive. Hobbes, a materialist, believed mind to be motion in the head. . . ."

Without completing the circuit of basic education courses as they are commonly taught, this may be enough to indicate what we found as we went our rounds and did our homework. There were some good courses and good teachers. I simply submit our testimony that nearly all of the courses were of the kind I have described and that we were struck over and over again by the fact that under the present system the colleges and departments of education do control a sizable block of time of the students intending to become teachers, for periods ranging from 20 to 30 semester hours of instruction, along with additional time for whatever practice teaching may be considered appropriate. Yet at no point, except for a few instances where comparative education courses were offered as electives, was there any indication that the study of education itself had within it some extraordinarily important areas for the study of foreign cultures and world affairs.

Some Suggested Reforms

If the development of the professional courses in education had all along been the work of diverse minds trained in a variety of fields, skilled in the arts of teaching, able and willing to bring the fruits of scholarship into the lives and working interests of students and teachers, we would already have had the rich blend of professional, vocational, and liberal studies our educational system so desperately needs. What makes a study liberal is not its detachment from something else called vocational or professional or from the cultural context in which it will be used. It becomes a liberal study by reason of the way in which it enriches one's understanding of man, nature, and society.

Academic study detached from aesthetic, personal, or cultural relevance to the life of the student and teacher is not liberal education; it is vocational. It gives him a stone when he asks for bread. Vocational training detached from intellectual interests and cultural concerns is not preparation for teaching; it is technical training for doing something other than teaching—for performing the duties of a paid employee. In a broader conception of teaching the college student who listens in class to a record of Dylan Thomas reading his poems is learning to hear, to feel, to understand the words and the truth the poet has to tell, not learning how to use the phonograph to teach poetry. The student who spends time in class with children who tell stories, draw, paint, and sing is not being technically trained to teach, but is learning to understand children and the arts through being in the presence of children. Is one liberal and the other vocational? They are both valuable kinds of experience in practical learning. What they are depends completely on the way they are done and on the way the teacher who is inducting the student into the world of teaching can make the experience of working with children a liberating art and can make study in the liberal arts a liberating experience.

The most natural thing to do in the development of education courses that will bring the full variety of the world into the consciousness of the student is to use the approach of the cultural anthropologist, which in essence is the approach of comparative education. If we examine the curriculum of education courses from this point of view, internationalism, or the study of American values and ideas in a world setting, is badly served. There are only seven centers of research and teaching in the United States where serious work in comparative education is now going on; and even in the case of those centers, which only have from one to four faculty members each, the influence they exert on the main body of education students is minimal.

Approximately 700 faculty members teach comparative education in all schools and departments of education in the United States. Most of them teach only part-time in one course in the field; their main work is in the foundations courses and the conventional curriculum. The history of the comparative education movement within the educating community has been relatively short—having begun to take shape in the late 1940's—with an emphasis on the philosophy and history of education in various countries. Since then, the movement has broadened its interests and increased the scope of its research, but not in any way comparable to the speed of the advance in institutes and centers for area studies and for economic and social development, which are, in many ways, supporting and complementary disciplines to the study of education.

The hope for the future of comparative education lies in the possibility that the social and behavioral scientists will see in the cross-cultural study of educational problems an opportunity for the advance of knowledge within their own fields and that more and more of them will become interested in comparative studies of educational systems, with education thus introduced into the general curriculum of undergraduate studies, both in the social sciences and in the schools and departments of education. In the meantime it is possible through new M.A. and doctoral programs in comparative education and the appointment of more faculty members with experience of foreign educational systems to the colleges of education to replace many of the present education courses with others of wider cultural content.

An Introductory Course

Suppose as an introduction to education, the students were invited to consider the school as it functions in three different cultures—Nigeria, the Soviet Union, and the United States; or Ghana, Indonesia, and the United States. Suppose, to suggest an example, selected Nigerian students, graduate students in comparative education familiar with Soviet materials, and the instructor were to plan a course in which the students carried out their own research on one of the three societies in teams, with leadership and supervision by the graduate students. The instructor would act as coordinator for their work and would supervise and present the research results, along with representative students from the study groups. Some of these representative students could be recruited from the local foreign student population or, through collaboration with the Educational and Cultural Affairs Bureau of the U.S. State Department or the Center for Educational Cooperation, directly from the home country from the ranks of student teachers in the teacher education institutions and schools. Materials could be collected not only from a bibliography provided by the instructor and the graduate students, but from materials supplied by the Soviet Union, the Nigerian government, and UNESCO and by written materials prepared especially by the Nigerian students.

Suppose, following the work of the first semester, the students were to continue as a class with the same or another instructor. Research teams would do field work in the sociology, political science, or psychology of the American school or on specialized topics, such as the role of the American teacher or the place of African studies in the elementary school curriculum. At the end of the year of work in the six semester hours of education, the student teachers not only would have furnished themselves with some degree of insight into the reality of a foreign culture but would have broadened their conception of education, would have acquired some skill in finding out things for themselves, and would have deepened their interest in further enquiry into educational questions. Having been thus introduced to foreign studies and world affairs by their concern for teaching and for education, the students might then become interested in taking other work in the field.

A similar approach to other cultures in the study of philosophy, anthropology, psychology, history, curriculum making, methods of instruction, child development, and the arts would not only complete the official task of meeting certification requirements but would extend the range of student knowledge in education and in foreign cultures in ways that would lead the students to become interested in traveling abroad, in studying indigenous American as well as foreign cultures, and in finding ways of teaching what they had learned to the elementary and high school students with whom they did their practice teaching.

Again, following the idea of open initiatives by the faculty, three or four faculty members teaching in the same or an allied field (one of the many mixed-material courses in the foundations of education, for example) could prepare themselves—through seminars, independent study, summer travel, NDEA Institutes, or summer institutes of their own devising with invited foreign graduate students—to study selected developing countries in Africa, Asia, or Latin America, concentrating on one such country and its regional area. The faculty could make themselves responsible for acquiring the basic knowledge necessary to an understanding of how the educational system worked in relation to the social, economic, and political factors in the country chosen.

Students in research teams would then be asked to emulate in some measure the same process through which the faculty had gone, using materials already turned up or produced by the faculty, meetings with visiting foreign experts and students on the campus, and tapes made by interviewing university faculty members and others. Each of the student research groups would present its findings to the others. The three faculty members would coordinate their teaching and, on occasion, would work with each other's students or bring the three classes together for a group meeting. The course might culminate in a summer travel-study project (arranged through one of the international organizations) in which a group of the students travel abroad with a member of the faculty for two months of study extended from the beginning work in the course. Or the process might be reversed; and the student travel-study project would come first, thus making it possible for those who were included in the trip, along with the three faculty members, to serve as discussion leaders for the other students in the course when they returned in the fall.

In an experimental program in teacher certification for early childhood education at Sarah Lawrence College, we found that one of the best ways of giving the student teacher a chance to work in the philosophy, history, or psychology of education under the state requirement was to arrange for her to enroll for work in philosophy, history, or psychology with a faculty member in one of the courses in those fields. In connection with the course work, the student would undertake an independent project in research on one or another issue or topic having to do with education. This, as was true of many of the other regular courses, often involved field work; and it was thus perfectly appropriate for a student to be carrying out a project in comparative study of the social attitudes of eighth graders in the Bronxville and Yonkers schools, or Indian and American children, as part of a course in psychology. This meant in many cases that other students and faculty members became interested in education through being exposed to the results of the study project.

In larger institutions with colleges or departments of education, the situation might be reversed. Students from political science, for example, might come to courses in education specifically designed in collaboration with political scientists to introduce the political science student to the politics of education. The mixture of students from inside and outside the field of education working together on common problems of interest to them all has an enlivening effect both on their work together and on the faculty members who teach them. The main thing is to get the initiatives going and to fill the existing course offerings with new content, thinking of the 20 to 30 credit hours of required education as a beautiful chance to extend the meaning of education to include a world content and a world perspective. There is no reason why the requirements have to remain chopped up into three-credit courses; a minimum of six hours for a single course in the psychology of education makes much more room for a sensible content of materials drawn from around the world—for example, a study of national character in three different cultures—than does the rush of a three-credit course through something called "learning theory."

The Education Curriculum

It seems to me, as I have said elsewhere, that rather than relying on the rest of the university faculty to provide courses in world affairs, foreign cultures, and international issues and trusting to the luck of the elective system and the counseling services to determine whether or not students actually worked in them, the college of education should develop its own curriculum—with the help of members of the university faculty and selected students and scholars from abroad—right in the middle of its own courses. Otherwise, it is unlikely that the intellectual vitality which can be developed through the introduction of ideas from outside the usual pattern of American educational thinking or the content of knowledge which could enrich the student's understanding of foreign cultures and world affairs will ever become available within the present structure.

My colleagues among the professional educators, many of whom make the same criticism of the pattern of professional courses as does the present Report, have informed me that the main obstacle to change in the international direction I have urged them to take lies in the fact that colleges and departments of education are mainly staffed by persons who have taken higher degrees in education to prepare themselves to teach the departmental courses already offered in their present form and that there is thus a self-perpetuating quality in all the required education courses. More than this is the matter of faculty assignments. Too often a person trained, for example, in curriculum development will be asked to teach a beginning course in educational psychology or introduction to education and will simply follow the syllabus and the text customarily used in such cases. The superficiality of the text then becomes a characteristic of the course.

The answer to that problem is the same answer that must be given to the problem of improving teaching throughout the entire educational system—new appointments of persons with a serious interest in educational change and the improvement of student learning; new forms of collaboration with scholars in the universities, foreign students, and scholars from abroad; research seminars for faculty members already teaching in the colleges of education—all of them based on a clear-cut decision by those in authority to alter the content and form of the present courses in education. Someone is going to have to make the moves.

We have the evidence of the brilliant work of those psychologists, political scientists, sociologists, and historians—men like Nevitt Sanford, James Coleman, David Riesman, and Henry Steele Commager—who, once they become involved in the study of education, bring to the field the knowledge and insight of their own kind of intellectual experience to show what can be done in breaking the bonds which hold tight the study of education within the province of its own practitioners. I have found that a great deal of the time the social scientists with a concern for social change and a high level of research intelligence have not become involved in educational questions in general and international education in particular simply because of prior interests in other matters. But I have also found that when they do become involved, as is the case with James Coleman and his editing of *Education and Political Development,*[5] the study of education immediately jumps to a new range of significance in its political and social content. We have yet to see much of this talent applied to international education *per se,* although the *Education and Political Development* book, containing valuable essays by political scientists, shows the way in which an important contribution can be made. So does the work of Seymour Martin Lipset, in his empirical studies of international politics and culture and student movements. But again, the major initiative in getting the contribution made will have to come from the educators. It cannot wait for the political scientists or anyone else.

The Removal of Obstacles

If, as I am constantly assured, the "system" is such that the moves will not be made from within the faculty membership of the educational establishment, that they will not be made by the state departments of education through changes in their requirements, or that they will not be made through progressive or radical proposals from the certification and accrediting agencies, then they can only come from three sources:

1. Students, both graduate and undergraduate, who demand broader and better work in an international dimension in their preparation as teachers—those who intend to serve abroad in the Peace Corps or in other volunteer services

---

[5] Coleman, James S., editor. *Education and Political Development.* Princeton, N. J.: Princeton University Press, 1965. 620 pp.

2. Individual faculty members who have had experience abroad and who simply undertake the reform of their own courses by new methods and new content

3. Deans of colleges of education and chairmen of departments who have a clear idea of the direction in which they want their institution to go and who make new appointments to match—both joint appointments with other departments, of anthropologists, foreign scholars, experts, and graduate students or, preferably, appointments of their own men and women—those who have had overseas experience, are familiar with other educational systems, are interested in educational reform and the education of teachers, and can simply remake the education courses under their present titles.

To such teachers will come many of those students who want to teach but do not want to lull themselves into a stupor while learning how to do it; others who seek some way of using their talents in foreign service; and others who, not knowing what it is they want, are just meeting their certification requirements. There is absolutely no doubt that at present the education courses are driving away most except the latter group. Neither is there any doubt that the whole area of education courses is one of the most fertile places for new growth in international education that exists anywhere in the system. A rich reward waits for any man who cultivates that area. He will not only have the undying gratitude of generations of students, he will have the reward of answering the academic critics—not by meeting their terms of surrender to the ubiquitous all-university committees, but by converting the wasteland of undergraduate education in the universities to an oasis where good teaching and good teachers grow.

Accreditation and Its Effects

Another way of looking at the state certification requirements is to consider them as an expression of what a given state considers to be the proper content of a teacher's preparation for teaching. In the requirements for the accreditation of institutions that educate teachers, the states usually call for a "broad liberal arts training" and for basic requirements in social sciences, with the usual inclusion of American history, occasional inclusion of state history, and even more occasional inclusion of world history or non-Western culture. Since the mental set of most of the requirement makers and curriculum developers is to think of college education as being divided into departments and courses, the idea that materials from the world's cultures should be an integral part of the entire curriculum has not penetrated the system of requirements and regulations. Mississippi and Hawaii are the only states requiring world history for the preparation of social science teachers; Oregon requires either European *or* world history.

I have read carefully the statement *Standards and Guide for Accreditation of Teacher Education* prepared by the National Council for Accreditation of Teacher Education and used for the instruction of insti-

221

tutions that wish to receive national accreditation for their work in preparing teachers. The intention of the statement is to provide a "guide to an institution in developing a report to the Council prior to a visit by a team of out-of-state and in-state evaluators" and to give "illustrations of possible ways of meeting standards." The sole purpose of NCATE, says the statement, is "to improve teacher education through accreditation."[6]

However, the standards and guide deal exclusively with a system of organization, facilities, and educational programs that certainly do give guidance, but guidance toward a standardized as well as standard program. The frame of reference of the statement rests on the assumption that there is an accreditable pattern for the education of teachers that consists of three parts—general education, academic studies relevant to the kind of teaching the students will do, and professional education, unspecified except as to the need for "laboratory" experiences including practice teaching. If it took the document with the seriousness with which it is obviously intended, the institution applying for accreditation would do its best to fit into the conventional pattern, including the acceptance of the philosophy that separates professional education and professional educators from their academic or "liberal education" counterparts.

It seems to me that if the Council's sole purpose is "to improve teacher education through accreditation," something more interesting and provocative than the present organizational outline must be provided to those seeking the approval of the Council and of the regional accrediting agencies. If the Council in its guidance toward improvement of the education of teachers bothers to ask about "the arrangements for transporting college supervisors and student teachers to and from the laboratory schools and the arrangements for housing student teachers while away from the campus," could it not ask the question, "What arrangements have been made to ensure that the student has a direct experience with how his society functions, or how local politics affects the quality of education available to poor families, or what it is like to live in a culture other than one's own?"

When we look for leadership in the improvement of education we have a right to expect that the agencies that have the power to control the way education is carried on will make a serious and continuing effort to assert such leadership right at the point where it matters most, that is, where the power is being administered. Although my concern here is with the question of how accreditation procedures can stimulate the imagination of educators in developing a world perspective in the education of teachers, that question can only be answered by reference to the whole framework in which the question is asked. The approach of the Council is juridical, didactic, organizational, administrative, and regulatory. Why not turn it around and prepare a statement to serve as a guide and

---

[6] National Council for Accreditation of Teacher Education. *Standards and Guide for Accreditation of Teacher Education.* Washington, D.C.: the Council (1750 Pennsylvania Avenue, N.W.) 24 pp.

standard for fresh thinking, raising the question of standards in a wider setting? The standards at present have to do with the qualifications of professional educators and the nature of the standard curriculum. When analyzed in practice, the standard turns out to be whether or not the faculty members teaching "professional" courses have themselves taken the right number and sequence of professional courses.

Would it not be useful to raise the questions of how well the students being graduated from the institution can teach, what breadth and depth of experience have they had in the world, what interest do they demonstrate in possessing an intellectual life of their own, what leadership have they shown in improving the quality of education, their own and that of the children they have been teaching? Otherwise one can only conclude that accreditation procedures are not designed to improve education but to imprison it within the status quo of professional education.

The *Proposed Standards for State Approval of Teacher Education*, published by the U.S. Office of Education in 1967, lists among its desirable goals in curriculum planning to "encourage discernment in examining the values inherent in foreign cultures to the end that a clearer understanding of other peoples will reduce world tensions." Among the proposals in this document are listed courses in contemporary world culture, world geography, and "the growth and development of the United States as a nation and its place in world affairs."[7] The findings of the present study indicate that until now, this section of the *Proposed Standards* has had no effect in changing state requirements, although it is too soon to draw the conclusion that there will be no effect in the future.

In the meantime the American Association of Colleges for Teacher Education has completed the first year of a comprehensive study of the criteria for evaluating teacher education programs and institutions to work out and recommend appropriate changes in present accrediting standards, to cite the areas where continuing research is needed, and to make a plan for the continuing review of whatever standards are adopted by the accrediting agencies. After a series of five regional conferences in 1967 and responses to an opinionaire on key issues from more than 1,500 educators, the AACTE drew up a preliminary draft of a statement on proposed standards,[8] which has now been circulated to a cross-section of the educating community.

An analysis of the draft statement shows that the basic framework of academic and professional courses has been retained and that preparation for teaching is still conceived as a process of taking courses within the subject matter of the arts and sciences and of taking other courses in

---

[7] U.S. Department of Health, Education, and Welfare, Office of Education. *Proposed Standards for State Approval of Teacher Education.* 0-243-517. Washington, D.C.: Government Printing Office, 1967.

[8] American Association of Colleges for Teacher Education. *Standards and Evaluative Criteria for the Accreditation of Teacher Education.* A draft of the Proposed New Standards, with Study Guide. Washington, D.C.: the Association, December 1967. 39 pp.

educational theory linked to "laboratory and clinical experience." That is to say, teaching and preparing to teach are conceived as classroom activities within educational institutions; and the element of direct experience in the world and the idea of cultural immersion and social involvement as a factor in the student's development have not yet found their way into the conceptual framework.

On the other hand, the statement reveals some welcome shifts of emphasis within the present system toward greater flexibility in the evaluation of the qualities of graduates, the use of continuing research to review present educational programs in the light of subsequent performance of the teacher, the inclusion of students in educational policy making, and greater encouragement for the development of ideas that break with standard practices. To those of us not directly involved in the day-to-day work of administering change within the teacher education movement, the process of change seems slow, cumbersome, and overwhelmingly circumscribed by professional and organizational interests. Yet the circumscription is a fact, the organizational problems are real, and the question of how to speed up the process of change and to free the imagination of educators for a wider range of ideas and practices is itself a matter of study in the formation of new strategies and a question that cannot be answered by frontal assaults on the bureaucratic structure. In fact, that structure seems strong enough to withstand almost any amount of attacks from outside.

What is called for is a deeper and more thoughtful strategy that turns the attention of educators toward the reality of the cultural and social conditions of their own society and the people in it and calls upon them to find ways in which the entire apparatus of institutional life in the schools and universities can minister to the changing needs of a younger generation and a new society into which the generation has so recently been born. The levers of change certainly do exist inside the universities and schools, but the fulcrum lies outside the institutions in the society at large; and it is there that the force must be applied at places indicated by the living reality of human need.

Stated in the broadest terms, our problem in America is to rouse up the initiatives of indigenous leadership, to give our people the impulse and the tools to educate themselves with the help of their teachers. Society is the ultimate teacher, possessed of new and enormous powers in its economic and social rewards and punishments, equipped with instruments of communication more powerful and far-reaching than those in the hands of schoolteachers. Whatever the regulatory organizations can do to release the energies of students and teachers to solve their own problems and to enhance the quality of their own lives will help to restore the balance in favor of the individual citizen and the individual teacher.

224

The Possible Role of State Departments of Education

One of the most encouraging things in our findings is evidence of the open possibility for new international work sponsored by the state departments of education, where there is leadership from the department and cooperation from the colleges, teachers, and schools. Fifteen states have worked out at least the beginning stages of individual international programs. As a minimum, some of the states have been conducting state-wide curriculum revision in which the world affairs element is a consideration; others have brought in foreign consultants to the department of education staffs.

A summary of present efforts as revealed in the replies to the questions raised in our letter sent to state departments is as follows:

• Five states report the appointment of foreign staff members or consultants in non-Western areas to the state department of education: Alaska, Connecticut, New Jersey, New York, Virginia.

• Two states—New Jersey and Ohio—report state-sponsored community projects in world affairs.

• Four states—Arkansas, New York, California, Michigan—report programs and conferences in international education, including foreign languages, area studies, and the like on a statewide basis.

• Eight states—California, Colorado, Connecticut, Hawaii, Michigan, New York, Pennsylvania, and South Dakota—are working on curriculum revision to include world affairs and non-Western cultures. Pennsylvania has changed its curricular requirements to include a unit in world culture in the high school curriculum.

• Two states—Colorado and North Carolina—report cooperation with colleges and schools in arranging teacher and student exchanges, travel programs, and the like; in North Carolina, credit is given to teachers by the Department of Education for foreign travel.

• Four states have established language and area studies centers in collaboration with universities in their states: Hawaii, Indiana, Maryland, Rhode Island.

• Connecticut and New York have started in-service programs in world affairs and related areas.

The above list is not intended as an exhaustive one; it is drawn only from replies made to the survey and is indicative of the kind of things now going on which could be extended on at least this minimum basis to all the other states. The above summary, it should also be remembered, does not take account of initiatives already taken by the schools, colleges, and universities in developing educational programs for teachers and for high school and college students under present certification rules.

An illustration of the situation that exists in most Eastern states can be taken from New Jersey where, 10 years ago, the State Board of Education developed suggestions for including non-Western material in the curriculum, although these were not turned into state requirements. However, several of the colleges where teachers are prepared worked in this direction on their own, and the encouragement of the State Department has resulted in various new programs. One typical example is the plan for an M.A. in social studies education at Paterson State College in Wayne, New Jersey. The plan calls for a fairly straightforward M.A. degree, except that it draws more than the usual amount of its material from non-Western cultures and aims at developing a knowledge of world affairs and an ability to carry out independent research. The professional work includes psychology and education; area studies in either Latin America, the Far East, the Middle East, Africa, or the Soviet Union; and a seminar in social science in which each student carries out his own research project. The new plan came as the result of faculty initiative and the pooling of existing faculty resources.

In smaller colleges of 3,000 students or less, public or private, it is unlikely that programs in area studies could be financed from regular budgets because of the cost of bringing in additional faculty members. The only way to handle that without additional money is to take every opportunity to bring in a qualified person with foreign experience and interests whenever new appointments are being made or, as is the case at Earlham College, to start seminars, travel-study projects, and the like which will develop new areas of interest and competence in the present faculty.

On the other hand, collaboration with the Peace Corps and the Center for Educational Cooperation to develop summer training programs for volunteers to a given area—Thailand or Malaysia, for example—could result in building up a special faculty and student competence in Far Eastern affairs. If a college specialized in one area, rather than in an entire continent or several continents—as is the case in some of the larger universities—a useful arrangement could be made for special studies and travel within the cultural and geographical limits of that area, especially if it were possible to use and receive help from the fairly extensive training facilities of the Peace Corps.

Another example, this one more typical of the present stage of development at New Jersey colleges, is Glassboro State College, where a Committee on World Education has been formed by the faculty to do six things:

1. Develop new courses in world cultures and world affairs

2. Develop new materials for all sectors of the elementary and secondary school curriculum

3. Hold campus lectures and discussions on issues in the world and on various of its areas

4. Organize field trips and film showings

5. Organize special projects in the extracurriculum

6. Establish contacts through visits, conferences, travel, and study abroad.

During the past two years this has been the extent of its program, and what happens next will be up to the faculty and administration. There is no obstacle in the State Department as far as requirements are concerned.[9]

International Programs Sponsored by New York State Department of Education

The survey shows that the most comprehensive effort by a state department to increase the international component in the education of teachers is to be found in New York State.[10] Although obviously the state has certain advantages not shared by others by reason of its geographical location and cultural setting, most of the items on the New York agenda could be transferred to other states, at least for discussion and intended action.

In their set of proposals made in 1961 for the "expansion and improvement of education in New York State," the Board of Regents of the state said flatly, "The proper dimensions of general education in our schools and colleges are global in nature."[11]

Since the state commissioner and his colleagues of the State Department of Education share this view and took the Regents' statement seriously, an Office of Foreign Area Studies at State Department headquarters in Albany was organized in 1963 to take statewide action in creating the global dimension, with a staff directed by Ward Morehouse. The Office has a New Delhi Educational Resources Center, where Mr. Morehouse and colleagues are working with Indian educators to develop new curricular materials for use in the New York State public schools; it has a Foreign Area Material Center in New York City; and it has a Center for International Programs and Services. After the new office was started in the State Department, the State University of New York

⁹ After the above was written, Mr. Kosygin and Mr. Johnson visited Glassboro State College for their discussions, suggesting by their presence there how quickly a college can become connected to a concern for world affairs by visiting speakers and organized discussion groups. It would now be appropriate for Glassboro State College to memorialize the Kosygin-Johnson meeting by establishing an International Study Center in Education, where the problems of elementary and secondary school curriculums and teacher education in the Soviet Union and in the United States could be studied by visiting Soviet and American educators and students. A memorandum to this effect was prepared for the Glassboro State College officials as part of the present study. It contains a preliminary outline of ways in which the College might extend its present interest and that of the community of Glassboro in Soviet-American relations into travel-study programs involving summer visits to the Soviet Union by student teachers and in other projects, including a comparative study of the Glassboro educational system and that of a counterpart Soviet city. A copy of this memorandum is available in the study files and at Glassboro State College, Glassboro, New Jersey, c/o Professor George Geng.

¹⁰ For survey of the work of state departments of education in promoting studies in foreign cultures as of 1964, see note 4, pp. 1-14.

¹¹ University of the State of New York. *Investments in the Future: The Regents' Proposals for the Expansion and Improvement of Education in New York State, 1961.* Albany: the University, 1960. p. 28.

installed an International Center in Planting Fields, Long Island, New York, with Glenn Olds as director, to do work in world affairs in the 58 colleges and universities in the state system. Since 14 of the 58 institutions are state colleges with a major interest in teacher education and most of the other institutions in the university system produce a fair proportion of candidates for teaching, the State Department of Education and the university will obviously have many ways of collaborating in the future.

An explicit definition of the role of the New York State Department of Education in international education is contained in a Department statement issued in 1963 entitled *The International Dimensions of Education in New York State: Guidelines for the Development of Foreign Area Studies in New York Schools and Colleges and for Strengthening the Role of International Education in the State Education Department.*[12] A fuller description of the whole program is available from the Department, although what follows can serve as a general outline of the program that Mr. Morehouse and the others have planned and are carrying out after having analyzed where the main points of action should be.

The guidelines, said Mr. Morehouse, "summarize possibilities for further development of the international dimension of education in New York State. They focus on needs and opportunities for strengthening the study of the world beyond Europe in our schools and colleges, as well as on ways of organizing the State Education Department to meet more effectively its growing international responsibilities."

Here, in summary, are the guidelines:

Certain resources essential to successful academic programs in non-Western studies may be more effectively developed cooperatively among several institutions.

No college or university education for Americans can in fact be complete without some systematically developed points of reference beyond the Western tradition.

While colleges and universities should be encouraged to make new faculty appointments of individuals with specific training in some aspects of the world beyond Europe, efforts need also to be made in strengthening existing faculty resources. Summer seminars in foreign area studies, programs of intensive study of non-European languages . . , and study abroad are all approaches which should be developed.

Libraries are the cornerstone of academic enterprise and require substantial development if programs of study on non-European areas are to be effective. . . . Bibliographical services and guides to teaching materials for use in colleges should be made available by the Department. (The foreign area material center mentioned above is responsible for distributing such bibliographies and materials and is financed by a Ford Foundation grant and by support under a contract with the U.S. Office of Education.)

For teachers already in service—a vast majority of whom did not have such opportunities [for the study of the world beyond Europe] in their own preparation for teaching—and even for future teachers who will not be able to take the option [for area studies in the certification regulations]. . . . Because of the

---

[12] New York State Department of Education, Albany, N.Y., 1963.

228

pressure of other requirements, additional opportunities for study need to be provided.

In the future, emphasis on foreign areas in teacher education should become increasingly flexible. Thus, opportunities for groups of key teachers and supervisors in the social studies and in other fields to become intellectually involved in some aspect of the world beyond Europe should be provided through special summer conferences and other programs.

A reexamination of the formal curriculum in the social studies as a whole is vital to further progress in strengthening the study of non-Western peoples and cultures.

While the social studies program will be more involved in study of the world beyond Europe, contributions of other subject matter fields should not be ignored. Art and literature provide important opportunities for study of the cultural accomplishment of other peoples. . . . Instruction in the major non-European languages should be offered to a limited number of high school students.

It is crucial that . . . our educational leaders have an opportunity to develop their own leadership in efforts to study other peoples and cultures. Regional conferences, seminars, and similar programs should be developed for school administrators and board members of School Study Councils and other means.

To administer various . . . [the international programs proposed above] an Office of Area Studies and Educational Exchange should be established within the Department. This office would also aid other units in the Department in meeting their international responsibilities more effectively through provision of specialized personnel and similar services to develop long-range policies and procedures in the international field.

Since 1963, when it began, the Office of Foreign Area Studies has already added substance to projects carried out under the above guidelines. A full account of practical things that have been done since the Office started is contained in the 1965 Progress Report.[13] Although the numbers of teachers and students who are involved in the programs for which these guidelines have given direction are comparatively small, the progress in finding ways to affect the whole New York State system has been remarkable. Financial support has come mainly from State Department funds, supplemented by funds from foundations and government agencies.

For example, in the summer of 1965, four summer programs in the study of Asia, Africa, Latin America, and the Soviet Union were offered at Columbia, Cornell, New York, Hofstra, and Syracuse Universities, with more than 200 teachers from the sixth and secondary grades attending (supported by tuition grants). Two visiting Indian scholars traveled throughout the state during the year to meet with teachers and students and to work in in-service conferences and workshops with teachers in more than 150 schools. Other teachers and administrators were sent abroad for summer study on travel grants financed by the U.S. Department of State, the budgets of local schools, and the private resources of the teacher.

Special arrangements for financial support of students interested in studying Chinese, Japanese, Burmese, Malay, Tagalog, Thai, Vietnamese, Dutch, Hindi, Pali, Sanskrit, Swahili, Portuguese, and Hausa have been made by the Center for International Programs and Services. Independent

---

[13] New York State Department of Education, Albany, N.Y., 1965.

study supervised by local faculty members is also available. Other arrangements are made for support to college faculty members on sabbatical for a year at a major university center for study, research and teaching in world affairs, international relations, and the like and for elementary and secondary school teachers in summer institutes.[14]

When the State University of New York International Education Center at Planting Fields goes into full operation, there will be a marked increase in the rate of growth of all these projects. Conferences with administrators and faculty members from the 58 institutions, which include community colleges as well as the state colleges and universities, have already been held; and some effects are already visible on those campuses. One example of collaboration in teacher education is to be found at the State University of New York at Plattsburgh, which is cooperating with the Glens Falls school system to try out new curriculums while the materials and methods are being developed in a program on the Plattsburgh campus. The role of initiative by educators outside the State Department is well demonstrated by the International Program in Glens Falls started in 1957 by Harold Long, superintendent of the Glens Falls High School, and George Angell, president of the State University of New York at Plattsburgh. Their work in the field antedates the formation of the State Department's Office of Foreign Area Studies but has benefited a great deal by that Office since it was founded.

The State of Indiana

Using the results of the survey, I would cite Indiana as one of the best examples of what state departments of education can do in international education and as an example of the collaboration possible between the state universities and state boards of education if both are willing. At Indiana University there is a special chance for that kind of collaboration since, by law, the University is head of the public school system of the state and therefore has responsibility for improving the quality and content of the educational system as a whole. Another special condition lies in the fact that Herman B Wells was president of the University from 1939 until 1962 and has been chancellor since then. There is no more active educator in the entire country than Herman Wells in pressing for and arranging for an American educational system that provides its students with a world perspective. Of the faculty of 3,000 part-time and 1,900 full-time members at Indiana University, more than 300 have had experience in foreign countries. As early as 1954, the first technical assistance contract abroad with a university was arranged by Whack Wright, vice-president of the University and dean of the School of Education, who went to Bangkok and worked out a proposal to help the Prasarnmitr (college of education)

[14] See: Morehouse, Ward. "Provincialism and Constitutionalism: The Role of the States in Foreign Area Studies." *Annals of the American Academy of Political and Social Science* 356: 119-25; November 1964.

there. There have been other relations with Southeast Asia ever since, in addition to direct connections in other Asian and in European countries.

At the Airlie House Conference on World Education, Professor Robert F. Byrnes described a study he had conducted in 1958[15] in the State of Indiana which showed that of the 65,000 students then in institutions of higher education in the state, only 300 at any time would take or had taken a course that dealt either specifically or substantively with a non-Western culture. With some Ford Foundation help, the University and the school and college system of the state, in collaboration with the State Department of Education, developed a statewide program to improve and expand the training of teachers, scholars, and students in foreign languages and non-Western cultures. The program includes, among other items, institutes for history and language teachers; the services of eight university faculty members who spend most of their time visiting high schools in the state for work on curriculum development in foreign languages and world affairs; a project in which 90 high school students from the state spend the summer abroad living with families and studying the language in France, Spain, and Germany; and a project supported in part by the Ford Foundation, in part by the state to help the other 34 colleges and universities of Indiana develop their faculty and add to library holdings for education in the non-Western world.

Among the joint efforts by the State Board of Education and the University are included a series of summer institutes in world affairs from 1958 to 1962 and, more recently, conferences on non-Western cultures held under the joint auspices of the state, Indiana University, the North Central Association, and the Asia Foundation. The State Board of Education has also been working with foreign language specialists from all four of the state universities to improve the state's language program. In addition, the State Department of Public Instruction is revising the social studies curriculum for the public schools and is working out the details of a seventh-grade course in non-Western culture.

While it is true that special advantages of the Indiana State Board of Education accrue from the constitutional responsibility of the university system for leadership of the state system of education, many of the things that Indiana and New York State are doing can be done and are being done in other states. If what we want is change in the public schools, the experience of Indiana and New York would indicate that one of the fastest ways to get it is to form a coalition between the state department of education and state university leadership.

There is, of course, the usual danger in assuming that a world dimension is being introduced into the educational system of Indiana when foreign languages are more widely taught and when area studies courses are offered to teachers. The danger is illustrated by the fact that in the

---

[15] Byrnes, Robert F., editor. *The Non-Western Areas in Undergraduate Education in Indiana.* Slavic and East Europe Series, Vol. XV. Bloomington: Indiana University Press, 1959. p. 8.

town of Nashville, Indiana, in the spring of 1967 a high school teacher was dismissed by his school board without any protest from his colleagues or the public because he had attended the "Spring Mobilization To End the War in Vietnam" in New York City on April 15, 1967, on his own time. The teacher was said by his principal to be one of the best teachers in the school, but after he had written a newspaper account of the peace march, in which he reported the views of the participants about war and about the demonstration, he was denounced by the townspeople for going to the march and for reporting on it in the local newspaper. His contract for the coming year was dropped. No amount of non-Western study and foreign language can ensure that principals and teachers, aside from the citizens, will understand the necessity of taking an interest in the actual affairs of the world and not merely in the affairs of the academic curriculum. They seem to need a World Affairs Center right there in Nashville.

Hawaii

In reviewing other work by state departments of education, I found that Hawaii has developed one of the most comprehensive programs of social studies in the country in bringing the concept of world cultures into the school curriculum. Here again, as in the case of New York State, Hawaii has special advantages—a culturally heterogeneous population; the East-West Center as a university focal point, where there are hundreds of foreign students and visiting professors; and the additional consciousness of world affairs that comes to a community when a Peace Corps training center is established in it on a continuing basis. It is also true that the small size of the community in the Islands makes it possible for easy communication among local world affairs clubs, school programs, and the State Department of Education. The University of Hawaii is able to act as coordinator for a great deal of the international studies in the educational system. The East-West Center has a community relations office and can help the schools by arranging for foreign scholars and teachers to visit the schools and make talks.

The state's own Pacific and Asian Affairs Council runs a Pacific and Asian high school program on world affairs which, from the accounts I have, is a successful extracurricular and interschool program active on all four islands. The local activities in the communities are mainly discussions, although the meetings are coordinated with the Pacific and Asian Affairs Council branches, which in turn get cooperation from the East-West Center in the matter of speakers and conferences. The Council is unusual in that it is completely voluntary, that it maintains a high level of active student participation, and that it is financed by the business community.

The Department of Education is at present revising the secondary school curriculum to include ninth-grade courses on Asia, Africa, and Latin America; a tenth-grade world history course; and a twelfth-grade course in

American foreign relations. The following is the skeleton outline of the required social studies program[16] in the Hawaii schools:

Kindergarten	Social Development at School and in the Community
Grade 1	Home and School Relationships
Grade 2	Community Helpers
Grade 3	Community Organization—How Basic Needs Are Met
Grade 4	Hawaii Long Ago and Now
	How People Live in Different Parts of the World Today
Grade 5	Our Country, the United States
	How Our Country Grew
	Living Together in the United States Today
Grade 6	Our Neighbors: Neighbors to the North and South and in the Pacific
Grade 7	Geography (a one-semester course)
	Hawaii (a one-semester course)
Grade 8	United States History and Government
Grade 9	Asia, Africa, and Latin America
Grade 10	World History
Grade 11	United States History
Grade 12	American Problems

Possible Initiatives

Since there is a considerable body of literature about certification, and information is available elsewhere on the programs of state departments in the individual states, I will rest content with mentioning New York, Indiana, and Hawaii as states that have taken initiatives and are doing more than most of the others. In many instances the departments of education do not think it their business to start up programs of the sort New York has organized, and in general the assumption is made or implied that the state department is an administrative and regulatory agency whose business happens to be with education.[17] This makes it even more important that the educators in the colleges and universities stay in touch with the need for change in requirements, curriculum, programs, and the whole apparatus of licensure. Otherwise, there may be no motion forward in international education at all, or it may be motion backwards should the state legislatures decide that they do not want international points of view officially installed in the educational system. The problem arises in its

---

[16] State Department of Education, Honolulu, Hawaii, 1966.

[17] According to the New York State Education Department survey already referred to, 19 states have some provision for leave for foreign teaching, although in most states leave is granted not by the departments but by the school boards. There is no record of any travel grants or Department initiatives for such teaching.

Thirty-seven states allow transfer of foreign credit; nine states have in-service programs sponsored by the State Education Department, mostly in the regular foreign languages. Only New York and Connecticut are recorded as running programs in the non-European areas and languages. Sometimes local school boards and districts do their own in-service work, are approved for credit, and, if they wish, can deal with non-Western areas.

most extreme form when in a given state there is no initiative taken by the faculty, the teachers in the schools, the students in the colleges, *or* the people in the state departments of education.

A different kind of problem arises when, as is frequently the case, there is not much connection among the community organizations; World Affairs Councils; United Nations Associations; Foreign Policy Association branches; and the work of the schools, universities, and state departments. In the department offices (usually placed in one building or set of buildings as part of the state civil service and quite often geographically removed from the main centers where the universities and colleges of education operate) the members of the departments see more of each other than anyone else. When the staff members travel to the schools and campuses, they usually see administrative officers on administrative and business matters rather than about anything to do with the teaching or with the curriculum in world affairs or other areas.

If we can find some ways to distract the attention of the bureaucracy from its unavoidable concern with rules and regulations and can turn that attention to substantive issues in education and the world, there will be at the very least more openness to change and at the very most an intelligently planned program to create a world dimension in the educational system.

The general need is for members of the state departments of education to break out of the routines of the department and of the colleges of education and to travel to universities and schools outside their state and outside the country. One of the best ways of bringing the state department of education more closely in touch with the ongoing educational issues and problems in the education of teachers would be to arrange for key people in the certification and accreditation sections to spend sabbaticals overseas visiting Peace Corps teachers and others involved in education and community development abroad. If this is not possible, these key people should at least spend a semester on a campus where some very good work in world education is under way. Projects could be organized on American campuses with foreign students who are articulate on the subject of their own education and its social and cultural setting and with persons on the faculty who would agree to work on a team research project having to do with developing new programs in the state department of education, with or without change in certification requirements.

It would be of great use to the state department of education to have for a semester or a half-year, well-qualified faculty members who would join the state department staff to study the problems from that side of things and to organize some research on curriculum and other matters. It would be even better if two or three faculty members at a time joined the staff on a temporary basis, since one person has only a minor amount of impact, everything else being equal, to do the sort of loosening up and looking around made possible in a group of interested persons who work together with the staff of the department of education.

Another useful idea would be for one or two key staff people from various state departments to spend three or four weeks working with their counterparts in the New York State Department or the Pennsylvania, Connecticut, Indiana, or Hawaii programs, comparing notes, carrying out informal research by collecting information, and visiting recommended schools and colleges where new international programs are in effect.

In extension of the idea of making many more direct relationships between state department staffs and the inside of the educational system, a great deal could be done by arranging for graduate students of education to serve as interns in departments of education to carry out research and study of the problems of the departments. The students could bring to the departments the fresh outlook of those who have been in the middle of the system and have been looking at the bureaucracy from the outside. Some of these interns should be foreign students and foreign educators, whose purpose would be to look at what we are doing and to join in the plans for what to do next.

Key people of the state department staffs should go abroad for six to eight weeks on study trips to foreign countries where they could work on questions having to do with the way cooperative programs can be arranged for curriculum development (the New York State Center in New Delhi is a good case in point) and would visit the foreign schools and teacher education colleges to see what they are doing and how they are doing it in relation to the administrative problems of their governmental services. It would be a good idea for such persons to travel with graduate students and faculty members interested in educational matters, since the department traveler would then have the privilege of thinking about what he was seeing with the additional perspective of those from outside his own administrative orbit. The idea of volunteering for the Peace Corps would also be made a great deal more attractive to teachers if they could be granted a two-year leave of absence from a present teaching post in order to go abroad. At present very few public schools grant such leaves.

Conferences for State Departments of Education

Over the past year I have been part of two conferences organized for their staffs by state departments of education, one in Educational Reform, the other in The Role of the Humanities in the Schools. Representatives from the colleges and universities were present as speakers and panel discussants. There was also a large representation of state department staff. When I asked elsewhere whether or not there were many such conferences on substantive issues as well as on state department problems, I learned that department members seldom meet together with university or public school faculty members for discussion of substantive issues in the reform of the curriculum, the problems of world education, or even new forms of collaboration with university scholars in foreign cultures. A lack of budget for the purpose was usually given as the reason.

At the conferences I attended, some interesting questions on educational policy came up; and it was obvious that the participants from the state departments were not at all familiar with what is happening on the campuses—where young student intellectuals have serious criticism to make of current educational policies and where critics on the university faculties have been writing and talking seriously about education in the humanities, the arts, and the social sciences. All the state department relationships seemed to be with those campus personnel who are teaching or administering education courses and who are insulated from the ferment of educational discussion going on in the activist groups of students and faculty. The main questions at the humanities conference, I discovered to my alarm, were about how units of credit might be given for new humanities courses in the high schools, how these additional hours could be fitted into the present schedules, how computers might be used for rescheduling units of time (an important matter, but only after some priorities of time allocation have been decided), and how, if at all, courses in the humanities could be organized before the publishing companies had produced the necessary course outlines and textbooks.

Teachers and state department officers alike seemed to feel helpless before the idea that new materials and activities in the arts and humanities can and should come from the efforts of teachers themselves and that to postpone action until the textbook, electronics, and audiovisual industries came to the rescue was in effect a confession of trained incapacity among teachers of the arts. Faced with this situation, most university critics of teacher education simply write off the state departments and their personnel or content themselves with denunciation or cite evidence that the whole system is hopeless. But how could it be assumed to be otherwise if the scholars and critics from outside the state departments make no effort to reach those on the inside or if there is no program with a serious intellectual content through which the staff members of the state departments can break out of their cultural isolation?

If the practitioner of education in the teacher education institutions or in the state departments has no serious interest in issues and ideas, he does his work according to rules that he did not make and that he has no special wish to change. If, at the same time, there is no way in which he is confronted with serious issues, the resolution of which can determine what rules are actually desirable, he accepts whatever rules and attitudes are in effect. It does no good for publicists, journalists, admirals, and others to denounce, deplore, and view with alarm. What is needed, aside from serious analysis of where the problems are, is a program of education and action. If education is needed among the educators, the point is to find out what kind is needed and to set to work to provide it.

Conferences of state department officials with teachers from the colleges and schools and with historians, sociologists, psychologists, and others interested in education are one kind of answer. Another approach could be the use of weekly seminars, possibly related to an ongoing research project carried on by a mixture of staff members, one or two graduate students, and university faculty members. The subject of the seminar would then relate to the ongoing research. It would also be useful to have elementary and secondary school teachers join such seminars or, if geographical distance prohibited this, to arrange for some form of internship by selected teachers in the state department.

As a bare minimum of action that state departments of education could take to encourage awareness of and participation in programs of world affairs and the education of teachers, the following might be done:

1. Depending on the mood and constituency of the state legislature and its committee on education, initiative might be taken for the passage of enabling legislation on certification requirements which gives explicit latitude for innovations within the teacher education programs of the state. In most cases this would not make a basic difference in the latitude already existing, although it might. The main point is to use the legislation as an invitation for the development of new kinds of programs.

2. There could be unofficial or official liaison with local World Affairs Councils, United Nations Associations, or similar organizations in the state, thus providing school systems with the resources of the organizations— library and information centers, state or regional activities, panel discussions, television forums, speakers, and whatever else the world affairs organizations had to offer.

3. Foreign specialists in education from non-Western countries could be invited to join the staff of the state department of education for a half-year to a year, perhaps longer if the particular job to be done required it. Some states have already done this by appointing foreign educators to state department staffs.

4. Members of university faculties who have had experience abroad or possess a particular knowledge of international education and foreign cultures could act as consultants to the staff and could work on the development of new programs.

5. The state department could make itself responsible for the organization of statewide conferences on world education which could take advantage of the presence in the state of foreign students, teachers in the teacher-exchange programs, films, and the personnel from language and area studies centers.

6. Specially qualified professors from the state or from other states or, for example, representatives of the Educational Development Center in Newton, Massachusetts, or information officers from the United Nations Association or the Foreign Policy Association, could be invited for one or two days of discussion with state department staff to review issues in education and world society which suggest needed changes in the educational system as a whole.

In general, the effort should go in the direction of breaking down the isolation between the state department staff and the reality of contemporary issues in world society as these relate to educational change.

An International Project Organized by Four States

A good example of an existing design for accomplishing many of the objectives discussed in the previous pages has been developed in a regional four-state project in Texas, Alabama, Louisiana, and Tennessee organized under Title V, Section 505, PL 89-10, the federal legislation established for improving state departments of education. Texas made the original application and started the project in motion on behalf of five states, although North Carolina, one of the original group, has not been active since the project began. To simplify the description of the design, I will take Tennessee as an example of the possibilities for coordinated action that links together not only a group of states, but a statewide system of schools, universities, community groups, and state departments of education within each state.

The Tennessee project began to take shape in March 1966 when James K. MusKelley was appointed as state coordinator by the Tennessee Department of Education. Mr. MusKelley received a leave of absence from Memphis State University, where he was a member of the faculty in the Spanish Department. He had traveled a good deal in Europe and had lived in Mexico for two years. Therefore, he was familiar with many of the problems in the exchange of ideas and persons and had a working knowledge of a culture other than his own.

In the year and a half Mr. MusKelley has been in office, progress in Tennessee has been remarkable. The following outline[18] served as the basis for programs developed in Tennessee throughout the year:

Outline of Elements Expected in a State Plan

I. *The improvement of the State Department of Education through international education.*

Curriculum development:
- Bulletins
- Textbook selection
- Staff involvement in international education

Certification of teachers:
- Recognition of overseas experiences in teacher education
- Injection of international education in courses of study in teacher preparation courses

Development of teaching aids and techniques:
- Specific items to aid in international education or language teaching
- Bibliographies and the like for teachers interested in international education
- Aids for non-English speakers

Staff seminars regarding international affairs and education:

Gathering information on current activities and relating them to proper departments:

---

[18] MusKelley, James K. *Outline of Elements Expected in a State Plan.* Memphis, Tenn.: Memphis State University, 1966 (Mimeo.).

238

II. *Development of international educational projects in local schools and in institutions of higher learning.*
- Get local groups to aid in development of specific projects
- Use presently organized educational groups, such as principals organizations
- Promote "sister school" relationship through Department of State
- Develop pupil and teacher exchange programs
- Aid local groups in developing international education concepts in local courses of study
- Exchange of educational materials
- Exchange of consultants

III. *Working with other agencies.*
- Promote international ideas in local and state meetings, fairs, and the like
- Get governmental groups, service clubs, and so forth to promote and support international projects

IV. *Assisting schools abroad.*
- The American-type school
- The school that is a part of the ministry system
- Reciprocal scholarships

Each of the items in the above outline was developed more fully as a design for specific action in the state. The budget for the work of the year was modest—approximately $35,000. An office was established at Memphis State University for the development of special projects—seminars, travel throughout the state and the country, visits abroad, and expenses for a statewide committee of five persons composed of public school administrators, university faculty members, and State Department of Education personnel. This committee is the primary working group in the program and has established connections in every sector of the state's educational system from public schools to teacher education institutions.

Mr. MusKelley reports that—

> The highlight of the project has been the response that I have found in asking people at all levels of education to participate. Universities over the state have been quick to respond. . . . It is evident that many college faculty members have wanted to work with public schools but did not know how to establish such a relationship. This problem has not existed with regard to schools of education, but in the other academic areas. By establishing closer relationships between higher education, the public school systems, and the State Department of Education, a much better system of education could be the result, and not only in the area in international education.[19]

The Procedure

Each of the states in the project requested each of their school systems to appoint one person in each district to act as liaison and to receive information about the international educational activities sent from project headquarters. Such information includes, for example, a newsletter and new materials and methods in social studies and the humanities. Of

---

[19] Letter to Harold Taylor, in study files.

the 155 school systems in Tennessee, one third of them appointed such persons, who are now actively involved in spreading the information to their own districts. In some cases, superintendents act personally in that capacity.

W. R. Goodson, project officer for the overall four-state project and chairman of the Latin American Committee for the Southern Association of Colleges and Schools; Severo Gomez, state coordinator for Texas; and Mr. MusKelley traveled together in Brazil, Chile, and Ecuador for a month to visit 13 schools to evaluate them for accreditation through the Southern Association and to establish ties with the schools in each of the countries. Memphis had already had experience with this kind of work through a direct school-to-school project between the American School of Guatemala City and the Memphis City Schools, under a grant from the Overseas Schools section of the U.S. Department of State.

Although this project has been in operation only one year, the Memphis superintendent of schools, several board of education staff, and supervisors of the Memphis City Schools have visited the American School in Guatemala as consultants, while three teachers from Guatemala have been enrolled in courses at Memphis State University and are reviewing, observing, and participating in all phases of the educational system of the city. There has been exchange of curriculum materials, newspapers, films, and other information between Memphis and the American School, as well as the use of consultant library services and materials. Exchanges have been arranged for teachers to work in Memphis and Guatemala; the Guatemala school program is accredited by the Southern Association and has 1,000 children, working both in Spanish and in English. Plans are presently being made for exchange arrangements with the Ministry of Education in Honduras. Three members of the Tennessee State Department of Education have already visited Honduras to work out the details for statewide collaboration between Tennessee and the countrywide system of Honduras.

On the community side, a group of Memphis citizens organized the International Group of Memphis in 1958 to put visitors from abroad in direct contact with citizens of Memphis and to find ways in which the 250 students and temporary residents who come from abroad each year can become directly involved in American life. Among many other projects, the International Group sponsors English teaching for the visitors and arranges a tutorial program so that any person wishing language instruction can hold regular meetings with an assigned tutor. During the past year 609 Memphis citizens were involved in helping in the program with a total budget of only $1,000 to maintain all its services.

Funds have been received by the State Department of Education and from the U.S. Office of Education to hold seminars on Latin America in the three major regions of the state during the coming year. In preparation for the seminars, college teachers who are experts in Latin America have submitted lists of books recommended for junior and senior high school libraries. Six hundred teachers, supervisors, and State Department of Education personnel will participate in the seminars, 200 at each of the centers. Each successive year, the seminars will concern a different area of the world and will deal with contemporary affairs in the countries being studied.

A series of pilot schools will start to produce new materials in the social studies and foreign languages. There will be a comprehensive program from the first grade through the twelfth, and local colleges and universities and the State Department of Education will supply the personnel. An effort will be made to interest college students in becoming foreign language teachers. Foreign students from local colleges and universities will be appointed for in-service and classroom teaching in the materials of their own countries.

A full account of the activities under way in Tennessee is available from the materials prepared by Dr. MusKelley. Similar activities are under way under the direction of the state coordinators in the other states. Overall planning is done by the four coordinators, together with Dr. Goodson, the overall director. This kind of regional and statewide planning and action is one of the most promising lines of development the present study has uncovered.

The Reform of the Certification System

Most state certification officers and their colleagues say that whenever initiatives for changes in the system of certification or the content of requirements are made by the colleges and universities, the state departments are both willing and eager to cooperate, usually through the route of the approved program. In an experimental project involving five universities in New York State, for example, each university is putting together its own set of requirements in what it considers to be the best way of preparing elementary or high school teachers on the assumption that after some discussion of the individual plans by educators, including Mr. Conant and his colleagues, the State Department of Education will approve them.

In the early 1950's, without fanfare and in the regular course of conducting business with the officers of the State Department of Education of New York, we developed at Sarah Lawrence an experimental program for early childhood education that departed completely from the conventional type (for example, there are no subject matter requirements for graduation from Sarah Lawrence, no grades, no examinations, few lectures, and no departmental system) and found no problem in having the plan accepted by the state. The state seemed to us to be happy that we were trying so hard to invent a new kind of program in our own style. It did not occur to us that they would not be, since we held the notion that the program we were developing was a good one and was a serious contribution to educational experiment.

Whether or not the experience of other colleges and universities in other states is as congenial as this one was, in terms of the results of our survey of the attitudes of certification officers there is every indication that something approaching a national plan in international education could be developed through regional state projects with the initiatives from the state departments.

The starting point would be in these general propositions about student teachers and foreign experience:

1. It is perfectly legitimate for educators and certification officers to assert that blanket approval by state certification officers of all forms of foreign teaching and study experience is not necessarily the best way of dealing with the problem. Some differentiation needs to be made between the variety of forms that teaching overseas can take, from service in the Overseas Schools to work in Peace Corps teaching, International Voluntary Service teaching, private schools overseas, and programs conducted by organizations like the Experiment in International Living or the American Friends Service Committee.

2. Steps might be taken by state certification officers not only to develop general agreements in arranging credit for foreign teaching experience, but to initiate programs through which candidates for certificates in secondary and elementary education would go abroad for a year of study in a foreign language and culture as a regular part of their preparation to teach. This would be especially relevant, of course, for language and world affairs specialists, but it should also be considered as an irreplaceable asset for the education of teachers in general.

3. Supervision of teaching overseas by qualified persons in the field would not only help in the evaluation of practice teaching and related experience, but would be, if properly conducted, an important aid to the student teachers themselves. Since the Peace Corps idea (apart from the actual Peace Corps program) is a central concept in the preparation of teachers for service in American schools, the possibilities inherent in the extension of present liaison between the Peace Corps and the departments of education is obviously one place to begin.

4. Granted the value of overseas supervision of Peace Corps teaching, it is possible that state departments could agree to make a formal liaison with Peace Corps teaching supervisors abroad, by which, in individual cases, the Peace Corps district representative could observe, supervise, and evaluate the work of individual Peace Corps teachers, reporting both to the Peace Corps and to the state department of education simultaneously. There is no reason why a state department of education could not take the initiative in volunteering to prepare 100 students for Peace Corps or other teaching in a given country through cooperative arrangements with selected colleges in the state and appointed supervisors for the overseas teaching. Then the state, as well as the state department of education, would have a stake in the quality of the student teacher sent abroad and the possibility of his service as a teacher in the state when he returned.

5. When state department budgets or special grants allowed it, the

representatives from the states could go abroad as colleagues of the Peace Corps or college supervisors to gain direct experience of the practice teaching and the methods of evaluation presently in operation in a given country. Observers from the state departments could also attend Peace Corps training programs in this country to gain a direct knowledge of the approach to teacher education which the individual programs are taking.

6. Members of the faculty of approved programs in the universities and colleges could be made responsible for working out the supervision, which might involve individual cultural affairs officers or American educational attachés in foreign countries who could report directly to the home institution.

7. An evaluation center similar to the kind operated by New York State might be developed under the auspices of state departments, where both the subject matter and professional training of each candidate who had been abroad could be reviewed, with recommendations made to the certification officer.

8. Individuals abroad from universities who are on AID educational assignments might be recruited as the university representatives for review of the teaching as it is going on and would report back to the home campus.

9. Staff members of UNESCO and of the UN Institute for Training and Research might also be recruited for the task of observing and, in some cases, supervising the work of practice teaching abroad.

Looked at from the point of view of the student teacher who is studying and possibly teaching abroad, a great many possibilities can be seen in the student's use of his own teaching experience to sharpen his perception of the educational system in which he is involved and the educational problems that he meets from day to day. Regular reports from the student within a general framework established in advance by a member or members of the college of education in the United States could assume the status of research studies dealing with cases of individual children or the development of curriculums or the analysis of the social and political conditions affecting the foreign educational system.

Arrangements for such a program in advance of the service abroad would enhance the student's own education while in service and assure him of a link to the variety of careers open in the teaching profession on his return. The collaboration between the universities and the state department of education in these matters would ensure the development of more enterprising and imaginative teacher education programs in the future. Some of these future programs might include collaboration of the students abroad with foreign students in this country who could conduct comparative case studies, research projects, and practice teaching in world affairs and non-Western cultures as a regular part of their experience in American institutions. As already noted, principals and superintendents of schools throughout the states could become involved, wherever possible, in summer travel-study programs to acquaint themselves directly with the teacher education problems of teacher candidates abroad, so that there would be a direct relationship between local school systems and the work of the colleges and universities in foreign countries. There is a very simple mandate for progress in all this. The main effort should be toward making the whole matter of certification a positive instrument in the development of American education in a world perspective, not simply a regulatory device for licensing teachers.

Chapter 5.   The Cultural Element in Foreign Policy

> And, at last, after many devastations, overthrows, and even complete internal exhaustion of their powers, the nations are driven forward to the goal which Reason might have well impressed upon them, even without so much sad experience.
>
> Immanuel Kant
> *The Idea of a Universal History*

As I write this section of the Report on the relation between the education of American teachers and the conduct of American foreign policy, everything I am capable of thinking about the issues involved and the future of American and world society is confronted by the reality of a series of world events which have followed each other in rapid succession—the lies and furies of the Arab-Israeli war; the political confusion and organized violence in Nigeria, the Congo, Vietnam, Communist China, Hong Kong, the American cities; the disintegration of rational discourse at the United Nations; the malignant race policies of the Rhodesian and South African governments; the cursing and screaming of invectives in threats against America and the West by the Castroites, the Chinese, the Arabs, and the Africans—in short, the unleashing of new modes of violence and the decrease in the power of rational and enlightened authority everywhere. I would be foolish to believe that through the education of teachers in world affairs or foreign cultures a restoration of order and acceptable authority would be forthcoming, or that what we do in education in this country can have a direct and controlling effect on the creation of a new world order more congenial to the true interests of mankind than the present one.

But it would be equally foolish to ignore the fact that *without* a profound and rapid change in the quality and outlook of American education in its moral, social, and political dimension, there is little hope that America will, in the future, be able to influence the course of events in the direction of peace and international stability, aside from curing the problems of poverty, racism, and violence which wrack our own communities. There is no need to repeat the familiar argument which links the quality of educa-

245

tion and the reality of full educational opportunity to the moral and social health of all societies. I believe we can take as self-evident that education of quality for all is what gives cohesion to a society and provides, in Horace Mann's phrase, "the balance wheel of the social machinery." But it may be useful to trace, in specific terms, the way in which the education of American teachers in world affairs is related to the conduct of an enlightened and powerful American foreign policy.

Here I take, as my beginning, the action of the House of Representatives of the Ninetieth Congress in passing the foreign aid legislation in August 1967, with cuts of $283 million from a requested and already cut budget of $2.87 billion, by an eight-vote margin, 202 to 194. By that margin of eight votes, the major components of American foreign policy concerned with cultural, economic, and social amelioration of the problems of world society were saved from irreparable harm. The continuance of future threats to such policy was prophesied by the fact that previous to the passage of the foreign aid legislation, 98 votes were recorded in favor of a move to abolish foreign aid altogether.

There are complicated political reasons involved in the success or failure of foreign aid legislation, more complicated than usual in the present instance. But ultimately, the decision to vote in Congress for or against the support of educational and economic aid for other countries depends on a single fact. That is the degree of conviction held by members of Congress that the conduct of American foreign policy should be based on positive efforts to use American resources to improve world conditions, or on other factors—mainly military and economic power exercised on behalf of a narrowly construed national self-interest. The degree of that conviction depends on a variety of other factors, but in the final analysis on two—the influence of education in world affairs and liberal democracy on the attitudes and knowledge of Congressmen, and the influence of teachers and education on the attitudes of the electorate.

The educational system is responsible for the education of those who will become its leaders, in politics or any other field. It is also responsible for educating everyone else to become interested in paying attention to what the leaders are doing and how the world is being run. The simple proposition is that the teachers in the schools and colleges are the only ones who, in this society, are responsible for working full-time at the task of educating the citizenry to understand the nature of their world. The corollary proposition is that unless the teachers have an education which can enable them to reach some such understanding, they can do nothing but hand on to their pupils whatever is given to them through the myths, folklore, and conventional wisdom of their society. It is with this in mind that I have been looking at the relation between the education of American teachers and American foreign policy, and it is for this reason that I have been unable to think of the education of teachers in the field of world affairs separately from their total education as serious intellectuals and as men and women of moral and social concern.

Some General Considerations

The foreign policy of a country is determined at a given moment by any number of things over which the country has no control, including the accidents of its own history and the condition and power position of the rest of the countries of the world. Short of a policy of territorial aggression, a country can do nothing about its geographical location, about the existence and relative size of its natural resources, or even about the way in which its people have in the past created the particular cultural, moral, and social environment in which certain kinds of foreign policy decisions in the present are either possible or impossible. Foreign policy is conditioned by the size of resources in military power, nuclear and otherwise, the extent of industrialization and technology, and all the other familiar economic and social items in the calculation of power politics. But, in the long run, to speak in terms of pure power, the capability of a given country to influence world events depends on its educational system—without which there would be no skilled manpower, talented managers, large-scale agricultural production, foreign service officers, engineers, linguists, economists, or statesmen; only politicians trying to manipulate a tribal system of ignorant and untrained people.

There are, accordingly, a series of foreign policies of various styles and content available to various nation-states, based on their capacity to exert certain kinds of power, positively or negatively. The Soviet Union could not do what it does had it not taken over a manageable peasant population from the czars and transformed it into a national system of industrial and agricultural production through an educational system which produced what the Soviet government decided it had to have to achieve certain national and international purposes. There are things the government of the United States cannot do because it did not take over a population of peasants and has not had the control of the country's educational system. It is forced to do most of what it does at home by persuasion and social engineering. What it does abroad is subject to the same conditions.

The instruments of power available to the United States in exerting influence in world affairs include all the military, economic, and political factors available to other countries, but on a vastly larger scale. The difficulty is that the relative strength of these and other factors has never been calculated with a high degree of precision, and, in recent years, American foreign policy has followed a plain pattern of assumption common to those engaged in power politics—which places military and technological power at the first level of significance, with political and economic power serving as secondary and interlocking elements in the exercise of influence. We have learned, of course, as have the Russians, that you cannot do very much with nuclear military power except blow yourself up with it, and that seems now to have been clearly established in the lexicons of military strategy for all but the Chinese.

It is in the exercise of moral and cultural power—that is, the capacity to persuade and to influence world events by visible acts of humane principle

247

under the sanction of international law and humane custom—that American efforts have been sharply reduced, while the rhetoric of moral principle goes on.

Yet, American political theory and our stated international intent flow from a moral postulate—that the use of power must be in the interest of those for whom it is used, with military strength to support the rights and interests of those who do not possess the means to act in their own defense. In the long run, the moral act, committed according to an unexceptionable and clear humanitarian aim, has the greatest power to influence world events, while there are self-defeating and narrow limits to the effect of military force in achieving political or social objectives. The same is true of economic power in the exercise of influence, as we and the Russians continue to learn from day to day in experience with bilateral aid programs.

A more adequate analysis of how a foreign policy exerts influence in world affairs would scale down the importance of the military, considering it useful only as an international deterrent to potential and actual aggression and as a means of stabilizing the world's military environment. The way is then clear for a fresh conception of the interlocking use of economic, moral, and cultural power for the development of a world order. That conception would be based on the fact that as the quality and scope of democratic education increases within nation-states and throughout the world, it becomes increasingly difficult for any single power to take military action outside its own borders without strong negative response both inside and outside those borders.

Until very recently there has been almost no analysis of the concept of cultural power as a factor in American foreign affairs. The assumption has been made in public discussion and in arguments before Congress that this is mainly a matter of building American prestige by exchanging art objects, performers, ideas, books, suitable intellectuals, and distinguished persons with other countries and thus, with the help of the U.S. Information Agency abroad and American culture at home, to please and impress the foreign public and foreign governments with American accomplishments. The entire budget for the State Department's educational programs is $51,201,000 for 1967, enough to include $34,363,000 for exchange of persons—6,724 foreign visitors (731 of whom are teachers) and 2,378 Americans (of whom 305 are teachers). As far as teachers are concerned, we are working in the hundreds when we should be working and thinking in the thousands.

The pitifully low budget of $1.5 million for exchanges in the performing arts is some indication of the low regard in which the work of our artists and intellectuals is held as far as the representation of American culture abroad is concerned. In this is reflected a general public attitude to the arts as something practiced by artists and enjoyed by their admirers but irrelevant to the national welfare or interest. It is assumed that foreign policy is one thing and culture another, and that there is little relation between them, since foreign policy is a matter of politics, diplomats, public

248

statements, and government strategies having to do with wars, enemies, communists, and friends, while culture is what is done in concert halls and lecture rooms.

The failure is not simply a lack of public understanding of the place of the arts and ideas in the national life, but the lack of a coherent body of thought or consistent set of practices in the United States to deal with the relation of this country to the cultures, educational systems, and peoples of the world. There is, instead, a welter of different institutions and agencies, from the business community to the Department of Agriculture, the American Friends Service Committee to the moving picture industry, the Ford Foundation to General Motors, the universities to the Pentagon, the State Department to the Rotary Club, all of them with different programs, intentions, and degrees of success in communicating these intentions internationally.

In the case of activities outside the government, this is probably as it should be, since the spirit of volunteer action and the special interests of all kinds of people should be reflected in the variety of ways in which they can make direct connections with other persons and institutions in the total world community. But in the case of government action, by the Congress or the executive branch, the significance of the cultural element in national and international affairs cannot be left to the whim of individual Congressmen on appropriation committees or to the accidents of administrative initiative and decisions in individual agencies. The biennial struggle for allocation of funds to the foreign aid bill, the identification of foreign policy issues with military concerns, the mixing together of military and economic aid as if it were all to be used for the same purpose, and the cuts in the budgets of anything having to do with cultural and educational affairs abroad—all of this indicates the need for continuous and sustained effort on the part of government officials and their intellectual allies in the universities to create strong and vigorous partnerships in the task of educating Congress and the country.

It is not too difficult to think that if a sufficient number of educators and university scholars took a serious interest in research, writing, and speaking out on the subject of cultural affairs in relation to foreign policy and foreign aid, a gradual shift would come about in the attitude of key Congressmen and government planners as to what constitutes a wise and effective use of our cultural power in the achievement of enlightened foreign policy objectives.

A scholar reading the text of the hearings on budget appropriations in international, educational, and cultural affairs before Congress would be appalled to find that rather than discussing cultural, or even fiscal, policy, the hearings consist of a series of suspicious questions about whether or not an American scholar going abroad has or has not ever been critical of his government, or whether there are foreign students in this country who have ever participated in demonstrations. Since the Congressmen who hold the hearings are responsible to the American people for decisions they make

249

in cultural affairs, it would be most appropriate and immensely helpful if the academic profession, through its organizations and through its research and individual scholarship, followed the course of policy making closely and made known to the Congressmen, the public, and the university community the results of their enquiry. At the present time, few educators are even aware of how policy is made, aside from not knowing what happens at budget hearings.

At the moment, most of those at work in government agencies who wish to expand and clarify the role of cultural affairs in our relations with other countries are doing what they can without much help from the universities, the intellectuals, or the serious critics of foreign policy. Few of the latter are drawn from the field of education and cultural affairs. They are almost entirely social scientists and historians whose intellectual and research interests are political and economic; their preoccupation with problems in these areas excludes consideration of the broader issues of cultural diffusion and world change. Knowledge of foreign policy is equated with knowledge of political, military, and economic strategy, and it is difficult for most people in government agencies, or in Congress, or in the universities, unless already occupied with cultural issues and concerns, to associate those issues with the operation of a foreign policy.

The Power of Education

On the other hand, since knowledge is power, and education is the means through which knowledge is generated and distributed, the educational system of a country is a form of power which exerts its influence in determining both what kind of foreign policy is possible for a given state and what kinds of long-range goals are feasible for a society as a whole. I do not believe it is accurate, except in a general sense, to say with President Johnson that "our foreign policy will advance no faster than the curriculum of our classrooms." If we were to believe this literally, our foreign policy would be pre-World War II. It is more accurate to say that the educational system is the major resource for developing attitudes and values which permeate the culture and, in the long run, the educational system is what gives the society its national intellectual character and its moral and political point of view. The emotional content in the life of a country can be harnessed for political and military purposes by social engineers with talent. In large part that content is developed within the framework of the educational system by the teachers and what they teach and do not teach, and by what is taught in history—pride of conquest, of ancestry, and of power, victories, love of country, or love of humanity at large.

Yet, the entire educational and cultural affairs program of the State Department for 38 countries in Africa involves 39 American professors to teach in African universities, 9 American teachers to teach English in African secondary schools, and 37 African secondary school teachers coming to the United States, plus 200 college students. This does not, of course, include additional programs of education carried on by AID and other agencies and foundations, but it does indicate the place of teachers and teacher education in the cultural policy of the United States in relation to one of the most important areas in the world, and one which is currently very much neglected by American aid for educational and social development. The total AID budget for teacher education abroad amounts to $6,496,000 for 13 projects in all of Africa. The scale of effort does not even begin to approach either the need or the possible effects which large-scale effort might have.

Parts of the World System

When looked at from a world perspective, it is possible to think of the educational systems of individual states as parts of an interlocking world system in which the power of education can, if properly used, be placed at the disposal of the world community. If education is considered as a factor in the international power structure, it can be consciously used either to further national self-interest or to help construct a viable international community. In the best of circumstances, it can do both. It can, for example, reconstruct the content of its national curriculum in a way designed to develop a sympathetic and accurate understanding of other cultures and ideologies, including those developed by the "enemy." When observed and noted by the educated community and governments abroad, this kind of curriculum will be taken as an act of goodwill and, in the broadest sense of the term, a positive political action. Another step is to invent ways in which teachers and scholars around the world can work together on common problems within their national educational systems— ranging from the problem of teaching science in the elementary schools to writing new kinds of world history in which each culture has a fair and honorable place.

The most extreme negative example of cultural values as an instrument of policy can be drawn from the present program of Communist China, which includes teaching the Chinese to hate Americans, on the assumption that this is beneficial to Chinese interests. A middle-range example can be drawn from current French policy, which, in the absence of France's former economic and military power for use on a broad international scale, has concentrated on the exercise of political and cultural influence through a program of French nationalism and the Gaullist grandeur of France, involving, among other items, the financing of 45,000 French teachers in service abroad. The British, in a roughly comparable situation involving the loss of military and economic power formerly available for use on a world scale, must rely almost exclusively on political, economic, and cultural relations, particularly with the United States, in order to effect such influence as is now possible. The British are therefore turning more and more of their efforts toward the improvement of their educational system, both in making it more democratic, thus releasing more talent among wider sectors of the society, and in increasing the capability of its technological and scientific manpower.

One rapid way of making the point I wish to make is to ask what resources for the exercise of power and international influence are available to those countries whose economic, and therefore military, power is unavoidably kept to modest proportions—modest, that is, when compared to Soviet and American capability. In this instance, no matter what they would have liked to have done in a military way, the British at Suez or the French in Indochina were unable to do it owing to lack of military and economic resources. The creation of political and cultural ties then assumes the first level of significance.

In a different situation, in Indonesia, because the circumstances did not allow the United States to use military force to control the internal politics of that country, our policy did allow the uncompleted revolution of the Indonesians against outside control a chance to work itself out in its own terms. American cultural, political, and economic influence, exercised in an enlightened way through the preceding years mainly by the Ford Foundation and the American program of foreign aid [a fair proportion of which had to do with teacher education], was able to operate without the handicap of military intervention. The result was that after the change in political leadership, achieved not without violence and bloodshed, Indonesia created a new and viable political situation of very great consequence for the stability of the whole of Asia.

It is possible to argue, on the basis of the facts, that the subsequent change of Indonesian policy in international affairs in the direction of peaceful coexistence was in some part the result of the patient and clearly visible efforts of American educators and the American government, over a period of 15 years, in putting American funds and personnel to work on behalf of the educational, social, and economic welfare of the Indonesians. Indonesia's present leaders were conscious during those years of the continuing contribution made to their country through the use of American cultural resources; they knew at first hand that the educators and economic advisers were honestly working to achieve the goals of a self-sufficient Indonesian society. But they also knew that the CIA had been helping the rebels against Sukarno in the 1950's when our declared policy was one of Indonesian self-determination. It was our good fortune that this piece of clandestine intervention was defeated by the Indonesian government then in power, before it could throw the whole of our foreign aid and educational program into disrepute.

In the wars and conflicts of these recent years, the strongest elements in creating the conflicts have had to do with nationalism, not with communism, and it is to nationalism, combined with racism, that we need to look in the present and future for the most dangerous sources of war, conflict, and mass violence. The defense against extreme nationalism as a force in politics, war, and world affairs is, in the long run, the development of international, political, and educational instruments which can reach the root problems which produce the grievances and aggressions.

It is at this point that the United States, with its own particular form of nationalist fervor, is put to the test of international leadership. Unless our military power is used as a stabilizing force for a peaceful international order, it becomes simply another means of creating a greater intensity of nationalism everywhere else in the world. Unless our cultural policy is one which takes full account of the rich resources available within the United States for extending the advantages of education to a wider and wider sector of the world population, we will find ourselves using these resources to increase the spirit of nationalism, among ourselves and others.

Education and Colonialism

It may be useful to point out that the history of educational imperialism subsequent to military conquest has had grisly effects on the cultural and social developments of the countries thus colonized. Not only does it impose a false culture and a feudal social system on the country of occupation, but when the revolutions and revolts of liberation occur and the societies are free to organize their own affairs, not only is the educational system inadequate to deal with problems of the society, but there is no cultural base from which a new educational system can grow. The United States is now providing in Vietnam a classic example of the contradictions between the use of military conquest for the achievement of political aims and the administration of educational and social welfare programs to rehabilitate the people and the society being destroyed.

The educational system left by the French in Vietnam was based on concepts of elitism and of social class which led directly to the kind of military dictatorship it has been our decision to support in South Vietnam. The French left a curriculum and program of the most reactionary style of French pedagogy. It is perhaps too much to ask that a colonial system designed to subjugate and exploit a people should develop a democratic educational system which would enable the colony to determine its own cultural, political, and social future. However, in retrospect, that would be the wisest course of action any colonial power could have taken, since it not only would have made possible a transition from a colonial relationship to one of cooperative liaison, but would have provided the fabric from which a new society and economy could be built, without the revolutions and wars of liberation which are now the common lot of the third world. Turning this to a positive precept, it is now clear that whatever else the United States does in connection with its foreign policy in Asia and Africa, the central thrust should be in social and economic development through education, which means the education of teachers.

The irony in our present situation in Vietnam is too obvious for extended comment. While AID and the Department of Health, Education, and Welfare have limited programs for teacher education, we find our efforts and those of the Vietnamese frustrated in trying even to conduct classes for the millions of children, 60 in a class, with "unmotivated pupils, ill-prepared teachers, undelivered supplies, inadequate plants, and insufficient finances." The irony becomes tragedy when we think what could be done were we to spend even $3 billion of our $24 billion a year on education and social development rather than on the military, or when we think of what the French could have done had they given Indochina an educational system designed for the benefit of Southeast Asia rather than for its exploitation by the French.

Instead of a broad, large-scale, and effective Vietnam program of educational aid where it is most needed—in the education of teachers and in the supply of teachers and teacher aides—at a time so many young Americans are anxious to serve in that other kind of war, a total educational budget of $5,079,000 is allocated for South Vietnam from AID funds for fiscal year 1967. Of this, $1,780,000 is for teacher education, with the rest for rural trade schools ($40,000), hamlet schools ($500,000), instructional materials ($700,000), vocational education ($784,000), and leadership training (selected Vietnamese sent to the United States for professional and technical education, $1,275,000). Two modest programs of the colleges of education of Ohio University and the University of Southern Illinois are continually inhibited in their efforts to give support to and increase the supply of teachers and teaching materials by the internal politics and restrictions of Washington-Saigon policies. Again there is a failure in cultural policy. A great many of these restrictions have had to do with the freedom of Americans in Vietnam, or, upon their return to the United States after service there, to express their views about the war or to work in the ways in which some of the finest teachers in South Vietnam— the 170 volunteers of the International Voluntary Service—are most capable of working.

American cultural policy, as administered by the military and civilian officials, with the latter now integrated with the military, has created tensions between the administrators and the civilian volunteers, who are widely recognized as among the most effective teachers and workers involved in reconstruction, resulting in the resignation in September 1967 of four major leaders in the volunteer movement. In the words of one of them, "As individuals . . . we cannot become part of the destruction of a people we love."[1]

"If we started building schools as passionately as we build air bases," says John Naisbitt, "and training teachers as thoroughly as we train pilots, we might bring something worthwhile to Vietnam. If we do not, our defeat will be as profound as that suffered by the French at Dien Bien Phu."[2]

While the Vietnamese suffer the consequences of severe educational shortages, the children of well-to-do Americans and military personnel in Saigon experience a similar shortage. According to a *New York Times*

---

[1] *New York Times,* September 19, 1967; pp. 1, 16.

[2] Naisbitt, John. "America's Dien Bien Phu." *Saturday Review,* July 15, 1967, p. 72.

Mr. Naisbitt, who served as assistant to the former Commissioner of Health, Education, and Welfare, John Gardner, is now in private industry and visited Vietnam in the spring of 1967. His article reviews the educational situation in South Vietnam on the basis of that visit and available reports in the field.

report of October 1, 1967, 100 American students are attending a new school whose curriculum director is a man with experience in real estate and business who accepted the post because, as he put it, "I go where the money is." The report quotes one of the teachers as saying, "It's a kind of a funny place. The children are wealthy and no one ever talks about the war. The war doesn't exist in this school."[3]

That view is shared by at least one of the students who is reported as saying, "For most kids, it gets sort of dull in Saigon. We drive around in our Hondas in the afternoon, we go down to the USO sometimes, or we just walk around."[4]

In applying an American philosophy of education to a situation of this kind, it should be possible to organize educational projects in community aid and social service in Saigon which would put such 15-year-old Americans to work in ways which could not only teach them how to use their time profitably but could improve the quality of their understanding of Vietnamese society in the throes of its dissolution. Again, the need is for an American policy, and one which stresses the need for teachers, teachers who are themselves aware of the relation of social change and moral values to intellectual and educational growth.

Aside from the meager help being given to teachers and teaching in South Vietnam itself, there is little indication that a cultural policy which must obviously make direct links between the need for educational development abroad and the preparation at home of those who can help with that development abroad has in any way been adequate to the tasks with which the policy deals. The extent to which our educational strength in the United States is inadequate in the field of Southeast Asian studies was the subject of comment by Professor John K. Fairbank of Harvard University, at the International Congress of Orientalists at the University of Michigan in August 1967. It takes 10 years, Professor Fairbank points out, with work in the Chinese and Vietnamese languages, as well as the politics, history, anthropology, and economics of Vietnam, to produce a full-bodied scholar in the Vietnam field, and we have only recently begun to organize the research and curricular programs through which candidates can acquire the necessary training.

On the other hand, the necessity of teaching and learning in America about Southeast Asia will not wait for a 10-year period for the incubation of scholars. We know enough already about the way in which direct experience in the Asian culture, combined with language training, practice teaching, and community development projects, can quicken the process of preparation to teach about Asia. If we cared to do so, we could, through government- and foundation-sponsored teacher education programs, mount a major program of teacher education right now which could serve as an international example of what can be done when a powerful democratic

---

[3] Weintraub, Bernard. "Americans Study at Saigon School." *New York Times,* October 1, 1967, p. 5.

[4] *Ibid.*

country uses its resources to the full in an effort to serve the true needs of the peoples of the world. Aside from the immediate training of volunteers for Vietnam, we could develop one-, two-, or three-year M.A. and B.A. programs in Vietnamese studies, Peace Corps style, calling for volunteers through such organizations as the International Voluntary Service and the 22 other organizations already at work in South Vietnam with a handful of 350 teachers and workers.

We could finance hundreds of Vietnamese teachers and American student teachers to work together and would thus come to grips with the fact that for the years to come, no matter what the outcome of the war, we are going to need more and more teachers in Vietnam and in the United States who are able to teach intelligently about the Vietnamese, the American, and the Asian people. The sooner we begin to help the Vietnamese with a larger supply of teachers for their own country and a larger degree of understanding of their problems on our part at home, the sooner we can help to repair the damage they are now suffering. If the Defense Department can afford to train 9,000 to 11,000 servicemen in the Vietnamese language and culture, we can certainly afford to train an equivalent number of civilian volunteers. We should be planning at this moment for a federal program of subsidy for selected veterans of the Vietnam war, both Vietnamese and American, to become teachers in Vietnam in the crucial period of reconstruction following the war's end. Although we will not be able to put highly qualified scholars of the kind described by Professor Fairbank into the field, that is not the major problem facing the Vietnamese. They need a new educational system, and we should make a national and international project out of helping them to get it.

The Cultural Obligations Implied by the International Education Act

In view of the situation of the United States in contemporary world society and the negative mood of Congress, the formal action of the Congress in passing the International Education Act of 1966 can be seen to be nothing less than a radical move in the direction of a world concept of education and a new cultural policy for the government. If the implications of the Act are carried out in practice, education becomes, for the first time in the history of the United States, a major element in foreign policy. Conversely, foreign policy is subject to analysis and decision based on long-range world-inclusive educational goals. The intention of the new legislation, as construed by President Johnson in his public statements, is to advance the cause of education everywhere, in cooperation with "all nations, friend and foe alike," with a wish to "receive as much as we give, to learn as well as to teach."

While the Act directs attention to the necessity of building an international dimension directly into the American educational system and cites ways in which existing resources and programs of government agencies can be used for education in an international dimension, Congress has moved in the opposite direction, granting funds for military programs, cutting back or canceling funds for international, cultural, and social needs of all kinds. International education has no constituency in this country except among those educators and citizens who believe in it strongly enough to make their views known publicly and to work directly with Congressional committees and government agencies to press for its advance. It is time that that constituency took appropriate action.

Certainly, to repeat the findings already reported in the present study, as of now only a small part of the task can be undertaken through existing college resources. What is needed are funds and support from outside agencies. To put it bluntly, there is a wide gap, as yet unbridged, between the American educational system and American foreign policy. There are too many pressing problems already afflicting the educators in trying to meet what has to be done from day to day, with budgets and energies already stretched, to encourage the wider perspective and inspire action to suit it.[5]

I have remarked elsewhere in this Report on the lack of direct connection between the academic departments and the programs of teacher education; in essence, the task of preparing teachers in subject matter areas has been handed over to the departments, whose members have seldom given reconsideration to the content of the academic disciplines in the light of the new roles the teacher is asked to fulfill—one of which is to act as interpreter of the new situation of America in world society and the new situation of mankind in the world revolution.

The emphasis in the work which has already been done, and done well, by Education and World Affairs and other organizations has been on the analysis of undergraduate and graduate liberal arts curriculums and the need for their reform by the inclusion of materials in world affairs and non-Western cultures. But the unsolved problem of EWA and of the organizations, associations, and government agencies which are developing ideas and policies in international education is how to inject these ideas into the educational planning of the schools, colleges, and universities. The relation between that emphasis and the work of the colleges of education is slight, even in cases where colleges of education have held AID contracts for the development of foreign educational systems.

The problem before us is one of stimulating interest and initiative within the colleges and universities so that they become active in considering a total shift in attitude toward the content of contemporary culture and whatever, of all the things which can be taught to the contemporary student, is most worth their knowing. Coupled with that shift must be another one, toward a concentrated and continuous interest on the part of the colleges of education in the policies and decisions about education and international affairs made by Congress and the Administration. This means the inclusion in education courses of materials drawn

---

[5] A full discussion of these matters is to be found in the Proceedings of the Conference on World Education, *op. cit.*

directly from government documents, reports of hearings, statements, and speeches of government officials on cultural policy at home and abroad—ranging from the reports of the National Endowment for the Arts and Humanities to the International Cooperation Year, government conferences on education, White House Conferences, and research publications of the U.S. Office of Education and the Department of State.

Those of us who believe that the entire content of the arts and sciences curriculum should be reshaped to bring it in touch with advances in the state of contemporary knowledge, including knowledge of contemporary world society, are at present in the minority. The curriculum makers in the colleges and universities are concerned mainly with variations in the sets of requirements for general and special education to achieve a proper balance between them, rather than with an analysis of the content of the curriculum itself to determine whether or not it is drawing upon resources of knowledge now available and relevant to the needs of the student and the citizen in the 1960's. The universities and the colleges of education need, as much as does the government, a reformulation of cultural policy. At present, few universities think of themselves as parts of a cultural system which has direct connections with the conduct of American foreign policy in its intellectual and cultural aspect. The government governs and the schools and colleges educate according to general assumptions laid down by national policies in the formulation of which educators of teachers seldom share.

One would assume that in the educational system of a democratic society in which there is no sharp division between the university and the society it serves, the colleges and universities would instinctively take part in efforts to formulate and to influence the conduct of foreign policy, particularly in its cultural dimension. But this is seldom the case. It is customary among intellectuals, when considering matters of power and the power structure of a given situation, to question the motives and intentions of those who use the power. Among liberal intellectuals in particular it is usual to find a sharp distinction made between idealists without power and politicians or government officials who exercise it, with suspicion of the latter and praise for the former.

The Role of the Intellectual

If one considers the political process from the point of view of the intellectuals, their role is to act as critics of existing policies and to raise the question as to whether a given policy or act is consonant with professed ideals. Every society thus has trouble with its intellectuals, no matter how authoritarian the society may be—as one can see in contemporary conflicts within the Chinese political apparatus, in Spain under Franco, in Yugoslavia under Tito, in the Soviet Union from Stalin to Kosygin, and, in a different context, in the United States.

In the liberal democracies, the problem is handled by assuring freedom of expression to the intellectuals and the universities and taking the position before the world that such freedom is an ideal for all societies.

258

It is for this reason that the United States, for example, is most often criticized for its failure to solve its own social and political problems, whereas the less open and more controlled societies, which do not make the same claim for individual freedom, receive milder criticisms in the court of world opinion, partly because political repression of intellectuals is considered normal in those societies. In fact, a good deal of the criticism from abroad, including much of that produced by writers in the Soviet Union, is based on prior criticism of American policy and action developed by American intellectuals writing for American readers.

What is seldom noticed is that a large portion of the world's intellectuals have a psychic investment in the cultural and political life of the United States and often use it, either consciously or unconsciously, as a testing-point, not only for our intellectual and social behavior, but for the values and validity of their own political and social structures. I wish to persuade the reader that the very openness of American society to the intellectuals who denounce it and the continuous flow of criticism we receive from abroad are not only signs of political strength, but indications of a cultural power which is the envy of the propagandists who inveigh against it. I would also wish to persuade the reader that American citizens, teachers, intellectuals, and artists who travel abroad, with or without government subsidy, have the same rights to express their opinions about American ideas and policies that they have at home, and that it is a favorable sign of the strength and value of a democratic society when these rights are freely granted and fully exercised.

Another part of our cultural power lies in the sheer amount of interest the world takes in us, with our daily lives and government actions scrutinized by a stream of foreign experts and the whole world seeming to feel free to take part in our politics, liking or disliking our Presidents, our habits, our films, our arts, and ourselves. My hope is that we can manage to go on being as interesting to the world as we now seem to be, and that the beginning we have made in developing new cultural policies designed to develop an international context for American ideas can be extended radically in the future.

Cultural Power and Internationalism

The circumstances demand a shift in cultural policy in the direction of internationalism and away from the notion that we should urge the American case on everyone who will listen. We need a more precise definition of what the policy is intended to accomplish. It has been assumed for years that it would be good for American relations abroad if courses and institutes in American culture, American literature, and American studies could be organized on foreign campuses in order that American ideas and values should become known and understood and that students abroad would have direct access to the materials of American life.

It has also been assumed, implicitly when not explicitly, that the main purpose of bringing foreign students and scholars to this country is to give

259

them direct access to the reality of America, its culture, and its educational system, in order that a better and more favorable understanding of our aims and values might exist abroad. There has always been an implicit political motive which, in broadest terms, could be described in the conventional phrase, "strengthening the forces of democracy by building friendship with foreign countries," or, in the language of the Bureau of Educational and Cultural Affairs in explaining its student programs with African countries, "improving the competence of friendly regimes and . . . increasing their understanding of American values, policies and actions."[6]

I am not suggesting that there is anything base in these purposes or that there is any harm in being friendly and wanting others to be, except that the emphasis has been so heavily in this direction that it has obscured other important aims. The kind of intellectual and social experience available to the visiting scholars and students has been too limiting, and, in a sense, too artificial.

I can recall, for example, speaking to American studies classes in universities abroad, where the students either had no particular interest in the subject of American philosophy, culture, and education, or were taking for granted that the American professor in their midst was there to persuade them of the virtues of American life and letters and to act as an apologist for its political and social system. The students were much more interested in the relations and comparisons between American ideas and those of other cultures, especially their own, much more interested in an opportunity for criticism and discussion than in academic exposition. My experience with intelligent foreign students in this country has been that the stereotypes of American ideas and cultural deficiencies which students bring with them from abroad are often reinforced by their experience on the American campus and within the American community.

It is true, of course, that the operation of any government, abroad or at home, reflects the cultural habits and social preconceptions of the people whose government it is. Americans are accustomed to competing with each other in the normal course of their lives and to judging people and institutions according to competitive ranking—in baseball, tennis, scholastic averages, television programs, or public opinion polls—with a national and personal desire to be first, to score the highest. American institutions of all kinds, including the educational and cultural, are rated according to their prestige, fame, productivity, wealth, and size.

In their personal lives and social customs, Americans seek recognition for their virtues and freely bestow such recognition on others as a normal part of their personal and social relationships. We want to be the first—first in space, as President Kennedy once said, without saying why we should be—first in whatever we do. We have built one of the most comprehensive systems of mass communication and image making the

---

[6] Hearings before a Subcommittee of the Committee on Appropriations, House of Representatives, Ninetieth Congress, Part 2, Department of State. Washington, D.C.: Government Printing Office, 1967. p. 575.

world has ever seen, and we are the home of advertising and public relations. We tend to believe that virtues, talents, skills, and capacities go unrecognized if unpublicized.

It would be odd, therefore, if a large part of these elements in the national character were not expressed in the American conception of cultural policy and educational operation abroad, if we did not demand results from those policies, results measurable by explicit admiration for our cultural artifacts, the approval of our ideas, appreciation for our performers, and support of our policies. In any number of ways we look for a return on our cultural investments in terms of political approval, "friendly relations," understanding. We want answered the question, Are you pro- or anti-American? without realizing that even to raise the question in part falsifies the answer.

On the other hand, the policies as they are administered suffer the defects of the culture, defects so endlessly described by American social critics. The policies suffer from the inability of most Americans to distinguish between holding an idea oneself because one believes it and "selling" it and oneself to others. The purpose of cultural exchange, and the reason for developing a cultural policy in the first place, is to advance the cause of education and of the intellectual and cultural interests of all concerned. This is an end in itself, from which may or may not flow other advantages to the sponsors. The appearance of the American Ballet Theatre Company before Soviet audiences is a gift from our dancers to the Soviet people which they accept gladly, as do Americans the art of the Bolshoi. The dancers happen to be American or Russian. When Andrei Voznesensky declaims his poems before Americans or cries in protest in Russia, "I am . . . a human being made of flesh and blood, not a puppet to be pulled on a string," he strikes a response in our country, because we recognize in him, and he in us, the common bonds which exist between one man and another, the common modes of experience through which we can share each other's bounty.

If, in consequence, certain political or other advantages accrue to either country, if Americans and Russians can learn to admire and understand each other through the arts, this is the natural and happy result of all experience in the arts. But this has little to do with the quality of wisdom in the ideologies or foreign policies of our respective governments. The arts bring the world's people together on common ground, as do science, education, and the sharing of all mutual interests. The ideal cultural exchange is of the kind represented by the Montreal Exposition, where the arts, ideas, and architecture of the world came together freely in an atmosphere which allowed each object, performance, and idea to make its own statement before an international community.

I am arguing for a total foreign policy based on cultural values which inform and enlighten its decisions and acts, and against one which considers the arts, education, and cultural affairs to be merely instruments of support for a foreign policy and national posture already decided upon by the government. The intellectual, cultural, and moral values are primary; the foreign policy must flow from them, not the other way around.

The Neglect of the Cultural Element

In the continuing stream of analyses of how American foreign policy is made and administered, the whole question of cultural policy as a factor in foreign relations has been, in the title of Charles Frankel's book, *The Neglected Aspect of Foreign Affairs*.[7] One of the neglects lies in what the cultural policy fails to include. The policy concentrates on the formal educational and cultural institutions in our own and other countries and neglects to include, for example, American scientific and technological advisory services abroad, the Atomic Energy Commission, the Arms Control and Disarmament Agency, the Atoms for Peace program, and the variety of programs run by government agencies—Labor, Agriculture, Commerce, etc.—through representatives in the embassies abroad. The intellectual community of foreign countries is organized much more tightly as an elite body than is the American and is much more in touch with itself. Scientific advisers working with foreign governments are directly involved with problems of disarmament, arms control, nuclear proliferation, the peaceful uses of atomic energy, education, and international research. They usually have direct and indirect connections with other scientists and scholars not in government service who are interested, or who could become interested, in problems of this kind.

The members of the scientific sector of the intellectual community in foreign countries seldom have any direct relation to American cultural activities abroad, partly because they lie outside the regular institutional arrangements for the activities, partly because science is not considered a part of culture or its affairs, and partly because the cultural affairs officers too seldom hold an interest in or knowledge of the larger questions raised by philosophers, scientists, and men of letters. Their interests are more likely to be administrative than intellectual, and their work, accurately described in Mr. Frankel's book, relates more to the disposition of administrative matters than to the discussion of cultural or philosophical issues with local intellectuals and educators. There is, for example, an international peace research movement in which Americans have played a leading part and which could become the basis for regional international conferences sponsored by the United States through its cultural agencies, or for visits by American specialists in the field.

Some of the same difficulties are to be found in the separation of cultural activities from education, since education is a body of practices, institutions, and curriculums in which experts are involved. There has been as yet no adequate clarification of the role in international education of the United States Information Agency, with its obvious involvement with American cultural institutions, of the relation between

[7] Frankel, Charles. *The Neglected Aspect of Foreign Affairs*. Washington, D.C.: Brookings Institution, 1965. p. 156.

its educational functions and those of the cultural affairs officers, or of the relation between the educational advisers and consultants in AID projects and the programs in cultural activities organized by the State Department. The visiting scholar with educational interests and knowledge who travels to foreign countries for lectures and conferences with foreign colleagues seldom meets the American educators who are at work there, nor do AID educators take part in cultural events dealing with broader educational and social questions.

The division of responsibility for "culture" between the USIA and its "fast" media—films, radio, magazines, public information—and the State Department's cultural exchange in the "slow" media—intellectuals, books, performers, exhibits, scholars, and teachers—is based on a fallacious distinction between the purveyors of information about American life and values and the exponents and practitioners of the arts, sciences, and education. An information service is neither a propaganda instrument nor a cultural eunuch. A Voice of America speaks for America and its democratic culture, and the information it conveys is loaded with values derived from the culture, including the values of objectivity and of truth telling.

In fact, the entire area of education has never been a central concern in foreign policy planning, especially as this has to do with the education of teachers and the kind of international cooperative research and teaching which could add a large and important dimension to the cultural element in foreign affairs. As is the case in the United States as a whole, the education of teachers has always been far down on the list of priorities; "education" has been separated from "culture," and the neglect at home is reflected in the neglect of a policy for teacher education abroad. The most promising development in the cure of such neglect is again the passage of the International Education Act and the location of the Center for Educational Cooperation in the Education Office of the Department of Health, Education, and Welfare, where specific and continuing attention can be given to international education in ways which link the American educational system to systems and persons elsewhere in the world.

The State Department and the Educators

As of now, the relation between American education and American foreign policy has been one in which students and faculty members in the colleges and universities consider the State Department, as the operating agency for the administration and manufacture of policy, to be the main force, for better or for worse, which determines the actions of the United States in the world. Yet, the relationship between the State Department and the intellectual community, both inside and outside the universities and schools, remains at best uneasy and, normally, unsatisfactory. Part of the unsatisfactoriness is unavoidable, since the State Department is an instrument for making policy according to certain views of what constitutes the national interest, and the university is an instrument for the development of informed opinion and critical judgment about all policies, in world affairs or anything else, and about what is in fact in the national interest. Those invited by the State Department to serve on advisory panels are drawn from a strong group of university research scholars and others whose work in the public interest is recognized, a good many of whom have interchangeable roles within the Department and the universities or are doing research in political and social issues as an extension of Departmental projects.

Again, an unavoidable problem arises in trying to maintain independent bodies of scholars in the universities whose research can produce fresh insight and thought *because* it is carried on outside and because its assumptions differ from those of the government, while at the same time maintaining on the part of the outsiders a degree of influence on the policy makers. I am thinking of issues such as U.S. policy toward Communist China, or toward Southeast Asia, or toward the antiballistic missile system.

But the center of the problem, as far as the entire educational system is concerned, lies in the relation between U.S. foreign policy and all its dimensions and the bulk of the university faculty members who are not on advisory panels and whose main intellectual and academic responsibilities lie in teaching undergraduates and high school students. At the time of the teach-ins on the Vietnam question, the feeling in the universities was that dissident views on the campus were considered by the State Department, the President, and his staff to be those of amateurs and bemused people without access to the cables and the inner circle of information and experts within the government. On the one hand, membership in the inner circle, when extended into the academic community, tends to neutralize the member as far as public disagreement is concerned; on the other hand, nonmembership disqualifies the critic, and the State Department takes the role of explaining its policies as if these were the only ones which could be held by reasonable men who understand the problems.

The approach is publicly evident in the foreign policy conferences organized by the State Department for the benefit of educators. Responding to a serious interest on the part of the Department in making its policies and procedures known to educators, Department officials, from the Secretary of State to the heads of various bureaus, have appeared these past two years before an invited national audience of administrators, professors, and teachers from a range of institutions, many of them colleges for teachers. I am prepared to believe in the sincerity of the motives of the government in providing the opportunity for educators to hear directly the rationale which the policy makers hold for the decisions they have made and are making.

The State Department has little enough opportunity for such explanation, and there is something incongruous in the fact that the military budget allows for the expenditure of millions of dollars for information services connected with its work, by which large numbers of newspaper and television reporters and influential persons, including educators, are flown to military installations and military briefings, while the State Department has an infinitesimal budget for its information services. The educators who attend the foreign policy conferences consist of those whose institutions or whose private means can provide the funds to make the trip possible.

Once they arrive, however, the educators enter a situation in which the Department spokesmen seem to consider themselves to be not partners in an intellectual and political enterprise but owners of a policy they must protect against harm. The result is that the educators are put in the role of potential purveyors of government policy, not as teachers concerned to consider world affairs from a broad international point of view. The fact that they seem to accept their role eagerly is one of the depressing items which must be conveyed in this Report. One senses that the educators feel grateful that they have been allowed to pay their own way to the State Department and that the State Department is willing to present its experts to expound on the validity of the policies it has adopted.

These conferences are enhanced by a sense of the reality of the issues, since they are presented to the audience by persons responsible for resolving them. This is an experience which few educators have the opportunity to enjoy, and it results in a heightening of interest in the issues themselves on the part of those who attend. But if the purpose of American education is to provide the teachers and students in the schools and colleges with an international point of view, it is difficult to see how the State Department contributes to that purpose simply by reciting the reasons why its present policies are correct and indisputable. One would hope that in subsequent conferences of this kind, university scholars whose qualifications for foreign policy discussion are equal to the occasion could present alternate views for discussion by State Department officials and that the central problem of increasing the flow of ideas between the educators and the policy makers on a whole variety of issues, including that of improving the teaching of world affairs and raising the level of informed criticism of government policy, could occupy the attention of the participants. Otherwise, such conferences give the impression of being the State Department's answer to the teach-in.

One of the most interesting examples of what might be accomplished by a change in format came in a panel discussion at the 1967 conference, in which a veteran reporter from the *Washington Post* challenged the entire information policy of the State Department before its principal information officer and raised fundamental questions having to do with the relation of national security to the free flow of information to the public. In the subsequent discussion, substantive issues were raised about the government's attitude toward freedom of the press and the right of citizens, students, and teachers to know more than they are ordinarily told on issues of serious importance to educators and of consequence to the education of teachers.

The State Department has a genuine role to play in the education of American teachers, both in the dissemination of information about government policies and the problems with which the Department deals and in the opportunity it has for working with the university community on the development of cultural policies relevant to the new position of the United States in world society. What is needed as the basis for a wider policy is the conception of the United States as an international culture, along with the idea that the American point of view is not "American," but international. Our purpose in America could then be seen, not as an effort to induct foreign scholars and students, or those we visit abroad, or ourselves, into an American culture and an American curriculum, so that we will all appreciate and support America and the West, but as an effort to enrich our curriculum and foreign cultures with the points of view, skills, and knowledge of scholars and students from everywhere. We should ask our visitors to join us in teaching Americans about the world, arranging our studies and theirs around sets of interests and common problems.

The proposal is that the United States should become a meeting ground for the people of the world, a place where we can pool the world's resources for the benefit of all. We should ask our visitors to bring their instruments and play their music, act their plays, read their poems, dance, sing, compose, paint, and write with us in our schools, colleges, and communities as resident artists and scholars, encouraging everyone to teach everyone else whatever it is he knows. Abroad, we can take the initiative in creating, not American outposts, but international centers where American students, teachers, artists, and scholars can work with their counterparts from elsewhere on common tasks for varying lengths of time.

The Idea of Regional World Centers for Education

The possibility would then exist of uniting the world's educational systems into one which draws on the intellectual and cultural resources of as wide a variety of countries as can be persuaded to join with us, and we would create a powerful counterforce to tendencies within the world community toward fragmentation and nationalist attitudes. We would also break down the conception of confrontation between East and West, by moving the center of gravity of Western initiatives into the African, Asian, and South American continents and helping to remove the distinction between We and They, the distinction, so often invidious, between a powerful industrialized West and an underdeveloped East and South.

We have already applied this point of view in certain parts of American foreign policy, in the Peace Corps, in the Atoms for Peace program, for example, and more recently in the proposal to create a world network of regional water resource centers to share scientific and technical knowledge and to develop cooperative research and study of present and future water shortages. At the first major international conference on the problem of the world's water resources, attended by 5,000 persons from 90 countries, in Washington, May 1967, President Johnson opened the proceedings by announcing the establishment in the U.S. government of a Water for Peace Office. President Johnson told the conference delegates that "the United States is prepared to join others in establishing a network (of regional water resource centers). We will provide our fair share of the expert assistance, the supplies, and equipment and the financing."[8]

This point of view about water is especially relevant to those matters having to do with the educational shortages, present and future, which afflict the contemporary world. It is time we announced that we were "prepared to establish a network of regional *educational* resource centers" where the education of teachers and of students in the problems of the contemporary world could be conducted as an international enterprise. President Johnson, at the water conference, raised the question, "How can we engineer our continents and direct our great river systems to make use of the water resources we now waste?", and, "How can we curb the filth that pollutes our streams?"[9] A revised version of these questions is equally relevant. If we were to construct a version of these questions in cultural terms, it would read, "How can we develop our continents and direct our great educational systems to make use of the educational resources we now waste?" and, "How can we curb the misinformation and bias which pollute our political and cultural relations?"

An example of what I have in mind can be drawn from an International Conference on Social Psychological Research in Developing Countries, held at the University of Ibadan, Nigeria, for a week in January 1967.[10] The Conference was organized jointly by the University of Ibadan and the Center for Research on Conflict Resolution, along with the Doctoral Program in Social Psychology of the University of Michigan in Ann Arbor. It was sponsored by the Nigerian Association of the Behavioral Sciences, the Society for the Psychological Study of Social Issues (United States), the Scientific Council of Africa, and the International Social Science Council.

Over 100 persons attended—50 of them official delegates, the rest observers from universities, government agencies, and research institutes in the African countries; the delegates included 21 social psychologists from Africa, 16 from the United States, 10 from Western and Eastern Europe, the rest from Latin America, the Middle East, Asia, and Australia. The symposia were organized around problems in education and the diffusion of knowledge, issues in social psychological research, and problems in development and social change. Aside from the papers read and the topics debated, plans were discussed for international cross-cultural research, regional workshops in teaching and research, teaching in the African universities, research on international tensions, and ways in which the

---

[8] Address to the International Conference on Water for Peace, by President Lyndon B. Johnson, May 23, 1967, Washington, D.C.

[9] *Ibid.*, p. 5.

[10] Further information can be obtained from Dr. Charles Pidoux, c/o United Nations, BP 492, Niomey, Nigeria.

resources of social psychologists could be applied to education and development problems in the new countries.

If even a limited number of scholars in this and allied fields—those having a direct relation to teaching and education, anthropology, sociology, political science, or philosophy—were to come together from around the world, taking time away from the home country on a planned international schedule for one month, three months, six months, or a year at a time, with graduate and undergraduate students as interns and research assistants, tutors, teachers, teachers' aides, etc., a whole new area of international cooperation could be opened up, through the efforts of Americans and other nationals of the kind who put together the conference in Ibadan. The Institute for Educational Research and Studies in Tehran,[11] on a very modest budget from the National Teacher's College in Iran, has already been one center of cooperation with the UNESCO Institute for Education in Hamburg, Germany, for a project in the International Evaluation of Educational Achievement. The use of American funds and American aid from the educational community, in combination with Iranians and others, could support very interesting and useful teaching and research in international education by building upon the present efforts of Dr. Iraj Ayman and others in the Institute in Tehran to make an international center for education in that country.

The Need for a Cultural Policy

Admittedly, it is easier, although still very difficult, to deal with the technology of water than it is to handle the relations between cultures, since political issues immediately intrude on the latter enterprise. On the other hand, the formation of a cultural policy consistent with President Johnson's point of view about water would give direction to a series of other international policies which are directly related to the American educational system. There is a marked difference between the tone and content of the President's statements at the water conference and at the International Conference on the World Crisis in Education in October 1967, although the emphasis on technology remained constant. The President, at the Education Conference, called for the use of the technologies of television, satellite communication systems, microfilming, etc., to extend education to the largest possible number of the world's people. But the President made no proposal about regional world centers for the study and promulgation of educational ideas and intercultural research, no declaration of policy of the kind which would have committed the United States to extending into reality the declarations and provisions of the International Education Act and of the President's speech at the Smithsonian Institution in 1965.

It may be true that the International Conference on the World Crisis in Education was not the proper place for an international policy statement by America. But without such a statement, or without some practical

---

[11] See *Progress*, newsletter (mimeographed) from The Institute for Educational Research and Studies, Box 3071, Tehran, Iran. 21 pp.

manifestation of the international intention of the United States in calling the Conference in the first place, the participants and those who took note of it in the educational community of the world could conclude that the Conference was either a propaganda device to draw attention to the American rhetoric of internationalism or a way of bringing together client countries for consultation about problems of mutual aid.

In any case, at some point and in some direct way, a statement of American cultural policy must be made if there is to be clarity about American intention before the world in supporting the cause of interna tional cultural self-determination and world education. One of the first items in need of clarification by a statement carrying the weight of the Presidency is the question of what kind of educational and social research is to be carried on by what agencies of the U.S. government, and what kind is the proper province of the universities and for what purposes. Such a policy statement, one would hope, would eliminate the colleges and universities from classified or secret government research of any kind and would eliminate the colleges and universities from all military research on whatever subject.

In positive terms, it would assign to the universities the area of research and teaching in the fields of world affairs, foreign policy, and international education, inviting the scholars of the world to join the American universities and their counterparts on other continents in an effort to find solutions to problems in international conflict and in international cooperation to avoid mass violence. I am thinking of a policy statement by the United States of the same degree of significance which marked the statement in the U.S. Constitution about the separation of church and state, in this case separating all military and clandestine government research from the free enquiry of scholars in the universities. One good way of identifying the areas of proper university enquiry would be to ask whether or not, whatever the research might be, it could be used as material for teaching in the undergraduate colleges. If, for security reasons, it could not be so used, it has no place in the life of the American university. If the results of university research could not be made available to the world community of scholars, "friend and foe alike," to use the President's phrase in justifying the International Education Act, and if the research itself could not be conducted anywhere in the world by any serious international group of university scientists and scholars, then it should not be done in American institutions of higher education.

Such a declaration of policy would have immediate effects, one of the first of which would be to assert a serious degree of control over the kind of research in the social sciences now being carried on by the Defense Department and its allied agencies, both public and private. We would immediately shift a large proportion of the $9 million spent annually by the Defense Department on the study of social conditions abroad to the State Department, which at present has less than $1 million for what can surely be called a major area of foreign policy. When only 1 percent of the

269

total government budget for the study of foreign societies is spent by the State Department, it is clear that the focus of effort in all these matters lies outside the scope of the very agency whose responsibility it is to understand the world before acting on it.

A Negative Example

The Camelot Project, for example, sponsored by the Defense Department with a staff of university social scientists organized to study ways of forestalling revolutions in selected Latin American countries, would never have been suggested or allowed had there been a strong overall policy based on a philosophy of democratic internationalism, and had this policy been properly administered by the State Department. Were such a study to be conducted, it would not have been put forward as a military-political project whose results might possibly be used against the country in which it had been carried out. If it were to be done at all, it would not have been the work of American social scientists or of university scholars employed by the military, no matter how honest their motives or their scholarship. It would have been carried out by a team of international scholars with the cooperation of the university community in the Latin American countries, and its results would have been published for the world community to read. In fact, a serious international study of the causes of revolution might produce some very useful recommendations for reorganizing the economic and social systems of the countries where revolutions are imminent. But it is unlikely that a unilateral study by the military of one country of the political conditions of another can be regarded as anything but disguised counterintelligence.

One would hope that a form of self-imposed discipline on the part of American educators and social scientists would prevent collaboration of the kind represented in the Camelot affair, or in the use of Michigan State University as a cover for intelligence operations in South Vietnam. In the absence of the discipline of scholars, and in the absence of restraint on the part of government agencies, an official policy for university research and American scholarship in foreign affairs is an absolute essential if cultural and educational affairs are to be considered a positive and honest element in American foreign policy.

One approach to such a policy can be found in the statement by the Fellows of the American Anthropological Association, in which the nature of international integrity in research and education is clearly described:

> The human condition, past and present, is the concern of anthropologists throughout the world. The study of mankind in varying social, cultural and ecological situations is essential to our understanding of human nature, of culture, and of society.
>
> Our present knowledge of the range of human behavior is admittedly incomplete. Expansion and refinement of this knowledge depend heavily on international understanding and cooperation in scientific and scholarly inquiry. To maintain the independence and integrity of anthropology as a science, it is necessary that scholars have full opportunity to study peoples and their culture, to publish, disseminate, and openly discuss the results of their research, and to

continue the responsibility of protecting the personal privacy of those being studied and assisting in their research.

Constraint, deception and secrecy have no place in science. Actions which compromise the intellectual integrity and autonomy of research scholars and institutions not only weaken those international understandings essential to our discipline, but in so doing they also threaten any contribution anthropology might make to our own society and to the general interests of human welfare.[12]

This is not the place to review at length the serious damage done to American cultural relations with other countries by the covert subsidies of the Central Intelligence Agency to educational and cultural organizations in the United States and abroad. It is enough to say that serious damage was done and that the CIA actions put in jeopardy the integrity of American students, scholars, teachers, Peace Corps volunteers, and every other representative of American culture who travels abroad for study, research, or public service. Many of the British and European intellectuals who had written for *Encounter* under the impression that it was an independent journal with American and British coeditors were outraged to learn that they had been writing for a magazine supported by CIA money.

The British editor, Stephen Spender, having heard rumors from other writers in the United States, Europe, and England of clandestine CIA support to his magazine, asked his American coeditor about it directly and was told that the rumors were false, when, in fact, the American knew that they were true. There is nothing I have seen in the magazine's publication record to indicate that the editorial policy was slanted in deference to American interests, and it is generally acknowledged that *Encounter* has been one of the most important intellectual journals in the West, one in which the most serious philosophical, literary, and political issues in Eastern Europe and the Western world have had a full opportunity for treatment by some of the best of contemporary writers.

But the attitude of the Europeans and British toward the episode is either one of cynicism that the Americans with their rhetoric of freedom and democracy should have been caught in a hypocritical counterintelligence act, a kind of intellectual U-2 incident, or a sense of betrayal in being tricked into writing for a magazine subsidized by a foreign government. At the very least, it is a naïve way for a country to run its cultural affairs, since any serious analysis of the idea of such subsidy, aside from rejecting its hypocrisy, would have indicated that eventually, among writers and intellectuals—the most sceptical and perceptive breed of all human kind where politics is concerned—this sort of secret would inevitably be exposed. What is now to prevent the assumption on the part of any country that Fulbright scholars, or any other Americans received into foreign universities as colleagues, are not gathering intelligence data on the people and institutions giving them hospitality?

---

[12] Fellows of the American Anthropological Association. "Statement on Problems of Anthropological Research and Ethics." Washington, D.C.: the Association (1530 P St., N.W.), 1967.

The point is that there has to be an American cultural policy, before the fact, not after, and that the policy has to be large-minded, consistent with the claims of a democratic society which says that it is concerned to be honest, open, and truly international in its relations with other cultures. We have to decide whether we want a policy designed to draw together the intellectual community of the world and to serve the world's interests, or one deliberately designed to work in the American self-interest as a combination propaganda and counterintelligence arm of the U.S. government. If it is neither one nor the other, it will be assumed to be the latter. Once we get a policy, we have to see that it is administered in keeping with its spirit.

The Role of Students

Again it is the lack of a clear understanding of the role of cultural and educational affairs in American foreign policy which makes it possible for decisions like that of the CIA and four Presidents of the United States on the covert subsidy of American students to be made at all. One of the deepest ironies in the relation of the Agency to the work of the National Student Association lies in the fact that at a time in the late 1940's and early 1950's when the U.S. Congress, the public, and the government were suspicious of political action of any kind by students and were unwilling to grant them responsibility for social or educational policy in the universities or to provide funds for independent student action, at home or abroad, the one organization in the entire country which did trust the students was the most sensitive of them all, the agency in charge of counterintelligence.

Those of us who were working in international and national affairs with students during those years found that it was nearly impossible to raise funds in support of international student projects, either from private sources, foundations, university budgets, or from the federal government. It is true that Congress, in the grip of the McCarthy disease of the 1950's, could not imaginably have been considered as a source of funds, nor could the State Department, then infected with the same ailment. But more than this, so little consideration was given at that time to the idea that students, or even educators, had anything to offer to the furtherance of American policy abroad or to the development of new patterns of thinking about foreign affairs at home that, with the exception of one or two of the smaller non-CIA foundations, it was unthinkable to most of those who might have furnished financial help to students and intellectuals that such help would serve a useful purpose.

The students have by now proven over and over again the quality of their ability, the degree of their responsibility, and the extent of their readiness to carry out tasks in cultural and social affairs far beyond the recognition they have received for the things they have already done. Most of it has been done without adequate support and against serious obstacles. The World University Service, with its worldwide projects in international education and community development, the Collegiate Council for the United Nations, the volunteers in the poverty programs, the

Peace Corps, the International Voluntary Service, aside from the National Student Association and the projects sponsored by many religious organizations, have all been part of an undefined cultural policy which the students have been carrying out. We can only imagine the power of action which would be released were there funds now available on a sufficient scale to finance properly the work of students in international education.

The Students and the Government

At this stage in the development of the student movement there are informed and serious persons in the U.S. Office of Education and in the Peace Corps who stay in touch with the student leadership, have direct knowledge of the student movement, and understand the enormous potential which lies in independent action through student-organized projects. Government grants for international student projects in teacher education are needed and should be administered on a broad scale. But we have had enough experience with the niggardliness and contentiousness of Congress in supporting budgets for cultural and international projects, even those which are in no way political, to warn us that appropriations adequate to apply a wide and generous policy of support for students in the field of teacher education and international affairs are going to be very hard to come by.

The idea proposed in government quarters for a public agency with a nongovernmental board of directors to make grants to student organizations and student-run projects in international affairs has merit, although it has the danger in it that its tie to the government would tie it to government policy. It is that danger which caused the National Student Association to cut back its international programs after canceling its CIA subsidies. Should an agency for the support of international projects in education by students and others be established, its administrators and policy makers would have to be at least as perceptive as the CIA in supporting students whose ideas run counter to those of the government. One model suggests itself in the format that the National Endowment for the Arts has taken, where a panel of distinguished artists, writers, performers, and cultural leaders are appointed by the President to a National Council on the Arts to make policy decisions about grants and to approve the ones presented to them by the staff. Education and World Affairs, drawing its financial support from foundation sources, is able to remain independent and forceful by reason of the distinction of its board of directors and staff, its financial independence, and its colleague relationship with government officers in the agencies and Congress.

Everything else being equal, the EWA model would be preferable to one which depended on Congressional appropriations. The danger is, in any case, that unless an enlightened attitude to cultural policy and international education is clearly established in the Congress and Administration, and unless there is strong national and Administration support for these policies, each time the appropriations come up for review the students and volunteers who have had fresh, interesting, provocative, or dissident

273

views to express will be attacked by Congressmen and hostile witnesses, and appropriations will be available only to conservative projects and compliant students and teachers.

It is literally true that as far as cultural freedom in international politics is concerned, we are still not very far from the McCarthy period, and the normal approach of government agency officials both to their own work and to Congress is one of caution. The caution has become more pronounced during the past two years as the government commitment to the military operations in Vietnam has grown in size and intensity. Since most of the major student leadership is on record as opposing government foreign policy, in Vietnam and elsewhere, it is doubtful that it would be possible to mount a serious student-run project in international education or cultural affairs without a staff composed of those students most likely to be attacked in Congress. The policies in foundation grant-making are very conservative when it comes to supporting student projects, especially those which have to do with international affairs and teaching.

What is true of the private foundations is even more true of the government foundations and agencies. As is the case in the Soviet Union, the scientific community in the United States has sufficient political influence in support of intellectual freedom to sustain a principled position about awards for scientific research, and it is unlikely that the National Science Foundation will ever be subject to the same threat of intellectual control which haunts the other organizations and agencies. When it comes to education, the humanities, and the social sciences, the situation is different, and it is more different still when independent student organizations and projects are concerned.

The Office of Economic Opportunity is one of the few government agencies to work directly with students without an intervening link to colleges and universities; an OEO grant supports the National Student Association's Tutorial Assistance Center through which more than 250,000 students across the country are helped, through an efficient, inexpensive, and well-run program, in the work of tutoring children in the inner cities and rural areas. The entire operation of the poverty program has given scope to student initiative which is rare in the operations of government— from Head Start teachers to VISTA volunteers, they command the respect of their government supervisors and have been given a large degree of autonomy and responsibility outside the conventional government and university supervision, sometimes with consequent political rumblings in the communities where they serve. Such rumblings are heard whenever young people concern themselves to take social action which has political effects. It is time for this country and its government to realize that if we mean what we say about creating a society for and of equals, we are going to have to support the right of young people to be equal and to act on behalf of equality and liberal democracy.

What is needed now more than anything else is a strong, positive, and convincing statement from the Administration, preferably from the

President, that this country trusts its students, that it wants to give them full support in funds and assistance to carry out the educational and cultural tasks abroad which they are fully equipped to do, and that not only do we not believe in turning American students into hidden agents of counter-intelligence, but we urge them to express their honest views about their government and its policies wherever they go. Unless support to students and their education in world affairs is given in this spirit and with this kind of clarity of purpose, no government-sponsored organization will have the mandate it needs in order to replace the CIA as the sponsor of student internationalism. Nor will the students believe that their government either needs them or wants them to represent America abroad, or that it trusts them to come to their own conclusions about the issues in world affairs which disturb their consciences.

The national policy for grant-making by all the agencies, both public and private, should be one which gives students consideration fully equal to that given to any other applicants in reaching judgments about the worth of a given proposal. Much of the best work by student organizations in teacher education and international affairs has been carried out without the supervision or control of university or government authorities; often its high quality is due to the fact that the work *is* unsupervised and not subject to the unnecessary inhibitions of academic convention.

An example of the kind of work in the international field which can best be done by students is to be found in a project, organized during the fall of 1966 by the National Student Association with support from the State Department, for a travel and seminar program involving 11 visiting Bolivian student leaders. The itinerary, personnel, and content were arranged by the students in consultation with the government, with a genuine international approach. One Bolivian student came in advance of the others to act as codirector of the seminar, the content of which was planned to include discussion of mutual problems in educational and social change in Latin America and the United States; the visitors had a chance to visit a cross-section of the activists in the American student body and to see what they were doing in community action, the poverty program, civil rights, and educational reform.

The Philosophy of Intellectual Autonomy

In a genuine sense, the students in this project and in others run by the National Student Association and comparable organizations were making cultural policy by the approach they took to their responsibilities toward the visitors and by the content of the program they planned. The particular character of the American student movement lies in its concern for social service and community action, as well as for the autonomy of students in running their own organizations. In contrast to student movements elsewhere which either are controlled by government officials or are tied to national political parties, the American student movement is honestly and fervently independent, unwilling to follow the guidance of the national political parties, even in those cases where they have formal affiliations.

American students also have a point of view about their relation to the society they are trying to change. Unlike most student movements abroad, most American students do not consider themselves part of an elite by reason of their university status, nor are they very interested in debating abstract political theory, except as a basis for social and political action. One of the main contributions they make in relation to American foreign policy is to demonstrate in action to those students with whom they work, here or abroad, a philosophy of social change in which the student becomes an ally of the members of his own community to achieve goals which they share. The concept of volunteer service in the public welfare is built into the student organizations, along with the policies of student autonomy. As part of the university system, they are now challenging their government and their society on a broad front of issues in world affairs and social change, particularly where these policies, as in the case of the CIA subsidy, seem to them a retreat from open democratic principles.

The university system has the major responsibility for preserving the integrity of American cultural policy, and university scholars and teachers have the duty of keeping themselves and their government honest. Their major instrument for doing so lies in their professional associations and in the work of the universities themselves. But they also have the duty, through their example and initiative, of helping to establish in the world community of intellectuals the standards of intellectual impartiality and honesty which are best developed through international communication and joint scholarship. The mere fact that American intellectuals are relatively free of political control and that they have access to sources of funds for open research which by comparison with foreign scholars are incredibly large, in itself lays a duty upon them to work in the interests of international scholarship and education, since the others are so much more limited in the conditions for their own initiatives. The world needs a world code for scholarship on the order of the Universal Declaration of Human Rights, and in the absence of an Eleanor Roosevelt as the American spokesman for a world point of view, the joint efforts of American scholars must be put into service on behalf of the international ideal.

It is no longer possible to assume the right of an American social scientist or educator to enter the culture of another country, to collect research data having to do with private interest or the interest of his government, and to return home with his booty, having done no more than to have taken the time of his colleagues and informants and to have accepted their intellectual and political hospitality. A cultural policy based on a concern for increasing the world's knowledge of itself and using knowledge for the international benefit would demand that the university community act as the major counterforce to the use of the sciences and arts for nationalist political gain.

In the interim stage toward full internationalism in scholarship, the increase in the study of American society by foreign scholars on a bilateral exchange basis would decrease the unavoidable insularity of American sociological assumptions. I am thinking, for example, of the contribution Gunnar Myrdal has made to American and world understanding of the American race problem, because of his ability to conceive the American problem in non-American terms.

This means cooperation among international scientists and scholars to produce work of use to all, with American subsidies to support the kind of open international research which enlightens and benefits the society in which it is conducted and the others to which its results are distributed. It is another reason for establishing regional education centers rather than conducting unilateral research projects along with bilateral exchanges.

The Teacher in International Affairs

But above everything else, it suggests a new conception of international education which starts with the idea of bringing together the teachers and students of the world to make common cause. In a different conception of the constituency of the world intellectual community, the teachers and students, rather than an elite of scientists, scholars, and writers, would be considered to be the fundamental element. The teachers and their students constitute the network of persons in whose hands lies the responsibility for teaching and learning what the world community needs to know. Or, to change the metaphor, students and teachers are the agents of transmission of the ideas and values which exist in any given cultural period or in any region of the world.

A culture consists of the body of ideas, habits, customs, and beliefs which hold a society together and give it its distinctive character. Not all of it can be conveyed to others, or even to itself, so much depends on what part of it is singled out. In the United States, for example, there is a youth culture, a Negro culture, a Puerto Rican, Spanish-American, Italian-American, and Indian culture, a culture of poverty, of the middle class, of the intellectuals. But when educators and others begin to do something about it, culture is always a matter of putting on art exhibits or adding courses in Western civilization or literature to the curriculum, or building cultural centers, or putting on performances of opera, music, ballet, plays. These are essential elements in the culture, but they do not begin to exhaust its content.

Similarly, the content of a culture does not become available either to its own members or to the members of other cultures until its words and ideas are transformed into meaning by persons who make the effort to learn what they mean. That is why so much is conveyed from one culture to another through the arts, particularly through plays, poems, and novels, where the reality of the lives of the characters in their own context is relatively easy to grasp. When the members of a national culture exchange words and ideas only with each other, or when only the elite understands what is being said either inside or outside a national culture, in science or in art, there is no serious means of communication across the world's cultures. The world's teachers supply that means.

For the teacher has a special privilege and a special role when he goes abroad to teach. To teach and to learn is to go to the heart of another culture, that is, to take one's place within the privileged situation of a company of friends who have something to give and something to learn from one another. To teach is to enter the lives of others at a level deep enough to make mutual understanding possible. To teach the children of another man is to enter his life as well as the life of his child and his family. To work with other teachers in their own schools is to join a community, not simply to take an assignment. The schools and colleges are the places where the cultural values and the true images of a society are represented in what is done there, and it is the intermingling of cultural values from the full variety of the world's people which can furnish the texture of a new kind of knowledge within the American educational system.

Further, when a nation-state deliberately conceives its cultural policy as an instrument for injecting its own point of view into the culture of another nation-state, it creates its own resistance to acceptance within the intellectual community at large, where the policy of using ideas as weapons or instruments is quickly noted and quickly suspected. Among the English language newspapers and magazines sent abroad by the Soviet Union, for example, the consistent policy of presenting facts and ideas about the Soviet Union in a favorable light not only gives the language of the presentation an unhealthy glow like that of bad advertising copy, but it makes it almost impossible for a reader to take it seriously.

Similarly, when by political selection the books in USIA libraries abroad are chosen with a view to including only those which present the United States in a favorable light, the library becomes in large degree useless to serious people. Or when most of the educators sent abroad on AID missions are administrators and educational practitioners, their presence generates no intellectual excitement which could produce fresh thinking in new dimensions of educational, cultural, and social change; there is discussion only of a series of practical solutions given to structural and organizational problems. To the intellectual community abroad, the educational practitioner from America then seems more to be a U.S. civil servant with anti-intellectual tendencies than a lively mind representing a lively democratic culture.

On the other hand, when the question is put in different terms, as, for example, How can the citizens of one country have open access to the ideas and culture of another country? it is not simply a question of the cultural apparatus in each country turning out new and approved products for export. It is a matter of how the educational systems can combine their own resources to develop materials which in the eyes of the teachers and educators of both countries can give a true insight into the character and quality of the cultures on either side. In the long run, this can be done only by the intermingling of teachers and students within a world educational system in which the national cultures are treated with a full degree of equality and a full degree of objectivity.

An example can be drawn from the work of the World Law Fund, which, on the basis of research studies of the kind produced by Louis B. Sohn and Grenville Clark in the field of world law, has developed new materials which deal specifically with international problems as part of an ongoing search for institutional ways of creating a stable world order.[13] Having developed new curriculums for teachers in universities and secondary schools in the United States, and having tried them out in more than 60 institutions, the Fund has conferred with Indian, German, Soviet, and Asian educators with a view to using international materials of this kind on a world scale within the universities and schools. No matter what the cultural or political differences may be from country to country, the common problems of international organization and the role of each culture in developing a world system can and should be studied, and should become part of the common body of knowledge with which the teacher deals within his own educational province.

It is for this reason that the intention of the International Education Act and the Center for Educational Cooperation can be realized only by paying direct and consistent attention to the problem of the education of teachers. The Act does not mention specifically the education of teachers, but it accomplishes little if it does not make that the major emphasis of its programs. At present, in American education, as far as the theory and practice of international education is concerned, the emphasis has been on the development of research centers in area studies and international affairs in the major universities and graduate centers, with a view to producing research scholars and experts whose interests lie, not in teaching, but either in government service or in research. Teachers in the primary and secondary schools of the world are the neglected element in international affairs. They are poorly paid, lacking in status within their societies, and in many instances poorly educated in comparison with their colleagues in the universities. In most countries the normal school or teacher training institute is still the established rule. When plans are made to increase the international dimension of education, either in this country or abroad, the teachers and their education are the last things which the policy makers take under consideration. The average number of teachers sent abroad annually for exchange of teaching posts and language and area studies instruction under the Fulbright-Hays Act is 700. The total number of teachers coming to the United States under the same program for instruction in American education is 400.

---

[13] See, for example, *Legal and Political Problems of World Order* (compiled and edited by Saul H. Mendlovitz), a reading and discussion guide for seminars in international affairs. Published and distributed by The Fund for Education Concerning World Peace Through World Law, 11 West 42nd St., New York, N.Y. 856 pp.

A New Emphasis on Teaching and Teachers

What is needed is a large-scale increase in the attention paid to the work of teachers of all kinds through the existing apparatus of cultural exchange and foreign aid. It is gratifying to report that following upon the recommendations of President Johnson's Smithsonian Institution speech of September of 1965 and the recommendations of Secretary Rusk's special task force for "a broad and long-range plan of worldwide educational endeavor," preceding the preparation and passage of the International Education Act, there has been a marked increase in such attention on the part of a group of government agencies. The work of the Inter-Agency Council for Educational and Cultural Affairs, whose chairman was Charles Frankel, has made a valuable contribution in coordinating the potential and actual operations of a series of government agencies which not only have a part to play in the expansion of international education, but have budgets with which to expand them. The Council includes the State Department; members from the Department of Health, Education, and Welfare, the Department of Defense, AID, the Peace Corps, and the U.S. Information Agency; and observers from the Bureau of the Budget and the Smithsonian Institution.

The major source of aid for international education, until the Center for Educational Cooperation receives its funds and begins to function, lies with AID and the U.S. Office of Education under the supervision of the Assistant Secretary for Education of the Department of Health, Education, and Welfare. This assures both the connection of international education with the ongoing work of the American educational system at large and the eventual protection of its budget from the biennial cuts administered by Congress to foreign aid projects of all kinds.

The Center for Educational Cooperation will do a number of things which badly need doing and will fill a set of needs fully recognized and described in John Gardner's report on AID and the universities in March 1964.[14] The Center will act as a channel for communication between U.S. missions abroad and the U.S. educational community, direct the programs assigned to it by the Department of Health, Education, and Welfare, and assist public and private agencies conducting international education programs.

One of the major concepts around which the Center will be built is that of a clearinghouse, a link between the domestic programs of schools, colleges, and universities concerned with world affairs and the kind of educational activities initiated by them abroad. The concept is based on the need for *continuous* interchange and cooperation between all countries, in education, cultural affairs, science, and technology, and will involve the selection and appointment of education officers in the U.S. foreign service and the development of new manpower within the American

---

[14] Gardner, John W. *AID and the Universities.* A Report to the Administrator of the Agency for International Development. New York: Education and World Affairs (522 Fifth Ave.), April 1964. 57 pp.

colleges and universities for service in international education and development programs in foreign countries. There will also be an American Education Placement Service, to give relevant information to Americans who wish to serve abroad—school and college teachers, professors and administrators, either retired or on sabbatical leave, Peace Corps returnees who wish to continue their work abroad, and others. The Service could eventually develop into a world teacher exchange through which the flow of teaching talent could move into multilateral channels through collaboration with foreign governments and their educational systems.

In the meantime, before the Center is established, the educational programs of AID, aside from the Peace Corps, have been the major source of funds and opportunity for conducting international education. The particular virtue of the educational work of AID lies in the fact that it is directly linked to the problems of social and economic development of the countries where aid is provided and is therefore involved in an immediate way with the problems of a viable social structure. Educational questions have to be answered in practical ways, including the basic question of how to educate teachers and how to get enough of them.

The increase in educational effort by AID over the past two years has gone unnoticed by American educators and the public, and, when analyzed within the limits of its policies, turns out to be a considerable one. The allocation of AID funds for education programs rose from $110 million in 1965 to $137.4 million in 1966 (25 percent), and from there to $166.2 million (another 21 percent) in 1967. A further increase of 50 percent to $250 million is planned for 1968 and depends on the appropriation of the total foreign aid budget by the present Congress.

The Educational Programs of AID

The following are some of the areas of education in which AID is now working in response to the new initiatives set in motion since 1966.

1. English language teaching and research for the Near East, South Asia, Africa, and the Far East have had a budget increase from $2 million to approximately $3.5 million.

2. The Summer Teaching Corps, for Summer Science Institutes and the National Education Association Teach Corps, sends American teachers abroad—to Latin America, Africa, and Asia (245 of them in 1967) —to carry on teacher education programs in intensive summer sessions.

3. Through School to School partnerships, in collaboration with the Peace Corps and the Partners of the Alliance Program, schools in the United States—120 of them in 1966, 503 in 1967—each provide approximately $1,000 in funds for building schools abroad and usually follow up that contribution with a continuing relationship in the supply of books and equipment. As this part of the program develops, there will be a great many more opportunities for collaboration between foreign and American schools by exchange of students, ideas, faculty members, and curriculums, with joint research projects included.

281

4. Through the Institutional Grant Program, AID will give support "to American research and educational institutions for increasing their capacity to deal with programs of economic and social development abroad," depending on the appropriations; the amount for this is calculated at $10 million.

5. A program of research and planning has begun for the use of new educational technologies, mainly television, in the developing countries, including Colombia and Jamaica, where projects have already started, and El Salvador, where a comprehensive educational system based on television is planned, to serve, with a five-year budget of $7.5 million, as a model for possibilities in other Central American countries and elsewhere in the world.

There are now teams from 71 American universities at work in 38 countries on AID educational missions, although as yet there is no comprehensive evaluation or even description of the overall policy and details of the educational programs themselves, especially as these apply to the education of teachers. One of the difficulties in the operation of AID educational programs lies in the fact that AID is a contracting agency for services and, unlike the Peace Corps, which has a self-corrective mechanism for evaluation of its educational work, has no research component to turn in judgments as to whether the programs contracted for are accomplishing what is needed and what was bargained for.

The Lack of a Research Arm

In the two educational fields in which AID research is done—education and human resources and institutional and social development—$6 million has been spent since 1962 for eight projects in the former and $2.75 million for 16 projects in the latter, on a range of topics from the feasibility of applying new educational media for use with large populations of illiterates to comparative social change in the developing countries. The contracts for the research have been awarded to universities and to independent research agencies and institutes; only one of the 24 projects has dealt with teacher education, and in this one case the research had to do with techniques for training teachers of English.

A typical instance of the difficulty already referred to in doing American-sponsored social research without international participation can be seen in the Brandeis University project to study the political attitudes of youth as a factor affecting economic development. As the official summary in 1967 points out, "no suitable location has been found for field trials. Difficulties with the problem of 'sensitivity' remain unsolved."

Aside from basic research, the results of which could be expected to help in giving direction to policy making for the use of educational and economic aid, there is at present no systematic way in which AID can evaluate the educational results of the teams from the universities at work in the 38 countries where they are located. When AID is faced with the assignment of particular contracts to colleges of education and universities for work abroad, it must simply work through the going establishment, rather than, as is the case with the Peace Corps, take part in developing its own educational and training programs for those in its service. As a result, whatever weaknesses or strengths exist in the philosophy and practices of teacher education in the United States, or in a selected college of education or university and its staff, are exported by AID to the country we are trying to help.

After reviewing the programs of teacher education conducted on the American campuses and described in the present Report, my concern is that we have no way of knowing—although we have any number of ways of suspecting—the kind of educational results being achieved by the help we are giving to foreign countries. If the philosophy and practices of the conventional American college of education are used as a model for the formation of new programs of teacher education abroad, then we can assume that the same programs of general education, education courses, academic credits, grades, examinations, lectures, and textbooks are being reproduced and that what is considered to be standard American practice is being presented to the developing countries as the best kind of modern education available.

Reports on the progress of AID educational projects abroad, prepared by those who are conducting them, do not give an indication of how the results would be judged by persons outside the field of professional education; thus we are back with the problem raised in Chapter Two of this Report, the problem of the closed system in which educators, most of whom accept a common set of assumptions about what constitutes good professional education, are the judges of what constitutes a good program and good results in the education of teachers. Although the officials of AID with whom I have been in consultation in conducting this study have been most cooperative and helpful, most of the answers to questions about the actual content of educational programs, the kind of teacher education being developed, the evaluation of them, the possibilities for educational research, international education, and student teaching by American students under AID auspices are simply not available to them, since no independent research has been carried on, even of the survey kind.[15]

Consequently, I am unable to report, as I hoped to do, on the possibilities for the use of AID projects in general as instruments for the education of teachers and as the means not only of giving help to foreign countries, but of learning as much as possible about the educational process in other cultures, the ways in which liberal and vocational education can be joined together in countries greatly in need of both, and the way in which scholarship and research in the social and behavioral sciences

---

[15] Since the above was written, a contract has been signed between AID and the American Association of Colleges for Teacher Education for an overall review of this kind.

can be joined with educational research and training in the field and at home. I have been able to find no particular point of view about the education of teachers in the plans being made by AID, nor have I found in the universities any point of view about the potential use of AID as a source of new curriculum development and teacher education. The policy suggested by a brief passage in John Gardner's *AID and the Universities*,[16] through which AID would take more responsibility for training people for the field and would work with the universities in doing so, has not been put into effect, except in the case of the half-dozen special programs similar to the Harvard, Teachers College-Columbia University, and Stanford projects already described in Chapter One.

AID as a Teachers College

If the full degree of importance which the education of teachers must command in AID planning is to be realized, it will have to come through considering the AID mission overseas as a breeding ground for new talent among the foreign students and teachers and among the Americans who go there to help them, rather than as merely a service mission by experts from America. As I have already argued in connection with the collaboration of colleges and universities with the Peace Corps, specific B.A., M.A., and Ph.D. programs should be organized by joint programs of AID and colleges of education where internships, which could well be arranged through existing funds already allocated to educational missions abroad, would give the opportunity for AID to have the help of young, enterprising, and educationally uninhibited student teachers abroad. They could work with their foreign counterparts on joint research and teaching projects as part of their preparation to teach from an international point of view at home and to prepare themselves for service abroad in the future.

In this way, AID would be able to recruit some of the most enterprising and interesting of the young people interested in education for future service in AID, while at the same time it would have the benefit of fresh thinking and educational help during the internship period. With a plan similar to the one already suggested for the colleges and the Peace Corps, student teachers and teachers from the host country could return with the American students to their home campuses, there to continue the joint research and teaching in local American schools as well as in the college where the American is taking his graduate or undergraduate degree.

In the long run, as well as the short, this would mean the development of a new kind of professor of education, as has been suggested in relation to the Peace Corps—one who is at home in a foreign culture, is skilled in the art of preparing and supervising teachers, and in possession of a body of knowledge based on direct experience and foreign study. Such professors would be the source not only of ideas and administrative talent for AID, but of fresh thinking in curriculum and teacher education on the

---

[16] *Ibid.*, pp. 36, 37.

home campus. A few such persons already exist, but they are so few and the possibilities are so great for increasing their number, that it is crucial that a new concept of AID as an instrument of cultural and educational development for teachers of all kinds be substituted for the present concept of a contracting agency for educational services.

I also like John Gardner's idea of increasing the two-way flow of people and ideas between cultures, in a style similar to that of the U.S. Geological Survey, which has direct relations with several hundred faculty members and graduate students who are on call for periods of varying duration.[17] If the colleges of education wished to start programs in which their faculty members and graduate students considered the experience abroad with AID as field work in education and as preparation for teaching, a new kind of base could be made within their own institutions for the spread of the whole concept of education as social development and for increasing the interest of the student body in foreign service within the social development agencies. This would immediately strengthen the quality of teacher education in world affairs, both in the kind of persons attracted into the field and in the content of educational experience available to them there.

I say this because in the literature of international education, both in government statements and elsewhere, more people show an interest in training manpower for overseas service than for the education of teachers. Over and over again, the teacher is omitted from mention, and it is assumed that to add an international dimension to education, it is only necessary to establish what are called "centers of excellence" for research, graduate work, and "international programs." One seldom sees recognition of the fact that it is the teacher who is at the center of the whole issue and that, unless the highest level of attention and effort is given to the education of teachers and the teachers of teachers, this kind of international center will have little effect on the educational system, either in providing intelligent and concerned young men and women for service abroad or for teaching at home. It will simply give us more research specialists.

The Filtering-Down Theory

While the colleges for teachers, the state colleges, and the undergraduate colleges and universities remain starved for scholars who can teach and who possess depth in knowledge of foreign cultures and world affairs, the assumption continues to be made that if research and scholarly exchanges occur at the university level, the results of that research and those projects will filter down to the public school teachers and find their way into the school and college curriculums. This is not what happens. As a matter of fact, even in those institutions where there are large numbers of American faculty members who have worked abroad on AID projects, on Fulbright grants, or in the foreign service at large, little effect can be

[17] Ibid., p. 37.

seen as a result of their experience and research on the undergraduate curriculums of their own institutions. As previously reported, even in those institutions where courses in non-Western culture are available to undergraduates, the students who are going to be teachers seldom take them, and the idea of filtering down is seen to be a baseless hope rather than an adequate concept.

Research Centers

A further neglect of the teaching system as an instrument of communication can be seen in the general American tendency of developing research centers and institutes for higher studies where scholars and educators can isolate themselves from the mainstream of education and carry out research on matters which may touch the educational system at its periphery but are seldom meshed with the ongoing life of the country's schools and colleges. The model of the Rand Corporation, with its system of contract research by experts who carry out their assignments and report to their sponsors, is the one which has most powerfully affected the university's role in international affairs.

Don Davies, of the National Commission on Teacher Education and Professional Standards, put the matter clearly when he asked, at the Conference on World Education—

> How do we influence 25,000 school systems, 150,000 school administrators, and 2 million teachers, all of them already in the elementary and secondary schools of the country? This is a problem that will not be settled merely by changes on college and university campuses. . . . If you are talking about such things as openness to differences in culture and ideas, you will have to remember that if the School Board and its staff does not accept that as a proper aim for the school, you are whistling in the dark. Whatever may be our strategy, it has to be one that includes a strategy for bringing about change in a very large and complicated system of public education.[18]

James Becker, speaking at the same Conference, referred to some of the practical projects now going on with teachers and communities:

> The work of these people makes a sharp contrast with the way the physicists went about forming the school curriculum with The Moses Approach—a few physicists get up on a mountain and come down with a curriculum. One of the main problems is that we have not yet found any effective ways of feeding the results of these special projects into the bloodstream of the elementary and secondary schools. . . . It is not a lack of research or a lack of ideas, it is the fact that you can't get any kind of hearing for the ideas in the climate that now exists. . . . The University may have a special project with social scientists working with the schools, but the project consists of a very few scholars who have a deep interest in it, and the rest of the institution pays little attention. . . .[19]

Mr. Becker's remarks confirm another finding of the present study, that the fragmentation of the university community into special subject matter areas, as well as the size and nature of the academic bureaucracy with its private departmental preserves, often extended into institutes and

---

[18] Taylor, Harold, editor. *Conference on World Education.* Proceedings. Washington, D.C.: American Association of Colleges for Teacher Education, 1967. p. 35.
[19] *Ibid.,* p. 36.

research centers, has the effect of isolating from the rest of the institution the very knowledge it needs in order to keep the university in touch with itself and its society. Foreign policy is studied in international relations courses centered in the specialities of the graduate school. Education is studied in a department or a school of education but has little relation to foreign policy concerns in spite of its central role in world affairs. The humanities and social sciences are segregated from both by the nature of their materials and the organization of the university. At the same time, teachers in the primary and secondary schools, where the flow of knowledge and ideas into the culture is the main potential for cultural change, are segregated from the universities and, except in a few instances, do not know or understand what is going on in them or in the fields of knowledge represented there.

The Example of an American Institution

An example of the problem as it is seen from the point of view of the kind of institutions in the United States where the majority of teachers are being prepared can be taken from the experience of Bloomsburg State College in Bloomsburg, Pennsylvania—a former teachers college—where there are now approximately 3,500 students, most of whom intend to enter the teaching profession. In its curriculum, its place in the educational system, and its educational point of view, it is typical of the majority of teacher education institutions. During a visit to Bloomsburg, I conferred with a cross-section of students and faculty members interested in how a college of this size with its particular resources could take steps to add an international dimension to the education of the teachers it is preparing. In the subsequent discussion, Craig A. Newton, chairman of the Department of History, described an approach being taken at Bloomsburg and the interest of present faculty members and the administration in trying to find ways of revising the curriculum and the total program of the College. The crux of the problem lay in the fact that there were too few faculty members who had had experience in foreign cultures or whose academic preparation had given them an opportunity to study outside the field of Western culture and history.

In a later statement, Dr. Newton put the problem for his institution as follows:

> The Pennsylvania State Department of Public Instruction has mandated a unit of "world cultures" in all secondary schools in the State. It is no secret that school instruction in this subject is wanting, nor is it too difficult to discover a major source of the weakness. Colleges often have been unable to provide either breadth or depth in non-Western culture because they lack available staff and the student body with representatives from these cultures. At this time this situation exists at Bloomsburg: our staff native to or professionally qualified in non-Western cultures have had full assignments in the standard collegiate fare and cannot be released for a special program, and we have had few students from other countries.[20]

[20] Letter from Dr. C. A. Newton to Harold Taylor—in study files.

Dr. Newton goes on to describe a program which his college wishes to begin in September 1968, concentrating on East Asia, giving the reasons for that concentration as well as for bringing East Asian postbaccalaureate students to the campus to assist in instruction in the history and culture of their native countries. The plan is to enroll the visiting students one-third time in a graduate program in American studies. Dr. Newton's reasons are as follows:

1. We have a member of the History Department professionally qualified who recently traveled in East Asia and will be free by September 1968 to assume a major portion of the responsibilities for coordinating the teaching by East Indian students. Also, he has a language competence that will aid him in communicating with the Chinese-speaking students.

2. Bloomsburg has been designated among the 14 state colleges and universities as the center for Chinese research material and study—as the China Culture Center.

3. The Departments of History and Geography offer four undergraduate courses in the area of East Asia. Potential enrollees in the program proposed may already have an introductory knowledge of the land and cultures to be studied.

4. Finally, our faculty have essential contacts to East Asia, people who will aid in the program. While we propose to treat only East Asia initially, if the program could be sustained, it would be expanded in future years to include other cultures.[21]

The idea presented would involve the services of six East Asian students, one each from Korea, the Philippines, Hongkong, Formosa, and two from Japan. The Korean student is already identified and willing to come. Negotiations are under way with a Japanese student. The instruction will involve Bloomsburg faculty members with the visiting students in seminars, and language instruction in Chinese. Yet the program can be carried out only if there are funds available outside the Bloomsburg budget for bringing East Asian students to the campus and for the appointment of either foreign scholars with competence in the history and culture of their own regions and/or American scholars with equivalent experience. Direct relations with one or two Asian universities for the exchange of students and faculty would be a natural development of this approach. What is needed is an international network of persons and institutions, built by the Center for Educational Cooperation, the State Department, the Peace Corps, AID, and other agencies, with help from existing international organizations and foundations and the funds to make exchange and collaboration possible.

When we project the situation of the American college for teachers into a world scale, from Pennsylvania to Indonesia, the problem to be solved takes on a different character. The problem is then to find ways of making direct connections among the world's teachers in order to carry on the work of creating new world curriculums and developing new world attitudes. If, within an affluent society, with more money to spend on education than any other country on earth, the American colleges for

---

[21] *Ibid.*

teachers are as hard pressed for funds to enlarge world understanding as the examples I have chosen and the results of this study indicate, some new international aspects of the problem become clear. They range from the scepticism engendered among educators around the world as to the sincerity of American intention to support world education in a truly international dimension, to the practical difficulties of institutions for teachers in other countries where the shortage of teachers, educational facilities, economic support, intellectual energy, and large-minded ideas about education prevent, among other things, the growth of internationalism in outlook and in curriculum.

Throughout this Report I have said over and over again in various ways that these present years are of unprecedented importance and unrepeatable circumstance in the opportunities they provide to the United States for educational, cultural, and political leadership in the world, and that these kinds of leadership are so closely intertwined that it is impossible to deal with one without linking it to the others. I would like to say it once more, this time in the form of a conclusion to the study itself. If we do not take advantage of these opportunities now, we will not have them again. The world will move past us.

What it finally comes down to is a matter of injecting a new and radical philosophy of internationalism into the stream of history. Throughout the slow movement of the centuries toward the present age, the philosophers, visionaries, and poets have put before the world the ideal of a common humanity, joined together in mutual concern for the welfare of all, assuring to each the protection and nurture accorded to him in the language of the most recent of these documents, The Universal Declaration of Human Rights of the United Nations. In previous centuries, and until now in this century, it has never been possible to construct a practical world program through which the ideals of the Declaration could be realized, or even to communicate between one part of the world and another as to the necessary working arrangements through which such fulfillment might be possible. Now, at least, we have the advantages of communication. We are all in touch with each other.

But there is one other item which is new and of transcendent importance. Until now, there has never been a country which has had at its command so incredible an array of powers and instruments for achieving a peaceful world order, and which at the same time has put forward the stated intention of achieving national security by international agreement rather than by conquest.

This is not the place to argue the honesty of that intention on the part of the United States. It *is* the place to point out that the honesty of intent will be proven or disproven by the reality of American acts and by the character of the opportunities seized or neglected. We have by now heard enough about the American commitment to share our cultural and educational resources with the world, and in so doing help bring about new forms of world education of benefit to all. There are now those among us, both here and abroad, who believe that without action in the very near future to put these intentions into effect, not only will the chance be lost, but the stated commitments will be clearly identified as the product of speech writers and not of the will of statesmen.

The American emphasis must now be completely practical. If there is to be world education rather than a series of bilateral cultural alliances calculated in the American interest, arrangements will have to be made for the use of American funds to support multilateral educational projects. There is no other country willing and able to take the necessary international initiatives.

To put it another way, the United States called an International Conference on the World Crisis in Education in October 1967, for the declared purpose of bringing the world's educators together to consider and to do something about a world crisis in education. There either is, or is not, a world crisis in education, and if a conference is called on that subject by the United States, the natural assumption on the part of those invited is that the United States thinks that there is one and therefore must have some notion of the nature of the crisis and the ways to its solution. Yet the stated American position was rhetorical rather than practical—"Can we train a young man's eyes to absorb learning as eagerly as we train his finger to pull the trigger?" asked President Johnson.

The answer is, of course, yes, provided we set about it properly. But nothing is decided or aided by calling for an International Education Year in 1970, unless an explicit plan is produced for the use of American funds on an international scale for making it possible for the teachers and students across the world to work with one another on the central educational problem—how to develop teachers whose teaching is relevant to the present and future lives of the world's students.

Everyone knows that the countries and people most in need of education are those least able to afford it. Everyone knows that the United States has the money to spend and is at present spending it at the rate of $28 billion a year on the war in Vietnam, for what it claims is an international purpose. We have now succeeded in demonstrating, to ourselves and to the world, the ineffectiveness of unilateral military force in solving political and social problems. This would be a magnificent time to make a different kind of demonstration, to show what could be done to create a viable world society by the use of our manpower, our technology, and our cultural and our economic resources. If, in order to do so, we were forced to seek a political solution to the present war in Asia, this would be greatly to our advantage. Until we try such a demonstration, we will never know whether it would work, or whether world education in the full meaning of the term is indeed possible.

Chapter 6. Summary of Recommendations

What teachers or anyone else can learn about world affairs depends on how sensitive they are to the political, social, and cultural life around them in their own society and in the world at large. Or, to put it differently, to understand the world's affairs and the nature of world society, it is necessary to be interested in and conscious of the issues which are alive in one's immediate society. In this, teachers are no different from the rest of mankind. It is everyone's educational problem to learn how to think perceptively and act intelligently in the context of modern society, with society now defined on a global and not a local scale.

The preparation of teachers in world affairs must therefore deal not merely with formal academic courses in foreign cultures, international relations, world history, and so on, but with the quality of intellectual and social experience available to those who are going to teach in the colleges and the schools. This applies whether or not their field is the arts, the sciences, or the field of world affairs itself. Whatever they teach, they should be educated in a way calculated to raise the level of their own awareness of what is happening in the world around them.

This means that those who are becoming teachers should have a chance to cross over, through their studies and their personal experience, to a culture different from the one in which they have been born and raised. This will provide them something to compare themselves with, and, by comparisons, they can learn to look at society from a broad perspective. Since most American teachers are unquestioning members of the white middle class who have seldom had a chance to move outside that class and its social milieu into a wider world, their educational need is for a broader range of experience with cultures and people unlike themselves. Without that, the academic studies designed to prepare them to teach in world affairs and other fields will have little effect on the growth of their understanding of social issues and human values, since the issues either will go unobserved or be considered from too narrow a perspective— a perspective limited by the student's own culture.

The recommendations of the present Report stem from the thought that education is the means by which societies and persons become conscious of themselves and of the changes going on within societies—the better to discover what kind of changes are desirable and how best to bring them about. The emphasis throughout the Report is on the quality of experience to be made available to the student who is becoming a teacher. No sharp distinction should be made between what is involved in learning to be a teacher and what is involved in becoming a person of intellectual and cultural substance, able to act in the world. For the educator of teachers, it is a matter of how, through arranging a series of appropriate experiences in intellectual, cultural, and social affairs, the student can learn to understand himself and others, to think clearly, to gain a body of knowledge about man, nature, and the world, and to teach what he has learned to others. The sooner he begins practicing the art of getting his own knowledge, thinking for himself, working and studying with other people, and teaching what he knows, the better will be his education and its eventual results in his work as a teacher.

General Recommendations

To begin, we can generally recommend—

1. That we stop thinking of the education of teachers exclusively in terms of formal academic requirements and professional courses and consider instead the ways in which their intellectual interests and experiences in the affairs of the world can be increased in range and quality.

2. That the study of world affairs not be considered a special area in international relations and world history for those being trained to teach in the field, but that the content of the entire undergraduate curriculum—particularly in the social and behavioral sciences and in the humanities—be revised to reflect a world point of view on man and society and to involve all students in ideas, materials, literature, and comparative studies from the cultures of the world.

3. That we shift the emphasis in teacher education away from the continual discussion of certification problems and procedures and place responsibility and support for new programs where it belongs: in the hands of students and teachers, working together in the academic *and* professional departments, in the schools, in the communities, and in the community agencies now cooperating with colleges of education, educational laboratories, and centers for the study of urban, rural, and international problems.

4. That the colleges and universities be reorganized to give students responsibility for conducting their own education, for developing their own study projects, for teaching themselves

through research projects, field work at home and abroad, student-led seminars, tutoring children and fellow-students, and inclusion in policy-making bodies within the colleges and universities. In this way, we can not only improve the quality of undergraduate and graduate education, but develop a higher degree of motivation and interest among students for careers in teaching.

5. That a nationwide volunteer Student Corps of 25,000 students be organized with government subsidy as an extension of the ideas and programs of VISTA, Head Start, the National Teacher Corps, and exchange Peace Corps. Service and study in foreign and American communities should be considered a regular part of teacher education programs.

6. That the American campus be considered a central place where students assemble to learn what they need to know in order to become educated and useful. The rest of the world, both inside and outside the United States, should be considered a general worldwide campus where students from the United States and other countries come together to educate each other with the help of scholars and teachers.

7. That the idea of the world as a campus become central in the thinking of those concerned with the education of teachers and that practical programs reflecting this idea become a central part of the work of educational planners.

8. That we take as models for new programs in the education of teachers projects developed within the Peace Corps, Exchange Peace Corps, National Teacher Corps, VISTA, Head Start, International Secretariat for Volunteer Service, International Volunteer Service, the Experiment in International Living, and other government and voluntary agencies concerned with social change and world affairs.

9. That the standard pattern of two years of general education requirements, an academic major, and a specified number of professional courses and practice teaching in the junior and senior year be radically modified (a) to allow the student to become directly involved in teaching, in the schools, in the community, and in his undergraduate college and (b) to allow for a high degree of flexibility in meeting the academic degree requirements. The new program would accept as meeting these requirements field work abroad and at home, Peace Corps and other kinds of voluntary service, independent study, student-run seminars, practical experience in research, and projects in the community.

10. That state departments of education take as their primary role—rather than the regulating of certification of teachers—the planning and initiating of new programs in international study (abroad and at home), international curriculums,

and international relationships with schools, teachers colleges, universities, and ministries of education in other countries.

11. That the education of teachers—for all levels of education, from nursery school to graduate study—be made a primary concern of the government and of the colleges and universities. The educational system of the public schools and the colleges, universities, and graduate schools can only proceed as far and as successfully as the quality of teaching in every part of the system.

12. That wherever there are programs and organizations with international connections—government bureaus, AID, Overseas Schools, the National Science Foundation, Institute of Mental Health, UNICEF, the Atomic Energy Commission, Experiment in International Living, university centers abroad, the Smithsonian Institution, the Council on International Educational Exchange—a component of teacher education be included in the existing structure. The intellectual and financial resources available to these organizations can be utilized to develop teachers with international experience.

13. That foreign students—both graduate and undergraduate—be considered a primary source when recruiting student teachers and teaching assistants for service in American schools and colleges, and that student teachers be recruited from foreign countries specifically for that purpose.

14. That international teaching centers be established on American campuses, with connections and exchange arrangements with institutions abroad for educational research, international curriculum making, practice teaching, and teacher education.

15. That educators of teachers turn their attention to the primary importance of the creative arts both in national and international education; and that the painting, sculpture, theatre, music, dance, and literature of other countries be presented to American students and teachers through visiting students, artists, performers, and scholars; and that international festivals of the arts—ranging from dance to films—be sponsored and arranged by colleges of education.

16. That the content of professional education courses be revised to include the study of foreign cultures and educational systems as a central component, coordinated with study and practice teaching abroad and the expansion of connections between American and foreign schools, teacher education institutions, and universities.

17. That serious and concerted political action be taken at the earliest possible moment to secure funds for putting into effect the legislation of the International Education Act.

18. That in connection with the administration of the Inter-

national Education Act and other government programs, 10,000 federal fellowships and/or scholarships be provided for student teachers — undergraduate and graduate — and young teachers already in service in the public schools and colleges, to make possible a year of study and practice teaching in foreign countries as a component of their preparation for teaching in the United States.

Specific Recommendations

In what follows, the more specific recommendations of the Report in relation to internationalism and world affairs are listed in summary form, according to the categories in which they fall.

The Peace Corps as a Teachers College

The ideal arrangement for the education of teachers in world affairs would combine direct experience inside the educational system and community life of a foreign country with a curriculum of studies in the history, language, social structure, and culture of that country, taught, preferably, by native scholars and teachers. This part of the teacher's education should be woven into his studies and his teaching experience in the United States, where he would prepare himself with a body of knowledge appropriate to the field in which he intended to teach and to his general development as an educated person.

An arrangement of this kind is possible through existing and future Peace Corps programs, as well as through other programs modeled on the Peace Corps concept. One of the principal recommendations of the Report is that through formal collaboration between the colleges and the Peace Corps, as well as through the invention of new models based on curriculums, and methods and approaches already tried by Peace Corps staff in the United States and abroad, educators of teachers should take full advantage of the possibilities for extending the Peace Corps idea into a wide range of new areas.

1. **New forms of collaboration with the Peace Corps should be worked out through state departments of education, colleges of education, and universities to include Peace Corps service as a regular component in five- and six-year curriculums leading to the B.A. and M.A. degree and the teaching certificate.**

2. **Taking the concept of Peace Corps service abroad as an organizing principle, existing curriculums and requirements for the teaching certificate should be modified to allow development of individual study programs during the undergraduate years for those intending to serve in the Peace Corps after graduation and for others interested in foreign affairs, international education, and international service of all kinds. This would include not only special junior-year-abroad programs for student teachers, but summer travel-study projects, international education workshops, and institutes in foreign countries and on American campuses,**

staffed by foreign students and teachers as well as their American counterparts. The courses and individual study plans in history, sociology, anthropology, foreign languages, literature, comparative education, and the arts would be chosen by the student and his faculty adviser to make up a comprehensive individually planned curriculum for that student.

3. Special graduate programs leading to the M.A. and Ph.D. degrees should be organized for returning Peace Corps volunteers. They would include practice teaching, flexible study programs, and curriculum development projects based on the previous experience of the volunteers in study and teaching abroad.

4. The Exchange Peace Corps idea should be extended, both through the expansion of government programs of the kind now being conducted by the State Department and by initiatives from the colleges and universities, to permit foreign students already in this country and others to be recruited from abroad to teach in the American schools and to participate in community development projects.

5. Individual faculty members in colleges of education should be assigned to liaison work with the Peace Corps for the development of study-teaching projects abroad for American student teachers. The Peace Corps could be of immeasurable help by virtue of its connections with foreign ministries of education and American embassies abroad. Foreign teachers and students would be recruited to work with their American counterparts in teaching and curriculum development both in the United States and in Peace Corps countries.

6. Returning Peace Corps volunteers should be recruited for teaching and research assignments in colleges of education which would collaborate with local school teachers, student teachers, and high school students interested in foreign affairs. The returned volunteers, selected on the basis of their ability and readiness for the work, would be asked to develop and test experimental curriculums—using materials and experience from abroad—in cooperation with elementary and high school teachers and a supervising faculty member from the college of education. Other volunteers should be recruited to serve in the college in developing new study programs and to advise students interested in entering the Peace Corps or similar foreign service projects.

7. The master of arts in teaching should be expanded in concept and program to include a three-year M.A. for the B.A. graduate. Six months of the senior year would be spent in preparing for Peace Corps service under special curricular arrangements; two years would be spent in service abroad, during which time the graduate student would submit research reports to and

exchange correspondence with a supervising faculty member at home and possibly a member of the Peace Corps staff in the resident country. The program would end with six months of study on the home campus and practice teaching nearby. Similar extension of the master of arts in teaching idea could be made with help from, although not necessarily service in, the Peace Corps in a two-year curriculum. One year would be spent in volunteer service abroad, with six months of preparation beforehand and six months of further study and teaching after the year abroad.

8. Four-year Peace Corps doctorate programs should be established. The two years of foreign service would be linked to a doctoral thesis based on field work, in a style similar to doctoral programs in anthropology.

9. The idea of the Stanford undergraduate regional centers abroad should be extended to include specific projects in teacher education for juniors and seniors taking the teaching certificate with the B.A. degree. This idea would emphasize the collaboration of foreign nationals who are student teachers and teachers with American counterparts.

International Programs Possible Through Existing Organizations with International Connections

1. Wherever there are AID programs in educational development, the sponsoring universities should include graduate and undergraduate students of education in the country teams. They would perform research, studies, and community development work as assistants to a university faculty member.

2. Faculty members serving abroad on educational missions for AID or other U.S. government agencies should, if possible, arrange for graduate students of education to accompany them in one or another capacity (on university fellowships or government and foundation grants) for the development of curriculum materials and direct experience with foreign educational systems.

3. Organizations like the International Secretariat for Volunteer Service or UNICEF should arrange for B.A. graduates from a number of countries, including the United States, to form volunteer international teams for work in education, teaching, and research. Academic supervision and credit would be given by the institutions to which the students are attached.

4. The Office of Overseas Schools, administered by the U.S. Department of State, should collaborate with colleges of education and U.S. school systems in establishing practice teaching and curriculum and research projects in U.S.-supported schools abroad in which student teachers could serve for periods from one semester to two years while remaining connected with their institutions at home.

5. Through consortia like those involved in the American Association of Colleges for Teacher Education, Great Lakes College Association, and the Regional Council for International Education, colleges and universities can combine their resources abroad and at home in developing educational programs for undergraduates and graduates who intend to enter the teaching profession.

6. Projects similar to that undertaken by UNESCO in its Education for International Understanding and Cooperation should be duplicated by other international organizations to create new links between teachers in a variety of countries for exchange of students, teachers, materials, curriculums, tapes, films, and other educational instruments.

7. International study projects similar to that sponsored by the UNESCO-International Universities Association on admission to universities should be organized on a broad scale through existing organizations with international connections: the World Academy of Arts and Sciences, Universities and the Quest for Peace, the World Law Fund, the World Confederation of Organizations of the Teaching Profession.

State Departments of Education; Certification and Professional Education Requirements

As indicated above under General Recommendations, state departments of education should shift their emphasis from defining course requirements and credit-counting procedures to planning and initiating new programs in the education of teachers. We can specifically recommend—

1. That special arrangements be made in cooperation with the universities and schools to evaluate foreign teaching experience by Peace Corps volunteers and others who have had teaching and educational experience abroad in order that (a) credit toward certification be awarded for bona fide work in education and teaching abroad, (b) students with foreign experience and interests be recruited into the teaching profession, and (c) regulatory programs of the departments exhibit a wider latitude in requirements for educational subject matter and practical teaching and field experience.

2. That the departments call upon colleges of education and universities for the development of new programs in international education for teachers and, as is the case in New York State, establish projects of their own for cooperation with educators and institutions abroad in the exchange of teachers and curricular materials.

3. That the courses in education accepted for the certification of teachers be thoroughly revised to include (a) comparative

studies of foreign educational systems, (b) field work at home and abroad in study and experience with a variety of forms of education, (c) material drawn from the social and behavioral sciences—particularly cultural anthropology—which can introduce the student to foreign cultures within the context of national educational systems.

4. That faculty members in colleges of education organize two- to three-year projects in the development of new education courses with content drawn from foreign educational and social systems, through summer travel and study and through cooperation with foreign educators, returned Peace Corps volunteers and staff, and faculty colleagues who are experts in foreign cultures.

5. That colleges of education appoint scholars in the social sciences and the humanities who have an interest in education and world cultures, rather than relying on other subject matter departments and research centers in the university to teach students of education to become aware of social issues and world problems.

6. That the process of regional and national accreditation of programs of teacher education be revised to emphasize and encourage variations in the standard pattern of curriculum to ensure the inclusion of a maximum of foreign experience and study on the part of the student body.

7. That staff members be appointed to state departments of education with specific responsibilities for international education throughout the state and that through connections established between institutions abroad, state school districts, colleges of education, and universities arrange for exchange of faculty, international summer workshops, international curriculums, and joint study projects with foreign scholars and students.

8. That summer travel-study projects aboard be arranged for groups. These would include members of department staffs, state school board members, graduate students of education, teachers, principals, superintendents, and college and university presidents and deans.

9. That the work of staff members of state departments of education be arranged to include (a) travel abroad to establish liaison with foreign institutions, Peace Corps staff and volunteers, ministries of education, and American cultural affairs officers; (b) the appointment of foreign students and scholars as interns in the department; (c) joint research projects in international curriculums with foreign educators serving as interns and staff members; (d) conferences with experts in foreign affairs and area studies for consideration of curricular changes and content in teacher education programs.

10. That official as well as informal relations be arranged

between state departments of education, the colleges of education, teachers of undergraduates, and community groups interested in international affairs—local World Affairs Councils, United Nations Associations, the Foreign Policy Association, the League of Women Voters, and similar organizations—so that the resources of these organizations can be put to use in the educational system and can work directly with teachers. This could include use of library and information centers, combined regional and state activities, conferences, panel discussions, television and radio forums with foreign students and scholars, visiting speakers, joint travel-study trips, etc.

11. That specially qualified professors from the state or from other states, returned foreign service officers, members of the United Nations Secretariat and delegations, staff members of nongovernmental international organizations be invited for one to two days of discussion with state departments of education staff members to review issues in education and world society related to the curriculum in international affairs.

Cultural Policy and Foreign Affairs

American foreign policy suffers from an underdeveloped sense of the importance of cultural power in the conduct of foreign affairs—the power, that is, of ideas and values in the arts and sciences to unite the international community around common interests and a concern for a peaceful world order. Nowhere is this underdevelopment more obvious than in the field of education and in the education of teachers, where the budgets for international work are low and the policies often contradictory.

The Report recommends—

1. That a major policy decision be made at the highest level of government on the purpose and character of the work in international education and cultural exchange, to emphasize the fact that—

(a) The use of American funds and educational manpower in international affairs should be to advance the cause of internationalism in the world community—not simply to cultivate friendly attitudes toward America, American culture, or American foreign policy.

(b) American education is part of a world system of education, and American resources should be used to the fullest extent possible to contribute to the welfare of all other educational systems.

(c) The education of teachers, in the United States and in all other countries, should receive maximum attention in practical programs designed to create a higher level of international understanding and cooperation.

(d) All government subsidies for American students, scholars, and intellectuals for service, research, and study abroad should be competely open and in no case covert, and that wherever possible teaching, research, and study on the part of Americans abroad be conducted in partnership with the nationals of the host countries, or with international teams in cooperative projects.

(e) The function of the university is to increase the store of knowledge and to teach and disseminate that knowledge for the benefit of mankind. Therefore, universities should not be used by their governments for research on military matters, either in secret or in open projects. The criterion for the selection of appropriate university projects should be whether they aid the spread of international enlightenment in the arts, sciences, and technologies and whether the results of the research could be taught to students in American or foreign universities and schools.

(f) Since the American universities are in a favored position in world society, with financial resources and a degree of intellectual freedom unknown in most other countries, they have a special obligation to set standards for intellectual behavior in relation to political and other controls which can give leadership to the world's intellectual community.

2. That university scholars take a more active role in following the issues and decisions in cultural policy as these relate to national and international affairs and take an active part in the formation of those policies by exercising their right of criticism, review, and political action where foreign policy is concerned.

3. That the AID program of educational assistance abroad shift its emphasis toward the education of teachers, and that this shift be reflected in the allocation of funds.

4. That the AID program in Vietnam be sharply increased in size and in budget to deal with the extreme educational problems now afflicting the Vietnamese people as a result of the war, and that a major part of the effort go into the recruitment and education of teachers.

5. That a government program be developed through which qualified Americans who have served in the armed forces in Vietnam and in other developing countries and are familiar with the language and problems of those countries be recruited as volunteers to carry out teaching, community development, and other duties as civilians following their military service.

6. That other programs for the development of teachers and scholars with a knowledge of Southeast Asia be established, with a view to preparing large numbers of potential aides in the rehabilitation of Vietnamese education once the war ends as well

as creating a larger body of scholarship and public understanding in the United States of the problems of Indo-China.

7. That the Educational and Cultural Exchange program of the State Department concentrate more heavily on the international education of teachers.

8. That plans be made for international festivals of the arts to be held in the United States and elsewhere, in which actors, composers, dancers, poets, painters, critics, and educators in the arts are brought together to share their performances, to translate each other's works, and to find ways of introducing their art forms into each other's educational systems.

9. That conferences of American educators be sponsored by the State Department to discuss issues in foreign policy, particularly in relation to cultural and social affairs.

10. That regional centers, initiated with American funds and administered by international committees, be established in various parts of the world for research and study of educational problems—curriculum making, teaching, translation, etc.—where an international student body could attend for periods from six months to two years, and the staff would be recruited on a worldwide basis.

11. That existing American institutions with international connections—the Smithsonian Institution, for example—organize joint projects with students and teachers from other countries for study and research in the natural and social sciences in order to improve the quality of teaching on an international scale.

12. That government subsidies be arranged for student-initiated projects in teacher education and international affairs through which American students could join forces with students from other countries in increasing their areas of common interest and common understanding, and that the former CIA subsidies to student groups be replaced by larger grants from open government and foundation sources—in each case administered through the authority of recognized educators, as in the case of the Fulbright awards.

13. That AID organize a research component in connection with its educational missions, in order that some objective evaluation may be made of the results of its educational work, and that the literature of educational research be expanded in an international direction. The research component could be built around projects carried out by qualified university and college of education faculty members, with graduate and undergraduate students of education recruited for the research staff as part of their work toward a degree in education.

14. That the American Overseas Schools be developed into

centers for teacher education and international research, for practice teaching by Americans and host nationals, and for international curriculum experiments.

The Role of Students

The recommendations having to do with students stem from the basic thesis of the Report—that the best way to learn to teach is by teaching and that teaching is not simply a matter of imparting classroom subjects skillfully but of entering the lives of other persons in order to help them fulfill their intellectual and personal powers. This means the reorganization of the whole style of instruction in the colleges and universities, with drastic modification of the lecture system. The lecture should be used only sparingly, in instances where it is appropriate. The main emphasis should be placed on making students responsible for teaching themselves and each other, whether or not they intend to become professional teachers when they graduate.

A corollary of this view calls for volunteer educational and social service in the community as a regular part of college education—particularly service in rural and urban areas, wherever student talents can be useful—not only to help in improving the quality of community life and education, but to give students a firsthand experience with the raw materials of the social and behavioral sciences. This calls for a more mobile style of college education in which summer experience, nonresident terms, travel-study projects, weekend institutes, a semester or a year of foreign study and experience, a semester or year spent at a college other than one's own, students from Negro colleges attending predominantly white institutions and vice versa, along with other shifts in cultural milieu, are included as a basic element in educational planning.

It also means giving major responsibility to student groups to plan their own courses, seminars, field work and study projects, and teaching projects in the communities. The two objections most often made to this form of education are that students are not capable of taking so great a responsibility without close supervision from the faculty and that academic credit toward a degree cannot be given for loosely supervised work whose main emphasis is on experience rather than on academic study. I have found both these points controverted by my own experience with students at Sarah Lawrence College and elsewhere. The kind of supervision to be given to student projects is of course crucial, since it must give the freedom and responsibility for intelligent educational work and at the same time provide some degree of guidance. But the principle is sound and very effective in practice. In the matter of awarding credits, the performance of students in the situations in which they are involved and the evaluation of educational results are revealed in the outcome of the projects, oral and written reports by the students, demonstrations, and evaluation by the students themselves.

Although this approach has relevance for all college students in improving the quality of their education and their ability to function as students, it has particular relevance to future teachers. In what follows, the recommendations are made with student teachers specifically in mind, although they apply to the education of students in general. If we educate all students as if they were going to become teachers, the quality of their general education would itself be improved.

Recommendations about a shift in the role of students have already been listed under the General Recommendations beginning on page 292. What follows are more specific proposals and suggestions.

1. **The opportunity for teaching should be extended into the elementary and secondary schools by organizing the teaching system to allow time for children to teach each other in tutorials with appropriate assignments made by the teacher, in team projects, in assignments of junior high school students to groups of elementary school children, and volunteer service by high school students in the community, especially in poor rural areas and urban slums.**

2. **Education students and others should be invited to act as tutors to foreign students and to work with them in educational and study projects connected with the country of their origin.**

3. **Selected sophomores, juniors, and seniors should be invited by university faculty members to serve as tutors and teaching assistants for freshmen, with three-year plans made in which foreign experience by the students during summer terms or nonresident semesters can then be put to use in adding additional materials to existing courses in the humanities and social sciences.**

4. **Study and, if possible, practice teaching experience should be arranged abroad or in a "foreign" culture in the United States for all students who expect to be teaching a foreign language or a foreign culture.**

5. **Special language and study projects for student teachers should be arranged from the freshman year on in geographical areas where direct collaboration between teachers and students in bilingual communities is possible, as in the Spanish-American region of the Southwest.**

6. **Through cooperation with service organizations like the Experiment in International Living, the American Friends Service Committee, Operation Crossroads Africa, the World University Service, etc., student teachers should be given educational experience abroad as part of their teacher preparation curriculum.**

7. **During one semester of nonresident education, junior and senior education students should be asked to develop teaching and community service projects in communities other than their own—for example among the Navajos, in Appalachia, in urban communities—and to carry them out under faculty supervision**

and with the cooperation of local educational authorities and teachers.

8. Through arrangements made with foreign students already in this country, international projects should be developed between the foreign students and their American counterparts for joint or parallel studies and practice in education in this country and in the country of the foreign student's origin.

9. Curriculum projects should be developed by student teachers studying abroad through which student film making can become part of their contribution to the curriculum in the schools and colleges back home.

10. Students should be asked—where the talent and the equipment are available—to prepare video-taped discussions with foreign students and scholars for use in the classroom and in the community, over local television stations, and closed-circuit television on the campus.

11. More projects should be initiated such as those developed by Nations Incorporated in San Francisco, in which high school students work in intensive summer sessions with foreign students and teachers already in this country on issues in world affairs. The foreign students can bring special kinds of insight and personal knowledge.

12. International curriculum-building projects should be initiated by American colleges of education by establishing connections between students in their institutions and students abroad, with exchange of tape recordings, short stories, plays, poems and other written materials, films, and comparative studies of family and social life. These could be similar to those conducted by the American Association of Colleges for Teacher Education in its interinstitutional affiliation project.

13. A United Nations Teacher Corps should be established through the extension of present collaboration between UNICEF and UNESCO in their work in teacher education. Internationally recruited student volunteers could spend two years in a foreign country teaching, studying, working, and living with their counterparts in order to render service to the host country, to develop an international point of view about education, and to prepare themselves through new curricular materials for service in their home countries.

Index

International Conference on Social Psychological Research in Developing Countries, 267
International Conference on the World Crisis in Education, 268-69, 290
International Education Act of 1966, 7-8, 10, 11, 38-39, 41, 74, 88, 123, 166, 256, 279
International Education Project, 63
International Education, Regional Council for, 71, 72, 173
International Education and Teacher Education Conference, 4
International Evaluation of Educational Achievement, 268
International House, 161
International Institute for Educational Planning, 158
International Programs and Services, Office of, 60
International Relations Committee, 1, 5-7
International Schools Examination Syndicate, 167, 175-77
International Secretariat for Volunteer Service, 149-52, 153, 159, 297
International Studies and World Affairs Center, 3, 169-72
International Teacher Development Program, 54
International Training, School for, 189
International Voluntary Service, 254
International Workshop, 164
Iowa, State College of, 3
Ithaca College, 164

James, William (quoted), 89, 90-91
Johnson, Lyndon Baines (quoted), 81, 166
Joint UNESCO-International Association of Universities, 180
Justin Morrill College, 136, 140, 186-88

Kalamazoo College, 173
Kant, Immanuel (quoted), 245
Keele, University of, 63
Kennedy, John F., 96
Kent State University, 3
Kentucky, University of, 3, 4
Kenya Institute of Education, 71
Kenya Plan, Government of (quoted), 151
Kettering Foundation, 171, 172
Kirk, Grayson (quoted), 75
Klassen, Frank, 2, 13
Kroepsch, Robert, 174

Lady of the Lake College, 3
Lall, Arthur, 152

Lamont Geological Observatory, 133
Landrum, Roger, 119
Lincoln University, 3
Lipset, Seymour Martin, 220
London University Institute of Education, 59
Long, Harold, 230
Los Angeles City College, 3
Lotspeich, William D. (quoted), 146, 147
Louisiana Four State Project, 238-40
Lowe, William, 164

McKinney, T. II., 140-41

Mankiewicz, Frank (quoted), 117
Malawi, 146
Martin Luther School, 10
Mead, Margaret (quoted), 19
Memphis City School System, 165, 240
Memphis, International Group of, 240
Memphis State University, 239, 240
Michigan State College of Education, 187
Michigan State University, 3, 9, 64, 186, 270
Michigan, University of, 62-64, 95-97, 267
Morehouse, Ward, 227, 228
Morgan, Arthur E., 183
Morse, Richard (quoted), 77-78
MusKelley, James K., 238-39, 240
Myrdal, Gunnar, 277

National Aeronautics and Space Administration, 133
National Committee for Support of the Public Schools, 35
National Council for Accreditation of Teacher Education, 221-23
National Council on the Arts, 273
National Council for the Social Studies, 6
National Defense Education Act, Title VI, 87
National Education Association Teach Corps, 281
National Endowment for the Arts, 273
National Institute of Health Administration and Education, 146
National Science Foundation, 126-32, 274
National Student Association, 93, 94, 95-96, 272-73, 274, 275
National Student Association Congress, 4
National Teacher Corps, 93, 142, 162-63
Nations Incorporated, 163-65
New Delhi Educational Resources Center, 227, 235

311

3837   0